Day b[illegible]
throug[illegible]
New Tes[illegible]

EDITED BY

DENIS CLAPHAM

JOHN HEADING

MALCOLM HORLOCK

PUBLISHED BY THE COMMITTEE OF
THE "PRECIOUS SEED" MAGAZINE—1979

Reprinted 1983

ISBN 0 900439 11 4

This Book, and the other *Precious Seed* Publications

Church Doctrine and Practice (336 pages)
Treasury of Bible Doctrine (468 pages)
Day by Day through the Old Testament (416 pages)

are obtainable from

ns,

PRECIOUS SEED PUBLICATIONS
P.O. Box No. 8
Neath, West Glam.
SA11 1QB

N, U.K.

The *Precious Seed* Magazine
is published bi-monthly
and is obtainable from
Mr. L. Cave,
175 Oxford Road,
Calne, Wiltshire, SN11 8AL, U.K.

Printed by The Cambrian News (Aberystwyth) Ltd.

Preface

THE EARNEST prayer of the Publishers of *Day by Day through the New Testament* is that God will use it to stir up any who are not enjoying and deriving benefit from the daily habit of reading His Word consecutively. We trust that it will also be of value to more mature believers, and that it will provide many a seed-thought for His servants as they prepare messages for many differing occasions in His service. Many other helpful books for devotional use are available, but few aim to act as a guide through the New Testament from start to finish, like this one. By way of short, daily comments, it offers help to a clearer understanding of the Word of Truth.

To take full advantage of this book, it is suggested that the Scripture portion for the day first be read, with prayer that God will reveal His truth and make one receptive to it. Then, as an aid to meditating on the portion, the reader will find the daily comments most helpful. Just as one might profitably talk over the Scriptures with an experienced friend, so here one will find a variety of Christian counsellors happy to share their understanding of the passages. They all have in common a love for that Word through which true peace and joy, and certain hope have come to them. The additional undated pages throughout the book may be read and considered when they are reached.

A great debt is owed to the twenty-five contributors for their cooperation at short notice, and despite many other demands on their time. Thanks are due also to the members of the *Precious Seed* sub-committee for their work in assisting the editors, namely to David Ainslie, Leonard Cave and John Williamson. We are glad to record our happy memory that our late brother Harold Hobbs, who used to be a member of the sub-committee, was of one mind with us in the project before passing into the Lord's presence. Our thanks are also due to others who worked behind the scenes, in additional proofreading and in manuscript typing. Our Aberystwyth printers have also cooperated to ensure that readers have the book in their hands by 1st January 1980.

May God graciously own and bless the book to His glory, and for the spiritual prosperity of all who willingly confess that Jesus Christ is Lord.

DENIS CLAPHAM
JOHN HEADING
MALCOLM HORLOCK

ABBREVIATIONS

A.V.	Authorized Version
R.V.	Revised Version
New Trans.	The New Translation by J. N. Darby

List of Contents

List of Contributors

H. Barnes	*Bromborough*	2 Peter, Jude
J. Boyd	*Holywood, N. Ireland*	James
D. Clapham	*Birmingham*	Galatians, Paul's four Personal Letters (p. 307)
R. V. Court	*Isle of Wight*	Luke 9. 51 to 24. 53
S. Emery	*Workington*	1 Corinthians
G. B. Fyfe	*London*	1 Timothy, Philemon
P. Harding	*Skelmanthorpe*	Philippians
M. Horlock	*Cardiff*	Matthew
C. S. Jarrett	*Malvern*	Titus
R. Jeffery	*Reading*	Luke 1. 1 to 9. 50
J. H. Large	*Seven Kings*	Romans
D. J. Lawrence	*Ammanford*	John chs. 13-21
A. Leckie	*Airdrie*	Hebrews
J. Marchant	*Cardiff*	Colossians
J. Mitchell	*Cardiff*	John chs. 1-12
K. T. C. Morris	*Southampton*	Ephesians
D. Newell	*Glasgow*	Acts
E. L. H. Ogden	*Poulton-le-Fylde*	Mark
B. Osborne	*Dinas Powis*	2 Corinthians
A. E. Phillips	*West Moors*	1 Peter
A. T. Shearman	*Worcester*	2 Thessalonians
E. R. Shotter	*Northampton*	1, 2 & 3 John
E. J. Strange	*Bridgwater*	Revelation
D. E. West	*Leicester*	2 Timothy
P. Young	*Coventry*	1 Thessalonians, Maps

All introductions are supplied by the contributors

Introducing Matthew's Gospel

BEFORE HIS conversion, Matthew the son of Alphaeus had collected taxes for the Romans in Capernaum. His name was then Levi, Mark 2. 14. The Lord commanded Levi to follow him, which he did. It is probable that he subsequently changed his name to Matthew, which means "gift of God". He had been a servant of the greatest earthly kingdom then known, that of the Roman Empire. It is appropriate therefore that, in his Gospel, he has much to tell us of a far greater kingdom—the kingdom of heaven.

The first Gospel records a high percentage of Jesus' teachings. Over half of the Gospel consists of His parables and sayings. The people were forever astonished at His doctrine, 7. 28; 13. 54; 22. 33. Apart from its introduction and conclusion, the Gospel can be divided into five sections, each ending with a discourse that is followed by words such as "when Jesus had finished these sayings". See 7. 28; 11. 1; 13. 53; 19. 1 and 26. 1.

It is practically certain that Matthew wrote his Gospel for the Jews. To such, the humiliation, rejection and death of Jesus was a very real stumbling block. They had expected a military and political deliverer, Luke 24. 21. Matthew set out to show that Jesus was indeed their Messiah. Chapter 1 shows that His genealogy was sound; He was entitled to the promises of Abraham and the throne of David. Chapter 2 shows that His infancy was in complete accord with the Old Testament. Chapter 3 shows that the foretold forerunner had come. Chapter 4 shows that His temptation proved Him competent to reign. Chapters 5–7 detail the principles according to which He would rule. Chapters 8–9 record the fulfilment of the Messianic signs of Isaiah 35 and 61. All the important events of Jesus' life took place to fulfil the prophecies of the Old Testament. Ten times Matthew uses words like, "that it might be fulfilled which was spoken by the prophets".

Notice the expression, "From that time began Jesus . . .", 4. 17 R.V., 16. 21 R.V. In broadest outline therefore the Gospel consists of three sections. An introduction, 1. 1 to 4. 16; Jesus' ministry, 4. 17 to 16. 20; Jesus' path of suffering and glory, 16. 21 to 28. 20.

Jan. 1st

READING : **Matthew 1. 1-25**

THE BIRTH OF JESUS CHRIST

THREE TIMES reference is made to Mary bringing forth a son, vv. 21, 23, 25. A woman had been instrumental in making man a sinner, Gen. 3. 6; a woman was instrumental in bringing him a Saviour. The "child", v. 18, was Mary's son, v. 25; the "fruit" of her womb, Luke 1. 42. Yet twice it is stressed that the child was "of the Holy Ghost", vv. 18, 20. This had to be, because the child was God, v. 23. We cannot comprehend how true and holy Manhood was united in one Person with eternal Deity, 11. 27; 1 Tim. 3. 16. Yet we gladly believe that which we cannot explain, for God has revealed it "unto us and to our children for ever", Deut. 29. 29.

In becoming flesh, John 1. 14, the eternal Word remained that which He had ever been and yet became that which He had never been. Melchisedec, a type of Christ, was "without father, without mother", Heb. 7. 3. The Lord Jesus became a Man and as such had no father, v. 18; He was God and as such had no mother.

The holiness of the child was secured by "the Holy Ghost". Jesus came "in the flesh", 1 John 4. 2, but was made only "in the likeness of sinful flesh", Rom. 8. 3. He shared our *human* nature but not our *sinful* nature. Mary was not perfect and needed a Saviour, Luke 1. 47, but the Holy Spirit brought a clean thing out of an unclean, Job 14. 4.

"A good name is rather to be chosen than great riches", Prov. 22. 1. The Lord was to be called by two good names, vv. 21, 23. Luke tells of a third, Luke 1. 35. The Lord was to be called "the Son of God", Luke 1. 35, because of what He had always been. He was to be called "Emmanuel", v. 23, because of what He became. He was to be called "Jesus", v. 21, because of what He would do. Isaac ("laughter") was named before his birth on account of something his father had done, Gen. 17. 17, 19; Jesus was named before His birth on account of something He was to do Himself. He was "to save", v. 21, He who began "the days of his flesh", Heb. 5. 7, by the momentous stoop from the throne of God to the womb of a woman, would therefore need to end those "days" by a further stoop to the fathomless depths of the suffering of the cross, Matt. 26. 38, 39; 27. 46.

Jan. 2nd

READING : **Matthew 2. 1-23**

BORN KING

THE YOUNG child Jesus is the centre of interest throughout the chapter. Every time the child and His mother are mentioned together, the child is given the first place, vv. 11, 13, 20, 21. After Christ is introduced as the "Governor, that shall rule", v. 6, Herod is no longer given his title of king; compare verses 1 and 3 with verses 7, 12, 13, 15, 16, 19, 22. The rightful "King of the Jews" has come!

The young child was also the object of Satan's interest. The Apocalypse draws the curtain aside and shows that the devil was the real instigator of Herod's attempt to slay the young child. The "dragon" stood ready to devour the child "as soon as it was born", Rev. 12. 4. Satan has set out from the beginning to oppose and frustrate God's purpose in Christ. God originally revealed that the coming Deliverer would be *the seed of the woman*, Gen. 3. 15. The devil therefore set out to defile and destroy the woman's seed. Satan used Eve's firstborn to murder her second son, but God answered with Seth, Gen. 4. 1–8, 25. The devil then masterminded an assault on the "daughters of men" to corrupt their seed, Gen. 6. 1, 2; Jude 6, but God answered with the flood. God later revealed that the Deliverer would be of *Abraham's seed.* The serpent attempted to defile this seed by the devices of the flesh, Gen. 16. 1–4, but God answered with Isaac. The Pharaohs were Satan's next unwitting tools to attack the seed of Abraham, but God answered with Moses, Exod. 1–14. God had also implied that the Deliverer would be of *the tribe of Judah,* Gen. 49. 10, and later, when one of that kingly tribe came to the fore, the devil used envious Saul to make several attempts on young David's life—but "God delivered him not into his hand", 1 Sam. 23. 14. It was then made known that the Deliverer would be of *the seed of David,* 2 Sam. 7. 12, 13. Of his many sons, David chose Solomon, 1 Kings 1. 17. Satan attacked through Adonijah but to no avail, 1 Kings 1. The devil made another assault on David's seed 150 years later through Athaliah, 2 Kings 11. 1, but God preserved the babe Joash, 2 Kings 11. 2, 3; 12. 1. Like so many before him, Herod acted the part of the serpent's seed but Mary's child was destined for God's throne, Rev. 12. 5.

Jan. 3rd

READING : **Matthew 3. 1-17**

THE BAPTISM OF CHRIST

JOHN'S MESSAGE was as simple and unpretentious as his clothing and diet, vv. 2, 4. Taking his marching orders from the words of the prophet Isaiah, v. 3; Isa. 40. 3; John 1. 23, he fearlessly announced the demand for repentance. Three different classes of men presented themselves for baptism.

There was *a vast crowd*, vv. 5, 6. Great numbers flocked to him from the city of Jerusalem, the province of Judaea and the neighbourhood of the Jordan. Among the crowd were many publicans and harlots who believed the Baptist's preaching, 21. 32. They came in genuine repentance, and their baptism was accompanied by the confession of their sins.

There was *a sizeable group*, vv. 7–12, comprising the Pharisees and Sadducees. This company included many hypocrites who took refuge in their national privileges and who saw no need of personal repentance. John had some severe and unsparing things to say to them.

There was *a solitary individual*, vv. 13–17. "Then cometh Jesus". Unlike the crowd, He showed no signs of repentance. He made no confession because there were no actions He needed to regret, no words He needed to withdraw, no thoughts of which He needed to be ashamed. Small wonder John hesitated to baptize Him, v. 14. Nevertheless it was right that Christ should identify Himself with His people, v. 15.

The Spirit descended and abode on Him, v. 16. As the meat offering baken in a pan was mingled with oil, Lev. 2. 5, so the human nature of Christ had its being and character from the Holy Spirit, 1. 18, 20, of which oil is the known symbol. As oil was subsequently poured on the offering, Lev. 2. 6, so the Lord was now anointed with the Holy Spirit, Acts 10. 38.

With words that echoed two Messianic prophecies, Psa. 2. 7; Isa. 42. 1, God testified that He was well pleased in His beloved Son, v. 17. Identical words were to be heard later on the Mount of Transfiguration, 17. 5. On the second occasion, the Father was to declare His satisfaction with the public ministry of the Saviour; at the Jordan, He declared His satisfaction with the years of privacy and seclusion at Nazareth. Blessed Lord; in public or private, ever perfect!

Jan. 4th

READING : **Matthew 4. 1-10**

THE TEMPTATION OF THE MESSIAH

THE DEVIL'S intention was to dissuade Jesus from His mission of Messiahship as mapped out for Him by the will of God. The popular image of the coming Messiah was that of a military deliverer who would liberate Israel and establish a great earthly empire with Jerusalem as its centre. God's programme for the Messiah also terminated in a throne—but it led via a cross, Luke 24. 26. The wilderness temptations would settle which kind of Messiah Jesus was to be.

Satan attempted to insert the thin end of his wedge first. Avoiding any direct reference to Christ's mission, he launched his attack on the seemingly unrelated issue of food, v. 3. It was unthinkable, Satan implied, that the King of Israel should be starving in a wilderness; surely He could use His Messianic powers to satisfy His humble needs! The issue, however, went beyond stones and bread. If the devil could persuade Jesus to act independently of God's will in a small matter, it was likely that he would succeed later with bigger matters—such as the cross.

The second temptation was more obviously relevant. If Jesus, in response to Satan's deft quotation of Psalm 91. 11, 12, had leapt down from the temple, Matt. 3. 5, 6, the crowd of worshippers in the court below would have supplied a captive audience. Witnessing His safe descent amid angelic presence, they would recognize the Lord who would have "suddenly come to his temple", Mal. 3. 1. He could have secured an immediate following if He had only conformed to the popular ideal of Messiahship and given some dazzling, spectacular display.

Finally, the devil dropped all disguise and came out into the open. He blatantly offered Jesus the world's kingdoms in exchange for His homage, v. 9. Compromise with him, Satan argued, was a small price to pay for avoiding Golgotha. The Son of man could enter His glory without suffering! But Jesus' future path was chosen. God's way was more costly, but it was the way He would take.

Jesus defeated the devil by three quotations from the last of the five books of Moses. Like David He carried five "stones" but only needed one, 1 Sam. 17. 40, 49.

Jan. 5th

READING : **Matthew 4. 11-25**

LEAVING

THE PASSAGE contains four instances of "leaving". Satan left the Lord, v. 11; Jesus left Nazareth, v. 13; Peter and Andrew left their nets, v. 20; James and John left their ship, v. 22.

Satan left, v. 11, because he had been *defeated.* His ammunition was exhausted. He had finished completely every form of temptation, Luke 4. 13 (Greek), but all his fiery darts had totally failed to discover any combustible material in the Lord Jesus! At the Jordan, Jesus had fulfilled "all righteousness", 3. 15; in the wilderness He had resisted "all temptation", Luke 4. 13. Once having bound "the strong man", Jesus proceeded to "spoil his house", 12. 29, by His ministry of healing and casting out demons, vv. 23, 24.

Possibly Jesus' withdrawal, v. 13, followed the events recorded in Luke 4. 16–30. If so, *Jesus* left, v. 13, because He had been *rejected.* On account of their unbelief, the men of Nazareth forfeited both His presence and blessings. Capernaum, and not Nazareth, was therefore to witness the majority of His recorded mighty works and was to be, in privileges as well as pride, "exalted unto heaven", 11. 23. Capernaum means "the village of Nahum". A Galilean tradition claims that it was the burial place of Nahum the prophet. It would indeed be appropriate that Capernaum's streets should be trod by the feet of One that brought "good tidings" and that published "peace" as expressed by Nahum nearly 700 years before, Nahum 1. 15. Now could Zebulun help itself to "treasures hid", Deut. 33. 19, and Napthtali was "full with the blessing of the Lord", Deut. 33. 23.

The *four fishermen* left, vv. 20, 22, because they had been *summoned.* He commanded them to quit their trade and to accompany Him constantly as His scholars and disciples. Peter and Andrew were called to a higher form of fishing, just as David had once been called to a higher form of feeding, Psa. 78. 70–72. They were not to be like the Chaldean "fishers" who scoured the land of Judah to lead the people captive, Jer. 16. 16. The disciples were to be fishermen of salvation. It is thrilling to note that Jesus called humble fishermen, and not angels, v. 11, to be His evangelists, 2 Cor. 4. 7.

Jan. 6th

READING : **Matthew 5. 1-16**

TRUE BLESSEDNESS

THE CONTENTS of chapters 5 to 7 are often referred to as the Sermon on the Mount. This Sermon is the Magna Carta of the kingdom of heaven. Jesus began His message as the book of Psalms begins—by describing the truly blessed (happy) man. The Lord's yardstick of blessedness was very different from that of the world. It congratulates and counts happy those who attain ease, wealth or fame. Happiness for the unconverted man usually lies in honour, riches or sensual pleasure. Christ's measure of blessedness was very different. His description of the ideal citizen of His kingdom contradicted popular ideas of what membership of that kingdom would involve. The Jews generally expected the blessedness of the kingdom to consist of authority, comfort and plenty. The Lord's manifesto delivered a full broadside to these expectations, vv. 3–12. Citizens of His kingdom would entertain humble opinions of themselves; would mourn over sin; would be mild and gentle; would passionately long to please God; would show sympathy and generosity to others in need; would be concerned with inward purity (rather than external cleanliness, like the Pharisees) and would be peace-loving and peace-seeking. Far from earning respect, such features would attract opposition.

Jesus had lived His Sermon for 30 years before He preached it, and, to some extent, the Beatitudes provide us with His self-portrait. He was lowly in heart, 11. 29. He mourned over the effect of sin on others, 23. 37, 38. He was meek, 11. 29; 21. 5. His meat was the will of His Father, John 4. 34. He showed mercy and compassion, Matt. 9. 27–30. He was, and is, pure, 1 John 3. 3, 5. He has made peace, Col. 1. 20. He was cruelly persecuted and reviled, 1 Pet. 2. 23. In many ways therefore, the description of the kingdom's ideal citizen was that of its King.

Disciples who live out the Beatitudes are salt and light in the midst of a world that is corrupt and in spiritual darkness, vv. 13–16. To hope to influence the world by conforming to its standards and ways is to forget the lesson of the salt; to withdraw from the world into monk-like seclusion is to forget the lesson of the light.

Jan. 7th

READING : **Matthew 5. 17-48**

FULFILLING THE LAW

THE LORD had not come to displace the law, vv. 17–19. He had come to "fulfil" it. That is, He would explain its true meaning and implications; penetrating beneath its words to its spirit and underlying principles. His quarrel did not lie with the law but with the scribes and Pharisees, v. 20. We should ponder the Lord's three "Excepts" concerning entrance to the kingdom. The essentials for entrance are repentance, 18. 3, new birth, John 3. 5, and right conduct, v. 20. Verse 20 states the theme of the whole sermon. The scribes were theological teachers who had received years of education. The Pharisees were groups of pious laymen from every section of the community; only their leaders were theologians. Jesus spoke of three kinds of righteousness: that of the theologians, that of the pious laymen and that of His disciples. He dealt first with the false interpretation of scriptural righteousness given by the theologians, vv. 21-48. Then followed His controversy with the righteousness of the Pharisees; almsgiving, prayer and fasting being the main characteristics of their piety, 6. 1–18. Finally, He developed the new righteousness that should mark His disciples, 6. 19 to 7. 27.

The Lord gave a spiritual exposition of the law, vv. 21–48. His authority to do so came over forcibly in His six-fold, "But I say unto you". He revealed something of the law's penetrating demands, which legalism had limited to mere outward conformity. Jesus spoke of the disciple's attitude to his brother, vv. 21–26, women, vv. 27–30, marriage, vv. 31, 32, truthful speech, vv. 33–37, violence, vv. 38–42, and his enemy, vv. 43–48. He warned His followers not to hate each other, v. 22; 1 John 3. 15, and gave them counsel how to act if they gave others cause to hate them. Take note of the "firsts" of reconciling an offended brother, v. 24, of seeking God's kingdom, 6. 33, and of judging one's own heart, 7. 5. Jesus urged unsparing severity with anything that proved a temptation to carnality, vv. 28–30. Private oaths, which had become a subterfuge for deceit, were forbidden. No resistance was to be offered in the case of personal wrongs; the disciple won by losing! There was nothing praiseworthy or Godlike in loving one's own kind.

Jan. 8th

READING : **Matthew 6. 1-18**

PRAYER

THE LORD spoke concerning almsgiving, vv. 1–4, prayer, vv. 5–15, and fasting, vv. 16–18. The first is an action directed at one's fellow men, the second is directed to God and the third at oneself. Christ condemned the man who accompanied his alms with the blast of a trumpet, the man who stationed himself to pray in places aimed at giving the maximum publicity and the man who disfigured his face to announce the fact that he was fasting. The first character desired "glory of *men*", v. 2, the second desired to "be seen of *men*", v. 5, and the third desired to "appear unto *men* to fast", v. 16. Of each, Jesus said, "They have their reward". His words signified, "they have signed the receipt of the reward". There was **no** balance to carry forward for heaven's approval! Religious acts which are put on show to win applause have no value in the sight of the Father.

Concerning prayer the Lord had something to say about the place, vv. 5, 6, the manner, vv. 7, 8, and the content, vv. 9–13. That is, He gave instructions where, how and what to pray. Jesus had place neither for play-acting, vv. 5, 6, nor for chanted and empty repetition, vv. 7, 8. The prayer, vv. 9–13, is impressive for its brevity, simplicity and scope. It contains only 66 words and can be repeated in less than 30 seconds. Yet it is a veritable compendium of prayer, with petitions which range from the common needs of the breakfast table to the eternal purpose of God. God's glory is put first and our needs second. While mundane matters are not too trivial for mention, the prayer recognizes the supremacy of the spiritual.

The prayer commences with an intimate, filial mode of address yet, at the same time, upholds the requirement for holy reverence, v. 9. The praying disciple then desires the all-embracing rule of God among men, when earth will yield a fair reflection of His will even as heaven does now, v. 10. Turning from the cosmic plan of the ages, he focuses on present, daily and physical needs, v. 11. Finally, he seeks forgiveness for any past, and deliverance from any future, faults, vv. 12, 13. Taking full account of his own weakness and the cunning and dexterity of the devil, the disciple exhibits a sense of total self-distrust.

Jan. 9th

READING : **Matthew 6. 19-34**

HEAVEN OR EARTH

THE EARLIER section of the chapter questions whether, in our religious activities, we seek the approval of God or men; of heaven or earth, vv. 1–18. The choice between heaven and earth occupies the remainder of the chapter also. Riches can be laid up in either, vv. 19–21. Treasure in heaven represents the best investment and offers the best security. The world says of earthly wealth, "You can't take it with you". How true, 1 Tim. 6. 7; but the Lord tells us that we can send heaven's riches on in advance!

The disciple ought to have one dominating purpose in life—to seek "the kingdom of God", v. 33. His eyes should be fixed unswervingly on heaven's approval and treasure. Selfishness, like a film, clouds the vision and prevents the true light from entering the soul. The Christian must choose who or what is to govern his life. He cannot serve God and gold, v. 24. Because the disciple cannot successfully set his heart on both heavenly and earthly wealth (note the "therefore", v. 25), he should devote every energy to the former and give up all worry and anxiety about the latter, knowing that God will provide for all his needs, vv. 25–34. Worldly cares can be just as detrimental to spiritual life as is the love of money, 13. 22. Anxiety is not only fruitless, v. 27, but unnecessary, vv. 25, 26, 38–30. We should not be troubled about what to put into or onto our bodies. God who gave both life and body will also provide the lesser gifts of food and raiment. We are "much better" than the fowls and "much more" to be clothed than the flowers. The things that matter most to the unconverted man are this world's goods; he seeks "all these things". The Christian seeks first God's kingdom. To him, spiritual things matter most; the rest are merely incidental. God looks after his earthly needs. The worldly man actively pursues the "things" of this world; the disciple receives them from the Father. He cares for God's interests and God cares for his. We should be free from earthly anxiety because God *knows* our needs, v. 32; because He *hears* our prayers, Phil. 4. 6; because He *cares* about us, 1 Pet. 5. 7. With such an unbreakable three-fold cord, Eccles. 4. 12, we can face "the morrow" without fear or care, v. 34.

Jan. 10th

READING : **Matthew 7. 1-29**

HEARING AND DOING

THE LORD'S comments on judgment, vv. 1–6, do not refer to civil courts, Rom. 13. 1–7, or church discipline, 1 Cor. 5. 1–13. His words relate to the private and petty judgment of others which springs from personal dislike, party spirit, envy, etc. Such unnecessary criticism finds no place in the life of a disciple with a humbling realization of his own faults. As the Christian grows in grace, he becomes more severe in his judgment of himself and more lenient in his judgment of others.

Trustful and persistent prayer is the disciple's resource in every need, vv. 7–11. God gives "good things to them that ask him", v. 11; James 1. 17. We often err in our requests and specify a wrong way to achieve a right end; in effect, we ask a serpent! God, however, has regard for our defective vision and, in His loving wisdom, provides something better, Eph. 3. 20. He never leaves us worse off and He never mocks us.

The Lord closes His sermon with a call to discipleship. He speaks of two ways, two trees and two foundations, vv. 13–37. No effort is needed to travel the broad way. It is entered through a gate wide enough to accommodate worldly ambition, lust, greed, etc. Purpose and decision are required to enter and pursue that narrow way which leads to the only life worth mentioning. The man on the broad way says that life consists of getting, being ruthless, hitting back. The man on the narrow way accepts Christ's teaching that life consists of giving, being meek and turning the other cheek. The first series of actions is "evil fruit"; the second is "good fruit". The fruit determines the nature of the tree, vv. 16–20. High profession and spectacular feats do not secure an entrance to God's kingdom; only submission to the will of the Father, v. 21. This will is made known in the "sayings" of Christ, vv. 24–27. The foolish man is the person who lives according to the standards of the world. The wise man is the person who practices Christ's teachings; who lives by His Golden Rule, v. 12. The Lord condenses the whole of the law and the prophets into one simple sentence, v. 12; Rom. 13. 8; it is love in action. Jesus does not demand that we just hear and understand His sayings, still less merely admire and applaud them; see Ezek. 33. 31, 32. He requires that we do them!

Jan. 11th

READING : **Matthew 8. 1-34**

HIS WORD AND HIS HAND

SEVERAL INCIDENTS are related which illustrate that "where the word of a king is, there is power", Eccles. 8. 4.

The authority of the King's word extended over the *ravages of sickness*, vv. 5–13. A servant was paralysed and grievously tormented, but his master had unbounded confidence in Christ. "Speak the word only", he asked. Great was the centurion's compassion, vv. 5, 6, great was his humility, v. 8 with Luke 7. 4, and great was his faith, v. 10. The Lord marvelled at "so great faith", much as His disciples were later to marvel at so great power, v. 27. The centurion's faith surpassed even that of the leper, v. 2, and totally eclipsed the "little faith" of the disciples, vv. 25, 26.

The Lord's word had power also over the *representatives of Satan*. "He cast out the spirits with his word", v. 16. One example is given of His mastery over Satan's forces and kingdom, vv. 28–34. The demons could submit their petition, v. 31, but ultimately they were dependent on His command, v. 32. One word from the King was sufficient. "Go", He said —and "they went".

Finally, His word controlled *the raging of the sea*, vv. 23–27. During the storm He slept "on a pillow", Mark 4. 38. We observe that, a little while before, He had stated that He had "not where to lay his head", v. 20. Possibly some devoted ear had heard, some loving heart been touched and some caring hand had supplied a cushion for His head. He arose and muzzled the tempest. It was a case of "stormy wind fulfilling his word", Psa. 148. 8.

His word was all powerful. He needed nothing more. It is delightful therefore to observe the two occasions on which He extended His hand, vv. 3, 15. How tender was His touch! How appreciated! As far as we know, Jesus had never cleansed a leper previously, and the man of verse 2 is unsure of His willingness to do so now. He has, however, confidence in His power. The leper's "thou canst" contrasts well with the "if thou canst" from the man in Mark 9. 22. Today the Lord still says, "*I will*", to those who have the leprosy of sin. They experience His cleansing, Matt. 8, 3; they enjoy His presence, Heb. 13. 5; and they expect His return, John 14. 3.

Jan. 12th

READING : **Matthew 9. 1-38**

THE PHYSICIAN

ATTENTION IS drawn to the effects of the Lord's miracles on those that saw or heard of them, vv. 8, 26, 31, 33. Great must have been the joy of those who personally experienced His power. Had they chosen to express their merriment in song, James 5. 13, no better words could have been found than those of Psalm 103. 3–5 where David gave five descriptions of the Lord.

To the palsied man, He was the God "*who forgiveth all thine iniquities*", vv. 1–7. The man owed much to the faith of his friends which overcame all obstacles and secured him a blessing even greater than hoped. The couch which had been the symbol of his sickness became the symbol of his cure—and forgiveness! To the woman with the issue of blood, He was the God "*who healeth all thy diseases*", vv. 20–22. Such was the Lord's overflowing compassion that He performed one act of grace on the way to perform another. To the daughter of Jairus, He was the God "*who redeemeth thy life from destruction*", vv. 18, 19, 23–26. Jesus described her death as sleep. It was His pledge of her awakening. "She arose". To the two blind men, who called for mercy, He was the God "*who crowneth thee with . . . tender mercies*", vv. 27–31. The eyes of the blind were opened by the Son of David, come to save, 20. 30; Isa. 35. 4, 5. Finally, to the dumb demoniac, He was the God "*who satisfieth thy mouth with good things*", vv. 32, 33. The man could speak!

In the heart of the section which records these mighty works, the Great Physician likens the sinful outcasts around Him to sick men. He regarded sickness, then, as a suitable picture of sin in its effects. Several representations are given of the sinner. He is without strength to walk aright, v. 2, but the gospel is God's power, Rom. 1. 16; 5. 6. He is defiled, v. 20, plagued, Mark 5. 29, unclean, Lev. 15. 25–30, but the gospel cleanses, 1 John 1. 7. He is dead, v. 18, in sins but the gospel quickens, Eph. 2. 1–5. He is blinded, v. 27, by the god of this world but the gospel enlightens, 2 Cor. 4. 4–6. He has nothing to say, v. 32, by way of confession, Rom. 10. 9, or praise, 1 Pet. 2. 5, but the gospel looses his tongue.

"Bless the Lord, O my soul", Psa. 103. 2.

Jan. 13th

READING : **Matthew 10. 1-42**

ALL NEEDS MET

THE LORD commissioned His apostles; "Go", He said, v. 6. Before they were ever "sent forth", v. 5, however, He first "gave them power", v. 1. The Lord always provides a supply of strength proportionate to the task He sets. From the day that David was anointed king, the Spirit of the Lord came on him, 1 Sam. 16. 13. If Elisha was to be prophet in Elijah's "room", 1 Kings 19. 16, then he would receive Elijah's mantle and a double portion of his spirit, 2 Kings 2. 9–15. When the Lord calls He always equips and meets all needs.

Jesus told the apostles to whom to go, vv. 5, 6, what to do and say, vv. 7, 8 and how they would be supported, vv. 9–13. Then He told them how they were to act if people rejected both them and their message, vv. 14, 15. He would later go on to speak of the eternal rewards in store for those who cordially received His ambassadors, vv. 40–42. But first, vv. 16–39, He paused to warn the disciples of the severe opposition which they would face and to give them some words of encouragement.

The apostles were to be as shrewd as the serpent and guileless as the dove, because they would be exposed to the slaughter as sheep, unable to protect themselves, v. 16. They could expect trouble from both civil and religious authorities, from both Jews and Gentiles, vv. 17, 18. The Lord assured them that they need not be *over-anxious*, vv. 19, 20. Although "unlearned", Acts 4. 13, they would be able to withstand their superiors in authority and knowledge by reason of the Spirit's guidance. Neither need they be *fearful*, vv. 26, 28, 31. Why should they fear suffering when it conformed them to their Master?, vv. 24, 25. They could also look forward to a time when their integrity and triumph would be openly acknowledged, vv. 26, 27. They need not fear foes whose power was limited; those who could harm the body and no more, v. 28. Fear has no place in the heart which realizes that the most trivial incidents of life work only for good. God cares for details, v. 30. He cares too for the common sparrows; how much more for His children, vv. 29, 31. Without anxiety about their words or fear for their safety, the disciples should confess Christ and love Him above all others, vv. 32–39.

Jan. 14th

READING : **Matthew 11. 1-30**

A SOUL AT REST

STRESS IS laid on the time and setting of Jesus' prayer, vv. 25, 26. The expression, "At that time", directs us to the dark background described in the earlier part of the chapter.

The faith of John the Baptist had faltered, vv. 1–15. John had been in the prison of Machaerus for a considerable time. News was carried to him of Jesus' works, v. 2, notably the raising of the son of the widow of Nain, Luke 7. 18. John had no doubt that Jesus was a great prophet but was now less confident that He was the Christ, v. 3. The Messiah was "to proclaim liberty to the captives, and the opening of the prison . . .", Isa. 61. 1. John had announced that the kingdom of heaven was imminent, 3. 2. If Jesus was the King, where was the freedom, fire and fan?, 3. 11, 12. Jesus invited John to reconsider His works, vv. 4–6 with Isaiah 35. 3–6; 61. 1, 2.

The generation which Jesus served was critical and scornful of both His own and John's ministries, vv. 16–19. John failed to please them because he refused to enter into their self-indulgent pleasures. John would "not dance". They dismissed him as a demon-possessed fanatic. Jesus did not satisfy their wishes either. He refused to adopt the rules of their oral tradition with its hypocritical washings and fastings. He would "not lament". They dismissed Him as an glutton.

The cities, where Jesus had performed the majority of His signs, refused to respond with repentance, vv. 20–24. The most favoured area on earth remained in unbelief.

All these circumstances were calculated to discourage. It seemed that He had spent His strength "for nought, and in vain", Isa. 49. 4. But He would "not fail nor be discouraged", 42. 4. "At that time", Matt. 11. 25, He turned to God in praise. When Jacob had crossed his hands while blessing Joseph's sons, Joseph had exclaimed, "Not so, my father", Gen. 48. 17, 18. The Lord could see that His Father likewise crossed His hands, revealing His secrets to infants and hiding them from the wise. But He responded, "Even so, Father". In the face of His trials and rejection, the Lord manifested an entire submission to the will and yoke of His Father and therein found rest for His soul. Amidst all, He remained composed and at peace. Today He offers the same rest to us.

Jan. 15th

READING : **Matthew 12. 1-21**

LAWFUL

THE PHARISEES were concerned to safeguard the interests of their day of rest, vv. 2, 10. Jesus had, however, already offered men a far better rest, 11. 28, 29.

The Pharisees criticized the disciples for satisfying their hunger by plucking and eating ears of corn on the sabbath; it was "not lawful", v. 2. In reply, Jesus cited two cases; that of David, for whom it was technically "not lawful" to eat the shewbread, Lev. 24. 9; 1 Sam. 21. 6, and, just as relevant, that of the priesthood who served in the temple on the sabbath, Num. 28. 9, 10. In both cases the letter of the Jewish law came into collision with higher laws and principles. The action of David was justified by the priority of need, and that of the priests by the priority of God's service. The Pharisees had their set of values all wrong. If they had grasped the true essential of pure religion they would have pitied the disciples and not condemned them, Matt. 12. 7. The priests' involvement with the temple exonerated them from blame. How much more therefore were the disciples absolved from guilt by their association with One "greater than the temple"! The angel had said of Jesus, "He shall be great", Luke 1. 32. In His priestly office, He was greater than the temple, v. 6; in His prophetic office, He was greater than Jonah, v. 41; in His kingly office, He was greater than Solomon, v. 42. The Messiah had full authority to direct the manner of the sabbath observance and to sanction acts of necessity on that day, v. 8.

Asked by the Pharisees, "Is it lawful *to heal*" on the sabbath, Jesus responded, "it is lawful *to do well*", vv. 10, 12. They regarded healing the sick as a work which could be avoided; He regarded it as a duty which could not. To leave undone any good work which lies in one's power to perform, is to do evil. Having therefore to "do" something, Jesus would "do well"!

Contrary to the popular expectation of a Messianic conqueror, the Servant of the Lord scorned self-advertisement and ostentation, vv. 16–19. Although severe with the hypocritical Pharisees, He would show extreme gentleness to the feeble and infirm, v. 20.

Jan. 16th

READING : **Matthew 12. 22-50**

THE POWER OF SATAN OR GOD ?

THE PHARISEES were dismayed because the people drew the proper inference from the Lord's mighty work of healing, v. 23. His power certainly could not be explained in merely human terms. Unable to question the genuineness of the miracle and unwilling to attribute it to the power of God, the Pharisees asserted that Jesus was in league with the devil. The Lord took up their charge and calmly tore it to pieces. He pointed to the absurd assumption involved in the accusation, namely, that Satan was acting against himself. No organized society (kingdom, city or household) can stand when it is divided. Satan's power was failing, Christ argued, not because of civil war within but because of an invasion from without. Satan had encountered a power stronger than his own. The power of God's Spirit had intervened; God's kingdom had burst upon men.

"He that is not against us is for us", Luke 9. 50, is the yardstick by which the disciple measures others. When examining himself, however, the test he applies is, "He that is not with me is against me", Matt. 12. 30. There is no neutral ground!

Rather than accept Christ's miracle as evidence of His Messiahship, the Pharisees would sooner distort good into evil by crediting the Spirit's power to the account of the devil. Such men were determined to reject Jesus and to shut their eyes to any evidence whatsoever. There was no hope for them. Nothing further could be done to convince them or move them to repentance—without which there could be no forgiveness, vv. 31, 32; Mark 3. 28–30. Consistency demanded, Jesus continued, that the tree and its fruit be of the same character. If casting out demons (the fruit) was a good work, the power to do it (the tree) must also be good, Matt. 12. 33. The Pharisees' charge revealed the true state of their heart. Words were an index of character and, as such, would count as evidence "in the day of judgment", vv. 34–37.

The Lord refused to perform a wonder with the object of dazzling people into accepting Him. Men should have read by faith the Messianic signs already given and responded with repentance, vv. 38–42.

Jan. 17th

READING : **Matthew 13. 1-23**

THE SOWER, SEED AND SOIL

THE SEVEN parables told by Balaam concerned the nation of Israel, Num. 23, 24; the seven parables told by Jesus in Matthew 13 concern the kingdom of heaven.

The first of the Lord's parables is that of the Sower. Its importance can be gauged from the fact that it is one of the only two parables common to all the Synoptic Gospels. The parable challenges men as to whether they are receiving the "seed", which is "the word of the kingdom", to good and lasting effect. Given that the sower does his work well and that the seed is good, the results of the sowing depend on the kind of place where the seed falls.

Jesus describes four types of ground: the wayside, the stony places, the thorny soil and the good ground. With the first, the seed went on but not in; with the second, it went in and on but not down; with the third, it went in, on and down but never came up. Only with the fourth did the seed go on, in, down and come up in an abundant harvest; it was not eaten, scorched or choked but fruitful. The first represents the case where "the word" lies on the surface of a man's memory. Its meaning is never really grasped by the mind, and it therefore falls an easy prey to the devil. The second is the case where "the word" is eagerly received but is not taken deeply to heart. The hearer is therefore altogether unprepared to face the subsequent testing that comes in the form of opposition. The third is the case where "the word" is received and gives every appearance and promise of life. As the days go by, however, the effect of that word is checked and frustrated by the preoccupations of the present life; by worry, wealth and worldliness, Luke 8. 14. The fourth represents the case where "the word" is not only heard and understood but abides and yields lasting results in the life. The man is "saved". See Luke 8. 12.

One practical point: Jesus said that a sower "*went forth* to sow". The sower did not merely put an advertisement in the local newspaper announcing that Mr. So-and-So would be sowing the seed at 6.30 on the next Lord's day and saying, in effect, "Now, all you ground, come and be sowed". Neither Jesus nor the apostles worked that way!

Jan. 18th

READING : **Matthew 13. 24-58**

THE KINGDOM OF HEAVEN

THE READING contains six parables. The first three parables were spoken, as was that of the Sower, outside the house and were addressed to the multitude, vv. 1–3. The last three parables were spoken inside the house and were addressed to the disciples, v. 36. The first three parables are concerned with the appearance and character of what is outwardly the kingdom of heaven. The last three reveal God's thoughts about the kingdom, and show that He has an answer to all the wickedness and failure associated with the false profession described in the three public parables. The One who told the parables possessed great authority, claiming that the world, the angels and the kingdom were all His, vv. 24, 37–41.

Each of the last three parables corresponds closely to one of the first three. There is a close similarity between the interpretation of the first and last parables, vv. 40–42, 49, 50. The "*tares*" teach that the devil introduces his agents alongside "the children of the kingdom", vv. 38, 39. The "*net*" teaches that the Lord will, in His own time and manner, separate out the bad from the good, vv. 48–50.

The "*mustard seed*" describes how, from humble beginnings, the movement professing the name of Christ would become an impressive and imposing organisation in the world, vv. 31, 32. For the symbolism of the tree, birds and boughs, see Ezekiel 31 and Daniel 4. Possibly the "birds of the air" represent Satanic influence, Luke 8. 5, 12. The "*one pearl*", vv. 45, 46, is the true church (the "one body", Eph. 4. 4–16) which, though remaining comparatively small, is immensely valuable in the sight of the Lord. In the language of the parable, He "sold all that he had, and bought it". See 2 Cor. 8. 9; Eph. 5. 25. One day the "pearl" will be presented to Him in all its flawless perfection, Eph. 5. 27.

The "*leaven*", v. 33, speaks of corruption which works subtly; both evil doctrine, 16. 6, 12, and wickedness, 1 Cor. 5. 8. If the "mustard seed" describes the external growth of the professing church, the hiding of the "leaven" describes its inward corruption. But the Lord has something hidden too, v. 44. Israel is His "*treasure*", hidden now in the field of the world but precious to Him.

Jan. 19th

READING : **Matthew 14. 1-36**

FEEDING THE MULTIDUDE

THE VOICE that had once cried in the wilderness had been violently silenced. When Herod heard about Jesus, his guilty conscience concluded that John had come back from the dead and was performing miracles in resurrection, something he had never done in his life, John 10. 41. On hearing of John's martyrdom, Jesus sought out a place of solitude. He was, however, allowed no peace. The multitude followed Him and rudely interrupted His meditation. It is delightful to notice the manner in which the Saviour received them. There was no trace of irritation; no hint of annoyance. He was moved, not with feelings of resentment but, "with compassion toward them and, he healed their sick", Matt. 14. 14.

Later, He fed the whole company, which numbered over five thousand, with "but five loaves, and two fishes". We should observe the Lord's method of working. He first required the disciples to bring their limited resources to Him, then He wonderfully multiplied their contribution and finally returned it to them for onward distribution to the crowd. Today, He still wishes to employ His disciples in meeting the needs of men. He asks that we bring to Him the little which we have, He blesses it in His own unique way and then looks to us to hand it out. It is an unspeakable privilege to be thus used of the Lord. Yet it is also our responsibility.

> "Thou hast no hands, O Christ, as once of old
> To feed the multitude with bread divine.
> Thou hast the living bread, enough for all,
> But there's no hand to give it out save mine".

That night the disciples were rowing hard on the turbulent Sea of Galilee. Jesus approached them, walking on the water. To calm their fears, He said simply, "It is I; be not afraid". His words, "*It is finished*", John 19. 30, direct us to His cross and a salvation that is complete. His words, "*It is written*", Matt. 4. 4, direct us to His word and a weapon that enables us to overcome the wicked one. His words, "*It is I*", Matt. 14. 27, direct us to His Person and His abiding presence through all our struggles and anxieties.

Jan. 20th

READING : **Matthew 15. 1-31**

GREAT FAITH

THE WOMAN from Canaan clearly had a genuine need; her daughter was cruelly tormented by a demon. Yet it seemed at first that she was to be refused her request. Initially the Lord met her plea with silence and when He later spoke neither of His statements was encouraging. To His disciples, who took up her case, He said, "I am *not* sent. . . " and to her further appeal He answered, "It is *not* meet. . . ". It was not that He lacked compassion in any way for either the woman or her child. The stumblingblock to His helping her lay in the manner of her original approach to Him. She addressed Him as "son of David"—His most distinctively Jewish title. Others did so and were blessed without delay, 9. 27; 20. 30, 31. But they were Jews and she was a Gentile. She had no just claim on Him in His character as Son of David. Her ground of approach had been wrong.

The Lord gently brings home to her the outside place that was properly hers. He likened her position to that of the domestic pet of the household in contrast to that of the children (which represented the people of Israel). Her faith asserted itself magnificently in her reply. She did not contradict Him; she turned His own words around to support her case. She took up the very theme that He had directed at her, and with the humble boldness of faith sent it back again in her reply. Recognizing now her true place before Him, she pointed out that even the housedog could expect its portion. She did not intend to deprive Israel of any of its privileges. She was not claiming the share of the "children". Yet surely she was free to request the "crumbs". Her faith in Him was such that she likened to mere crumbs the power necessary for Him to deal with her child. Great was her faith and Jacob-like she wrestled and prevailed over Him. "Be it . . . as thou wilt", He said. At first it had seemed that she was to be denied the smallest boon; now He opens for her the vast treasure house of His resources and bids her take all she needs.

May God give us faith to "pray without ceasing", 1 Thess. 5. 17. Remember, His delays in answering are not necessarily denials!

Jan. 21st

READING : **Matthew 15. 32 to 16. 12**

FULL CONSECRATION

THIS WAS the second time that Jesus had fed a large multitude with just a few loaves and fishes. It is well known that the baskets which were filled with the remaining fragments on this second occasion were larger than those that had been filled on the first. Nevertheless the number of baskets involved have a simple but valuable lesson to teach us.

When the Lord had fed over five thousand with five loaves and two fishes, twelve baskets had been filled with fragments. Now He used seven loaves and a few fishes to feed a much smaller number. We might therefore have expected to find more than twelve baskets filled afterwards. In the event, only seven baskets were required. Why do the results of the miracle not appear to have been so great as before? The explanation lies in Mark 8. 10–14. Mark tells us that, immediately following the incident, the disciples had "one loaf" with them in their ship. Jesus had asked them plainly, "How many loaves have ye?" It seems that they either forgot or withheld one loaf in the boat. The blessing was reduced because, when asked, they failed to surrender and consecrate all they had to Him. If we are to experience full blessing in His service, He must have our all. Does He have it?

The Lord later warned His disciples to "beware of the leaven of the Pharisees and of the Sadducccs". He was referring to doctrine but the disciples mistakenly understood Him to refer to their failure to bring food. He reminded them of the two occasions on which He had recently fed vast multitudes. For Him to feed Himself and the disciples would therefore have been a relatively small thing. In the light of earlier events, they should never have imagined that the provision of a meal could prove a problem to Him. When faced with fresh needs, we should consider how the Lord has proved Himself on our behalf in the past and trust Him to do the same again. David provides us with an example of the reasoning of faith when he said, "The Lord that delivered me out of the paw of the lion, and out of the paw of the bear, he will deliver me out of the hand of this Philistine", 1 Sam. 17. 37. Paul followed the same line of reasoning, 2 Cor. 1. 10. Do we?

Jan. 22nd

READING : **Matthew 16. 13-28**

THE SUFFERINGS OF CHRIST

THE PERSONALITY of Jesus clearly made a profound impression on the people of His day. No doubt they discerned qualities in the Lord which led them to make the identifications which they did, v. 14. He shared the Baptist's uncompromising condemnation of sin and hypocrisy; He was marked by the same unflinching and fearless courage which men associated with Elijah and He displayed feelings of compassion similar to those of the weeping prophet. But Peter knew that the past and its notable figures had gone. Now they were faced with Him, who was none other than the Christ and nothing less than the Son of God. Through all that he had heard and seen of the Lord, Peter had been enabled by the Father to penetrate to the secret of His Person, v. 16.

Peter however had a long way to go. He did not share the popular views of Jesus' identity but he most certainly shared the popular views of what Messiahship involved. His conception of Messiahship fell hopelessly short of the truth and consequently, when Jesus spoke about dying at Jerusalem, he withstood Him, vv. 21, 22. Peter was right about His titles but wrong about His mission. The cross was a stumblingblock to Peter. This proved that his ideas of Messiahship were moulded by men and not by God. For, in the divine purpose, the suffering of the Christ was an integral part of His mission, 20. 28. Peter later came to understand all this. In his first Epistle, he speaks of the Lord's sufferings in every chapter—and every time associates them with the title Christ.

In the words spoken by Peter at Caesarea Philippi, Jesus heard two distinct echoes from the past. He recognized first the voice of His Father, which at His baptism had declared His divine and unique Sonship, vv. 16, 17. He recognized later the voice of the devil, which at His temptation in the wilderness had tempted Him to bypass the cross and take a short cut to the throne, vv. 22, 23. The same fountain (Peter's lips) sent forth sweet and bitter water that day, James 3. 11. But He was not fooled. He could not be sidetracked from His mission of salvation. He had a Church to build, v. 18. Such was Hi[illegible] for this Church that the Christ was willing to give [illegible] it, Eph. 5. 25.

Jan. 23rd

READING : **Matthew 17. 1-27**

JESUS ONLY

BOTH AT His baptism and on the mount of transfiguration, God singled out the Lord Jesus as, "my beloved Son, in whom I am well pleased", 3. 17; 17. 5. At the Jordan the Father distinguished Him from the worst of men. On the mount He distinguished Him from the best of men.

In every way the Lord is greater than either Moses or Elijah. They were both prophets who had spoken the word of the Lord. But God is now speaking "by his son", Heb. 1. 1, 2. "Hear ye him", He said, Matt. 17. 5. Moses and Elijah were both men of mountains (Sinai and Carmel) but on this mountain, they must retire and leave us to see "Jesus only".

Moses and Elijah both controlled the mighty waters. Moses needed a rod, Exod. 14. 16, and Elijah a robe, 2 Kings 2. 8. Jesus too controlled the water: His word was sufficient, 8. 26.

The exit of Moses and the exit of Elijah from the world were both unusual to say the least! Moses died on a mountain on account of a sin he had committed, and had God for his undertaker. Elijah was translated direct to glory. The Lord's departure was the sum of both. Like Moses, He died on a mountain (though for *our* sins) and the circumstances of His burial were all arranged by God, Isa. 53. 9. Like Elijah, He was "carried up into heaven", Luke 24. 51.

In the face of the many problems confronting him, Moses was all set at one stage to give in. Concerning his task, he said, "*it is* ' *heavy*", Num. 11. 14. On one occasion, Elijah likev nd the way too hard, and cried, "*It is enough*", 1 K' The Lord faced waves of opposition altogether
'ier prophet, and yet He continued until He
'inished", John 19. 30.

h were able only to direct and influence the
of he people. They were unable to change
'ly the most outspoken of the people's
' confessions, 1 Kings 18. 39, came
d a new covenant in His blood.
' is written in our hearts.

'lassed the Lord with Moses
sson. In his account of the
s only", 2 Pet. 1. 16-18.

Jan. 24th

READING : **Matthew 18. 1-14**

THESE LITTLE ONES

When the disciples queried who would be greatest in the kingdom, a little child provided the Lord with an apt illustration for His reply, vv. 1, 2. A child is a total stranger to pride, haughtiness and selfish ambition. The Lord warned the disciples that, unless they reversed the direction of their thinking and learned the trust and humility of a child, they could never begin to learn what the rule of God meant. Unless the disciples turned from their self-seeking ambition, they would not enter His kingdom, let alone be the greatest in it.

True humility does not consist in thinking bad things about ourselves; it consists in not thinking of ourselves at all. Disciples need this kind of humility if they are to attain greatness in the kingdom of heaven, v. 4.

Not only, however, must the disciple be humble and unassuming himself, but he must adopt the right attitude to others who believe in Jesus. For him to receive one of them is to receive the Lord Himself, v. 5. To make the path of the humble more difficult to tread is the direst sin. It is better not to live than not to love, v. 6. Any tendency in the disciple that proves a cause of temptation and stumbling to others must be dealt with ruthlessly—whatever the personal cost, vv. 7–9.

The passage emphasizes that humble believers are usually of no great account in the eyes of the world; it describes them repeatedly as "little" children, vv. 3, 4, 5, 6, 10, 14. The besetting sin of many Pharisees and teachers of the law was contempt for the unlearned and those they considered to be unworthy of notice. The disciple, however, must be careful not to despise any of the Lord's "little ones", v. 10. The Lord gives three reasons. They are ministered to by high and noble beings who enjoy God's presence and favour, v. 10; they have been sought and saved by the Son of man to whom they are unspeakably precious, vv. 11–13; they are the objects of the preserving purpose and grace of the Father, v. 14. The "little ones" may be viewed with scorn and disdain by the men of the world but their well being is of supreme importance to the holy angels, to the divine Shepherd and to the Father who will allow none to be lost. May the Lord deliver us from trampling on those He describes as "the apple of his eye", Zech. 2. 8.

Jan. 25th

READING : **Matthew 18. 15-35**

FORGIVENESS

PETER INTERRUPTED the Lord to request clarification of a point, v. 21. The Lord had been outlining the procedure to be followed if one Christian wronged another, vv. 15–17. He had implied that a repentant brother was to be forgiven, v. 15. That was fine but what, Peter wanted to know, if the brother committed a second offence . . . and a third? How many times should the Christian forgive another before he decided that enough was enough? Peter suggested that seven times might not be unreasonable, v. 21.

The Lord replied with a parable, vv. 23–34. The servant of a certain king had owed him a fabulous sum of money and had begged for time to repay it. In the event, the king went much further than the servant asked. He did not give time for the servant to discharge his debt; he freely forgave him and cancelled it all. The servant was free. Soon after, this same servant discovered a fellow servant who owed him some trivial amount. His colleague begged for time to pay his debt but was sternly refused and harshly treated. When the king became acquainted with the facts of the case, he dealt with the merciless servant in an appropriate manner.

No matter how often our brothers and sisters may sin against us, their indebtedness to us will always pale into insignificance when compared with the number of sins which God, in His grace, has forgiven us. We can usually count on one hand the number of times other saints have wronged us. Yet an electronic calculator would fail to keep pace with the number of times we have offended our Lord. And He has graciously forgiven all!

We need to remind ourselves constantly of the cost and of the importance of our forgiveness. It will prompt us not only to love the Lord more, Luke 7. 41–43, but also the more readily to forgive those that sin against us. No numerical limits can be placed on forgiveness in the kingdom of heaven, when the only means of entry into that kingdom is forgiveness unlimited. If we always forgive our brother *from the heart*, v. 35, we will never even know how often we have forgiven him because we will not have been keeping count!

See to it then that you follow Ephesians 4. 32.

Jan. 26th

READING : **Matthew 19. 1-15**

FORBID THEM NOT

A QUESTION asked by the Pharisees gave rise to the explanation by the Lord of His doctrine on marriage. He turned away from the law, Deut. 24. 1–4, which had been given on account of the hardness of their hearts. He referred back to God's original intention, according to which one man and one woman united together and became one in His sight. The Lord therefore re-established the true character of the marriage bond. The bond was indissoluble apart from the exceptional ground of fornication. The disciples expressed the view that if marriage was so binding then it was better never to get married! Some men, the Lord explained, certainly would never marry and help bring children into the world. The highest motive to this was that of those who renounced family life for the sake of the kingdom of heaven. The apostles clearly took this to mean that marriage and family life constituted an undesirable "second best" for a disciple.

It was "Then" that the children were brought to Him. We are not told by whom, v. 13; Mark 10. 13; Luke 18. 15, but no doubt parents were involved. In any case, the Lord's self-appointed bodyguards were swift to act. It seemed obvious to them that He, who had just spoken of marriage in such terms, would not thank them if He was pestered by a company of parents and children. They therefore "rebuked them". They felt sure that Jesus would have no interest in children. How wrong they were! He was very angry about it all, Mark 10. 14. He called the children to Him, Luke 18. 16, and rebuked the disciples. To avoid any misunderstanding, He expressed His interest in the children by both positive and negative commands; they were to be allowed to come and they were not to be prevented from coming. Then He not only laid His hands on them, v. 15, but also folded them in His arms and blessed them, Mark 10. 16. We can associate this with the interest He took in the games the children played in the market place, 11. 16, 17. His very last message before He was crucified included a reference to children, Luke 23. 28.

Let all those who work with the young, in the Sunday School, children's meeting, classroom or home, take encouragement. The Lord is interested in children.

Jan. 27th

READING : **Matthew 19. 16 to 20. 16**

MY MOTIVE IN SERVICE

THE LORD told the parable of the labourers, Matt. 20. 1–15, to illustrate and explain His saying, "Many that are first shall be last; and the last shall be first". The point of the parable lies in the way in which the wages were paid at the end of the day, v. 8. Those men were paid first who had worked for the shortest time. When the turn came for those to be paid who had worked twelve times as long, they received the same payment—and were not impressed, vv. 11, 12. The men who started work first had become last; they were paid later than the others and paid less in proportion to the work they had done. But they had "agreed" their wages in advance, v. 2. It had all been conducted in a very business-like manner. They had wanted to know then what they were going to get for their labours. The later workers, on the other hand, had not insisted on negotiating a rate of payment; they had been prepared to trust in the honesty and goodness of the vineyard owner. This latter attitude paid high dividends! He was just with the first, v. 13, but with them he was generous, v. 14. The bargainers ("the first") found themselves "last" in the queue where to be first was to benefit most.

The parable was aimed at the disciples. They had heard Jesus require the rich young man to forsake all and follow Him; in exchange for which He had promised "treasure in heaven", 19. 21. The young man had not been prepared to pay the price—but they had paid it. Having fulfilled the Lord's conditions, they wanted to know more details about the "treasure" to which they felt entitled, v. 27. First, the Lord graciously promised them places of authority in His kingdom and a hundredfold compensation for all earthly relationships they had sacrificed. Then He told the parable. In effect it warned them not to become over-occupied with the details of their reward. A little done in the spirit of love and devotion was worth more than much done in the spirit of an hireling. Heavenly reward is promised us as an encouragement in our service for Christ—it should not be the motive. "The love of Christ constraineth us", 2 Cor. 5. 14. We can safely trust the Lord to reward fairly. He "is not unrighteous to forget . . .", Heb. 6. 10.

Jan. 28th

READING : **Matthew 20. 17-34**

TRUE GREATNESS

LIKE so many others, Salome expected the Lord Jesus to redeem Israel from the hated Roman oppressor, and to establish an earthly, political kingdom. She coveted prominent places of authority and power for her sons in that kingdom. Her sons shared her aspirations for them. Jesus questioned their ability to share His cup and baptism. He was referring to His forthcoming suffering but they completely misunderstood Him. Drinking a cup in the Old Testament could imply good or ill, and James and John interpreted His words as referring to blessings and responsibilities in the kingdom. They therefore asserted that they were able to share His rule in it. Sadly, Jesus confirmed that they would both experience "the fellowship of his sufferings", Phil. 3. 10. The position of eminence, however, was not His to give.

The other apostles were aggrieved at the selfish petition; deeply resenting the attempt to secure the chief places in the kingdom. Yet the resentment of the ten men was rooted in precisely the same soil as the request of the two. Clearly all twelve disciples pictured Christ's kingdom as similar to the Roman Empire with its procurators, puppet-kings and Emperor. The self-seeking of the two brothers and the displeasure of the other disciples stemmed from the same worldly conception of greatness; the man with authority being considered the greatest. But they all had it wrong! The rules of Jesus' kingdom ran in the opposite direction. The greatest of all was the servant of all. James and John should not have sought a position where they would be served and the others should not have been so angry at the prospect of serving them. The Lord cited His own example—in life and death. He had come to serve and to give His life for others. His words find an adequate commentary in today's reading. His readiness "to minister" is illustrated in verses 29–34. Others thought that the blind men did not merit His attention; He stopped and gave them sight. "What will ye that I shall do unto you?" are the words of one who ministers. His willingness "to give his life" is explicitly affirmed in verses 17–19.

A question faces us today. Would we rather be a servant or a ruler among God's people?

Jan. 29th

READING : **Matthew 21. 1-16**

THE KING COMES

THE LORD'S entry to Jerusalem was accompanied by considerable excitement and enthusiasm. May God give us to capture a little of the thrill that always comes with seeing "the king in his beauty", Isa. 33. 17. We should notice the King's

Poverty. The Lord had a genuine "need", Matt. 21. 3. He rode a borrowed ass for the obvious reason that He owned no ass of His own. Nor does this surprise us. He preached from another man's boat, illustrated His message with another man's coin, ate the Passover in another man's room and, following His death, lay in another man's sepulchre. The disciple's garments provided His only saddle. Yet He who rode on an ass doubtless could have created a diamond-studded chariot of the finest gold. Truly, He who was rich had become poor!

Tenderness. The prophet had foretold that Christ would use two animals. Jesus rode on the younger of the two, John 12. 14, but had the older beast brought also. It is likely that the ass and her colt had never yet been separated and He was concerned about the feelings of both. Few men would have given this a second thought. Such consideration was, however, characteristic of Him who brought water out of the rock for beasts to drink, Num. 20. 11, and who spared Nineveh on account partly of its "much cattle", Jonah 4. 11.

Lowliness. The King was entering His royal city. He possessed kingly authority, an authority which was recognized not only by men, Matt. 21. 3, 6, but also by beasts, v. 7. In this connection it is significant that the colt had never been broken in, Luke 19. 30. Nevertheless His approach was marked by the total absence of any ostentation or pageantry. For the Lord, greatness went hand in hand with lowliness.

Courage. He had no gleaming sword in His hand, no helmet on His brow, no prancing charger beneath Him. He rode an ass, such as monarchs in ancient times rode on missions of peace. Yet His face was altogether that of a warrior. He had come to the holy city to fight for a kingdom—albeit not of this world. In five days time He must die. A cross was to be the triumph chariot from which He would lay low our many foes. Knowing full well the battle that lay ahead, John 18. 4, the Lion of Judah turned "not away for any", Prov. 30. 30.

Jan. 30th

READING : **Matthew 21. 17 to 22. 14**

ONLY LEAVES

JESUS AND His disciples left Bethany early one morning. In the fresh, spring air, He became hungry. A solitary fig tree grew in the rocky soil by the roadside. It was not the season of figs but the tree, covered with leaves, attracted His attention. It is well known that the leaves of the fig tree develop after the fruit. Out of season, this tree had precociously put forth its leaves, giving every promise of fruit beneath.

The Lord, however, found "leaves only", 21. 19. Its foliage lied. There was no fruit! Jesus uttered a command and immediately it began to dry up. The disciples noticed nothing unusual and passed on. It was the following morning that they observed the effect of Christ's word, Mark 11. 20, 21.

In the Old Testament, the fig tree had been used as a symbol of the nation of Israel, Joel 1. 7. The Lord therefore selected the premature and barren germination of the fig tree as an emblem of a people who, for all their high profession and ritual formality, were totally destitute of fruits of righteousness, without which the mere external forms were worse than useless. Israel's fig leaves were an attempt to cover its true nakedness before God, just as fig leaves had been used to cover the nakedness of the man and the woman in Eden, Gen. 3. 7. The tree must therefore be destroyed.

It is thrilling to remember that to us who once had "leaves only", God revealed "Jesus only", Matt. 17. 8. He demanded, "believe only", Luke 8. 50. Yet the question faces us—are we all talk or is the fruit of the Spirit, Gal. 5. 22, 23, really being produced in our lives?

The Lord then spoke about the failures of His self-righteous people, and of their leaders in particular, 21. 45. In the parable of the two sons, 21. 28–32, He contrasted them and their loud *profession* of obedience with the outcast multitude who repented and found salvation under John's ministry. In the parable of the vineyard, 21. 33-46, He spoke about their *responsibility* and their failure to fulfil it. In the parable of the marriage feast, 22. 1–14, He described their gospel *privileges*. They were the guests who were called first but refused to come.

Let us see that our profession is real, that we rise to our responsibilities and that we value our many privileges.

Jan. 31st

READING : **Matthew 22. 15-46**

WHOSE IMAGE ?

THE LORD was confronted by a number of Herodians and disciples of the Pharisees, v. 16. The question which they put to Him, v. 17, was not however their own. It was the brain-child of the nation's religious leaders; the Pharisees, v. 15, the chief priests and the scribes, Luke 20. 19, 20. The question they had selected was one on which the nation was divided. They arranged for representatives of both parties to the controversy to be present. The Herodians represented the party loyal to the Roman government. The Pharisees were strongly opposed to it and felt a quiet sympathy for the many rebellions that had arisen against the emperor. The intention was to ensnare and entangle Jesus in His words.

Palestine had been ruled by the Romans through its procurators since A.D. 6. The payment of tribute was one of the most tangible—and most resented—symbols of that rule. The Jewish delegation came with their honeyed words of flattery, v. 16, intending to disarm any suspicions Jesus may have had. He saw through it all!, v. 18. They aimed to face the Lord with a deadly dilemma. It would have been fatal to have answered either way. To have said, Yes, would have been to recognize the royal authority of Caesar, and to give the lie to any claim of His to be Messiah. The Pharisees were then ready to accuse Him to the people as an enemy of their national hopes. The rulers expected, however, that He would have said, No. The Herodians were then ready to accuse Him to Pilate as an enemy of the Roman state, Luke 20. 20; 23. 2. Their plans were cunningly laid and skilfully executed!

The Lord answered them with perfect wisdom, as He did the later questions, vv. 23–40. He pointed them to the image, name and titles on their coin, which broadcast the fact of Roman domination. The Lord argued the propriety of paying tax to Caesar on the ground that it was only giving the emperor back his own property. But He went further. Man also bore an image—albeit defaced and soiled, v. 21; Gen. 1. 26, 27. Jesus reminded the men of God's rights over them. They left Him; their purpose frustrated, v. 22.

We, too, must render "unto Caesar" his things, Rom. 13. 1–7, and "unto God" the things that are His, 12. 1, 2.

Feb. 1st

READING : **Matthew 23. 1-39**

BLESSED IS HE

THE CLOSING verses give us the last words which the Lord Jesus addressed to His nation. It is very moving to see His compassion for Israel revealed as He surveyed His ministry among them. How sad that He needed to speak also of wilful rejection by those who chose not to be saved.

A hen and her chickens provided Him with an exquisite picture of the protection and care which He had offered, v. 37. But, oh, the fearful resistance of which the human will was capable! Israel "would not". How much more happy are they to whom it can be said, "He shall cover thee with his feathers, and under his wings shalt thou trust", Psa. 91. 4. Jesus had earlier spoken of *a gnat and a camel*, v. 24, to highlight the inconsistent actions of a people who concentrated on relatively trivial matters to the exclusion of the important issues of spiritual life. He had also mentioned *serpents and vipers*, v. 33, as best describing the wicked character of those who were like their "father the devil", John 8. 44 with Rev. 12. 9.

The nation would no more see Him as a merciful Saviour offering redemption; yet one day they would recognize and welcome Him as their Deliverer, v. 39. Then the earlier acclaim of the multitude, 21. 9, would be heard again!

The Lord's sad lamentation followed immediately on a scathing denunciation. The works of these truth-hating, God-rejecting hypocrites were performed only to win the applause of men. The woes Jesus pronounced against them provide us with a full length portrait of the hypocrite, with all his false profession and shameful inconsistencies.

There were eight woes in all, vv. 13, 14, 15, 16, 23, 25, 27, 29. They remind us of the eight woes which Isaiah the prophet uttered against his contemporaries, Isaiah 3. 9, 11; 5. 8, 11, 18, 20, 21, 22. There was, however, one important difference between Isaiah and Jesus. Faced with the majesty and holiness of the Lord of hosts, the prophet was forced to pronounce one more woe—on himself, Isaiah 6. 5. Not so the Lord! He closed His address not with a woe but with a beatitude, v. 39. Isaiah had eight woes for others and then added "*Woe* is me", Jesus had eight woes for others but then, concerning Himself, He added, "*Blessed* is He".

Feb. 2nd

READING : **Matthew 24. 1-51**

THE COMING OF THE SON OF MAN

THE PAGES of world history are turning swiftly. They are often red with blood. Our civilisation is shot through with barbarity and savagery; in many places the foundations of human government and society are shaking; man's powers of destruction are horrific. Small wonder, therefore, that people today often call out with God's prophet, "What shall be the end of these things?", Dan. 12. 8. The Lord's description of the end of the age provides part of the answer.

The disciples had asked Jesus two questions. First, "When shall these things be?", referring to the downfall of Jerusalem and the overthrow of the temple of which He had just spoken. These events were to take place about 40 years later. Second, "What shall be the sign of thy coming, and of the end of the world?", a double event which has not taken place even yet. His answer therefore embraced events which were to span many, many centuries. He answered the first enquiry by describing the general signs of the present age, vv. 4–14, and the second by naming the special signs of the end of the age, vv. 15–51. We also must distinguish clearly the characteristics of the whole age from those which will precede His return to rule. "Wars and rumours of wars", etc., are *not* indications of the Lord's return. Of such things, Jesus said distinctly, "the end is not yet", v. 6. The warning signs of His coming to reign as Son of man are "the abomination of desolation" and the "great tribulation", vv. 15, 21.

Although the primary reference throughout is to Israel, there are several practical applications for us. Great stress is laid on men's ignorance as to the time of the Son of man's return, vv. 36, 42, 44; 25. 13. We are no wiser as to the time of "the rapture". We should therefore remain in a state of constant expectation also, so as not to be caught off guard, v. 43. The belief that the Lord could return at any moment affects one's attitude towards others, vv. 45–51. The evil servant suspected that his lord "delayed his coming". When Israel doubted that Moses would return they too started misbehaving, Exod. 32. 1–6. Unless we live in the light of the Lord's return, we are liable to be ashamed before Him at His coming, 1 John 2. 28.

Feb. 3rd

READING : **Matthew 25. 1-30**

OPPORTUNITIES REDEEMED

THE PARABLE of the virgins, vv. 1–13, teaches us to be watchful and prepared for the Lord's return. The parable of the talents, vv. 14–30, teaches us the importance of serving Him well while we await His coming.

The "talents" represent the opportunities of usefulness and service which the Lord gives to us. They do not represent our ability. They represent the scope He affords us to serve Him which, in fact, is determined by our ability, v. 15. He neither requires us nor expects us to do more than we are able. In their limited spheres, the first two servants acted in an energetic and trustworthy manner. Their lord praised them and decided to make more extensive use of them by putting them into greater positions of trust and responsibility, vv. 19–23. The third servant had no gains to offer the master, v. 18. He maintained that he had done nothing with his talent out of fear of enraging his lord. The master exposed his claim for the lame, deceitful excuse it was. The truth was that he had shrunk from the effort involved in using his talent. He was "slothful", sluggish, lazy! The unused talent was taken from the idle servant and given to him that had served well.

The proper and energetic use of our opportunities and potential in this world will earn us a reward that will partly consist in extended, increased and permanent opportunities of serving our Lord in His glorious kingdom. The full and faithful use of our capacity now will secure for us greater and ampler opportunities of pleasing Him then. Our reward for work well done will be more work, on a scale far beyond our dreams, in that day when we see His face and serve Him. Rev. 22. 3, 4. In this life we are able to enlarge our service in heaven!

On the other hand, opportunities unused and capacities undeveloped will then be lost and gone for ever. It is a divine law that what one servant forfeits through folly and neglect will pass to another. The individual will suffer; God's work will not. Saul's throne passes to David, and Judas' office to Matthias. The strenuous worker can gather to himself the heavenly service that is being lost by the idle. Our place and status in the kingdom will not be allocated or settled in any arbitrary way but on the basis of our proven worth now.

Feb. 4th

READING : **Matthew 25. 31-46**

INASMUCH . . .

THE LORD concluded His discourse on the mount of Olives by describing a day of examination and review. There is little doubt that the passage envisages the judgment by Messiah of the Gentiles in respect of their attitude towards the Jews during the tribulation period, Joel 3. 1–8. Nevertheless we must be careful that we do not use its accurate dispensational interpretation to evade the force of its conscience-searching application. The principle stated in verses 40 and 45 holds true of the people of God today; indeed it applies to the very "least" of them! The Lord regards all that we do to His "brethren" as done to Himself. This truth underlies His challenge, "Saul, Saul, why persecutest thou me?", Acts 26. 14.

We can draw comfort from the fact that the Lord Jesus knows who among His people are hungry, thirsty, naked, etc. vv. 35, 36, 40. He takes full account of the circumstances surrounding the lives of all His saints. He can say, "I know thy . . . tribulation, and poverty," Rev. 2. 9.

Christ's blessing is reserved for those who are compassionate, generous and concerned about the needs of others. Their services are not rendered for reward or because they know that the Lord will reckon their works as done to Himself. They are startled by such developments, vv. 37–39.

The Lord Jesus proceeds roundly to condemn the sin of neglect, vv. 41–46. Here it is not those who neglect to prepare themselves, vv. 1–13, nor those who neglect energetically to use their opportunities of serving Him, vv. 14–30, but those who neglect the needs of others. It is the sin of doing nothing. He does not accuse those on His left hand of stealing the food of the poor, but of failing to feed them. He does not accuse them of poisoning others, but of failing to give them drink. He does not accuse them of stripping others naked, but of failing to clothe those that are. He does not accuse them of injuring His brethren, but of failing to visit them when sick. He does not accuse them of persecuting others, but of failing to visit them when in prison. "Therefore to him that knoweth to do good, and doeth it not, to him it is sin", James 4. 17.

Feb. 5th

READING : **Matthew 26. 1-35**

THE ANOINTING AT BETHANY

THE ANOINTING of Jesus took place in the house of a leper, v. 6. It was appropriate that He who was about to be rejected by His nation and its rulers, vv. 1–5, should be entertained by a man who knew something of being "despised and rejected of men" himself.

Mary willingly lavished on the Lord precious ointment worth some 300 pence, John 12. 3, 5. It was an expensive gift; a similar jar of ointment had once been presented by the emperor of Persia to the king of Ethiopia! Mary encountered a storm of criticism from the disciples, headed by Judas; cf. v. 8 with John 12. 4, 5. Ostensibly, Judas was concerned for the poor but, in truth, he was aggrieved that he would be unable to divert any proceeds of sale in his own direction, John 12. 6. His estimate of the Lord's worth was very different from Mary's. She gladly bestowed her costly gift on Him. To Judas this was "waste", v. 8; he valued Christ no higher than the price of a slave, thirty pieces of silver, v. 15. Judas was interested in what he could get *for* Him; Mary was concerned with what she could give *to* Him. Yet even the spikenard which Mary gave up for the Lord was as nothing compared to what He was shortly to give for her, vv. 26–28. His "body" and "blood" were given for us too. What therefore should He mean to us! Mary poured the ointment on the Lord's body as a preparation for burial, v. 12. It is significant that she does not seem to have been among the womenfolk who later went to embalm His body, Luke 24. 10.

Mary anointed His head, Matt. 26. 7, and His feet, John 12. 3. They were worthy of anointing. Isaiah had described the nation of Israel as corrupt and vile from the "foot" even to the "head", 1. 6. The world-empire image of Nebuchadnezzar's dream included a head of fine gold and feet of iron and clay, Dan. 2. 31–33. But if Judah was defiled in head and foot, and if there was deterioration between the head and the feet of successive Gentile world-powers, things are very different with our "beloved", Song of Songs 5. 10–16. His head is as the most fine gold and His legs are set upon sockets of fine gold. With the Lord, there is neither corruption nor deterioration, "yea, he is altogether lovely".

Feb. 6th

READING : **Matthew 26. 36-75**

THE UNPRAYED PRAYER

PETER WAS a better fisherman than he was a swordsman. When he lashed out at Malchus with a sword he managed to sever only an ear and not a head, v. 51.

The Lord rebuked His loyal but misguided disciple. He first stated, as a general principle, that those who lived by the sword would perish by the same, v. 52. Secondly, He told Peter of a prayer which He could have prayed. Had He prayed such a prayer, He would have been spared His recent agony in the garden, vv. 36–44; He would not have needed to drink the cup from which He had shrunk; He would have avoided the indignities, the insults and the base violence He suffered before Caiaphas, vv. 57–68.

What was it for which He could have prayed? "*Angels*"! The Saviour was in the garden of Gethsemane, in the area described by the prophet Joel as "the valley of Jehoshaphat". It was there that the Lord would sometime cause His "mighty ones to come down" to do battle with the assembled Gentile forces, Joel 3. 9–13. Possibly Michael and his angels, Rev. 12. 7, were poised at that very moment to sweep Judas and the "great multitude" with him, Matt. 26. 47, into eternity. But it was not to be.

For what could He have prayed? "*Legions*"! Alongside the temple police and the servants of the chief priests and elders, there stood before the Lord a Roman captain and his band, John 18. 12. At the very most, this "band" comprised a full cohort; being one-sixth of a legion. The Lord was telling Peter that He could have summoned support which would have vastly outnumbered anything His foes had to offer.

For how many legions might He have asked? "*Twelve*"! Eleven of His apostles stood with Him. They could have each had an angelic legion to defend them.

In a single night, one angel had destroyed a hundred and eighty five thousand Assyrians, 2 Kings 19. 35. On that basis, twelve legions (seventy two thousand) could depopulate over three and a half worlds the size of ours today! Such dynamic aid lay only a prayer away from Christ, but it was a prayer that He would never pray. His hour had come. God's will must be done, Matt. 26. 42. The Scriptures must be fulfilled.

Feb. 7th

READING : **Matthew 27. 1-32**

IN PLACE OF BARABBAS

PETER CLAIMED that the men of Israel "denied the Holy One and the Just, and desired a murderer to be granted" to them; "and killed the Prince of life", Acts 3. 14, 15. Peter was saying that they had given life to the one who had taken life, and they had taken the life of the One who had given life. The irony of the situation did not, however, stop there.

The Jewish council had condemned Jesus for blasphemy, 26. 65-66. Knowing that such a charge would mean nothing to Pilate, they had heaped up political charges against Him. Pilate could not afford to ignore their claim that Jesus had said He was "Christ a king", Luke 23. 2. The leaders of Israel falsely imputed to Christ their own political expectations of the Messiah. The Lord had scrupulously avoided giving any encouragement to an uprising against Rome, John 6. 15, but He now stood charged with being the very kind of Messiah He had refused to be, 4. 1–10; 16. 21–23. Pilate found it incredible that this poor, bound, Galilean preacher should have ever laid claim to any sort of royalty, and cross-questioned Him as to the nature of His kingship, v. 3; John 18. 33-38.

Satisfied as to Jesus' innocence and confident of the result, Pilate offered to release for the people either Jesus or Barabbas, v. 17. Due largely to the subtle influence of the chief priests and elders, the people chose Barabbas. To both the people and their leaders a patriotic adventurer, who recognized no Messiahship but that of the sword, was more attractive than the Man who had so recently suffered without resistance, 1 Pet. 2. 23. The rulers had claimed Jesus was a threat to Rome; they turned from Him because they knew He was not. They claimed they wanted Him crucified because His kingdom was of this world; they were happy to see Him die because they knew it was not. The final irony lay in the fact that the governor was forced to release a man who was guilty of the very form of crime which the leaders attempted to fasten upon Jesus. The Lord was led out to be crucified in the place of a man who represented the kind of Messiahship which He had persistantly refused to accept.

Barabbas must have known that Jesus died in his place. We too know that He gave "himself for us", Eph. 5. 2.

Feb. 8th

READING : **Matthew 27. 33-66**

OPENINGS

THERE WERE four immediate effects of Christ's death. First, His death served to *open* a way into the holiest part of the temple, v. 51. The rent veil demonstrated that the sacrifice which Jesus had offered was sufficient to "bring us to God", 1 Pet. 3. 18. The unrent veil, along with many other features of the Jewish system, had indicated, "that the way into the holiest of all was not yet made manifest", Heb. 9. 3–8. All this was now changed. Before the cross of Christ, it was death to enter inside the veil, Lev. 16. 2; since the cross it is death to stay outside! When God had rent the heavens, 3. 16, 17, it was to declare His pleasure in the Person of His Son; when He rent the veil, He declared His pleasure with the work of His Son.

Second, His death served to *open* the tombs of the saints, vv. 52, 53. Although the graves were opened then, it is clear that the bodies of the saints rose and came out of the graves only after the resurrection of the Lord. Jesus then appeared personally, "not to all the people, but unto witnesses chosen before of God", Acts 10. 41. The presence of the resurrected saints in Jerusalem acted as a witness of His resurrection to those also who had rejected Him.

Third, His death and its circumstances served to *open* the heart of a Roman centurion, v. 54. Perhaps he had heard the Jews tell Pilate that Jesus claimed to be the Son of God, John 19. 7. Certainly, he came to believe that He was the Son of God, which the Jews refused to accept, vv. 40, 43, 54. To Paul, it was the resurrection which declared Jesus to be the Son of God, Rom. 1. 4; to the centurion, His death did so.

Fourth, His death led to an *open* confession by Joseph, Matt. 27. 57, 58. This rich man had previously been a secret disciple, John 19. 38, but the cross "makes the coward spirit brave"! The Lord rested in Joseph's tomb on the seventh day of the week. He had similarly rested following the creation of the world. Then He rested because His creative work was "finished", Gen. 2. 1–3. Now He rested because His redemptive work was "finished", John 19. 30. When the Lord created Adam, He gave man his life, Gen. 2. 7; when He redeemed man, He gave His own life, 20. 28.

Feb. 9th

READING : **Matthew 28. 1-20**

THE GREAT COMMISSION

THE STONE was rolled back to reveal to mankind what angels already knew—that Jesus had as much power to take His life again as He had grace to lay it down, John 10. 18. The angel "sat" on the stone. Contrast the elaborate precautions which men had taken over the door of the tomb and the ease with which he swept them all aside. So much for the sentry and the seal . . . and Caesar! At the angel's intervention the guards quaked as much as did the ground, vv. 2, 4 R.V.

The angel spoke to the women of "the *place* where the Lord lay", v. 6. This place holds memories for us of His victory over death; the grave was still there but it was empty. Matthew has mentioned other sacred scenes. The "*place* called Gethsemane", 26. 36, recalls Jesus' agony in anticipation of the cross. The "*place* called Golgotha", 27. 33, reminds us of His suffering for sin. Angelic appearances led to similar actions by the Roman guards and by the women. The awe-inspiring developments were announced to the chief priests by the guards, v. 11, and to the disciples by the women, v. 8. Sadly, the former announcement was believed more readily than the latter, Luke 24. 11.

The Gospel closes with "the Great Commission", vv. 18–20. We read of an infinite resource—"*all power*". Satan had asserted, "All this power . . . is delivered unto me", Luke 4. 6. The Lord rightly claims it as His own. He had said that all was delivered to Him and invited men therefore to "come" to Him, Matt. 11. 27–29. Here He says that all is given to Him and commands His disciples therefore to "go" for Him. All effective servants of Christ must first "Come, see" before they "go . . . tell", vv. 6, 7. We read of a universal mission—"*all nations*". The disciples' parish is no longer confined to Israel 10. 5, 6; it is the whole world. They face all peoples with the challenge of discipleship and baptism in the name of the Holy Trinity. We read of an unqualified obedience—"*all things*". We are not free to pick and choose which commands we obey, Psa. 119. 128. The New Testament has no place for an *à la carte* Christianity. We read of an abiding Presence—"*always*". Jesus gives His assurance, "I (who have the power) am with you (who have the task)". It is enough.

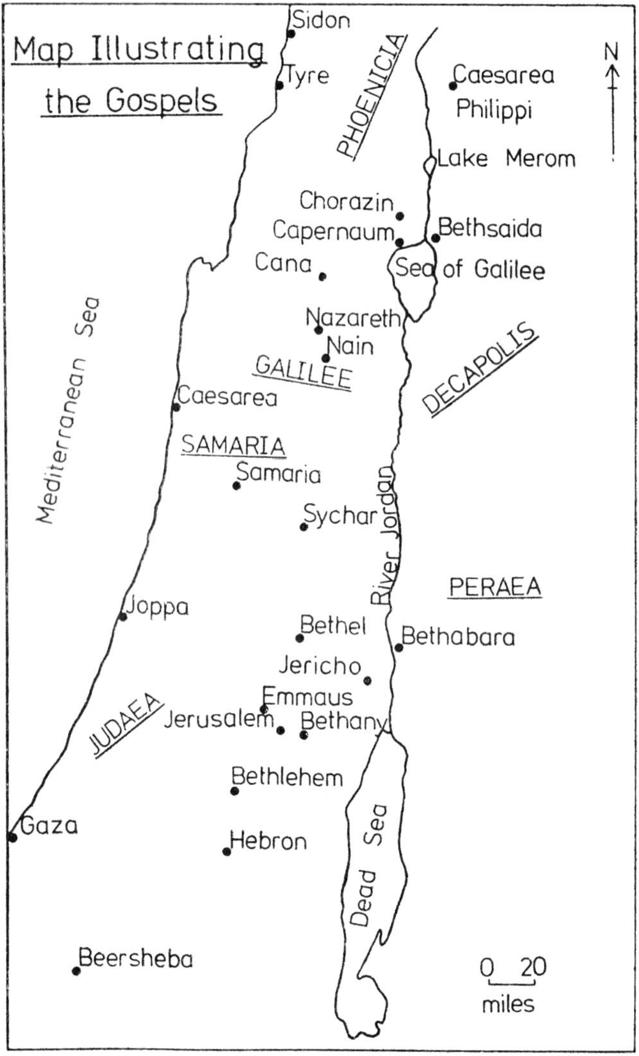
Map Illustrating
the Gospels
Sidon
Tyre
PHOENICIA
Caesarea
Philippi
N
Lake Merom
Chorazin
Capernaum
Bethsaida
Cana
Sea of Galilee
Mediterranean Sea
Nazareth
Nain
GALILEE
DECAPOLIS
Caesarea
SAMARIA
Samaria
Sychar
River Jordan
PERAEA
Joppa
Bethel
Bethabara
Jericho
Emmaus
JUDAEA
Jerusalem
Bethany
Bethlehem
Gaza
Hebron
Dead Sea
Beersheba
0 20
miles

Introducing Mark's Gospel

THE FULL name of the writer of this Gospel is John Mark, and he is referred to nine times in the Scriptures. Listed chronologically the references are: Acts 12. 12, 25; 13. 5, 13; 15. 37; 1 Pet. 5. 13; Col. 4. 10; Philem. 24; 2 Tim. 4. 11. Additionally, the "certain young man", Mark 14. 51–52, may have been Mark himself. We have then a little glimpse of his life, and his ministry to the apostles Paul and Peter, and also to Barnabas. His failure gives a balanced record of this servant of the Lord who was entrusted with the holy task of writing a Gospel. It is generally accepted that under the inspiration of the Holy Spirit, Mark's main source of information was Peter, and there are many details in his Gospel to confirm this.

Mark, as a servant of those who were called to highest service with, and for, their Lord, was the Holy Spirit's choice to portray the Servant character of the Lord. This he did in a simple, vivid and direct style. Phrases become little pictures. This Gospel is full of action. For example, in the course of chapter 1 the Lord is seen in the waters of Jordan, in the wilderness, by the sea, in the synagogue, in a house, in a solitary place, and in the towns of Galilee.

His programme may be broadly analyzed:

The Servant's Commendation	1. 1–13
The Servant Himself	1. 14–45
The Servant's Authority	2. 1 to 3. 6
The Servant's Friends	3. 7 to 6. 6
The Servant's Influences	6. 7 to 8. 26
The Servant's Instruction	8. 27 to 10. 52
The Servant's Pathway	11. 1 to 12. 44
The Servant's Prophecy	13. 1–37
The Servant's Dismissal	14. 1 to 15. 47
The Servant's Exaltation	16. 1–20

This Gospel is like a swiftly flowing river as it moves into the area of Galilee, 1. 14 to 9. 50, and then into Transjordania, 10. 1–31, and finally into Judaea, with Jerusalem the focal point, 10. 32 to 16. 18. Moving out to Bethany, 16. 19–20, His work perfectly accomplished, the Lord returned to heaven to commence new work through others.

Feb. 10th

READING : **Mark 1. 1-45**

THE DAWN OF THE SERVANT'S DAY

HOW SIGNIFICANT is the opening statement of this Gospel. Objective in its style, and direct in its message, the servant character of the Lord is immediately emphasized by the absence of genealogy and record of birth. To show that the beginning of which Mark writes is not the origin of the glad tidings he is going to present, there is heard, through Malachi's prophecy, Jehovah speaking to His perfect Servant, and Isaiah speaks of the voice of the One who would follow in the way prepared, vv. 2–3.

It was the responsibility of John, to whom the prophetic utterances refer, to introduce his Lord. He was content to be the messenger and the preparer of the way; the voice of the One for whom the way was prepared. He had a sense of vocation; he knew his mission; he knew his message. He also recognized the authority that God had bestowed upon him. Yet this prophet of whom, the Lord said, none was greater (see Luke 7. 28), confessed himself unworthy to serve his Lord even in the capacity of the lowest slave.

Mark now turns to the Servant Himself. Already acknowledging Him as Son of God, v. 1, He is Lord, v. 3, the Mighty One, v. 7, and the Beloved, v. 11. Attention, divine, satanic and human, was centred on Him. The Spirit alighted upon Him, identifying Him with divine activity, v. 10. The Father acclaimed Him, declaring His holy pleasure, v. 11. The devil attacked Him, emphasizing His absolutely sinless character, v. 13. The disciples accepted Him, acknowledging His Lordship, v. 20.

Now follows in quick succession the account of three specific miracles and a summary of many others at the eventide of a Sabbath day. In casting out the demon, the Lord's authority over evil was manifested, vv. 23–28. In curing the fever, His authority over sickness was witnessed, vv. 29–31. In cleansing the leper, His authority over impurity was experienced, vv. 40–42.

Thus in clearly defined word-pictures Mark has sketched many and varied activities of God's perfect Servant. His work was effective. Knowledge concerning it was extensive. "and they came to him from every quarter", v. 45.

Feb. 11th

READING : **Mark 2. 1-28**

CONVERSIONS AND CONTROVERSIES

CAPERNAUM HAS already been prominent in the previous chapter, and again the house is the scene of a further miracle. The narrative makes this house the focal point of attention, vv. 1–12. It was *the house of attraction.* "It was noised that he was in the house", v. 1. It was *the house of the word.* "He preached the word unto them", v. 2. As the result of the interruption which led first to the forgiveness of sins of the helpless man who was lowered through the roof by four friends with faith, and then to his restoration to strength, it became *the house of blessing*, vv. 5–11. As God was glorified by the amazed onlookers, it was *the house of praise and testimony*, v. 12. We could not offer a more Christ honouring prayer than that our own homes may be so identified in spiritual character.

The Lord's electing grace is seen in the conversion of Levi, the consequences of which were very far reaching, for this man was none other than Matthew the apostle and writer of the Gospel.

In the remainder of the chapter two criticisms are made. To the question why His disciples did not fast, the Lord's reply showed the contrast between legal conformity and the liberating grace of God revealed in Himself. The Lord having come, a new relationship was possible and was being enjoyed by His own, v. 19. Not only that, but the truth He revealed could not be put like a patch on the old cloth of Judaism, but was like a new robe of righteousness; see Phil. 3. 9. The old wine skins represented Judaism. The new wine of the Gospel could not be contained in such vessels, but brought the experience of "the liberty wherewith Christ hath made us free", Gal. 5. 1. So the perfect Servant taught true liberty in Himself.

The criticism of the plucking of the ears of corn by the disciples on the Sabbath day received a reply from the Lord which put the law into its right perspective in relation to His Lordship even over those traditions to which the Pharisees had put themselves into bondage, Mark 2. 23–28.

The recognition of the Lordship of Christ over every matter will solve the problems which can arise from day to day.

Feb. 12th

READING : **Mark 3. 1-35**

GRACE AND AUTHORITY

IT IS a sad reflection on the nature of the Pharisees that when they saw the Lord and the man with the withered hand in the synagogue, they watched for an opportunity to accuse Him of healing on the Sabbath day, v. 2. It was this attitude that filled the Lord with anger and grief, v. 5. This was righteous anger which is not sin; see Eph. 4. 26,—anger at the state of their minds, accompanied by grief because of the hardness of their hearts.

After healing many, Mark 3. 7–12, the next task of God's perfect Servant was to appoint twelve men who would be His close companions. The choice was outstanding in importance and lasting in impact. Mark includes the Lord's two fold purpose (i) "that they should be with him"; this was His desire for them, (ii) "and that he might send them forth to preach"; this was His commission to them, v. 14. The order is important, establishing the necessity for communion with the Lord before service for Him. It is still a basic principle. Mark's list of the names of these men differs from that of Matthew (10. 2–4) and Luke (6. 14–16) in that each is stated separately, "and" linking them. This teaches that every servant is responsible to the Lord for his calling.

Entering a house, the Lord was confronted first by friends who tried to restrain Him, v. 21, and then by the scribes who came to judge Him, vv. 19–30. These made a very serious charge concerning the power by which He cast out demons. The Lord's answer implied (*a*) that if a demon cast out demons their realm would fall, and (*b*) the casting out of demons is positive proof of the Lord's power over Satan, being able to bind him, the strong man, and that His power would eventually destroy his house. The Lord's warning in verse 29 concerning blasphemy against the Holy Ghost must be read in the context of the entire paragraph.

His mother and brethren could not comprehend His work. His relationships extended beyond the levels of natural ties to embrace all who do the will of God, vv. 31–35. Faith, not family, is the basis of this eternal relationship which enables the Lord to say of the church "Behold I and the children which God hath given me", Heb. 2. 13.

Feb. 13th

READING : **Mark 4. 1-34**

THE SOWER, THE SEED AND THE SOIL

OUR SECTION today contains three parables, all of which relate to sowing and growing. The first is generally known as the parable of the sower, but is sometimes called just as accurately the parable of the soils. Mark opens his account with the words "Hearken; Behold", v. 3. This is the key. The parable is about the reception of the Word of God distributed as seed by the faithful servant of God. Even the good ground was not equal in production. We have a responsibility as to how much of what we receive in ministry and teaching we are prepared to put into practical effect. Is the yield thirtyfold, sixty or one hundred? The Lord amplified the message of the good ground by referring to the uselessness of a lamp underneath a measuring container or a bed. Attitudes to responsibility will be manifested with the personal realization of what greater production there could have been. What light we have we must display. The more we share the knowledge of our Lord the more we shall receive. Indifference or indolence will prevent the light from shining, and we shall suffer loss, vv. 21–25.

The next parable, vv. 26–29, is the only one recorded by Mark alone. Once more the sower, the seed and the soil are prominent, but here the Lord is only concerned with the receptive earth and the development of the seed in it. The sower has discharged his responsibility. The seed has life and will grow imperceptibly. Its development is illustrated in three stages, and in the context of the gospel, shows the simple beginning, the mysterious process and the mature issues of spiritual life. Let all faithful sowers of the Word take heart; see Isa. 55. 10–11.

In the third parable, vv. 30–32, to illustrate the kingdom of God the Lord chose out of His entire creation a grain of mustard seed. The kingdom of God had an insignificant beginning through twelve men with little apparent potential from whom, nevertheless, there shot out branches throughout the world, attracting by its unique character in Christ all who will come. The metaphor of the fowls of the air is used in a similar context with the goodly cedar in relation to Israel; see Ezek. 17. 23.

Feb. 14th

READING : **Mark 4. 35-41**

WHAT MANNER OF MAN IS THIS ?

IT IS always illuminating and instructive when studying the Gospels to have open the relevant portion of every account that is recorded by more than one of the evangelists. To do so with the narrative of the Lord stilling the storm will show that Mark includes five observations which are omitted by Matthew (8. 23–27) and Luke (8. 22–25). These are: "They took him even as he was in the ship"; v. 36, "And there were also with him other little ships"; v. 36, "And he was in the hinder part of the ship, asleep on a pillow"; v. 38, ". . . carest thou not that we perish?", v. 38; "And he arose, and rebuked the wind, and said unto the sea, Peace, be still", v. 39.

It is not difficult to picture the graphic description Mark gives. How caringly would the disciples have led Him just as He was into a quieter part of the ship, and there the Son of God who had willingly subjected Himself to the human limitations of physical rigour, tired after the activities of the day, pillowed His head on a cushion and slept. He had no cares about the tempestuous sea which arose. He, the disciples and the other ships that had accompanied Him, would reach the other side. He had said so. This fact was quickly forgotten in the panic that ensued when the storm was at its height and the ship was filled with water. The Lord's presence did not bring immunity from the adverse conditions but it guaranteed them security.

Fear so often distorts perspective, and they rudely awakened Him with the question "Carest thou not?". Yet how often does a child of God doubt in times of adversity. It is easy, and yet so wrong, to forget that the storms encountered in spiritual experiences are under His supreme control. Let us remember the exhibition of His power in the storm, and the "nevertheless afterward" of the chastening; see Heb. 12. 11. He rebuked the storm and commanded the sea to be still, and at peace. This incident brings two facts of Himself together. Though truly Man, He showed Himself to be truly God that evening. No wonder the disciples feared exceedingly before the display of such authority, and said among themselves, "What manner of man is this?", Mark 4. 41.

Feb. 15th

READING : **Mark 5. 1-20**

POWER OVER DEMONS

MARK NOW centres attention upon the tumultuous circumstances of demon possession; immediately upon Jesus coming out of the ship there emerged from the tombs among which he dwelt a man with an unclean spirit, v. 2. His form of address to the Lord indicates that even his voice was under demon control, and the name "Legion" which he used was that of his oppressors, vv. 7, 9. The power of demon possession is made very obvious in the narrative, and yet they themselves acknowledged subjection to the authority of the One whom they recognized to be "Son of the most high God", v. 7. They were unable to resist His command to come out of the man, and besought Him that they may enter the herd of swine feeding near the mountains. It is important to note that the Lord did not send them; He gave them leave. Having done so, thus proving that the activities of evil are under divine authority, they, of their own volition, entered the beasts with disastrous results to the means of gain of those who owned them. The deliverance of this man with the subsequent peace it brought not only to his tortured mind, but to the terror-stricken neighbourhood when he was running wild, was of more value than the swine whose unclean meat, for whatever purpose it was used, should have been offensive to their Jewish owners, vv. 13–14.

The depraved subject of the Lord's compassion underwent a wonderful change, and he is found with his Deliverer "sitting", which speaks of restfulness, "clothed", which speaks of readjustment, and "in his right mind", which speaks of restoration, v. 15. The repercussions led to the gracious Saviour being asked to leave the district.

There was one, however, who had no such desire, and the renewed man acknowledged his gratitude and showed his devotion by requesting that he be with Him. The Lord had been rejected by the Gadarenes, and there was none to speak to them of His compassion and power, except he who had experienced them. Graciously the Lord showed him that his place of testimony was among his friends, and what a great missionary he proved to be, vv. 18–20. Sometimes, the greatest service can be performed nearest home!

Feb. 16th

READING : **Mark 5. 21-43**

JAIRUS' DAUGHTER AND THE DISEASED WOMAN

THESE MIRACLES interlock in a manner unique in the Gospel records, the incident concerning the daughter of Jairus being interrupted by the healing of the woman with the issue of blood. The period of twelve years remarkably connects them, in that the synagogue ruler's fear and sorrow ended twelve years of joy (see Luke 8. 42) and for the woman, twelve years of suffering and despair were terminated by recovery and peace.

What Jairus had seen or heard had impelled him to meet this mighty miracle worker as He disembarked on His return from Gadara, vv. 22–23. His prayer showed reverence for the Lord, a regard and concern for his little daughter, and faith in the Lord, whose coming to her bed-side he besought. The Servant-Son who was always about His Father's business, unhesitatingly went with him, v. 24. Jairus' concern for his child may be a present reminder of the parental responsibilities today to bring one's children before the Lord daily in believing prayer, that they may be preserved in all the moral and spiritual dangers with which they are so constantly beset.

The Lord was delayed in His journey but not deterred in His purpose, by the intervention of the woman who, determined to reach Him, had made her way through the crowd, possibly on her hands and knees, and was able to touch the hem of His garment. The virtue lay, not in the hem, but in her faith which the Lord immediately acknowledged. These verses may be summarized by noting (*a*) her condition, vv. 25–26; (*b*) her coming, v. 27; (*c*) her conclusion, v. 28, and (*d*) her cure, v. 29. Receiving the title "daughter", she became the only woman to whom the Lord is recorded as giving this title. Not only did she enjoy this affectionate relationship, she also entered into peace, v. 35.

Informed at that time that the daughter was dead, the Lord, notwithstanding, continued His journey to the house. There He displayed His power over death, vv. 37–42. The Lord's concern for the child's after-care speaks of the need today for the exercise of shepherd care toward those who are newly alive from the dead, ". . . something . . . to eat", v. 43.

Feb. 17th

READING : **Mark 6. 1-32**

REJECTED PROPHETS AND SENT APOSTLES

FOLLOWED BY His disciples, the Lord came into His own town where He and His family were well known. Here he exercised His authority by teaching in the synagogue. There were those who heard Him who did not understand the source of His knowledge, wisdom or power, vv. 2–3. They would not recognize that in their midst was the Son of God; "they were offended at him". The word means "scandalized" derived from *scandalon* which was that part of a trap which, when struck by the animal, ensnared it. The people ran up against His words, and were caught by them. The controversy was that when they, the imperfect, challenged Him the perfect One, they had no answer. They would not believe the divine source from whence His knowledge, wisdom and authority came, and in consequence His work was limited, v. 5. The prophet was indeed without honour in His own country.

The time had come when the second reason for the calling of the twelve was to be fulfilled. They had been with Him learning; they were to go forth preaching; see 3. 14. The principles He gave them only applied until His own ministry on earth ended; see Luke 22. 35–38. Nevertheless there still remains the basic principle of faith. The words "he . . . gave them" are in the imperfect tense, which implies a constant supply of power from the Lord, vv. 7–13.

The Name and the works of the Lord soon reached the ears of Herod whose guilty conscience concerning the death of John the Baptist evidently troubled him, vv. 14–16. In parenthesis Mark relates the evil deed; his narrative encircles a wicked woman, a degraded girl, a misguided ruler and a noble martyr. Verse 20 is an eloquent expression of Herod's personal opinion of this mighty prophet. Here was a man under conviction of sin through the life and preaching of John. Yet he became the tool of an unscrupulous woman.

The lesson of verses 30–32 is the necessity for times of being apart with the Lord in restful dependence upon Him. It is possible to be so busy in the Lord's service that there is no time to hear His voice. How we need the quietness of the solitary place with Him. Let us all beware of barrenness in a busy life!

Feb. 18th

READING : **Mark 6. 33-56**

COMPASSION AND CONTROL

THE DEPARTURE of the Lord and His disciples by ship was seen by many who knew Him, and these apparently headed them off so that a great congregation were waiting as they reached the shore. His shepherd heart was moved with compassion as He saw them, v. 34, and He began to feed them with spiritual food. Toward the end of the day, the disciples would have sent them into the villages for food, but the Lord placed the responsibility for feeding them upon the twelve, v. 37. The Lord never applies a test without having the solution Himself at hand. All He asks for is absolute trust. He would have them in personal exercise about the problem, and as a result they brought Him five loaves and two fishes. Meagre, but, brought in faith, sufficient. The principle of order, which is the hallmark of a good servant's work, is very evident by the Lord's command, v. 40. Note in verse 41 five acts of the Lord. The first four were complete, the fifth was continuous until all were satisfied. This was not a miracle of extension. It was a miracle of creation! The part of the disciples was to distribute to others what the Lord first gave to them. There was a basketful for each of them also. The Lord will always recompense His servants.

After this tremendous happening, the Lord sent the twelve away in the ship. He Himself went into a mountain to pray. During the crossing a storm arose. Yet they had acted in obedience to His command, and it had led them into the teeth of the storm. It sometimes does today. The loss to them would have been great had it not been so, however; in the storm and because of it, Jesus revealed Himself as Lord over all disturbing elements, and the restless waves became as a silver pavement to His feet. Matthew 14. 28–31 adds the incident of Peter walking with Him too. Their fear was dispelled by His presence, and the storm calmed by His power; they came with Him to the other side, Mark 6. 50–53.

These two miracles form one parable. The Bread of Life by His death brings hungry souls who receive Him into eternal blessing. As High Priest He intercedes for His own, soon to come to where they are amid the storm scenes of this world, and take them to be for ever with Himself.

Feb. 19th

READING : **Mark 7. 1-37**

TRADITION AND REALITY

THIS CHAPTER opens with the Pharisees criticizing the Lord's disciples for eating with unwashed hands in contravention of the tradition of the elders, v. 2. In reply the Lord quoted Isaiah 29. 13 and Moses, Exod. 20. 12; 21. 17, thus exposing their empty shell of hypocrisy by the very law to which they gave lip service. Clean hands will never compensate for an unclean heart! Privately the Lord explained that man is not polluted by what he eats but by what he is, and illustrated the point by noting thirteen poisons which proceed from the heart of men, Mark 7. 17–23.

The incident concerning the Syrophenician woman who pleaded with the Lord to cast out the demon from her daughter is outstanding, vv. 24–30. As a Gentile she had no claim upon God's grace. Salvation was for the Jew. The time of gracious invitation to all nations would not arrive until after Pentecost. His reply was not encouraging for it was based strictly upon that principle. It was for her a test of her faith, and while accepting the Lord's parabolic answer that, as a Gentile, she had no right to partake of the children's bread, she completed the illustration by claiming access to the crumbs under the table, vv. 28–29.

The miracle of the recovery of the man who was deaf and had an impediment in his speech is recorded by Mark only, vv. 32–37. The methods the Lord used were unique. The reason may be that as the man could not hear any word the Lord might speak to him, he would understand the process. First, the Lord took him away from the crowd. It was an unspoken rebuke to those who were seeking a sign. Moreover, His contacts with him were of a personal nature. Those fingers with which the Lord accomplished the heavenly work of creation, Psa. 8. 3, were employed in the healing of one of His creatures. The use of the Lord's saliva underlined the fact that healing power was not only in, but of, Himself. His cry "Be opened", v. 34, was a fiat to the latent organs to become attuned to hear the Restorer's voice, and to sing His praise. To the Lord, the perfect Servant, was accorded the highest acclamation that could be given for service accomplished: "He hath done all things well", v. 37.

Feb. 20th

READING : **Mark 8. 1-38**

COMPASSION, CURE AND CHALLENGE

COMPARING THE two separate incidents of feeding the multitudes as recorded by Mark, the reader will observe different features such as the place of the miracles, the period of time the people were with the Lord, the number fed, the fragments that remained, and the containers in which they were collected, the words translated "basket" being quite different. (See Acts 9. 25 for the same word used in this chapter.) Of the comparable features we may remark on two only; the compassion of the Lord, Mark 8. 2; 6. 34, and the satisfaction of those fed, 8. 8; 6. 42. Why was the feeding of four thousand a problem to the disciples?, 8. 4. Had they forgotten that the Lord had fed five thousand? Or did they limit the Lord's ability to repeat that miracle?

The miracle that followed, vv. 22–26, is the second and last exclusively recorded by Mark. Although instantaneous in itself, the effect was gradual. The lessons we may learn are (*a*) spiritual light increases little by little; (*b*) the imperfect will one day be complete. There is a real sense in which we can pray that the Lord will increase our spiritual vision with the unseen touch of His hand.

From verse 27 a very definite change in the ministry of God's perfect Servant will be seen, as He finally prepared for the fulfilment of the work He came to do. The confession of Peter that He was the Christ, v. 29, recognized, although the implications were not understood, that here was God's Anointed in whom all Scripture would be fulfilled. This confession provided the occasion from which the Lord began to teach the disciples concerning His death, v. 31. They too must each take up his cross and know the cost. This did not, neither does it now, mean the personal and physical enduring of hardship or infirmity for which bearing one's cross is sometimes interpreted, but rather the bearing of His reproach, Heb. 13. 13. As then, the Lord still calls for a denial of self, an identity with the cross and its reproach, and a committed following for His sake and the gospel's, to "lose" one's life in relation to the pursuit of that which is spiritual, and by gaining spiritual treasure to "save it", Mark 8. 34-38. Are we willing for this?

Feb. 21st

READING : **Mark 9. 1-29**

THE CONTRAST OF EXPERIENCE

THAT THE three synoptic writers record the incidents which immediately preceded and followed the transfiguration of the Lord in the same sequence makes a comparative study a simple exercise (see Matt. 17. 1–8; Luke 9. 28–36). Verse 1 is linked with those things of which the Lord had been speaking in the previous chapter; yet it fittingly introduces the subject of the transfiguration as the occasion which pointed onward to the manifestation of His glory, the result of His death of which He had told them. Mark relates that the Lord led them "up . . . apart by themselves", v. 2. The conditions of elevation and separation must be satisfied before the Lord's glory can be seen. It is so today in a spiritual sense. Ponder the description of the scene. Consider the company assembled, and the voice from the cloud. It is noteworthy that Peter, when describing his experience, is no longer concerned with Moses and Elijah, but speaks only of His Lord of whose majesty he was an eye-witness "when we were *with him* in the holy mount", 2 Pet. 1. 16–18.

During the happenings in the mountain, the disciples below were involved in an incident out of which they had not come at all well, vv. 14–18. Mark emphasizes the condition of the lad, and the efforts of the demon to destroy him. The Lord's arrival from the mountain brought relief to all concerned. His sympathetic enquiry and His assurance of power through believing, mentioned only by Mark, repay thoughtful reading, vv. 21–23. The disciples knew they had themselves failed where power had been known (see 6. 13), and asked the Lord the reason. His reply was clear, v. 29. Matthew includes the further reason of unbelief; see Matt. 17. 20. Prayer and faith cannot be separated in Christian experience. If we do not believe we cannot pray. If we do not pray we lose our power. Like the disciples, we too face the forces of evil. "For we wrestle not against flesh and blood, but against principalities, against powers, against the rulers of the darkness of this world, against spiritual wickedness in high places," Eph. 6. 12. We ask "Why could not we . . . ?". Faith is the door to power of which prayer is the only key. May we use it constantly. Alone in His presence is where we learn the reason of our failures.

Feb. 22nd

READING : **Mark 9. 30-50**

LESSONS IN HUMILITY

It is a sad commentary on the twelve that, during the journey in which the Lord had again told them of His death and resurrection, they were only concerned with their own ambitions. The Lord's teaching that followed centred upon the phrase repeated three times, "in my name". With a little child in their midst He taught them the lesson of humility of *position*, vv. 35–37. The simplicity of a childlike faith is the mark of spiritual greatness. Paul spoke of the "simplicity that is in Christ" in relation to a steadfast testimony, 2 Cor. 11. 3. In reply to John's report that they had forbidden one who had cast out demons in the Lord's name because he did not follow them, He taught the lesson of humility in *relationships*, Mark 9. 38–40. This incident is used to support ecumenicalism, or by whatever name it may otherwise be called. We have no authority to treat the Lord's words in this way. This man had his own part with the Lord, and the Lord acknowledged it, but He did not bid the disciples go out and join him. The principles of local church character are in God's Word, to be followed in humility and simple obedience to it. We nevertheless rejoice in the oneness of the body of Christ, and should love all who love Him. In the figure of the cup of water given in His name, the Lord taught the lesson of humility in *works*, v. 41. We learn here the importance in the eyes of the Lord of the smallest deed performed in His name. It takes a humble spirit to make a small gift unknown to any, rather than one which because of its quantity attracts attention, if done for that purpose.

"Be clothed with humility", wrote Peter, 1 Pet. 5. 5.

The Lord summarized His discourse, first by warning against stumbling others, embodied in the figure of a child who can be easily influenced. He then referred to the possibility of personal hindrances through the instrumentality of the hand, the foot and the eye, vv. 42–48. These powerful figures of speech teach the need for rigorous self-discipline which can only be experienced by the crucifixion of the flesh; see Gal. 5. 24. The Lord clarified His illustrations by expressing fire and salt as refining and purifying character, the salting bringing mutual peace, Mark 9. 49–50.

Feb. 23rd

READING : **Mark 10. 1-52**

WORDS OF WISDOM

THE CHAPTER opens with the familiar phrase "he taught them". However, the Pharisees who came did not want to be taught, but rather to test Him on the question of divorce. The Lord referred them first to Moses and then to creation, and reiterated the principles of marriage in the eternal purposes of God, vv. 2–9. Later, He told the disciples the position of adultery into which persons would bring themselves if they violated those principles. The Lord's words have never been abrogated.

The beautiful incident of the little ones in the arms of the Lord will always be a source of inspiration to parents and others who have the spiritual wellbeing of children upon their hearts, vv. 13–16.

The young man who came running to the Lord asking what he should do to inherit eternal life received a gracious but challenging response. Although claiming to have observed the commandments, he lacked that sacrificial love for the Lord which would have caused him to take the five steps required of him; go, sell and give; come and follow. The Lord, who beholding him loved him, saw *one thing* he lacked, but that was *everything* so far as his conversion was concerned, and he went away grieved, vv. 17-22.

When James and John asked to sit nearest to the Lord in His glory, He used two symbols in His reply; a cup and a baptism. The first spoke of receiving, the second of an entering into. This is what the Lord sustained on the cross. He received the judgment of sin; that was the cup. He entered into the death of the cross; that was the baptism. In persecutions and sufferings they would indeed drink of the same cup, and be baptized with the same baptism, but the positions they sought were not for them, vv. 35–40. Their service was higher, following the example of the One who "came not to be ministered unto but to minister", v. 45. Their ministry in the name of Him who would give His life a ransom for many would follow.

In graphic word pictures Mark tells of the restoration of Bartimaeus' sight, vv. 46–52, the most eloquent being "Jesus stood still" when He heard the cry of a blind beggar.

Feb. 24th

READING : **Mark 11. 1-33**

IN JERUSALEM

THIS CHAPTER contains events which occurred on three successive days in the all important week opening before us. The entry of the Lord into Jerusalem is recorded in all the Gospels, vv. 1–11; Matt. 21. 1–11; Luke 19. 29–44; John 12. 12–15. The prophetic pen also wrote of it, Zech. 9. 9. He who had told His disciples of His rejection briefly received the people's acclamation. The triumphant procession ended, not in the palace, because His kingdom will not be established on earth until a future day, but in the temple where His all-penetrating eyes "looked round about upon all things" where there was but a formal representation of the glory of God. Then, with the twelve, He returned to the love of Bethany's homestead.

The second day in the sequence is covered by two incidents; the judgment on the fig tree, vv. 12–14, and the casting out from the precincts of the temple of the marketeers and money changers. We see here a perversion of the law of God which made certain provision for purchasing that which was required for sacrifice, Deut. 14. 25–26. Deviation had led to dishonesty and desecration, so that the house of prayer had been made a den of thieves.

The sequel to both these happenings occurred on the third day of this momentous calendar of events. The fig tree had withered away, having failed to fulfil its function bearing fruit. The Lord made the occasion a spiritual lesson from which personal applications can be made today. Failure to bear fruit in one's testimony can be overcome by faith in God. Inward dependence can become the means of outward achievement. Such dependence is itself manifested by prayer conditioned by a forgiving spirit.

In the temple the Lord received a double challenge from the dignitaries there. First, on the nature of His authority and then on the source of it. The Lord turned the question by asking them the source of John's authority and teaching. They knew the source was of God. They knew too that he had introduced the Lamb of God, who now stood in their midst. They resented His authority, and they rejected Him. But perhaps in their hearts they knew the answer to their question.

Feb. 25th

READING : **Mark 12. 1-44**

PARABLE, PRECEPT AND PRAISE

FOLLOWING THE silencing of His critics, the Lord told them a parable the effect of which is clear from verse 12. The scene is a vineyard. They would know God's song of the vineyard concerning Israel and her privileges and responsibilities, Isa. 5. 1–7. The planter of the vineyard is God. The hedge is the middle wall of partition between Jew and Gentile, Eph. 2. 14. The husbandmen are themselves, the Jewish rulers; the servants are the prophets, and the well beloved son speaks of the Lord Himself. The stone also speaks of the Lord, and is enlarged upon in other Gospels, Matt. 21. 42–44; Luke 20. 17–18.

The reply the Lord made to the Pharisees and Herodians who were sent to ensnare Him in His words placed human government in its proper position, and at the same time made the observance of its authority subject to the higher claims of God, vv. 13–17.

The Sadducees then approached Him on a hypothetical question involving personal relationships after death, vv. 18–23. The Lord in His reply set a wonderful example of the use of the Scriptures. How much more authoritative an answer is today when it is based solely upon the Word of God, and not on the thoughts of men. God, the Lord concluded, is the God of the living, v. 27. He was referring to those who had died. What comfort this knowledge brings in times of deepest sorrow, and how blessed is the hope it establishes.

Then followed a question from a scribe interested and perhaps concerned, vv. 28–34. Once more the Lord's familiarity with the Scriptures provided a complete answer. The basis of love is sacrifice. Love is an attitude of heart that controls the thoughts and inspires the actions. Love for one's neighbour is beholden upon the children of God. Such was the Lord's grace, that the common people heard Him gladly; yet so full of truth was He that He was unsparing in His judgment of the scribes, vv. 35–40.

The chapter ends with the account of a poor widow who received the Lord's commendation because, having only two mites, she cast into the treasury all that she had, vv. 41–44. The value of the gift is measured by what remains!

Feb. 26th

READING : **Mark 13. 1-37**

WHEN SHALL THESE THINGS BE?

THE PROPHETIC utterances of the Lord to four of His disciples were made in answer to two questions they asked Him following His pronouncement of the overthrow of the temple, vv. 1–4. Commencing with conditions on earth immediately after His absence from them, He unfolded the order of events which will culminate in a period of time, the severity of which will be noted in verses 19–20, never seen before and never to be seen again. The Lord called it "great tribulation", Matt. 24. 21. See also Rev. 7. 14. It is "the time of Jacob's trouble", Jer. 30. 7. There are many scriptural assurances that the Church will not experience this, having been raptured into the Lord's presence before it takes place. The Lord then foretold the coming of Himself, the Son of man, in the clouds with great power and glory for His elect Israel, Mark 13. 24–27.

Whatever the nature of the Lord's teaching to His disciples, it always carried with it practical exhortations and sometimes warnings. These are as appropriate and necessary for His Church today. In the context of this discourse, Mark records two parables which the Lord interpreted with one word, "watch".

(*a*) *The fig tree*, vv. 28–32. Once more this tree is used as a symbol of the Jewish nation which is to be the outstanding sign of the approach of these things. There is of course no authority for applying interpretations to specific incidents of today, but it serves to show the development of prophetic truth as it begins to unfold. Today Israel is the truest signpost of things to come that the world has ever had. This parable taught the relative imminence of them.

(*b*) *The porter*, vv. 33–37. The exhortation to watch and pray with which this parable is introduced envisages the traveller encamping in open country where unseen and unknown dangers abound, necessitating watchfulness at all times. The parable itself is of servants working in the house, the porter watching at the gate envisaging the daily fulfilment of the work to hand with an expectancy that the master of the house may arrive at any moment. May we be marked by these same attitudes of watchfulness!

Feb. 27th

READING : **Mark 14. 1-31**

THE OINTMENT, THE ROOM AND THE MOUNTAIN

WHILE VERSES 1–2 tell of the determination of the chief priests and the scribes as to what they could do to the Lord, verses 3–9 relate what Mary of Bethany did for Him. In her act of anointing Him with very precious ointment is seen the quality of a love which did not consider anything too costly for Him, as she broke the box and poured its contents on His head. This deed brought from His lips two commendations: first, "she hath wrought a good work on me", v. 6; second, "She hath done what she could", v. 8. This was, as the adjective implies, a beautiful work, which true worship always is, and it was made so because of her motive. The Lord interpreted the expression of her heart, and she erected a memorial that day that will never be removed wherever the gospel is made known throughout the world.

From this incident of adoration, Mark points to an incident of participation in which two unnamed men are involved in the preparation for the event that has been commemorated since the Lord's death and will be until He shall come, vv. 12–25. The pitcher-bearer led the way. The owner of the house made his contribution in three ways: the room was large, furnished and prepared. To all who love Him, the Lord is asking "Where is the (my) guest chamber?" We do well to ask what preparation we make for Him daily, so that He can have communion and fellowship with us. Our hearts should surely be large, our minds fully furnished, and our entire beings exercised by spiritual preparation as we too make ready. Everything prepared, the Lord came with the twelve. Reference to the presence of a betrayer among them brought the sorrowful question, "Is it I?" Although Mark's record is short, it is complete. Never let us tire of reading verses 22–25, or neglect any opportunity so to remember our Lord on the first day of the week.

In the quietness of the mount of Olives, the Good Shepherd told His sheep of His smiting and their scattering, with the promise of reunion after His resurrection, vv. 26–28. Despite Peter's protestation, the Lord foretold his denial, and our reading which began with silent worship concludes with loud assertions of loyalty, v. 31.

Feb. 28th/29th

READING : **Mark 14. 32-72**

THE GARDEN AND THE PALACE

GETHSEMANE! The garden where the depth of the personal emotions and experiences of the Lord were revealed, vv. 32–42. The phrases "sore (greatly) amazed, very heavy, exceeding sorrowful" are sufficiently eloquent to make comment unnecessary in this devotional study as He went forward and fell on the ground and prayed. He prayed three times. Mark includes "Abba, Father", v. 36. Upon no other occasion is the Lord recorded as using that address, and it is only used upon two other instances in the Scriptures; see Rom. 8. 15; Gal. 4–6. W. E. Vine says, "'Abba' . . . betokens unreasoning trust; 'father' expresses an intelligent apprehension of the relationship" (*Expository Dictionary of New Testament Words*). With the awful reality of the cup before Him, we adore Him for saying "nevertheless', v. 36.

In contrast to the faithfulness of One in the fulfilment of His mission was the faithlessness of another in the fulfilment of his greed, vv. 43–52. The means by which Judas betrayed the Lord makes the incident obnoxious as the token of affection became the sign of diabolical evil on that unique occasion, as with "Master" on his lips he betrayed Him.

The Gospels report that the Lord was subjected to three trials at the hands of the Jews. The first was before Annas; the second, which Mark records in some detail, before Caiaphas, vv. 53–65; and the third was before the Sanhedrin. In these the accusation was blasphemy. The faithful Servant had been dismissed, and they sought to discredit him. The Lord was silent before all their questions until, adjured by the high priest about His person and relationship with God, He claimed His Messiahship and predicted Himself as their judge, vv. 61–62.

All the Gospels tell of Peter's denial of His Lord, vv. 66–72. Mark's record is of great interest because it may well be Peter's personal account. Poor dear Peter! Yet have we never denied our Lord, if not as directly, just as effectively by a silent reticence to declare that we know Him? Thank God for the weeping, v. 72. We should never be ashamed of the tears of true repentance. They are precious in God's sight, and pave the way to restoration.

Mar. 1st

READING : **Mark 15. 1-47**

THE PLACE GOLGOTHA

ALTHOUGH THE Jews had already condemned the Lord Jesus to be "guilty of death", the travesty of justice continued under Roman jurisdiction. These, like the Jewish trials, were also in three stages. Mark records the two appearances before Pilate, Herod's part occurring between verses 5 and 6. The charge was different. Blasphemy would have had no influence upon Pilate, but he would listen to a political accusation, and this was the course the Jews pursued. Pilate knew the Lord was not guilty of treason and would have released Him had he not allowed the circumstances of the situation to control him. His final attempt by offering the choice between Barabbas and the Lord was rejected, and he delivered Him to be crucified, vv. 1–15. Thus a procession wended its shameful way out of the city to the place Golgotha. Never before, or since, had heaven or earth witnessed such a scene: a mocking rabble, repulsive soldiery and gloating rulers. In utter weakness, Simon bearing His cross, the Lord came to that place, and there they crucified Him, vv. 16–27. Mark notes the time was the third hour, and for three hours the sinful eye of man was permitted to watch Him. But from the sixth to the ninth hour darkness covered the whole land. God was laying upon His beloved One the stroke of holy judgment, and no human eye must see the vital spiritual nature of His sufferings because of man's sin. Who would define the only cry recorded by Mark of the seven the Lord uttered on the cross? "My God, my God, why hast thou forsaken me?", v. 34. The holiness of God made the cross a dire necessity. The love of God made it a glorious possibility and an established fact in the accomplishment of the sinner's redemption. Having completed His work, Jesus Christ, Lord, God's perfect Servant, gave up the ghost, and the veil of the temple was rent from the top to the bottom as though an unseen hand had done it, v. 38. The temple, His Body, had been destroyed by man, v. 29. The temple of the law had been rendered ineffectual by God. There is now a new and living way, Heb. 10. 20. The events of that day were crowned by Joseph of Arimathaea who obtained the body of the Lord Jesus for his own personal and loving burial arrangements, Mark 15. 42-46.

Mar. 2nd

READING : **Mark 16. 1-20**

GOD'S VINDICATION OF HIS SERVANT

MARK OPENS his account of the resurrection with the very significant phrase "when the sabbath was past". Sabbaths had come and gone, but this one during which the body of the Lord had lain in the tomb was the last, because He was no longer there. The resurrection had brought to an end the ministration of the law, and in its place was the ministration of righteousness; see 2 Cor. 3. 9. A new day, the day of grace, had indeed dawned. To the women was given the glad news by the heavenly visitant with the message they were to bear to the Lord's disciples. Mark adds the words "and Peter", v. 7. How Peter would have cherished that very special mention of his name! Three of the occasions when the Lord appeared to His followers are stated in verses 9, 12, 14. Mary Magdalene had returned to the tomb, and was rewarded with a sight of her Lord and a brief conversation with Him; see John 20. 11–18. Her story was not believed. The two who saw Him in the country (see Luke 24. 13–35), also received the same treatment. That the Lord upbraided the eleven for their unbelief is not surprising. He had told them He would rise again on the third day.

Of the great commission with which the Lord entrusted His disciples, Mark records only part, and baptism is established as the consequence of faith, vv. 15–16. The signs of which the Lord spoke in verses 17–18 were transitional and mostly have no practical relevance today.

The Servant, perfect in character, diligent in service, faithful in death and triumphant in resurrection, then returned to the One who had sent Him, whose will He ever delighted to do, and at whose right hand He sat down, His work complete, v. 19. His is the place of honour and authority.

His servants then went forth, their source of power being stated in verse 20, "the Lord working with them". This expression is unique, linking the Servant with His servants in a very intimate way. Thus the beginning of the Gospel which Mark wrote had no ending when the Lord returned to heaven. His work continues, no longer through His own lips and hands, but through ours. The power for that work however is still His, and only in His name can it be done.

Introducing Luke's Gospel

THE GOSPEL of Luke stresses the humanity of the Lord, whose blessed mission was "to seek and to save that which was lost", 19. 10. Everywhere we come face to face with that One who expresses the divine love in "gracious words", 4. 22, and "glorious things", 13. 17. His compassionate heart for fallen man is manifest in His words as well as in His works. Who, with an enlightened mind, a mind illumined by the Spirit of God, would fail to see the deeper meaning of such parables as those of the prodigal son and of the good Samaritan? Seeking and saving is Jesus' peculiar work, and it is this of which we read right throughout the Gospel of Luke. As one who companied a good deal with Paul, and who is referred to as "the beloved physician", Col. 4. 14, Luke gives some beautiful details, especially when recording some of the miracles and acts of compassion, e.g. Luke 7. 12. Right to the end of his narrative, we are considering the Lord Jesus as the One who, by life and lip, speaks to us in terms we are able to understand and brings, as it were, God nigh to us. The Almighty Worker declares Himself, and Luke sets forth this declaration as he traces out accurately all things from the very first, 1. 3. Others had taken in hand to draw up a narrative concerning the things "believed among us" and Luke undertook to put these things in accurate order, being himself acquainted with them from their origin. The "beloved physician" is not content to leave these things in the form of oral tradition, but determines to set them out in a permanent and unchangeable form so that Theophilus might have more certainty about them.

We, likewise, do well to trace "all things accurately", 1. 3 R.V. As far as we are able to ascertain, Luke is the only Gentile writer in the Bible. He writes his narrative to another Gentile, Theophilus, and our interest deepens as we discover that the "glad tidings" is directed towards us Gentiles because Israel have turned their backs upon it.

Let us then, in the language of an old hymn, read what Luke has written, saying as we read:

> "My soul rejoices to pursue
> The steps of Him I love—"

Mar. 3rd

READING : **Luke 1. 1-38**

PURPOSE AND PERSONS

THE PERSONS WHO occupy a prominence in the narrative are: Herod, Zacharias, Elisabeth, Gabriel, Joseph and Mary. With the exception of Gabriel, we are introduced to a cross-section of humanity through whom God is going to work in bringing the glad tidings of salvation. A heathen monarch, a Hebrew priest and his childless wife, a man whose name was Joseph, a virgin whose name was Mary—not a very imposing array, but they were destined to be associated closely with the One who came "to seek and to save that which was lost", 19. 10.

Zacharias and Elisabeth "were both righteous before God", both morally and ceremonially, v. 6. They had, however, one great disappointment in life. They had no child; Elisabeth was barren. Their prayer in this matter was eventually heard, as Gabriel announced to Zacharias. Joy and gladness were promised by the heavenly messenger, but unbelief robbed Zacharias of any pleasure in anticipation (as unbelief must), and the angel pronounced dumbness upon him until the day when these things were to be performed, v. 20.

"The people were praying without at the time of incense", v. 10. The angel's assurance that the prayer of Zacharias was "heard" reminds us that, despite the fact that so many pray to God and so varied are their petitions to Him, "if we ask anything according to his will, he heareth us: and if we know that he hear us, whatsoever we ask, we know that we have the petitions that we desired of him", 1 John 5. 14-15.

Little did Zacharias and Elisabeth know that the child they were promised would grow up to be the forerunner of the Messiah, would make such an impact upon the society of his day and would be described by the Lord Jesus as the greatest prophet, 7. 28.

Gabriel's announcement to Mary, although astonishing, was received by her in the beauty and simplicity of true faith, "be it unto me according to thy word", v. 38.

We have discovered something of the writer's purpose, vv. 1-4, and some of the persons involved in what must ever be one of the most tremendous years in all the history of God's dealings with mankind, vv. 5-38.

Mar. 4th

READING : **Luke 1. 39-80**

BLESSING THE LORD

ELISABETH BLESSED her cousin with a loud voice; Mary magnified the Lord; Zacharias, being filled with the Holy Ghost, prophesied and blessed "the Lord God of Israel". Such ascriptions of praise take our thoughts to Psalm 34. 3, and the invitation of the Psalmist to "Magnify the Lord with me, and let us exalt his name together".

In such circumstances, and in this very remarkable introduction to Luke's Gospel, we catch something of the tremendous stir caused in the area where these events took place. A greater stir was yet to come, not only to "a city of Galilee, named Nazareth", v. 26, or to the hill country, "into a city of Juda", v. 39, for, as Elisabeth's son, John the Baptist thundered out words of warning to a "generation of vipers", and announced that "all flesh" should "see the salvation of God", 3. 6. This is the atmosphere which Luke catches as he brings before his friend Theophilus, and indeed all who read his Gospel, an accurate account of the incidents surrounding the birth of John the Baptist, and of the matters and circumstances leading up to the birth of Mary's son, Jesus.

There is always the element of gladness when the Lord blesses His people, and these humble folk had great cause to rejoice together when they witnessed with spiritual intelligence the beginning of God's gracious activities for the salvation of men. The references to rejoicing, gladness, and praise in the Gospel of Luke are frequent, as we should expect. The first chapter introduces two women, both having cause to rejoice; Elisabeth, v. 58, and Mary, vv. 46–47. Near the close of the Gospel, Luke writes of a little company in Jerusalem, nonplussed at the news brought by the two who had just seen the Lord Jesus after His resurrection, who "believed not for joy", Luke 24. 41. The Gospel concludes with the words they "were continually in the temple praising and blessing God. Amen", 24. 53.

The scene is now being set, as it were, for the demonstration of God's power and love which would bring salvation to all men through the Lord Jesus. The first chapter ends with a reference to the Baptist, as a child, growing in body and spirit preparatory to his public "showing unto Israel", 1. 80.

Mar. 5th

READING : **Luke 2. 1-39**

THE SAVIOUR COMES

THE WORDS of Paul, "he became poor", 2 Cor. 8. 9, come to mind when reading this account of the birth of Jesus. Following a decree made by Caesar Augustus, Joseph and Mary left Nazareth and journeyed to Bethlehem "to be taxed". It was while they were there that Mary "brought forth her firstborn son, and wrapped him in swaddling clothes, and laid him in a manger", v. 7. This was the beginning of the amazing story of how the grace of God, bringing salvation to men, came by "the man Christ Jesus", 1 Tim. 2. 5; Titus 2. 11; John 1. 17.

Notwithstanding the obscurity of Jesus' birth, the meanness of His surroundings and the total lack of celebration of such a momentous event, there were some, even men of low degree, to whom the angel of the Lord came, bringing "good tidings of great joy", v. 10. The shepherds, to whom these glad tidings were announced, were certainly "sore afraid", v. 9, and must have been even more greatly astonished when "a multitude of the heavenly host" joined the angel in "praising God", v. 13. Let us not let familiarity with the fact of His coming into the world dim our sense of delight and wonder. A true, pure, sinless man has been born into this world. He "came down from heaven", John 6. 38, to give His life "a ransom for all", 1 Tim. 2. 6. Let this be very much more to us than history. It is related to our personal need and our eternal salvation.

"The glory of the Lord" appeared, Luke 2. 9, as the Lord Jesus took up residence on earth "and dwelt among us", John 1. 14. This answers to glory filling the tabernacle and temple, Exod. 40. 34; 2 Chron. 5. 14, as the ark entered therein.

While many wondered, and some feared, the "Saviour of the world" came, John 4. 42. Shepherds glorified and praised God, Luke 2. 20; a man, "just and devout . . . blessed God, and said, Lord, now lettest thou thy servant depart in peace", vv. 25–29; an aged woman, Anna, "gave thanks likewise unto the Lord", v. 38, speaking of Him "to all them that looked for redemption in Jerusalem".

Luke knew that the coming of "the man Christ Jesus" was for the redemption of sinful men, and that this meant, ultimately, His vicarious death at Calvary, 18. 31–33.

Mar. 6th

READING : **Luke 2. 40-52**

LOST AND FOUND

IT WAS at the age of twelve years that Jewish boys began to go to Jerusalem to the festivals, and at this age Jesus was taken to the annual feast of the passover as commanded, Deut. 16. 1–2. It must have been a great attraction to Him to get among the great Rabbis as they sat and discussed matters of the law of Moses, together with the "tradition of the elders", and "the commandments of men", Mark 7. 5–7. It was men such as these who later bitterly opposed Him and clamoured for His death. He tarried behind in Jerusalem whilst Mary and Joseph, unaware of the fact, went "a day's journey", "supposing him to have been in the company", Luke 2. 44.

Disappointments often come when we "suppose" this or that concerning the Lord. See Luke 3. 23. Mary Magdalene's untold joy was delayed because she, when so near to Him, supposed "him to be the gardener", John 20.15.

The parents of "the child Jesus" suddenly became aware of His absence from the company of their kinsfolk and acquaintances. After a three day search with much sorrow, He was found in the temple, not teaching, but hearing the doctors, and "asking them questions", 2. 46. We shall read more of His wondrous words as we proceed through Luke's Gospel. They were amazed, including His mother, who, although inwardly perplexed, "kept all these sayings in her heart", 2. 51; see 2. 19. Those who should have known Him best on earth seem to have known Him so little. They knew little of the business that He was about and, when He stated this business, "they understood not", 2. 49–50. He would later tell His disciples that doing the will of His Father was His meat, the very inward sustenance of His life, John 4. 34.

Leaving Jerusalem behind, the company continued their journey, "and he went down with them, and came to Nazareth, and was subject unto them", 2. 51. Like the "handmaid of the Lord", 1. 38, there are many things which we do not understand. She "believed" the unbelievable, 1. 45, and "kept all these things, and pondered them in her heart", 2. 19. Where reason gives no help, love "rejoiceth in the truth" and "believeth all things", 1 Cor. 13. 6–7.

Mar. 7th

READING : **Luke 3. 1-38**

A VOICE IN THE WILDERNESS

IN THIS chapter a varied section of humanity is confronted by John the Baptist. There were Roman soldiers, "the people", tax-collectors, and some described as a "generation of vipers". John spared none. The voice crying in the wilderness was a warning voice; there were no pleasantries for sinners with this man's preaching. Time was running out for Israel, the Messiah was shortly to appear, and His winnowing fan would separate the wheat from the chaff, true from false. John likened this to: "Every valley shall be filled, and every mountain and hill shall be brought low", 3. 5–6; all flesh would be brought to a common level before God, that His salvation might be seen by all. Very much like Elijah, the Baptist's voice is a warning voice, 3. 7. His denunciations of the sins of the people were not modified when he reproved Herod "for all the evils" he had done, v. 19. A faithful man must often suffer for his faithfulness and Herod "shut up John in prison", 3. 20. Yet he had said to them all, "one mightier than I cometh", 3. 16. This One increased, while John decreased, and in this process John's joy was fulfilled, as the voice of the Bridegroom replaced the voice of the "one crying in the wilderness", John 3. 29, 30.

It is important to note that John's teaching could not take place at the same time as that of the Lord Jesus; similarly, the church on earth could not exist side-by-side with Judaism; the Lord Jesus had to return to heaven so that the Holy Spirit should be present instead.

This chapter, which mentions so many individuals and which closes with Mary's genealogy, speaks also of the Father, the beloved Son and the Holy Ghost. How delightful it is for us to turn away from man in his sin, bewilderment, falsities and pride, to contemplate "Jesus himself", declared to be the Father's beloved Son, in whom He was "well pleased", Luke 3. 22, 23. Luke separates, as it were, Jesus from all others. So it must ever be. While we rightly think of Him being presented in Luke's Gospel as "the man", let us never forget that He is also "the Lord from heaven", "the last Adam", "the second man", 1 Cor. 15. 45–47. He is unique in every way, the "Beloved", in whom alone a poor sinner can be accepted by God, Eph. 1. 6.

Mar. 8th

READING : **Luke 4. 1-13**

TEMPTED OF THE DEVIL

THE TEMPTATION of Jesus follows upon the testimony of God to His beloved Son. Being filled with the Holy Ghost, He "was led by the Spirit into the wilderness", v. 1. Immediately before His public ministry began He was confronted by the adversary. It was a fitting prelude to His work of destroying (undoing) the works of the devil, 1 John 3. 8. This wilderness temptation was not the only time the Lord was attacked by the enemy, for He later spoke of His disciples as those who had continued with Him in His temptations, Luke 22. 28. They were not present at the temptation in the wilderness. It seems that His only companions were the "wild beasts", Mark 1. 13. It was surely a temptation when, after He had fed the five thousand, men came to "take him by force, to make him a king", John 6. 15. Then He departed into a mountain alone. There was also the occasion when Peter voiced his displeasure at his Master's mention of His forthcoming death and resurrection, Mark 8. 31–33.

The Lord was "in all points tempted like as we are, yet without sin" (*lit.*, sin apart), Heb. 4. 15. The purpose of His temptation was not to discover if He could sin, but to show that He could not sin! "The prince of this world cometh, and hath nothing in me", John 14. 30. Whatever the bait was, He did not respond. Just as pure gold cannot be attracted by a magnet, so He was not drawn away or enticed by temptation and lust as we are, James 1. 14.

Bread would have been most acceptable in His hunger. The kingdoms of the earth and their glory were seemingly to be more desired than to be "despised and rejected of men". To engage in false heroics by jumping from a pinnacle of the temple would have put the word of God to the test. To all these insinuations the blessed Son of God quoted from one book of Moses, Deut. 8. 3; 6. 13, 16, in reply.

In spite of all the fierceness and subtlety of this threefold attack upon the Lord Jesus, He came forth unscathed, untainted and victorious.

We are reminded of His perfect suitability as our High Priest. He is able to sympathize with our weaknesses because of His understanding of the path we tread, Heb. 4. 14–16.

Mar. 9th

READING : **Luke 4. 14-44**

SYNAGOGUE, CITY AND SICK-ROOM

"IN THE POWER of the Spirit", Jesus returned to the place "where he had been brought up", to Nazareth. The synagogue was the place of testimony for Him, and although those within heard His "gracious words", they showed that they did not accept Him, v. 24.

Luke's account of this visit to the synagogue is fascinating because of the detail he gives. First, the book of Isaiah was "delivered unto him"; then He opened the book, found the place, and began to read from Isaiah 61. 1–2. Having completed His reading, "he closed the book, and he gave it again to the minister, and sat down". There was a dignity about the whole incident, and Jesus showed a deep reverence in reading the Scriptures in public. It is not surprising to read, that "all bare him witness, and wondered at the gracious words which proceeded out of his mouth", v. 22.

The psalmist wrote of the Messiah, into whose lips "grace" was "poured", Psa. 45. 2. Jesus said, "the words that I speak unto you, they are spirit, and they are life", John 6. 63.

Nevertheless, as He said, a prophet is not "accepted in his own country", v. 24. He only needed to speak of God blessing the Gentiles and the congregation was filled with wrath and sought to destroy Him, v. 29.

In the synagogue of Capernaum He cast out of a man "a spirit of an unclean devil" (demon), v. 33, and those present "were all amazed, and spake among themselves, saying, What a word is this!". Thus His fame followed Him. He entered the house of Peter, whose mother-in-law had been taken sick "with a great fever", v. 38. He rebuked the fever; she was restored, and immediately she ministered to those in the house.

The Lord was always quick to discern any discord in a home, 10. 40–42. He still restores tranquility and peace where there is any kind of "fever". "Fever" in the home is a common enough sickness in our day, and it too often seizes and agitates the mother! The mother is the heart of the family; the father is the head. We need love as well as leadership, so let us "beseech him" for the mothers, v. 38, in our prayers.

Mar. 10th

READING : **Luke 5. 1-39**

CATCHING, CLEANSING AND CALLING

A VARIETY of contacts and a diversity of needs are before us in this chapter, but the Son of man is ever greater than the needs of men.

Jesus borrowed Simon's boat and, thrusting out from the shore and using the boat for His pulpit, He taught the people. As a reward, or as strengthening Simon's faith after a night's vain toil, the net was let down to result in "a great multitude of fishes", v. 6. The incident provides something of an object lesson for Simon was told that, from henceforth, he would "catch men", v. 10; Acts 2. 41; 10. 44–48. Wherever there is a display of divine glory there is a sense of human guilt, v. 8; 7. 38; Isa. 6. 1–5.

The Lord's next encounters were with a leper and a paralytic, who together illustrate the corruption and impotence sin produces. In the case of the leper and his pitiable plight we see the grace and the power of the Son of man in touching him. His loathsome disease immediately departed.

Next, the paralysed man was brought before Him. The difficulty facing the four men, Mark 2. 3, who carried their friend to Jesus was overcome by removing the tiling of the house. They let him down "before Jesus", who saw what nobody else saw, namely "their faith", v. 20. Pronouncing "thy sins are forgiven thee", He gave a token of the reality of this to unbelieving onlookers by also saying: "Arise, and take up thy couch, and go into thine house", v. 24. The onlookers were amazed and said, "we have seen strange things today".

Levi was next confronted, and was called to "Follow me", v. 27. Rising up from his tax-collecting fellows, he spread "a great feast", v. 29,—and invited them all! The Pharisees and scribes murmured against His disciples because of the dubious guests, but He replied, "They that are whole need not a physician; but they that are sick," v. 31. His "call", He pointed out, was to sinners. His disciples ate and drank while "the bridegroom" was with them, and why not?

The chapter closes with a parable which, if understood aright, speaks of the old covenant and the new. These do not mix, and those attached to the old find it difficult to get attached to the new, saying "The old is better", v. 39.

Mar. 11th

READING : **Luke 6. 1-49**

TRUE OR FALSE ?

THE CHAPTER before us begins with two incidents which concerned the Sabbath. The disciples plucked ears of corn, rubbed them in their hands and ate the grains. An objection from the Pharisees to this being done on the Sabbath day was answered by reference to an action of David's, vv. 3, 4; 1 Sam. 21. 6. As the Lord of the Sabbath had been rejected, there could be no true Sabbath for these people, only an empty profession of obedience to God.

Jesus had perfect right, as Lord of the Sabbath, to allow His disciples to satisfy their hunger, and to heal a man of a withered right hand, vv. 6–11.

Following this, from an unnumbered company of disciples, He called out twelve, "whom also he named apostles (sent ones)", v. 13.

The sermon on the mount, which followed, was addressed to the disciples, vv. 20, 40. The Lord gave them instructions as to their attitude towards a world in opposition to them. To love one's enemies, to return good for evil, to be poor, hungry, and to weep, to be hated for the Son of man's sake, would bring suitable reward in heaven. Christianity *is* Christ and those who listened to His words were brought face to face with what would be the price of true discipleship in a world of false values and other loyalties.

The Son of man spared no one when the matter of hypocrisy was dealt with. The blind who presumed to lead the blind and the man with a beam in his own eye, who saw a mote in his brother's eye and offered to remove it, were His illustrations of hypocrisy. Sincerity must ever be the hallmark of Christian discipleship. Calling Christ "Lord, Lord" and failing to practise His teachings is a hollow sham, v. 46.

The chapter closes appropriately with the Lord's illustration of two builders, representing the man who hears His "sayings, and doeth them", on the one hand, and the man "that heareth, and doeth not", on the other, vv. 47–49. One had a "rock" foundation, the other built "upon the earth" with disastrous results.

Let us be sure that our "faith has found a resting place" in Christ, and not in mere religion.

Mar. 12th

READING : **Luke 7. 1-35**

THE GREAT PHYSICIAN AT WORK

THIS IS a chapter to rejoice the heart indeed. We find Jesus in the midst of the havoc caused by sin and His complete mastery in the midst of this havoc. "The blind see, the lame walk, the lepers are cleansed, the deaf hear, the dead are raised, to the poor the gospel is preached", v. 22. Did ever a surgery in the world see such a group of patients as this? No more groping for the blind; no limping for the lame; no banishment for the leper; no silent world for the deaf; and life for the dead who hear His voice, with "glad tidings" for the poor.

The centurion sent for the Lord to come and heal his servant, v. 3. The messengers testified to his worthiness, vv. 4, 5, and, incidentally, there are commendable things said about all the centurions mentioned in the New Testament, Mark 15. 39; Luke 23. 47; Acts 10. 1, 2; Acts 27. 43.

The sublime faith of this Roman centurion, as he measured his own powers of command with the "say in a word" of Jesus, v. 7, called forth Christ's testimony that He had "not found so great faith, no, not in Israel", v. 9. The servant "that had been sick", v. 10, was made whole.

On two occasions Jesus "marvelled"; once at the unbelief of His countrymen, Mark 6. 6, and once at the faith of this centurion.

Following on a situation in which a servant was about to die, v. 2, Jesus faced at Nain a sorrowful company carrying out the dead body of the only son of a widow, v. 12. His heart was moved with compassion and, touching the bier, He said: "Young man, I say unto thee, Arise", v. 14, and the one who had been dead "sat up, and began to speak", v. 15.

In the prison, Matt. 11. 2, John was wondering if, after all, the Messiah had come or not. Jesus did not tell John's messengers in so many words that He was the Messiah, but He sent them to tell John "what things ye have seen and heard", v. 22. His works were credentials enough, surely, to convince John that He was the One of whom he had spoken, John 1. 15.

When the messengers departed, Jesus began to tell the people of the greatness of His messenger, the Baptist, and the importance of his mission.

Mar. 13th

READING : **Luke 7. 36-50**

JESUS ACCEPTS AN INVITATION

"ONE OF the Pharisees", the sect which so bitterly opposed the Lord Jesus, invited Him to a meal. He accepted the invitation. The company was joined later by a woman known in the city as "a sinner". Luke provides us with a strange picture indeed; there is Jesus, the Righteous One; the Pharisee, the self-righteous one; and the woman, the unrighteous one.

Perhaps she looked at those blessed feet, so soon to be pierced for her sins, as for ours, and contrasted those feet with her own in the ways they walked. His were the beautiful feet of One who brought "good tidings", that published "peace", Isa. 52. 7; hers were the feet that, by inference, were restless and straying, Prov. 7. 11–12. Her standing, her weeping, her washing with her tears, and wiping with the hairs of her head, her kissing and anointing, all tell of a worshipful heart and a sense of guilt in the presence of divine glory.

The Pharisee, looking on, was questioning in his mind what sort of prophet "this man" was, since the woman who touched Him was "a sinner", v. 39.

Jesus read his thoughts, and it was this that gave rise to His parable, vv. 41, 42.

The creditor had two debtors, owing five hundred pence, and fifty pence respectively. The debt of the first was ten times as great as that of the second, but on one point they were alike . . . they were both bankrupt! "They had nothing to pay." Out of the generosity of his heart, the creditor "forgave them both". How like our God, "Who forgiveth all thine iniquities", Psa. 103. 3. The one who was "forgiven most", will naturally love most, and the actions of the woman had expressed her deep appreciation of Him who had authority "on earth to forgive sins", Mark 2. 10. In spite of the evident objection of those "that sat at meat with him", Luke 7. 49, Jesus announced her forgiveness and told the woman, "Thy faith hath saved thee; go in peace", v. 50.

The lesson emerging from this parable is that we are all debtors, some more, some less. The question is not so much the greatness of our sin, but the fact of it. May we all experience what this woman experienced and, being forgiven much, we shall love Him much in return.

Mar. 14th

READING : **Luke 8. 1-56**

SAYING AND DOING

THE GREAT Worker is likened to a sower, the seed being "the word of God", v. 11. His companions, as He went "throughout every city and village, preaching and showing the glad tidings", were those in whose hearts the seed had been fruitful, vv. 1–3. Then follow two parables in which He spoke of the natural to illustrate the spiritual. He pressed home the spiritual truth that those, who "in an honest and good heart" hear the word, should keep it and radiate the light of it to others. Such are brought into the nearest spiritual relationship to Himself, v. 21.

Then He entered into a boat with His disciples to "go over unto the other side of the lake", and they encountered a storm of wind. In distress the disciples cried, "Master, master, we perish". Arising from sleep at their cry, He "rebuked the wind and the raging of the water: and they ceased, and there was a calm", v. 24. It was a picture in the natural realm of what happens in the spiritual at His word of command, v. 29. The poor man, on "the other side", v. 22, was released from the powers of evil by His almighty word, and was found "sitting at the feet of Jesus clothed, and in his right mind", v. 35. Returning from "the other side", He was met by Jairus who fell at His feet and pleaded for his twelve year old daughter, who was dying.

As the Lord responded to this appeal, a woman moved out of the throng and touched His garment. Plagued by a seemingly incurable complaint she had said, "If I may touch but his clothes, I shall be whole", Mark 5. 28. Her healing was as immediate as it was startling, and she declared all to Him "before all the people", Luke 8. 47. Her faith had made her whole, and peace followed.

While speaking the word of peace, news was brought that the daughter of Jairus had died. There seemed no point in His going any further. He replied, "Fear not: believe only, and she shall be made whole", v. 50. He entered the house of death and took Jairus' daughter by the hand. He called, saying simply, "Maid, arise", v. 54. She was restored to life, power and thought, and her parents were astonished.

His word brought "calm", v. 24; a "right mind", v. 35; "peace", v. 48; "life", vv. 54, 55.

Mar. 15th

READING : **Luke 9. 1-27**

FORETASTES OF THE KINGDOM

JESUS CALLED "His twelve disciples together", and gave them power and authority over all demons and diseases. Their equipment for evangelizing was His authority. They were to "take nothing" for their journey; His power would suffice in every situation they met. The disciples, "preaching the gospel, and healing every where", gave Herod much perplexity. The tyrant said, "Who is this, of whom I hear such things?", v. 9.

Following all this activity and manifestation of His power with them, the disciples were taken aside by Him into quietness. Communion with Him keeps the servant calm, fresh in spirit, and prepares for further ministry. The feeding of the multitude followed. His compassion would not allow the people to be dispersed in hunger, so His command was, "Give ye them to eat", v. 13, and they "were all filled".

The world into which He came was not only a place of hunger and misery, with sin as the root cause, but a place where He was despised and rejected. We find Him in prayer *alone*, v. 18.

A lonely man, indeed, even though His disciples were with Him. The shadow of a great sorrow was over His soul. As the people speculated as to who He was and He, true man that He was, felt the estrangement, He asked His disciples, "But whom say ye that I am?", v. 20. Peter's answer, "The Christ of God", was true indeed, but He had to explain that there was to be suffering for Him before the glory. Peter learnt this lesson later through the tears of his own remorse, and the joy of Jesus' resurrection, 1 Pet. 1. 3; 5. 1.

A man would later say, "Lord, I will follow thee whithersoever thou goest", v. 57, but the price of discipleship was high, as He now explained. To deny himself, to take up the cross, and follow Him, was too great a price to pay in the reckoning of one man, Mark 10. 21, 22. How do we feel about it? Are we ashamed of Him in the world that crucified Him and cast Him out or do we "Stand up for Jesus", to receive His "well done" later on? To save one's life for self or lose it for Him—the choice is ours.

Mar. 16th

READING : **Luke 9. 28-50**

WE BEHELD HIS GLORY

AFTER THE scene of hunger, vv. 10–17, Luke now shows us a scene of glory, and the Lord in prayer. Taking the favoured three, Peter, James and John, He ascended a mountain and, while in prayer, "the fashion of his countenance was altered, and his raiment was white and glistering", v. 29. The glory which now radiates from His very garments is His proper glory, veiled hitherto for the sake of the companions of His grace and love that, with darkened glass as it were, they might see Him the better; compare 2 Cor. 3. 18.

With Jesus were Moses and Elijah, talking of His decease (*lit.*, exodus), His "going out" in death, v. 31. As representatives of the law and the prophets, they must pass. The disciples were now to "hear him", v. 35, the beloved Son of the Father, attested by the voice out of heaven. The scene was so overwhelming that, waking out of heavy sleep and seeing His glory, Peter wished to retain the wondrous spectacle within three tabernacles, "not knowing what he said", v. 33. To have retained Him thus ran counter to the divine purpose; the Christ was first to suffer and then "to enter into his glory".

The scene changes, for, on the next day, coming down from the hill, they were met by a man anxiously beseeching Jesus to look upon his son, an only child, who was taken by an evil spirit. The disciples had been of no help to the man in his desperation but the Master said, "Bring thy son hither", v. 41. Rebuking the unclean spirit, He "healed the child, and delivered him again to his father", v. 42. Impotent disciples; mighty Christ!

Manifesting "the mighty power of God", v. 43, to the amazement of all, He reminded His disciples of His coming trial and death at "the hands of men". This was a strange atmosphere, surely, in which to debate who should be the greatest among them, v. 46. Taking a child as His object lesson on humility, He said, "he that is least among you all, the same shall be great", v. 48. Another lesson on humility followed this when He answered their complaint about one using His Name in casting out demons although "he followeth not with us". There can be no neutrality where Christ is concerned. "He that is not against us is for us", v. 50.

Mar. 17th

READING : **Luke 9. 51 to 10. 42**

HE IS LORD

HOW EASY it is to call Jesus "Lord" and yet by our actions to deny our profession. James and John believed that they were acting according to the wishes of their Master when they said "Lord, wilt thou that we command fire to come down?"—after all, it was what they themselves were ready to do, and they thought that they were right. The Lord's rebuke, "Ye know not what manner of spirit ye are of", shows very plainly that such an attitude of anger and desire for judgment was not in keeping with acknowledging His Lordship.

The man who said, "Lord, I will follow thee whithersoever", v. 57, had not faced up to what was involved in such a claim. As many have found since then, to own His Lordship has meant following the "outcast stranger"; if necessary, suffering the loss of all things. It is well to find out what is involved before we take the term "Lord" lightly upon our lips.

In verse 59 another man said "Lord", but he added "let me first". It is not difficult to see the inconsistency here—if Jesus is Lord *He* must come first. His wishes, His directions, must have priority. Yet again we hear the word "Lord", v. 61, but, as before, with a condition. This time relatives came before instant obedience: again the claim of Lordship fell to the ground.

It may well be that as we read these words we can recall more than one occasion in our lives when the words of Peter, "Not so, Lord", Acts 10. 14, have been ours. This may be the position even today. May contemplation of the Saviour's blessed Person bring us to the place where we can say "Lord, what wilt thou have me to do?", Acts 9. 6.

The fact that He is Lord is clearly demonstrated later. In His sovereignty the Lord sent out seventy disciples to announce His coming, and He declared, "He that despiseth you despiseth me; and he that despiseth me despiseth him that sent me". He claimed the right to demand that He should be received, and He plainly declared that rejection of Him would result in judgment. How glad the disciples were to be able to return and say, "Lord, even the devils are subject unto us through thy name". Yes, even in the spirit world He is Lord.

Mar. 18th

READING : **Luke 11. 1-26**

ASK — SEEK — KNOCK

As Son of man the Lord Jesus took the place of dependence on God, and this is reflected in the frequent references to prayer in His life. The disciples saw Him at prayer (not for the first time), and what they saw convinced them that prayer was a vital factor in that wonderful life. This realization created within them a desire for a similar experience—"Lord, teach us to pray", v. 1. The life they witnessed was linked in constant contact with God, and they wanted to know the secret.

Very graciously He taught them that prayer was based on relationship—"Our Father". It is for the members of the family. True prayer gives God His rightful place—"Hallowed be thy Name", and longs for the day when the Son of man shall be seen as Lord in His own kingdom on earth. It embraces material needs—"our daily bread", spiritual needs—"forgive", and seeks help to live aright amid the constant pressure from the evil one.

Have you ever had a friend come to you, one "out of the way", v. 6 Gk., needing help, and you have felt so empty and barren that you could not do anything? Do you remember going to that other Friend who has an abundant supply, and obtaining help from Him? The fact that there is a Friend to whom we may go shines out of this passage, vv. 5–8, but there is the warning that God may test our earnestness by not giving at once, vv. 9, 10. He is not an unwilling God, but He knows best just when to give. Keep on asking. Everyone that keeps asking receives; he that keeps seeking finds; and he that keeps knocking finds the door flung open. It seems that Abraham finished asking before God finished giving, Gen. 18. 23–33. We must remember, however, that if God says "No" this is just as surely an answer as "Yes".

Leading on from this, the Lord draws a lesson from the way in which earthly parents normally give to their children. They are concerned with their good. They will not willingly give them what will prove to be harmful, or withhold from them what is beneficial. How much more shall your heavenly Father, who is essentially good compared with men who are essentially evil, give that which is good.

Mar. 19th

READING : **Luke 11. 27-54**

GREATER

AT THE OPENING of our reading a woman pronounces blessing upon Mary because she was the mother of Jesus, vv. 27, 28. This is in keeping with the angelic declaration to her, "blessed art thou among women", 1. 28. Some have raised Mary to a completely unjustified height. We note that the Lord's words rectify this, because He puts into a place of greater blessing them "that hear the word of God, and keep it". Natural relationship is not as important as spiritual, James 1. 1; Jude 1. The Lord claimed for Himself the dignity of being "a greater than Solomon" and "a greater than Jonas", vv. 29–32.

A queen travelled many miles to have conversation with Solomon, having heard of his fame. A wicked city repented at the preaching of Jonas the prophet. How did the Lord's contemporaries treat the One who was greater than both? "Though he had done so many miracles before them, yet they believed not on him", John 12. 37. Sadly the Lord made the solemn declaration that greater light involves greater judgment. How have we reacted in response to His revelation?

Verses 37–54 take us into the home of a Pharisee who condescendingly invited the Lord to dine with him. Immediately the Lord broke one of their first rules: He did not wash before the meal. This had nothing to do with hygiene, but was a purely ceremonial requirement. In response to the Pharisee's astonishment, the Lord drew attention to the hypocritical practices which exalted outward behaviour above inward condition. They gave tithes but failed to love God. They put themselves on a pedestal to be seen of men, but God knew their hearts. There are "Pharisees" still, and God is still more concerned with the "inward part", v. 39. "Man looketh on the outward appearance, but the Lord looketh on the heart", 1 Sam. 16. 7.

The Lord's rebuke stung a listening scribe into response. He felt that the criticism of the Pharisees had also been directed at him. The Lord agreed that it had, and very firmly He denounced a company of men who claimed to be teachers of the Word of God, but who surrounded that Word with man-made rules. He charged them with taking away the key of knowledge, that is, withholding God's Word.

Mar. 20th

READING : **Luke 12. 1-34**

DIVINE PROVIDENCE

OUR PORTION today, apart from verses 13–21 (spoken to the man who interrupted the Lord's words), is specifically stated to be for the disciples. As we take our place in that category today, the words of comfort and assurance are ours. What a God we have—He was even interested in the free sparrow cast in when four were purchased; compare v. 6 with Matt. 10. 29. Even the hairs of our head are numbered, so detailed is His knowledge of us. When the Lord said, "ye are of more value than many sparrows", He knew that very soon His own precious blood would be shed for the redemption of His disciples. We are precious to Him.

His care would extend to those testing experiences when, because of faithfulness in confessing Him, His disciples would be brought before those in authority. In such circumstances, said the Lord, leave the matter of defence in the hand of God. He will give words to utter when preparation proves impossible.

The interruption at verse 13 gave the opportunity to warn against covetousness. Covetousness implies that we are not satisfied with God's provision; that we could do better than He. Verse 22 returns to the discourse to the disciples and again we are brought into the realm of divine providence. The ravens, unclean birds, have no barns, but their daily provision by God is assured, and the disciples are "better than the fowls". The lilies of the field, toiling not, spinning not, yet maintained in such glory as to surpass Solomon, are a testimony to the Father's faithfulness. We are better than the lilies. The grass of the field, so common to us, is maintained by God. God "clothes" it. How much more His own!

Trust in our God will prevent anxious care. We know we have need of material things, but more important, He knows it, v. 30. Anxious care then should be absent, and the main thrust of our daily living should be seeking the kingdom of God, v. 31. In this we are contrasted with the "nations of the world" who devote their energies to "what shall we eat, and what shall we drink?". Seeking His glory first means that "all these things shall be added" to us; not necessarily what we want, which might prove harmful, but what God sees to be good for us. He knows best.

Mar. 21st

READING : **Luke 12. 35-59**

HE IS COMING

THE LIFE of trust (yesterday's reading) is also a life of watchfulness and faithfulness. The Lord frequently made reference to His coming, and urged that His disciples should live in the light of this important event. If He is coming there can be no slackening of effort—there must be girded loins and burning lamps, v. 35. The girded loins speak of readiness for labour, and the burning lamp of a testimony to be maintained in the darkness. This is against the background of His coming, concerning which we must say that He has given no dates.

A ready welcome for the coming One is followed by indications of approval by the Lord, vv. 36–40. "Blessed are those servants"—who can explain all that this means? Then the staggering statement that He, the Lord, shall "gird himself . . . and serve them". Unspeakable humility, and yet in that humility His greatness shines out. He had said to His disciples, "Whosoever will be chief among you, let him be your servant", Matt. 20. 27. Still taking the place of service He demonstrates His right to be chief.

Verses 42–48 move into the realm of faithfulness, and we are introduced to a "faithful and wise steward", who accepts responsibility during His Lord's absence. Paul spoke of stewardship and emphasized that "it is required in stewards, that a man be found faithful", 1 Cor. 4. 2. During the time our Lord is away we have all had a charge committed to us, in relation to which faithfulness is required. Verse 43 tells us of the Lord's reaction to that faithfulness "when he cometh". What depths there are in those words "Blessed is that servant"! But the sad fact remains that faithfulness will not be found in all His servants, and we see the Master dealing with unfaithful servants accordingly. John spoke of the possibility of being "ashamed before him at his coming", 1 John 2. 28.

Faithfulness and watchfulness will cost something. The Lord speaks of division because of Him. If we are faithful to Him we must not expect that all will be in agreement; even in the family circle there may well be opposition. The Lord, the Faithful One, knew what this meant for Himself; a "baptism" of suffering at the hands of men and God, v. 50. Yet to the end He remained the Faithful and True.

Mar. 22nd

READING : **Luke 13. 1-35**

EXCEPT YE REPENT

REPENTANCE IS a change of attitude which leads the individual to trust in God and abandon sin. It has a vital part to play in God's dealings with men. Some told the Lord of those who had been slain by Pilate, and of those who died when a tower fell on them, implying that those who suffered in this way were outstanding sinners, and had been judged. "Except ye repent, ye shall all likewish perish": the response of Christ looks away from those who had suffered in those incidents and is directed to His hearers, and to us. Repentance is vital, or all will perish. Christ accepts the universality of sin and there is therefore no exemption from the requirement to repent.

The parable following, vv. 6–9, is linked with our first passage, but includes the additional truth of the patience of God. In the fig tree planted in the vineyard (a place with nourishing soil), we see the nation of Israel cared for by God. The vine-dresser (the Lord Jesus) had been tending it for three years (His public ministry). The owner looked for a return, but, alas, there was none. There was no fruit, in spite of the fact that the Son of God had been among them in grace. The "vine-dresser" pleaded for another year before judgment, but it was in this fourth year that the nation revealed itself in all its wickedness and crucified their Messiah. The words "cut it down" were fulfilled in A.D. 70 when Jerusalem was destroyed. No repentance means that there is nothing for God and the position is hopeless.

Verse 34 can be linked with these two passages. This outburst of the Lord reveals His compassionate heart. He saw a city which would not repent, He saw a fig tree that would not bear fruit, and the divine Son of God could see no alternative to the impending tragedy. "I would, but ye would not". Oh, the sorrow of it all. The Lord did not immediately write off those who would not repent and those who did not bear fruit, but there comes a time when He must, and He does it sadly.

"Are there few that be saved?", v. 23. The Lord does not say "yea" or "nay". He told the questioner to ensure that he entered in at the strait gate. This involves repentance.

Mar. 23rd

READING : **Luke 14. 1-35**

CHALLENGE

SEVERAL PARABLES flow from an invitation from a Pharisee to the Lord to partake of a meal. The guests are the "upper crust", and the Lord notes the jostling going on to secure the highest places at the table. Although Himself a guest, He challenges this attitude and says in effect, "take the humble place—the only move must then be upward". He emphasized what is clearly a divine principle, "whosoever exalteth himself shall be abased; and he that humbleth himself shall be exalted". He is the supreme example of this in self-humbling and divine exaltation, Phil. 2. 5–11. His further instruction as to who should be invited to a meal (that is, those unable to repay) leads to a comment by one of the guests, "Blessed is he that shall eat bread in the kingdom of God". The Lord's response is another parable concerning a feast, made by God and to which men are invited. It may be that the first ones invited were the Jewish nation. There was certainly a general refusal to take up the invitation. The excuses for refusing are paltry and clearly indicate an unwillingness to accept. As Paul pointed out, "the fall" of the Jewish nation would be "the riches of the world", Rom. 11. 12, and God flung the door of blessing wide open for the Gentile world; for the unworthy and the outcast who would respond to the invitation.

Introducing the next three parables, the Lord discourages "easy" discipleship, vv. 25–27. The multitudes were following Him, but not out of conviction. The Lord pointed out the challenge of discipleship. He must be supreme in the life. Love for Him must be so great that all other loves pale into nothingness. The most difficult part of discipleship concerns "his own life also", v. 26. It is easier to set others to one side than self.

Two of the parables show that Christ does not want followers who rush into discipleship unthinkingly, vv. 28–33. The parable of the man building a tower and the king facing invasion, while similar, are yet different. "In the first parable Jesus says, 'Sit down and reckon whether you can afford to follow me'. In the second He says, 'Sit down and reckon whether you can afford to refuse my demands'.", (A. M. Hunter). Both considerations are important.

Mar. 24th

READING : **Luke 15. 1-32**

A SEEKING GOD

THERE IS a close link between the end of chapter 14 and the beginning of chapter 15. The Lord had spoken of salt which had lost its savour and consequently had become useless, and He urged His hearers to give heed to what He said. The publicans and sinners agreed that this description fitted them, and drew near to hear Him. This brought forth complaints from the Pharisees and scribes, who could not understand how the Lord could have dealings with such people. They did not understand that it was the eternal purpose of God to seek and to save such. To explain this, the Lord spoke this incomparable parable, vv. 4–32; it is really only one, in three sections. It seems that His purpose is to show that the whole of the Triune Godhead is closely interested in and concerned with those who are lost. He, the Son, is seen in the first section, vv. 3–7, as the Good Shepherd going out to find the lost sheep. The Holy Spirit is depicted in the second section, vv. 8–10, where we see the woman seeking with a light to find her lost coin. The Father is seen in the final section welcoming home the lost son, vv. 11–32. Each section emphasizes the joy that comes through finding that which was lost.

The Son sees of the travail of His soul and is satisfied, Isa. 53. 11. Surely when the Lord Jesus later entered paradise from the cross and took with Him a sheep whom He had rescued from the fangs of death, He could have called the heavenly host and said, "rejoice with me; for I have found my sheep which was lost". The woman rejoices in finding the lost coin (a dead thing) and the Holy Spirit rejoices as dead souls are quickened into life. The Father sees the lost son brought back into the family circle and we listen to His words, "It was meet that we should make merry, and be glad". The parable reveals that there is a sense in which God has a loss while men are away from Him. The shepherd had lost his sheep, the woman had lost her coin, the father had lost his son. It was this sense of loss that brought the Son of God into the wilderness to "seek and to save that which was lost".

"And the angels echoed around the throne,
Rejoice! for the Lord brings back His own!"

Mar. 25th

READING : **Luke 16. 1-31**

DEFECTIVE STEWARDSHIP

THE STORY of the unjust steward presents us with problems of interpretation, due largely to our failure to understand fully the transactions in which the steward engaged to safeguard his future. His stewardship was at fault and dismissal faced him, with gloomy consequences. The purpose of the adjustments mentioned in the story was to obtain favourable treatment for himself later at the hands of those he had thus benefitted. It is possible that the adjustments were not in themselves dishonest, but merely a putting right, by way of deduction, of transactions which were previously doubtful. The man's master commended his wisdom in the matter, not of course any dishonesty of which he may have been guilty. The Lord points to the action of the man and says in effect, "Look, that man, a worldling, acted sensibly in the time of crisis, and in so doing he secured a measure of security for the time following his dismissal". If the "children of this world" act wisely in the handling of material things, how much more should the "children of light". The principle is stated, "he that is faithful in that which is least is faithful also in much". Clearly, however, the individual must be devoted to God and not to the material things, and they must be handled in the light of that devotion, v. 13.

In verses 19–31 we see another man guilty of defective stewardship. He uses God-given wealth for self alone. We cannot imagine a greater contrast than that between "fared sumptuously every day", v. 19, and "desiring to be fed with the crumbs", v. 21. Yet the rich man is not charged with wickedness. The scene changes. The rich man dies, has a splendid funeral but, in hades, is in torment. Lazarus also dies. We read of no funeral, but he is in the place of blessing, paradise. We should consider the solemn truth that there comes a moment when destiny becomes fixed and unchangeable. As we listen to the conversation between the rich man and Abraham we discover that, if the rich man had given heed to the teaching of Moses and the prophets, he would not have entered the place of torment. He lived for self. The implication is that Lazarus, though poor in this world's goods, was rich in faith.

Mar. 26th

READING : **Luke 17. 1-37**

IN THE LIGHT OF HIS COMING

AN UNFORGIVING spirit is a problem, vv. 3–6. The Lord says that, if one offends against us and repents, we must forgive. It could be argued that, if there is a repeated offence (seven times), some doubt may be cast upon the professed repentance. But the lesson is plain—if he repent, forgive him. We may doubt the genuineness of the repentance but our business is to forgive. We can understand the disciples' request, "increase our faith", for this attitude of continued forgiveness lies beyond human power. The Lord replied that it is not the amount of faith that is important, but the quality of faith. He spoke of a sycamine tree, believed to be a mulberry, a tree with very deep roots. It is a fitting picture of a deeply rooted unforgiving spirit. By faith this can be dealt with.

The slave, vv. 7–10, had no right to expect thanks for what he had done, he had only done his job. Let us remember that, in the light of Calvary, we can never do too much, indeed never do enough, for our beloved Master. We see our service as unprofitable; may God keep us from looking at it otherwise. The divine viewpoint graciously sees it differently, and the faithful servant, even though he views his own service as unprofitable, will hear the words "Well done".

Ten lepers are cleansed but only one returns to give thanks vv. 11–19. The Lord is looking for the gratitude of those whom He cleanses. Do we fail here? Do we take our salvation for granted? The man who came back received a deeper blessing. While the nine were healed of their leprosy, the tenth was saved from his sin as well, and enjoyed a yet closer relationship with his Master.

The Lord now directs the thoughts of the disciples to the day of the coming of the Son of man, vv. 22–37. Israel and the world are in view, not the church, and we see the Son of man intervening sharply and in judgment. The world will be absorbed in its own affairs, and will be shocked by the suddenness of events. Before all this happens, however, the church will be taken to be for ever with the Lord, 1 Thess. 4. 17. It is against the background of this happy event that we seek grace to exercise a forgiving spirit and to give acceptable service.

Mar. 27th

READING : **Luke 18. 1-43**

HOW DO WE PRAY ?

IN TODAY'S passage we read of the prayers of a widow, a Pharisee, a publican, and a beggar. Verses 1–8 are introduced by the words, "men ought always to pray, and not to faint". We see a widow who went through a testing time and sought legal aid to set the matter right. Receiving no satisfaction, she came back again and again until the judge gave way and granted her plea. Persistence pays. Is our God unwilling to act? No, His giving will be out of a heart of love. Yet He will give at the right time; not too soon, and not too late. Keep on praying.

A Pharisee prayed, vv. 10–12. But was this really prayer? Boasting of what he was, of what he did, he had neither time to confess any need nor to worship God. For such a man there was no response from heaven. Do we pray like this?

A publican prayed, vv. 13–14. He was a man with whom the Spirit of God had been working, a man who saw himself as God saw him, *the* sinner. How could a man who was so corrupt dare approach a holy God? In the courtyard outside he had seen the smoking altar, telling of sacrifice, and in the most holy place was a mercy seat covered with blood from the altar. Here was hope. "God be merciful (lit., propitious) to me". It was enough. God, who read the hearts of Pharisee and publican alike, graciously stepped in and "this man went down . . . justified". God answers real prayer.

A beggar prayed, vv. 35–43. This beggar must have heard stories of the prophet of Nazareth, and what he heard convinced him that He was the Messiah, the Son of David. Now He was within reach and, ignoring all attempts to stop him, the beggar cried for help. "And Jesus stood". The Maker of heaven and earth, the Sustainer of the universe, stood still at the cry of a beggar! What grace! And what did Jesus say? "What wilt thou that I shall do unto thee?" "Lord, that I may receive my sight." It was not a long prayer, but it was very effective. Maybe the Lord is saying to you today, "What do you want me to do for you?". Tell Him plainly all your need and watch Him work. What you see will lead to praise.

"Unto him that is able to do exceeding abundantly above all that we ask or think, according to the power that worketh in us, unto him be glory . . . by Christ Jesus", Eph. 3. 20-21.

Mar. 28th

READING : **Luke 19. 1-48**

SALVATION AND DOOM

WE READ of a publican, vv. 1–10. The interesting suggestion has been made that this is the same man the Lord talked about in the previous chapter, 18. 13–14. Whether this is so or not, the Lord had come specifically to seek him, v. 10, and He invited Himself to his home. We would love to know the conversation in that home but we only know subsequent events, and these prove that a wonderful change had taken place in the man. He was not only a tax-gatherer but the chief tax-gatherer, and in his progress upward he had become a very rich man. Now as an indication of a changed nature he declared his intention to disgorge his ill-gotten gains. This is what happens when a sinner finds mercy; he not only goes to his house "justified" but the very course of his life is changed. And the words of the Lord in verse 10 indicate that He came for this.

In verses 11–27 we find servants with their master's money, which they should have used for his purposes while he was away. Maybe in the money we see the basic commitment to all servants, to live out their faith. As individuals they varied in their response to their master's requirements. To one we hear the words of the master, "thou good servant", and see opportunity given for wider service. To one, who had taken no action at all, we find words of reproof and the loss of what he failed to use. "Shall I go and empty-handed; must I meet my Saviour so?".

The Lord was ascending up to Jerusalem, vv. 28–40, and He must enter as foretold by the prophetic Scriptures, Zech. 9. 9. In a nearby village were some folk who owned an ass between them (a sign of poverty) but the word came, "The Lord hath need of him". There was no hesitation and the ass was released. Had these people been blessed by the Lord, having come to recognize the Lord's claim to all they had ?

With the solemn passage in verses 41–44 we link Luke 13. 6–9, especially "cut it down; why cumbereth it the ground?". And yet, as the doom of the city rose up before Him, He wept. W. H. Griffith Thomas has said, "Let us sit at Christ's feet until we learn the secret of His tears and, beholding the sins and sorrows of city and countryside, weep over them too".

Mar. 29th

READING : **Luke 20. 1-47**

A MATTER OF AUTHORITY

Our chapter touches on the matter of authority several times, and we see the Lord Jesus claiming authority in every department of His teaching. His authority was questioned, vv. 1–8, by what seems to be a deputation from the Sanhedrin. It could be that, in putting to them His question concerning John the Baptist, He was challenging not only their sincerity but also their competence as religious leaders. If in their official capacity and responsibility they had not been able to come to a decision concerning John, how could they guide the people, and how could they form a judgment on Him who was greater than John? If in fact they really knew the truth concerning John and were not willing to face up to the logical consequence of his being from God, the Lord was not prepared to countenance such dishonesty. He had previously told them "I came down from heaven", and they knew well enough from whence His authority was derived.

Jesus then asserts that, although some of the rulers knew that His claims were sound, they deliberately rejected His authority, vv. 9–18. The husbandmen in the vineyard were the leaders of Israel, responsible to God for the tending of the nation and producing fruit for God. They rejected the owner's servants (the prophets) and, finally, the One whom they recognized as the Son—the Heir. He was cast out and killed in order that they might remain in undisputed control. The Lord solemnly pointed out that such a course of conduct could not succeed, but that God would act in judgment.

His adversaries put Him to the test with a question about tribute money, vv. 19–26. With what wonderful authority He dealt with the catch-question. He taught that there were things which Caesar might demand and things which God might demand.

In His reply to the Sadducees' attempt to trip Him up, vv. 27–38, the Lord indicated that His knowledge extended also to the resurrection life.

How sad was this constant challenge to His authority. It is possible, however, that we also can be guilty of this. Look at verse 44, "David . . . calleth him Lord." May we do this in every realm.

Mar. 30th

READING : **Luke 21. 1-38**

LITTLE IS MUCH

It is interesting to note how the Holy Spirit has placed together an apparently insignificant event and the discourse about tremendous events to take place in the history of Israel. Few would have perceived what the Lord noted, v. 2. Verse 1 tells us that He "saw the rich"; verse 2 that He "saw also a certain poor widow". He could have observed without comment, but He chose to draw attention to the woman, and pointed out that her tiny offering far outweighed the gifts of the rich. After all, when they had finished giving they had plenty left; when she had finished giving she had nothing left. Her giving was 100 per cent, but behind the gift was a believing heart which was prepared to trust God for the future. Dr. Joseph Parker has said, "The gold of affluence which is given because it is not needed, God hurls to the bottomless pit; but the copper tinged with blood He lifts and kisses into the gold of eternity".

The record moves into the Lord's discourse concerning the future, both near and more distant. He appears to have alternated between the two as He talked to the disciples. History was going to be the explanation of His words. In verses 5, 6 the destruction of the temple in A.D. 70 is in view; verses 8–11 would seem to have reference to the days immediately preceding Christ's coming in glory; verses 12–19, "Before all these", tells of the experience of the disciples in the time up to the fall of Jerusalem; verses 20–24 speak again of A.D. 70; verses 25–28 move on again to the days preceding His coming as the Son of man.

In the parable of "the fig-tree, and all the trees", the Lord gave a sign as to when "summer" for Israel would be nigh. The fig tree will begin to show signs of growth, but so will all the trees. Looking to the land of Israel, we see the fig tree putting forth its leaves. Looking further afield we see the emerging nations bursting out with evidences of new national life. Beloved, "the kingdom of God is nigh at hand", v. 31. Note the authoritative nature of the Lord's words in His claim in verse 33.

Dwell upon the words, "at night he went out and abode in the mount", v. 37. Was this for prayer in view of Calvary?

Mar. 31st

READING : **Luke 22. 1-38**

IN THE UPPER ROOM

As THE TIME draws near for the offering up of the Saviour, Satan is very active. In verse 2 we see the chief priests and scribes in the midst of their plotting, and in verse 3 Satan is seen taking possession of Judas, who became a willing accomplice. In the background to all this is the divine foreknowledge, and we can compare Psalm 2. 4, "He that sitteth in the heavens shall laugh: the Lord shall have them in derision". God is going to work all things after the counsel of His own will—what can men and demons do?

With perfect assurance the Lord moves on His way, vv. 7–13. He sends His disciples to prepare for the Passover feast, knowing all that will happen, and that an unnamed disciple will gladly place his premises at the disposal of his Lord. Note the words "they went, and found as he had said".

The Passover feast merges into something new, the Lord's Supper, vv. 19-20. The bread and cup of the feast suddenly gain new meaning as the Lord takes them both and points to them as symbolical of His body and His blood. Satan may be plotting but, in spite of this, the Lord can see that there will be a church established, and that believing souls down through the centuries will rejoice in the simple remembrance feast. "This do in remembrance of me", v. 19.

In verses 21–23 reference is made by the Lord to the treachery of Judas, although Judas is not named. In perplexity the disciples enquire which of them can be meant; they do not know. The Lord had known his true identity when He originally called him, John 6. 64, but by neither word nor hint had He betrayed Judas to the others.

How sad that in such circumstances His disciples should be thinking of earthly grandeur, vv. 24–27. Jesus is thinking of a cross, they are thinking of position. The words spoken by the Lord to correct this attitude come to us today, "let him . . . that is chief (be) as he that doth serve", v. 26.

Satan again comes into the picture, v. 31, as one who requests permission to have the disciples so as to sift them. He has to ask because God is supreme. Directing His remarks at Peter, the Lord utters comforting words, "I have prayed for thee, that thy faith fail not". Praise Him!

Apr. 1st

READING : **Luke 22. 39-71**

DESPISED AND REJECTED

THIS IS holy ground. Note verse 39, "as he was wont". He was no stranger to Gethsemane as a place of prayer, and Judas knew this, John 18. 2. But never before had the Lord such an experience as then. Calvary was before Him. The judgment for sin was now very close, and the horror of it all enveloped Him. It may well be that there were also Satanic pressures, but we hear Him say "not my will, but thine". Meditate for a moment on the words, "being in an agony he prayed more earnestly". Dr. Luke draws attention to physical results of the pressure, "his sweat was as it were great drops of blood falling down". How great were His love for us and devotion to the Father's will!

The betrayal, vv. 47–53. It was now revealed fully who the traitor was, but the Lord looked beyond Judas as He uttered the words, "this is your hour, and the power of darkness", v. 53. It is difficult to understand how he could have dwelt in the presence of perfect purity and love for three years and yet have been guilty of such baseness. J. S. Stewart says, "It was the crowning touch of horror, the last point of infamy beyond which human infamy could not go, when out in the garden Judas betrayed his Master, not with a shout or a blow or a stab, but with a kiss".

Judas betrayed Him, Peter denied Him, vv. 54–62. Do not be too critical of poor Peter. If we have never denied our Lord (and this is doubtful) let us remember, "there, but for the grace of God, go I". Peter was restored, the gaze of the Lord broke him down, v. 61. Later, in resurrection life, the Lord sought him out, 24. 34.

As we read verses 63–65 let us remember who this was they treated so—the Son of God. It was death for a man who in error gripped the ark of the Lord, 2 Sam. 6. 6–7. Here men did the equivalent yet God withheld His hand.

Note the calm dignity of the rejected One before the Sanhedrin. He was unwilling to discuss their question, "Art thou the Christ". He knew their insincerity. When, however, they asked Him, "Art thou then the Son of God?" He answered, in effect, "what you are saying is correct". This was enough—what they were seeking to justify the charge of blasphemy.

Apr. 2nd

READING : **Luke 23. 1-56**

BEHOLD THE AMAZING SIGHT

As WE behold the Saviour in this chapter we see an "amazing sight" in all the situations depicted. He was sent to Pilate, vv. 1–5, because the Jews had no power of putting to death. For Pilate to give a death sentence it was necessary for them to concoct a charge with which he could deal, so they charged Him on political grounds. Pilate soon realized there was no substance in the charge and sent Him to Herod, vv. 6–12, who also found "no cause of death in him". As we look at Jesus before these two rulers, we note the moral superiority of the Prisoner over His judges.

The moment came when Pilate "gave sentence that it should be as they required", v. 24, and "when they were come to the place, which is called Calvary, there they crucified him", v. 33. There had been divine movement toward that place ever since the forming of the eternal counsel and determination that man should be redeemed. In a sense it was not Judas, Pilate, Herod and the Jews who put Him there, or arranged the timing. All was divinely ordered, Rom 5. 6. This was in mind when the Son of God came into the world and declared "Lo, I come to do thy will", Heb. 10. 9.

It is possible to come very near to the Saviour and yet be lost, and to be far off and yet be saved, vv. 39–43. No one that day who saw the malefactors on their crosses would have dreamed that before the day closed one of them would be in paradise with the Lord of glory. His heart touched by the Spirit of God, the man acknowledged his sin and sought the Lord's help. In these circumstances the Lord would surely bless; He had come to seek and save that which was lost. The man's companion in crime, equally near to the Lord, died unrepentant.

Human imagination is useless when trying to understand the mystery of "darkness over all the earth", v. 44. The eye of man was not permitted to witness what took place when God dealt with His Son on account of sin. We stand afar off. We try to fathom the mystery. We hear His cry from the darkness, "why hast thou forsaken me?" and later, "It is finished". Away in the temple the veil is rent and the way into God's presence is suddenly flung open.

Apr. 3rd

READING : **Luke 24. 1-35**

HE IS RISEN

LOVE OVERCOMES difficulties. It was "very early" when those dear women made their way to the tomb to carry out the ministrations which their love had planned. It was still dark, John 20. 1. There was the problem of the "great stone" to be overcome, but still they came. They found this problem dealt with, entered the tomb and saw the linen grave-cloths still there, but no body. Two of God's messengers were there to speak to them and they gently chided them for seeking "the living among the dead". The angels then reminded them that their Lord had told them this would happen. Their thought seems to have been "because Jesus said it, it must be". The women remembered and, with hearts filled with a new hope, they returned to Jerusalem. Sadly, "their words seemed . . . as idle tales and they (the disciples) believed them not", Luke 24. 11. Peter ran to see, wondering but not wholly convinced.

The Lord wants us to know He is alive. It is interesting that He should choose two unknown disciples (were they husband and wife?) for a special revelation that first day of the week. To their sad hearts He opened up the Scriptures, vv. 27, 32. Leon Morris says, "We should perhaps understand this not as the selection of a number of proof-texts but rather as showing that throughout the Old Testament a consistent divine purpose is worked out, a purpose that in the end meant and must mean the cross".

It was a long walk, about 7½ miles, but, as they moved on together, all tiredness and despondency went and their hearts were thrilled. The Stranger went in with them for a meal and, taking the place of the host, He broke the bread and gave it to them. They recognized this action and possibly saw the print of the nails in His hands—and then He was gone. What should they do now? With such news, they must return that 7½ miles through the darkness of the night to tell the others, "He is risen". On their arrival they found rejoicing hearts, and were greeted with the news of the resurrection. Among the things they were told was this, "The Lord . . . hath appeared to Simon". Yes, Peter had received a personal revelation from the Lord he had denied. We wonder what they had talked about. What wondrous love the Lord had showed to Simon.

Apr. 4th

READING : **Luke 24. 36-53**

OH JOY !

WHAT AN exciting day! As the two from Emmaus were telling their story and the others in the room were telling theirs, suddenly the very Subject of their conversation was standing among them. He did not need to open the door—the resurrection body, while being a real body, was not subject to the natural laws that had previously governed it. Some have since denied that the body was raised and have argued that only the spirit left the tomb (was it ever there?) and that the body turned to gases. The Lord knew there would be such arguments and forestalled them by saying, "handle me, and see; for a spirit hath not flesh and bones as ye see me have", v. 39.

The disciples were terrified and affrighted, v. 37, a natural reaction to the supernatural. But this soon passed, and then the disciples were "glad, when they saw the Lord", John 20. 20. Fear was replaced by joy. The Lord was alive and with them. As He had done with the two on the way to Emmaus, so now the Lord takes the assembled company back to the Old Testament revelation, and then He opened their "understanding, that they might understand the scriptures". This was not only for their personal spiritual profit, but also because they were to use these Scriptures in preaching the gospel.

It is likely that verses 46–48 are a summary of the Lord's teaching over the next forty days. In these verses He told the disciples that what they now knew was not for them alone; it was to be preached among all nations, beginning at home. The Lord knew that this was an impossible task for men in their own strength. Graciously, therefore, He spoke of the Holy Spirit, the promise of the Father, who would endue them with power. Note the words of the Lord, "tarry . . . until ye be endued with power". Beloved, do not dare to go without it.

What a wonderful climax. They were on the hillside, talking, when suddenly He began to rise. The disciples watched Him go, hands outstretched in blessing, until He was out of sight. Was this to be the end? No! Luke tells us in his second book (The Acts) that, as they were gazing heavenward, a voice said, "this same Jesus . . . shall so come . . .", Acts 1. 11. A risen Saviour, a Holy Spirit, a coming Lord! Hallelujah!

Introducing John's Gospel

THE APOSTLE John is next only to Paul in his contribution to the New Testament Scriptures. We accept his authorship of the Gospel for a number of reasons, not least of which is his intimate acquaintance with the Lord Himself, 2. 24; 4. 1; 19. 28, as well as his detailed knowledge of the holy land, 1. 28; 2. 1; 3. 23. He is also extremely well acquainted with the disciples, denoting the testimony of an eye-witness, 1. 40; 6. 8. John is a self-effacing writer. When we consider his accuracy in the giving of names, we can only conclude that the unnamed person in 13. 23; 20. 2, etc., is the apostle himself. If another had written the Gospel it would be most unusual if he had omitted the name of so well known a person as the apostle John.

The Gospel would have been written towards the end of the first century in John's old age. He vividly recalls the momentous days of his youth when he was in company with the Son of God. His is the last of the Gospels and he assumes that his readers are already familiar with certain well-known facts. He gives the reason for his writing in 20. 30–31. Out of the abundance of material available, the apostle carefully selects certain things in order that we might believe that Jesus is the Christ (the fulfilment of the ancient prophecies) and more than this, the Son of God. To John, the Messiah has the nature of God Himself and by believing in Him men can rejoice in the possession of eternal life.

Chapter 21. 24–25 could be seen as a brief summary of the Gospel. It reminds us of the reliable witness of John and of the wonder of Christ, for if everything which He did was recorded the world would not be able to contain it. Chapter 20. 30–31 tells us why John wrote—so that we might believe to be blessed, whereas 21. 24–25 gives us what the apostle wrote—his witness and the fulness of his inexhaustible Subject. John employs a limited vocabulary, using the same words repeatedly. Nevertheless, he has profound insight regarding the uniqueness of God's revelation in Christ.

A suggested main outline of the Gospel is His Person Declared, chs. 1–4; His Power Disputed, chs. 5–12; His Passion Described, chs. 13–21.

Apr. 7th

READING : **John 2. 1-11**

THE FIRST SIGN

IT WAS a time of rejoicing that Christ selected for the occasion of His first miracle. John vividly recalls the memorable day when a marriage took place in Cana of Galilee. The Lord was "acquainted with grief" but also knew times of gladness. The next sign in chapter 4 regarding the healing of the nobleman's son is associated with grief. Whether in a situation of gladness or sadness He is still Lord. How interesting to observe that the place of His first miracle was not the capital city but rather an obscure village. It is so like Him to order events in this way, and in it we see His deep humility and total lack of ostentation.

The Lord proved to be thc ideal Guest. The best way to commence married life is with Him! When the wine failed He was more than equal to the situation. John explains very simply how He changed water into wine. It symbolises the replacing of the outward cleansing of Judaism by the surpassing inward joy which only Christ can give, Psa. 16. 11; Rom. 5. 11. We notice the wine came after the water—was from it and better than it!

John speaks of Christ's miracles as signs—miracles with a message. In this first sign the long process involved in producing wine is done away with, and by His word the Lord directly changes water into wine and that the very best of wine. The result of the manifestation was the deepening of the faith of His disciples. Others witnessed the remarkable happening, but it was the disciples who really reaped the benefit. Others may be affected by Him, but only those who love and trust Him really learn the truth about Him.

Those present on this occasion have lessons for us. The mother of Jesus (we note John's respect for her, vv. 1, 3, 5; 19. 25–27) had implicit trust in His ability and word, v. 5. The servants obeyed the word of Christ, literally, promptly and without question. Do these features characterize our service? Whilst the master of the feast was ignorant of the miracle, the servants knew very well how the water became wine. Knowledge of Christ is the starting point of true wisdom, Col. 2. 3. Finally, at this manifestation of His glory the disciples came to appreciate in a fuller way the One whom they had followed. How much do I appreciate His glory and His grace?

Apr. 8th

READING : **John 2. 12-25**

THE SEVERITY AND SINCERITY OF CHRIST

AT THE PASSOVER the Lord publicly condemns those who make a living from religion. In accordance with the prophecy of Malachi 3. 1, He comes suddenly to His temple in judgment. Some are only interested in Christianity for what can be made from it. Beware—remember Judas. We note the Lord made a scourge of cords, v. 15. It was necessary for Him to cleanse the temple but the scourge He used was not a permanent feature of His ministry. This was not the only occasion He cleansed the temple, but we see here His goodness as well as His severity. The disciples recognized His zeal for God's house; cf. v. 17 with Psa. 69. 9. We do well to ask ourselves whether we share something of the Lord's zeal for His house. This has a direct bearing on our contribution to the establishing and continuance of the local church, 1 Tim. 3. 15. We need to distinguish between an enthusiast and a fanatic. A fanatic is someone with a hot head and a cool heart. An enthusiast is someone with a cool head and a hot heart!

For other references to divine zeal, see Numbers 25. 13 marg.; 2 Kings 19. 31; Isaiah 9. 7; 37. 32.

If the Father could not be at home in the temple building, He certainly did find a home in Christ, John 2. 19. The Lord speaks of His resurrection, and only after it did His disciples comprehend the significance of His words, v. 22. When He said, "Destroy this temple, and in three days I will raise it up", v. 19, the Jews misunderstood Him. He was later misquoted by His opponents, Matt. 26. 61; 27. 40. He often spoke on a higher plane than men readily understand. He meant something vastly different with regard to birth, ch. 3; water, ch. 4; bread, ch. 6, and here concerning the temple. Are we in tune with Him, or do we think and act merely as carnal men?

Although Jesus did not respond to the challenge of the Jews to produce an authenticating miracle, He did many miracles which are not recorded by John. Although many trusted in Him, He did not trust them. Why? Because He knew them. Their interest was in what He did and not in Him, v. 23. It was the faith of the curious not the committed. He had no faith in their faith. His attitude towards us is determined by His infallible knowledge of us, vv. 24, 25.

Apr. 9th

READING : **John 3. 1-36**

ETERNAL LIFE THROUGH THE ETERNAL ONE

THE CHAPTER contains the best known verse in the Gospel, if not in the whole Bible—"For God so loved the world, that he gave his only begotten Son, that whosoever believeth in him should not perish, but have everlasting life", v. 16. Chapters 3 and 4 illustrate that the scope of the Gospel is for the whole world. In chapter 3, we find a leading Pharisee from Judaea; in chapter 4 a woman from Samaria and a nobleman from Galilee—see 4. 42. The portion reveals the necessity of new birth. The learned Nicodemus did not understand the Lord's teaching, although the Old Testament witnessed to the truth of the new birth, Ezek. 11. 19; 36. 25–27. He thought well of Christ, v. 2, but not well enough, v. 13. He moved from complimenting Christ, v. 2, to being converted to Christ. We note his desire for Christ, ch. 3; his defence of Christ, 7. 45–52; and his devotion to Christ, 19. 38–42.

The serpent on the pole, Num. 21. 9, is typical of the greater salvation available through faith in the One who was lifted up on the cross, John 3. 14. It was necessary for Christ to go to Golgotha—notice the sinner's imperative, v. 7; the Saviour's imperative, v. 14; and the saint's imperative, v. 30. He who went to the cross was the Son of God, and in this the greatest demonstration of God's love to men was expressed, v. 16. This classic verse tells of many great things. A great source of love—God. A great object—the world. A great gift—His only begotten Son. A great possibility—whosoever. A great condition—believeth in Him. A great deliverance—shall not perish. A great possession—have everlasting life. John is the apostle of sharp antitheses: death and life, v. 16; condemnation and salvation, v. 17; belief and unbelief, v. 18; light and darkness, v. 19; love and hate, vv. 19, 20; doing evil and doing truth, vv. 20, 21. The Gospel knows no neutrality. Men are either for or against Christ.

John the Baptist again bears eloquent testimony to the Lord, and has a fine understanding of his own position in relation to Christ, vv. 29, 30. He points men to Christ and then retires. It is possible to point to Christ and then hinder those who wish to follow Him. Not so with John—as Jesus moved into the foreground, he gladly receded into the background.

Apr. 10th

READING : **John 4. 1-54**

THE WELL IS DEEP

THE WOMAN of Samaria was amazed when the Lord, being a Jew, asked her for a drink. When He spoke subsequently of the living water which He could give, she totally misunderstood. She thought He referred to the water in the well and, as He had nothing to use to obtain the water, she exclaimed, "the well is deep", v. 11. Of course this is literally true for the well was over 100 feet deep, but still more is it true in a spiritual sense. In fact, that which Christ provides is much more than a deep well; it is a spring of water issuing in eternal life, v. 14. During the ensuing conversation the woman's thoughts were turned from the well and even her waterpot, v. 28, to consider the remarkable Person by whom she was confronted. He showed His knowledge of her past and present life, and revealed the true meaning of worship as well as plainly stating that He was the Messiah. Many of the Samaritans believed on Him as a result of the woman's testimony, vv. 29, 39–42. The disciples, too, learned that the Lord was sustained by that which is not connected with physical need but rather through accomplishing the will of the Father, v. 34.

The second sign in the Gospel is in this chapter. The Lord again visited Cana, and was met by an officer of king Herod. He had a son who was seriously ill in Capernaum about twenty miles away. The nobleman evidently expected Christ to make the journey from Cana to Capernaum in order to heal his son, vv. 47, 49. However, the Lord, after challenging the sincerity of the man, told him to go his way because his son was healed. The Lord cured the boy without seeing him and thus showed He was Lord over distance. The nobleman expected a gradual cure, v. 52, but he was informed by his servants that the fever left him instantaneously. He then realized that his son was healed at the precise time when Jesus spoke the word. As a result, the nobleman believed with his household. The son had been in a desperate state at a distance from Christ, and yet was wonderfully delivered by the Lord's word. The believer likewise was once in a desperate state, Eph. 2. 1–3, at a distance from Christ, 2. 11–12, and has been delivered, 2. 4–10, 13–22. If the first sign, John 2. 11, was a manifestation of Christ's glory, this second sign shows complete trust in Him.

Apr. 11th

READING : **John 5. 1-47**

CHRIST IS EQUAL WITH GOD

THE HEALING of the infirm man is the third sign in the Gospel. Chapter 2 presented Christ as the Lord of quality when He changed water into wine; chapter 4 saw Him as the Lord of distance as He healed the nobleman's son. The opening of Chapter 5 shows Him as the Lord of time, for 38 years is no difficulty to Christ when healing the man at the pool, vv. 5, 9. Whether it be the young, 4. 46, or the old, 5. 5, Christ has the ability to meet the need. It was the Sabbath day when the man was cured, and this caused the Jews to persecute Jesus. When the Lord said, "My Father worketh hitherto, and I work", v. 17, the Jews tried the more to kill Him; not only because, in their opinion, He had broken the Sabbath, but by calling God His own Father, He made Himself equal with God. The Lord answered them and showed He was equal with God:

1. *In working*—"Verily, verily, I say unto you, The Son can do nothing of himself, but what he seeth the Father do: . . . these also doeth the Son likewise", v. 19.

2. *In knowing*—"For the Father loveth the Son, and showeth him all things that himself doeth: and he will show him greater works than these, that ye may marvel", v. 20.

3. *In raising the dead*—"For as the Father raiseth up the dead, and quickeneth them; even so the Son quickeneth whom he will", v. 21; also vv. 28, 29.

4. *In judging*—"For the Father judgeth no man, but hath committed all judgment unto the Son", v. 22; also v. 27.

5. *In honour*—"that all men should honour the Son, even as they honour the Father. He that honoureth not the Son honoureth not the Father which hath sent him", v. 23.

6. *In regenerating*—"Verily, verily, I say unto you, He that heareth my word, and believeth on him that sent me, hath everlasting life, and shall not come into condemnation; but is passed from death unto life", v. 24.

7. *In self-existence*—"For as the Father hath life in himself; so hath he given to the Son to have life in himself", v. 26.

The Jews were right in their observations but wrong in their unbelief. The Son did and taught nothing of Himself, vv. 19, 30; 8. 28; 12. 49. The only act He claimed as altogether His own was that of laying down His life, 10. 18.

Apr. 12th

READING : **John 6. 1-21**

LORD OF QUANTITY AND LORD OF NATURAL LAW

THIS PORTION contains two more of the signs included in the Gospel. In chapter 2 we saw Christ as Lord of *quality* whereas here, in connection with the feeding of the five thousand, He is Lord of *quantity*, vv. 1–14. The second sign is Christ walking on the sea showing Him to be Lord of natural law, vv. 15–21. A great multitude had followed Jesus, and He now wished to give them something to eat. He asked Philip regarding the matter, full well knowing exactly what He intended to do, v. 6. He had no need of Philip's advice, but Philip needed testing. Philip dwelt on the vastness of the need as he considered the problem. Unfortunately, he left Christ out of his calculations. Do we? Andrew offered a suggestion but stressed the smallness of the provision. For Philip it was a matter of deciding between the Master or the multitude. Which is greater? Whereas for Andrew it was a question of the Lord or the lad. That the Lord was more than equal to the situation is evident in that He not only satisfied the multitude but there were also fragments remaining which were surplus to the requirements of the large company. There is satisfaction and surplus in Christ. In connection with this miracle, the reader may care to consider pages 26 and 28 again.

The effect of the miracle on the people was that they were determined to make the Lord their king, v. 15. After all, what a boon He would be to them. Therefore the Lord withdrew into a mountain. In the evening of that day the disciples went to the lake of Galilee and intended to cross over to Capernaum. It was now dark and the sea arose because of a strong wind. With much effort they rowed about three miles across the lake and then they saw Jesus walking on the sea, v. 19. His glory is revealed in His treading on the waves of the sea, Job 9. 8, and in His seeing in the dark, Psa. 139. 12. We also see His grace in His words of power and peace, "It is I; be not afraid". The disciples were assailed, v. 18, afraid, v. 19, but then assured, v. 20. The Lord had been *for them* in the mountain but He was now *with them* in their difficulty. He refused the throne from the crowd, but He proved to His own that He really was King—the ruler over wind, darkness and sea. Is He all this to you?

Apr. 13th

READING : **John 6. 22-71**

CHRIST THE SUSTAINER OF LIFE

CHRIST HAD claimed to be the *source* of life, 5. 24–26. In chapter 6 He showed and taught that He was also the *sustainer* of life.

We see that the majority had wrong motives in seeking Christ. It is not a matter of *working* for that which is only of temporal value, but of believing on Him who can *give* that which is eternal in its nature, v. 27. The Lord Himself was the true bread from heaven of which the Old Testament manna was typical. In fact, He is the bread of God, v. 33. If He satisfies God, is He not more than able to satisfy us? The Lord claimed to be the bread of life and promised that those who came to Him would never hunger, and by believing on Him they would never thirst. The complete answer to genuine spiritual hunger and thirst is Christ Himself. Are we enjoying being sustained by Him? The Lord promised that if a man ate of the bread which came down from heaven, he would not die, v. 50, and further if any man ate of this living bread from heaven, he should live for ever, v. 51. In fact, He said that except by faith we eat the flesh of the Son of man, and drink His blood, we cannot have eternal life, vv. 53, 54. The climax of His teaching is in verses 56–57, "He that eateth my flesh, and drinketh my blood, dwelleth in me, and I in him. As the living Father hath sent me, and I live by the Father: so he that eateth me, even he shall live by me". Many of the disciples found this teaching of Christ offensive and walked no more with Him. However, Peter showed that he truly grasped Christ's meaning when the Lord said, "It is the spirit that quickeneth; the flesh profiteth nothing; the words that I speak unto you, they are spirit, and they are life", v. 63. For Peter's reply is a high water mark in the apostle's experience—"thou hast the words of eternal life", v. 68. Jesus is not only able to satisfy His people. He is also the One who will ultimately glorify them, vv. 39, 40. It is indeed a necessary exercise to analyze what we believe, but it is only by personal appropriation to ourselves of His Person and His work that we receive the assurance of eternal blessing. Is Peter's magnificent confession, v. 69, ours too ? Compare this with his other great confession in Matthew 16. 16.

Apr. 14th

READING : **John 7. 1-53**

NEVER MAN SPAKE LIKE THIS MAN

THIS CHAPTER presents Christ speaking to various groups of people.

To His brethren. They advised the Lord to go up to the feast of tabernacles in order to manifest Himself to men. However, He would not go with them, saying, "My time is not yet come: but your time is always ready", v. 6. Of course, He knew the best course of action to take far better than His brethren did. We ever need His grace to act correctly towards other members of our families, especially if we find we have unbelievers within that circle.

To the Jews. The Lord subsequently went to the feast privately. When it was about the middle of the feast, Jesus went up into the temple, and taught. The Jews considered it marvellous that He should speak as He did, having never learned from the schools of the Rabbis. The Lord claimed, "My doctrine is not mine, but his that sent me. If any man will do his will, he shall know of the doctrine, whether it be of God, or whether I speak of myself", vv. 16, 17. As we marvel at the Lord, we should move from admiration to adoration!

To the multitude. They are challenged by the Lord regarding His healing on the Sabbath day. But if circumcision could take place on the Sabbath why not the complete restoration carried out by the Lord? He concluded with, "Judge not according to the appearance, but judge righteous judgment", v. 24. Religion without reality is not to be confused with the truth expressed through love.

Further notable words of Christ are contained in verses 28, 29, 33, 34. We especially mark His words on the last day, that great day of the feast, in verses 37, 38 (with the important explanation in v. 39).

There was a division among the people because of Him, and this is ever the case. It was the officers who uttered the words used in today's heading, when they returned to the chief priests and Pharisees, v. 46. At this point Nicodemus stood up in defence of Christ. He was later to express his devotion to Christ, 19. 39. May our appreciation of the Lord cause us to do the same as Nicodemus; to defend the validity of His Word and to express to Him our thanks for enduring the cross.

Apr. 15th

READING : **John 8. 1-11**

THE LORD IS FULL OF GRACE AND TRUTH

THE LAST verse of chapter 7 belongs properly with the start of chapter 8. The Lord was ever in communion with His Father—what an example to us! While He was teaching in the temple, the religious leaders brought to Him a woman taken in adultery. They asked Him whether or not the woman should be stoned in accordance with Deut. 22. 22. They sought to place the Lord in a dilemma. On the one hand, if He affirmed the binding validity of the law it would, in effect, have encouraged action contrary to Roman law, as capital punishment was withheld from the Jewish authorities. On the other hand, to set the Mosaic law aside would have been to give up any claim of His to fulfil the law. The Jewish leaders were well aware of the problem, and made the most of the opportunity in order to accuse the Lord.

The Lord stooped down, and with His finger wrote on the ground. In so doing He took their eyes from her. They were keener in exposing the sins of others than confessing their own. The Lord, therefore, revealed to these men the depths of their own sinful nature. His statement, "He that is without sin among you, let him first cast a stone at her", v. 7, raised the matter from the legal to the spiritual level. They were made to realize that freedom from outward guilt was not a claim to sinlessness. Would any of the accusers dare to be the first to cast a stone at her, like the witnesses of Deut. 17. 7? He stooped again to write on the ground and this gave the accusers the opportunity to withdraw. This left Jesus and the woman alone. Her accusers could not condemn her, and Jesus would not condemn her. The law was unable to make a distinction between the sinner and her sin; it had to condemn both. But He could make just that distinction. His words to her were, "go, and sin no more", v. 11. The woman was led to see that the Lord did not condone her sin, that He did not condemn her.

The finger of God had written the law, Exod. 31. 18; Deut. 9. 10. He wrote again that day in the temple. The Lord not only knew the law, He had originated it. He also knew the hearts of those about Him on that day. There He stooped down and raised Himself. To deal with sin He died and rose from the dead.

Apr. 16th

READING : **John 8. 12-59**

THE UNIQUE SON OF GOD

THE LORD refered to the Father as "My Father", thereby denoting a unique relationship which existed between the Father and the Son. We note references in the section to— "the Father", "one Father" and "thy Father", but Christ claimed that God is His own Father in a peculiar sense. Christ shares the nature of God. He used the expression, "I am", a number of times in the chapter. He has a personality which defies complete explanation. Certainly His opponents could not understand Him because of their unbelief. How awful are the eternal consequences of refusing to believe in Christ.

In view of His unique relationship with His Father, He could claim to do always those things that pleased Him, v. 29. He could challenge His opponents regarding His sinlessness, v. 46. Such was His confidence in completing the programme set before Him that men held no fear for Him, vv. 20, 59. He could even prophesy concerning the type of death to which He would submit Himself, v. 28, another evidence of His deity.

He referred to His followers as "my disciples". They will enter into the fulness of what it means to follow Him if they abide in His word, v. 31. We observe the importance of heeding and keeping His word, vv. 31, 51, and the effects of resisting His word, vv. 37, 43. Is His word highly esteemed by us? Do we abide in His word? Those described as "my disciples" by the Lord, not only abide in His word, v. 31; they also love one another, 13. 35, and bring forth fruit, 15. 8.

Although the Pharisees would not accept His witness, the Lord said, "my record is true", v. 14. He could make such a claim because He came from heaven and was to return to heaven. He could also call on the Father as bearing witness of Him, v. 18.

The Lord spoke of "my day", v. 56. It was this day that Abraham had anticipated long before the Lord was born into this world. Bethlehem was not the beginning of Jesus' existence. The Lord could say, "Before Abraham was, I am", v. 58. He speaks not only of His pre-existence but also of His eternal pre-existence. The wonder of His majestic Person causes us to bow before Him and say, "for he is thy Lord; and worship thou him", Psa. 45. 11.

Apr. 17th

READING : **John 9. 1-41**

LORD OVER MISFORTUNE

As the Lord passed by He encountered a man who had been blind from birth. This man was a beggar, v. 8, and provides a picture of the sinner, both in nature, Eph. 2. 3, and in practice, Rom. 3. 23. However, the Lord made it clear that the man's physical condition was not connected in any way with either personal sin or the sin of his parents. The Lord who is the Light of the world, John 8. 12; 9. 5, gave the blind man his sight. How beautiful to note that it was by His word that the Lord changed water into wine, 2. 7–9, but He anointed the blind man's eyes with clay and told him to wash in the pool Siloam. The man could not see the Lord's face, but he could feel His touch of compassion! The man was an unfortunate individual, but found that Jesus was Lord even over misfortune.

The sequel to the miracle reveals the exceptional stir it made. John shows how people's minds reacted differently to the healing. The neighbours displayed the usual curiosity and scepticism. The Pharisees showed their prejudice against Christ, on the grounds that the healing took place on the Sabbath day, vv. 14, 16. They opposed the man and tried to intimidate and make him submit to their authority, v. 24. When all their abuse and threats failed, they cast him out of the synagogue, vv. 22, 34. They said that they wanted to honour God, v. 24, and Moses, vv. 28, 29, but at the expense of the Lord Jesus. How foolish!

The parents of the man appear in a poor light. Frightened from any public sympathy for their son when up against the leaders, they adopted a mean-spirited neutrality and put the responsibility on someone else. Yet, in spite of all the opposition, the man's testimony was outstanding, v. 25. To him, Christ was greater than his problem and all opposition. The man advanced from wonder, v. 25, to worship, v. 38. The man's growth in appreciation is noteworthy. To him Jesus was a man, v. 11; a prophet, v. 17; the Son of God, v. 38. The man had lost the synagogue of the Jews, vv. 22, 34; he had found the Son of God, vv. 35–38. He had lost a place where he could worship, but he had found a Person whom he could worship!

Apr. 18th

READING : **John 10. 1-42**

THE GOOD SHEPHERD

THIS CHAPTER refers to five different types of men who have a relationship to the sheep.

The stranger, v. 5. He could perhaps attempt the shepherd's work but in fact he would be trying to do what was not his calling. In vain he would approach the flock. They would not know or trust him and so they would flee from him.

The hireling, v. 12. Whereas the stranger might assume duties to which he has not been called, the hireling does have a duty to the flock, but his character is revealed by the way he fails to discharge that duty. The flock flee from the stranger, but the hireling flees from the flock when they need him most. He flees because his main concern is the salary, not the sheep.

The thief, v. 1. He is worse than either the stranger or the hireling. The thief comes with deliberate evil intentions, v. 10. The hireling was after gain and rendered his services as long as there was no personal danger involved. However, the thief sees the flock as a prey. The next two men are very different.

The porter, v. 3. He is not necessarily a shepherd himself but can identify a true shepherd. John the Baptist was a porter indeed, but unfortunately many who considered themselves porters in Israel's flock failed to recognize the Good Shepherd when He came, 1. 11.

The Shepherd, v. 2. Unlike the thief, He comes not to take but to give, v. 28. Unlike the hireling, He does not sacrifice the sheep to save Himself, but sacrifices Himself to save the sheep, v. 11. Unlike the stranger, His voice is known by the sheep, v. 27. They are His own sheep and He knows them by name, vv. 3, 14. Only of Him can it be said, "he goeth before them, and the sheep follow him: for they know his voice", v. 4.

The Lord Jesus truly is the Good Shepherd. He knows His own sheep by name and they know Him. Such is His love for the sheep that He laid down His life for them, vv. 11, 15. In His care they are eternally secure, v. 28. The shepherds in the local church have as their supreme example the chief Shepherd Himself, 1 Pet. 5. 2–4. He reminds the under-shepherds of the great estimate He places on those in their care, for He describes them as "my sheep", v. 27. The under-shepherds love the Shepherd and they serve the flock because it is His, 21. 15–17.

Apr. 19th

READING : **John 11. 1-57**

LORD OVER DEATH

THE MIRACLE of the raising of Lazarus shows Christ to be Lord even over death. John writes that these signs are recorded that we might believe that Jesus is the Christ, the Son of God, 20. 31. In our meditations we have seen in the miracles of Christ proof that He is

Lord of Quality	by changing water into wine, ch. 2.
Lord of Distance	by healing the nobleman's son, ch. 4.
Lord of Time	by healing the man at the pool, ch. 5.
Lord of Quantity	by feeding the five thousand, ch. 6.
Lord of Natural Law	by walking on the sea, ch. 6.
Lord over Misfortune	by healing the man born blind, ch. 9.
Lord over Death	by raising Lazarus, ch. 11.

As in chapter 9, John is not only concerned with the actual sign in chapter 11 but also with the events leading up to it and its sequel. Prior to the miracle, on receiving the message from Mary and Martha regarding the illness of their brother, the Lord abode in the place where He was for two days. That He could have healed Lazarus, even from a distance, there is no doubt, 4. 47–54, but He did not and Lazarus died. The Lord knew of the death of Lazarus without any notification—yet another evidence of His deity, v. 11. When the Lord came to Bethany, both Martha and Mary felt that, had He been present earlier, Lazarus would not have died, vv. 21, 32. We may not always understand His will, v. 6, but we can always rest completely in His love, v. 5. He is too loving to be unkind, and too wise to make a mistake.

After the Lord's tremendous claim to be "the resurrection, and the life", v. 25, Martha responds with an excellent confession, v. 27. When He came to the tomb Jesus wept, v. 35. He was the Son of God, vv. 4, 27, but perfectly human also in the midst of grief. After prayer, the Lord cried with a loud voice, "Lazarus, come forth", v. 43. He did so, with the graveclothes on him, and the Lord gave the instruction, "Loose him, and let him go", v. 44. There is life and liberty in Christ.

Chapters 5–12 tell of the growing opposition to Christ, and it is at this point that counsel is taken to put Him to death.

Apr. 20th

READING : **John 12. 1-19**

WORSHIP AND WITNESS

THE CROSS was very much before the Lord when He retired to Bethany. At supper, Mary took very costly ointment and anointed His feet. She wiped His feet with her hair and the house was filled with the fragrance of the ointment. Mary's appreciation of Christ was so great she did not hesitate to anoint Him with that which was of considerable value. Others then entered into the preciousness of her worship of Christ. Do others come into the good of the fragrance as I worship Him? Martha worked for Christ, Lazarus waited with Christ and Mary worshipped Christ. Am I characterized by these features? Mary's act was costly, v. 3, it was criticized, v. 5, and it was commended, v. 7. She was often found at the feet of Christ. In a prosperous situation, Luke 10. 38–41, she sat at His feet, and heard His word. In John 11. 28–32 she fell down at His feet in circumstances of adversity. In John 12. 3 she anointed His feet in a scene of mystery which pointed to His suffering. Mary's example teaches us that whether we enjoy prosperity, endure adversity or find ourselves confronted with great mystery, we should be "at his feet", 11. 32.

Lazarus was a true believer in Christ. He had fellowship at the supper, v. 2, and was a means of pointing men to Christ, vv. 9, 17, 18. He also encountered danger because of his connection with the Lord, v. 10; compare 2 Tim. 3. 12.

The portion tells us of Christ's triumphal entry into Jerusalem, vv. 12, 13, in remarkable humility, v. 14, and fulfilling the prophecy of Zechariah 9. 9. The disciples failed to understand the full significance of this at the time, but learned the meaning when Jesus was glorified, v. 16. The ascension brought home to them the Lord's sovereignty—may it do the same for us! Note the repeated reference to "these things" in verse 16.

The passage closes with the despair of the leaders, v. 19. They felt that Christ was gaining popularity. How little did they understand God's plan, v. 23!

The disciples did not comprehend at the time the momentous happenings of those days. It was only on reflection that the apostle John came to appreciate the significance of "these things", v. 16. May we, too, grow in our appreciation of Christ and His achievements.

Apr. 21st

READING : **John 12. 20-50**

WE WOULD SEE JESUS

AMONG THOSE at the feast were certain Greeks who approached Philip with a view to obtaining an interview with Christ. What an excellent desire—"Sir, we would see Jesus", v. 21. As servants of Christ, we should remember that He is what men really need—not good ideas or good advice but the good news concerning Jesus! Philip needed the support of Andrew in approaching Christ. Andrew was ever at hand in leading someone to Christ. He was a true Christian missionary—the first home missionary, 1. 41; the first children's missionary, 6. 8, 9; the first foreign missionary, vv. 21, 22. Andrew always had time and patience to listen to enquiries even from children and foreigners.

How appropriate that the Lord should speak then of the corn of wheat falling into the ground and dying in order that it might bring forth much fruit, v. 24. He also spoke of His soon approaching death which would draw all men unto Him, v. 32. Again, He indicated the manner of His death, v. 33; see Phil. 2. 8. Christ's sovereignty is by His sacrifice. Even in this dark hour, with the Lord's death soon to take place, John once more stresses the essential deity of Christ by pointing out that Isaiah saw His glory and spoke of Him, v. 41; Isa. 6. 1–10.

The Lord said that to believe on Him was to believe on God, v. 44, and to see Him was to see the One who sent Him, v. 45; 14. 9. He came with the purpose of saving, v. 47, but in rejecting Him men reject God and face judgment, vv. 46–48.

One of the great tragedies of human history is recorded in verse 37, "though he had done so many miracles before them, yet they believed not on him". With all the advantages of proximity, of sight, sound, of observation and conversation, these people "believed not on him". The Lord later said, in effect, that seeing was not believing but that believing was seeing, 20. 29. We thank God that the believer understands this reversing of human judgment by the Lord.

Throughout chapters 5–12, the Lord's power was disputed. Against this we see Him as the Source of Life, ch. 5; the Support of Life, ch. 6; the Source of Truth, ch. 7; the Source of Light, chs. 8, 9; and the Source of Love, chs. 10, 11, 12.

Survey of The Upper Room Ministry

The reference to the Lord's love, 13. 1, introduces, not only the feet-washing directly following, but the whole section, incorporating also the discourses, 13. 31 to 16. 33, and the prayer of intercession, 17. 1–26. Christ's loving concern, demonstrated in the outward act of service, is no less evident in the discourses which follow. We see Him caring for the disciples' welfare in view of His departure; preparing them tenderly for the bitter blow about to fall; hiding from them the most painful facts about the mode of His departure; providing them with thoughts of glory and a place in the Father's house, to support them in the crisis they were soon to face. All these things, and many more, combine to highlight the love of the Lord for His own.

"He loved them unto the end", 13. 1, means more than that He loved them up to the time of His departure. He continued to love them at the Father's right hand. His love is changeless and eternal. The statement concentrates on the character of the love rather than on the time factor. He loved them "to the utmost" is the idea. His was a divine love which knew no restraint, even to the point of washing the feet of the disciples. In a few hours, He was to stoop still lower to the shameful death of crucifixion.

If the words, "Arise, let us go hence", 14. 31, mean that Jesus and the disciples immediately left the upper room, it follows that the ensuing discourses and the prayer were spoken on the way to Gethsemane, which they entered when they had crossed the brook Cedron, 18. 1. Certainly, there is a change in the subject matter after chapter 14. The dominant theme thereafter is the world, with its evil and hatred, and the witness of the Spirit and of the apostles in it. As far as the Lord was concerned, of course, the words, 14. 31, indicated His readiness to go forth and meet the foe and to accomplish the will of His Father whom He loved.

These chapters, commencing with the ministry of cleansing and ending with the intercessory prayer, along with all the things that were spoken in between, throw valuable light upon the ministry in heaven of our Great High Priest.

Apr. 22nd

READING : **John 13. 1-17**

THE STOOPING LORD

THE WASHING of the disciples' feet was both an act of love and of service; two things closely associated which, in fact, cannot be separated when put in this order. It is possible to serve without love, I Cor. 13. 1–3, but not to love without serving. Love must express itself in action and always in the interest of others. Love is selfless but self loves to be served. This was perfectly displayed by Him, into whose hands the Father had committed all things, when He stripped, stooped and served. All the details of the loving act were performed by Himself—the laying aside of His garments; the taking of the towel and the girding Himself therewith; the pouring of the water; the washing and wiping of their feet.

The act appears more impressive when considered against the background of events which were developing and shortly to take place: the treachery of Judas; the denial of Peter; the arrest and trial. Foreknowledge of what was coming upon Him must have intensified His sorrow, yet, He was more concerned for them than for Himself, loving them unto the end.

There was, however, a deeper significance to His act. It was not understood then, but it was later, when the Spirit came. It was an action parable that taught practical sanctification. Christians are cleansed once and for all by the work of Christ on the cross, but they need a daily cleansing from defilement as they walk through this earthly scene. Peter objected to this at first, but had to submit to Christ or forfeit fellowship with Him, since there cannot be communion without cleansing. The water is symbolic of the Word, the means whereby cleansing is effected in believers, Eph. 5. 26; Psa. 119. 9, and the whole scene is illustrative of the unceasing ministry the Lord fulfils on our behalf as our High Priest in heaven above.

The moral lesson is summed up in verse 14, "*ye also ought*" and in verse 15, "*ye should*". The first involves obligation; the second, example. We owe it, not only as a matter of duty, but also because of His example, to do for each other what the Lord did. To fail in this is to put ourselves above the Lord who set the example. This service will not be carried out by censure but by love using the water of the Word.

Apr. 23rd

READING : **John 13. 18-38**

THE TROUBLED HOST

JESUS, TROUBLED in *soul* in the previous chapter, 12. 27, is now troubled in *spirit*, v. 21, the highest region of His being. Consequently, the sorrow He felt was more intense. The cause was the presence of the traitor. It was not anger at what Judas was contemplating, but anguish at the sorrow the son of perdition would bring upon himself. The Lord neither rebuked nor expelled him. When, finally, Judas left the company, it was of his own accord. The treachery of Judas, however, was no surprise to Christ. It was foretold in the Psalms and Jesus knew the character of Judas when He chose him, v. 18. His announcement that a traitor was among them should have made Judas blush, but it would appear that he showed no guilt. The others did not suspect him, even when he went out. They thought he had gone out either to buy or to give away, when, in fact, he had gone out to sell and to receive. In selling the Lord, he sold himself, and the small sum he received was worthless by comparison with the price he paid spiritually. He went out into the "night", v. 30, and, later, into eternal night. If the revelation, v. 21, failed to deter him from the path of ruin, it had a different effect on the rest and produced searching of heart. The tense atmosphere was governed by actions not words; even Peter is silent and beckons to John, vv. 22-23. If the Lord's Supper was not introduced until after Judas had left, then the heart-searching anticipates the exhortation to self-examination contained in 1 Cor. 11. 28.

After the exit of Judas, the anguish of Christ gives way to thoughts of glory. He was glorified in the death of Lazarus, 11. 4, but is now glorified by His own death. By accepting death through betrayal ("That thou doest, do quickly", v. 27) the Son of man attained glory there and then, v. 31. The glory in verse 32 was however future, referring to the resurrection which took place with no delay. Thoughts of His glory did not make him forget those He was about to leave behind. They had leaned on Him for support; now they must support each other by love. This, and nothing else, would mark them as His disciples. Peter wanted to mark his discipleship by dying for Christ, but was soon to learn how weak he was and that Christ, first, must lay down His life for him.

Apr. 24th

READING : **John 14. 1-11**

THE FATHER'S HOUSE

THE SUBJECTS introduced in this discourse are designed to comfort the sorrowing disciples. Jesus, troubled in body, 11. 33; in soul, 12. 27; and in spirit, 13. 21, now says to His own, "Let not your heart be troubled". The heart is not only the seat of feelings, but also of faith, Rom. 10. 10. They were now to walk by faith, and a troubled heart would make faith ineffective. Alas! their faith was shattered by the arrest, trial and crucifixion, but had they believed in God who willed all things, and in Christ who came to perform His will, they would have been kept from despair. The first item of comfort consists of opening up heaven to their faith. They cherished ideas of a place in an earthly kingdom, but there was something much better planned for them, namely, a place in the Father's house above. It was prepared for them, first, by the shedding of His blood, and then, by His presenting the value of it in the Father's presence. The certainty of Christ's coming again to take them there depended upon His going. If He were not to return it would mean that His work on the cross and appearance before God have completely failed. At present, the believer is *in Christ*, but the purpose of His coming is that he may be *with Christ*. Being with Him will involve two things: a glorious vision, 17. 24, and a glorious change, 1 John 3. 2. What a prospect this is in contrast to the portion of the unbeliever!, John 7. 34; 8. 21.

Going to the Father's house is yet future. Meanwhile, however, access to the Father can be had as the Lord shows by His reply to Thomas. Jesus said, "I am the way", not "I will be the way", which means that the way to the Father is present and permanent, Eph. 2. 18; Heb. 10. 19. To Thomas, knowing the end was essential to knowing the way. In matters of faith, however, the first essential is to know *the way*. Knowing Him, a person, not a method, is to know *the truth* about the end, v. 7, and also, *the life*, whereby the end, coming to the Father, can be realized. Philip thought that a vision could do more than three years ministry in word and deed by Him who was the revelation of the Father. By comparison, a vision could do little, no more, in fact, than it did in the case of Moses, Exod. 33. 18–23.

Apr. 25th

READING : **John 14. 12-31**

POWER THROUGH PRAYER

The Lord appealed to His works as proof of His oneness with the Father, v. 11; likewise the works which the apostles were to perform were evidence of their oneness with Christ. They would do even greater works; not in power, but in spiritual scope. The Lord's work was largely confined to Palestine, but the apostles had a wider ministry as recorded in The Acts. The works would still, in a sense, be the Lord's own, Mark 16. 20. The apostles' success rested on faith, prayer and the Holy Spirit. The importance of the first, "He that believeth on me", John 14. 12, is marked by the occurrence of the word "believe" or "believeth" seven times in the chapter.

Regarding prayer, v. 13, we have the scope, "whatsoever ye shall ask"; the condition, "in my name", and the motive, "that the Father may be glorified in the Son". "In my name" corresponds to the phrase "in Christ", often found in the Epistles and implies oneness with Him. Where prayer is consistent with this oneness, there is a guarantee of His active cooperation, "that will I do". Asking "in his name" also means to ask in the person of One who is on equal terms with the Father, making the outcome doubly sure.

The Holy Spirit, who would provide the power, is referred to as "another Comforter", v. 16, marking His divine Personality. He takes the place of Christ who had been with the disciples for about three years; the Spirit, however, would stay with and dwell in them for ever. Instead of losing by the Lord's going, they would be gaining an extra source of comfort. The word here translated "Comforter" is rendered "advocate" in 1 John 2. 1. It follows that there is One in heaven and Another on earth who plead our cause. The manifestation made to those who love Christ, John 14. 21, is not physical but spiritual. By the Spirit, communion is enjoyed, vv. 18–24. He teaches as well as comforts. Jesus taught *many things*; the Spirit of truth teaches *all things* and gives understanding about things said before by Christ, v. 26. In His farewell, Christ both left peace and gave it as a possession to be secured for them by His death. Being sinless, neither death nor Satan, who had the power of it, had any claim upon Him, v. 30; He died in love and obedience to His Father, v. 31.

Apr. 26th

READING : **John 15. 1-27**

THE TRUE VINE

CHRIST IS the *true* vine by way of contrast to Israel who failed to bring forth fruit for God, Isa. 5. 2; Psa. 80. 8. The disciples, being the branches, John 15. 4, were now therefore what the nation had ceased to be. The natural vine exists for one purpose, namely, to bear fruit. It is useless for anything else; even a pin to hang things on could not be made from the wood, Ezek. 15. 3. The disciples were chosen, John 15. 16, to fulfil this purpose. The unfruitful branch in verse 2 is said to be "in me"; the possibility of a fruitless Christian is, thereby, contemplated. The husbandman, clearly identified as the Father, v. 1, removes this branch; which act teaches us the searching lesson that it were better that fruitless Christians, with no desire to fulfil the function for which they were chosen, were not left here.

Increased fruitfulness results from two things: *purging* or cleansing, v. 2; and *abiding*, v. 4. The husbandman is responsible for the first of these; the believer himself for the second. The "more fruit" of verse 2, is brought about by skilful pruning, that all-wise discipline administered by a loving Father, Heb. 12. 9–11. The fruit for which the Father looks, and by which He is glorified, John 15. 8, is the reproduction of Christ, the Vine, in the branches, Gal. 2. 20; 5. 22, 23. To abide in Him is to allow Him to abide in us. In this connection the repeated pronoun "my" should be noted; "my words", John 15. 7; "my disciples", v. 8; "my love", v. 9; "my commandments", v. 10; "my joy", v. 11; "my friends", v. 14; "my name", v. 16. The degree of fruitfulness will be determined as Christ is allowed to dwell in the believer.

Belonging no longer to the world, John 15. 19, would make them the object of the world's hatred. This made love among themselves all the more necessary, vv. 12, 17. The world loves only its own, with a selfish love; they were to display a sacrificial love following the Lord's example, vv. 12, 13. Persecution would be directed against the name they bore, seeking to destroy it, v. 21; James 2. 7; 1 Pet. 4. 14. The attitude of the world would spring from ignorance, for which there was no excuse, John 15. 22–25. Despite all opposition, they were to bear witness to Christ as helped by the Holy Spirit, vv. 26, 27.

Apr. 27th

READING : **John 16. 1-11**

THE HOLY SPIRIT AND THE WORLD

THE HATRED of the world and the Holy Spirit's help in witness, which were referred to generally in the last chapter, are expounded in more detail in this passage. The persecution of the disciples would take the form of expulsion from synagogues and of violence, even to the extent of their being killed. Worse still, this fanaticism would be regarded as service to God and open to anybody to carry out, v. 2. Far from being an act of devotion to God, as these zealots presumed, their zeal only displayed ignorance of the Father as revealed by Him who was the Son, v. 3. The repeated expression, "These things I have spoken unto you", marks the means by which the Lord prepared His own in advance for the trials they would have to face. The most likely cause of stumbling to the disciples, v. 1, would be the rejection by their fellow-countrymen of their witness to that which was the fulfilment of the national hope.

Obsessed with sorrow, the disciples failed to appreciate the benefits that would result from the Lord's departure, or to consider what that departing would mean for Him. Consequently they did not ask Him, "where goest *thou*?". He had to endure a deeper sorrow than theirs before He entered into His glory, vv. 5–6. The ascension was expedient to the coming of the Spirit, v. 7, who would convict an unbelieving world. To convict is to expose, to confront with evidence, to condemn. The Spirit's conviction is concerned with three things; sin, righteousness and judgment. The Spirit continues what Jesus began on a wider scale, "the world", v. 8; as to sin, see 3. 21; 8. 9; 15. 22–24; as to righteousness, 7. 18; 8. 46; as to judgment, 12. 31. Sin concerns fallen nature, and the proof of it is unbelief, v. 9; righteousness is found, not in the natural man, Rom. 3. 10, but only in Christ, proof of which is the ascension, John 16. 10; judgment is the inevitable end of sin and alternative to righteousness, proof of which is the defeat of Satan at the cross, v. 11. It is the Spirit's work to bring a person to the knowledge that, to escape judgment, he must have the righteousness of God by faith, not that which is the result of legal obedience. An example of the effectiveness of the Spirit's work is seen in Acts 2. 37–47.

Apr. 28th

READING : **John 16. 12-33**

THE HOLY SPIRIT AND THE BELIEVER

THE "yet many things", v. 12, which could not be spoken to the disciples then, were spoken to them later through the Holy Spirit. That it was the Lord who spoke to them is confirmed by the following statements about the Spirit: "for he shall not speak of himself", v. 13; "for he shall receive of mine", vv. 14, 15. In relation to the believer, the work of the Spirit is threefold: He guides into the truth, v. 13; He reveals the glory of Christ, v. 14; He shows things to come, v. 13. The Spirit "guides", involving a willingness to be led on the part of the believer. This guidance is into truth, all and not part of it, as the sphere in which the disciple must walk. Knowing truth is not enough, 3 John 4. The way in which the Spirit glorifies Christ is by making Him better known. The word "show" appearing at the end of verses 13, 14, 15 means to declare. Where a desire to know the Lord exists, the Spirit actively responds to fulfil it. The Revelation of John cannot be excluded from the coming things that were to be shown, since, from the fourth chapter of the book, future events are recorded.

Two "little while's", are mentioned by the Lord, v. 17, which perplexed the disciples, v. 18. The first, during which they continued to see Him physically, ended with His death; the second lasted until the resurrection and ascension when they would see Him spiritually, transforming the cause of their sorrow into a means of joy, v. 20. The birth pangs of sorrow would issue in the joy of a new experience of which no one could rob them, vv. 21–22. That joy would be made full by yet another blessing, that of answered prayer, v. 24. At Pentecost, speaking "in proverbs" would no longer be necessary; the disciples would have a spiritual understanding of the Father, giving them greater boldness in prayer, vv. 25–27. The statement of verse 29 was said in ignorance, and the confession of verse 30 showed limited understanding. Jesus said, "I came forth from the Father", v. 28, conveying His divine nature; they say, "thou camest forth from God", v. 30, implying, a divine mission only. The scattering, v. 32, proved the weakness of their knowledge; despite their failure, however, the Lord assures them of His victory, v. 33.

Apr. 29th

READING : **John 17. 1-26**

THE LORD'S PRAYER

THERE ARE many occasions when the Lord prayed without our being told what He said. There are also a few cases where brief prayers are recorded, 11. 41, 42; 12. 27, 28; Matt. 11. 25, 26. The entire content of this prayer, however, is preserved.

Its *significance* is seen in that the teaching just concluded is crowned by intercessory prayer. "These words", v. 1, refer to what has preceded, not to what follows. The prayer was also evidence to the disciples of the High Priestly work that He was to take up in heaven on their behalf. The words spoken aloud were intended to give joy, v. 13.

The *scope* of the prayer is seen in that it spans divine revelation made through the Son, vv. 1–5; the apostles, vv. 6–19; the church, vv. 20–26. It begins with reference to Christ's essential and eternal glory, retained in glorified humanity, v. 5, and ends with the mention of His acquired glory, shared with and contemplated by His own, vv. 22, 24.

"That they may be one, as we are", v. 11, is the *substance* of the intercession. The unity of believers and the visible effect it has on the world is stated in verse 21. Christ prays for oneness in holiness by asking that they be kept from evil, vv. 15, 17. Whilst He was here, He kept them securely, v. 12. He also asks for a oneness in glory, v. 22, a oneness in love, v. 23, and a oneness in place, v. 24.

The *subjects* of the Lord's exercise are clearly stated in v. 9. Seven times in the passage they are referred to as given to Christ. They belonged to God by creation but were given to Christ by foreknowledge and election, v. 6.

The *style* is marked by a holy reverence; "O Father", v. 5; "Holy Father", v. 11; "O righteous Father", v. 25; He never addressed God as "Our Father", because His Sonship was unique. He enjoyed an intimacy with the Father as being on equality with Him, and the lifting "up his eyes to heaven", v. 1, indicates that the spiritual world was never far away from the Lord. "Holy Father" contrasts with the evil world in which loved ones would be left, with the defilements from which they needed to be kept. "Righteous Father" contrasts with the unrighteousness of the world that knew not God and rejected Christ.

Apr. 30th

READING : **John 18. 1-40**

THE BETRAYAL, ARREST AND TRIALS

JOHN'S GOSPEL has been called the spiritual Gospel. The facts which John records are revelations of spiritual truths, and this is to be seen even in his treatment of the passion. One of the main features of the Burnt Offering, Lev. 1, was the voluntariness of its offering, portraying Christ who "offered himself without spot to God", Heb. 9. 14. It is this aspect which John presents in his account. That Judas "knew the place", v. 2, is the reason for the Lord's going to the garden, not to hide but to make Himself accessible for arrest. He knew that the events to take place were according to the divine plan; hence He "went forth" to His enemies, v. 4. Twice He says, "I am he", vv. 5, 8; the first time, in order to identify Himself, the second, to urge them to proceed with their mission, which could not be carried out without His consent, and to secure the safe exit of His disciples. The rebuke of Peter, the mention of the cup, v. 11, and the statement made to Pilate, v. 36, display the voluntary character of Christ's sufferings. In view of these things, the bindings of verses 12, 24, were not necessary.

It appears that Peter's denials took place while the religious trials before Annas and Caiaphas were in progress, vv. 12–27. Had Peter gone in with John into the courtroom instead of lingering outside with the unsympathetic crowd, he would have been unmolested. Meanwhile, inside, the Lord is questioned about His disciples and His teaching, v. 19. His reply concentrated on His teaching and not on the disciples, most of whom had fled, and one of whom was outside denying Him. John is present at the trial and remains faithful to the end.

The civil trial before Pilate begins at verse 28 and ends at 19. 16. The majesty of Christ's Person dominates the scene, vv. 34–37. The real person under examination is not Christ but Pilate, whose spiritual indifference, vv. 35, 38, and moral weakness, v. 39, are exposed. The religious hypocrites who refused to enter Pilate's hall because of the feast about to begin, v. 28, were oblivious to their inner defilement of heart which clamoured for the death of the Sinless Lord, vv. 29–32. They had no scruples in choosing a robber, v. 40, instead of One who did no violence, Isa. 53. 9.

May 1st

READING : **John 19. 1-16**

PILATE'S DILEMMA

THE CIVIL trial, alternating from outside to inside the judgment hall, reflects Pilate's dilemma. Outside, he tries to conciliate the Jewish leaders without yielding to their desire. Inside, he is confronted with Christ who probes his conscience but to whose claims, likewise, he is not prepared to yield. Devoid of moral courage, he looks for a middle way out. Such a way was to offer Jesus to the people as an alternative to a notorious criminal, thus appealing to their sense of justice. This scheme failed when they opted for Barabbas, 18. 40. Scourging by the soldiers, vv. 1–3, is another attempt to achieve his end, calculated to move them to pity, v. 5. After His being made the sport of Pilate's soldiers, it must be a very moving sight to which Pilate directs the crowd with the words, "Behold the man!". The fact that Pilate subjects the faultless Lord to scourging shows that he, no less than the Jews, has small regard for justice. His hope is doomed to failure; instead of feeling pity, they shout, "Crucify, Crucify". Scourging was only a half measure; they insist on the whole punishment being carried out, v. 6.

Pilate tauntingly hands the responsibility for crucifying Jesus over to them. They reply that, contrary to his declaration of the innocence of Christ, their law condemned Him as guilty of death because "he made himself the Son of God", and, therefore, if permission is granted, they will carry out the sentence, vv. 6–7. Being responsible for the indignities meted out by the soldiers, Pilate, for all his impiety, had every reason to be more afraid on hearing this new charge, v. 8. He asks Jesus about His origin but receives no answer, v. 9, because the reply given to his earlier question had been met with contempt, 18. 33–38. Pilate's power over Christ was not absolute as he supposed, v. 10; he was responsible to a higher power, v. 11; Rom. 13. 1. As representative of the civil power, he fails to act responsibly, ultimately puts Caesar before God and delivers Jesus to be crucified, John 19. 13–16. Caiaphas, however, as representative of the theocracy, had committed the greater sin. He of all should have recognized the Christ.

"The rulers take counsel together, against the Lord, and against his anointed", Psa. 2. 2.

May 2nd

READING : **John 19. 17-42**

THE CRUCIFIXION

THE DETAILS peculiar to John's account of the crucifixion are instructive. "He *bearing* his cross *went forth*", v. 17, stresses the voluntary character of the death. Just as in the garden Jesus "went forth" to meet his foes, 18. 1, so now He left the city and went out to Golgotha. The exhortation, "Let us go forth . . . bearing his reproach", Heb. 13. 13, reminds us what our willing response should be. It is John who tells us that Jesus was crucified "in the midst" of the other two, John 19. 18. Even in the scene of His rejection He held the pre-eminent place.

Only in this Gospel are we told that Pilate wrote the title and refused to have it changed when requested by the Jews, vv. 19-22. The Jews had given their allegiance to Caesar and they had therefore to submit to Rome's representative. John informs us that the inner garment of Jesus was "without seam" and that it became the possession of one of the soldiers, vv. 23–24, illustrative of the imputed righteousness in which the Christian is arrayed. John draws attention to the devout women who, in sharp contrast to the crude soldiers who sat and watched, were standing there, including the mother of Jesus. Being her first-born, He discharged His responsibility for her welfare by committing her to John, vv. 25–27. In response to the fifth cry from the cross, "*I thirst*", we have the only act of mercy shown to the Lord, its record marking the tenderness of John, vv. 28–29. The loud cry reported by the other writers is said by John to have been a cry of victory, "*finished*". John observes that "he *bowed his head*". He who found no rest for His head in this world, found rest at last in the Father to whom He commended His spirit, v. 30. It is only John who records that His legs were not broken and that His side was pierced. He shows that these things fulfilled the Scriptures, vv. 31–37; the one fulfilled the law, Exod. 12. 46; Num. 9. 12, and the other the prophets, Zech. 12. 10. All four evangelists write concerning Joseph, but it is only John who adds that he was a secret disciple and that he was assisted by Nicodemus, whose first acquaintance with Jesus was at night. Both men found a new courage and openly identified themselves with Christ, John 19. 38–42.

May 3rd

READING : **John 20. 1-31**

THE RESURRECTION

JOHN CHOOSES four cases to show the different ways in which belief in the resurrection was brought about. The first example is John himself, who was the first to arrive at the sepulchre, v. 4, but the second to enter it. Peter entered first and contemplated the careful arrangement of the grave-clothes. This was evidence that the body had not been stolen. John, on entering, grasped the import of what he saw and believed, v. 8; something not said of Peter. To John, the linen-clothes were a sign of the resurrection. Had the disciples known the scripture (perhaps Psa. 16. 10), v. 9, the resurrection would not have been a surprise but a fact expected. To John at least, it was a matter of faith at this stage. Shortly, it was to become a matter of fact through the Lord's revelation of Himself.

The next example is Mary, vv. 11–18, who had been delivered from seven demons, Luke 8. 2. She was not only first to bear the news of the open tomb, vv. 1, 2, but also first to see the Risen Lord. The love that stayed to witness the harrowing scenes of Calvary kept her at the tomb, where her deep grief was expressed by tears, John 20. 11. The presence of angels should have reassured her that nothing untoward could have happened to the body with such in attendance, Psa. 91. 11, but no one except Him whom she called, "my Lord", John 20. 13, could assuage her grief. Such devotion could not go unrewarded; the supposed gardener called her by name and instantly she knew Him, as each sheep knows the voice of the shepherd, 10. 3, 4.

The third case occurred in the evening, when the Lord came and stood in the midst of the disciples assembled behind closed doors, vv. 19–25. Proof of the resurrection was given by displaying His hands and side. John mentions the side, and not the feet, because of the deep impression the side-piercing had upon him as an eye-witness.

The last example is Thomas, who was present when Jesus revealed Himself again a week later. He was brought to belief when given the chance to apply a test on the very terms he had proposed. The confession, "My Lord and my God", is the pinnacle of faith, and the objective to which the whole of the Gospel of John is intended to lead, vv. 28–31.

May 4th

READING : **John 21. 1-25**

THE EPILOGUE

JOHN HAS stated that his object in writing is to lead men to belief in the divine Christ, 20. 30, 31. In order to achieve this end, he selected eight of the miracles which Jesus did, the last of which is recorded in 21. 1–14. He calls the miracles signs because they are significant of deeper things. They are all demonstrations of Deity and, as Jesus is the Christ, they foreshadow Messiah's kingdom. They also contain lessons on Eternal Life. On the occasion of the first sign, Jesus manifested His glory by turning water into wine; now, in resurrection life, He manifested Himself, vv. 1, 14, by the draught of fishes. John perceived the stranger on the shore to be the Lord, v. 7. Peter's action was the result of John's remark, not from personal recognition. In connection with Messiahship, we note that the sea of Galilee is here called the sea of Tiberias, after Tiberius Caesar, and pictures the Gentile nations out of which there is yet to be a great in-gathering for millennial blessing. As to the teaching on Eternal Life, we learn that it is a life of *service*. Peter's going to fish of his own inclination, influencing others also, resulted in fruitlessness, but, when the Lord directed the work, there were positive results. Jesus standing on the shore in the morning, the haul brought to the land, and the counting of the fish, all prefigure the review of service at the Judgment Seat of Christ. The restoration of Peter which follows highlights the conditions upon which service depends, namely, love to Christ, vv. 15–17, and surrender to God's will, vv. 18-19. Three times the Lord asked Peter, "Lovest thou me?", corresponding to Peter's three denials. The first questioned his love in comparison with others, "more than these"; the second, his love for the Lord alone; the third, the reality of his love. Peter, informed that his end would be martyrdom, asked about John. The answer given was a reminder of the Lord's sovereignty over His servants. John's service was no concern of Peter's, vv. 20–22. The Lord who directs our service, vv. 1–14, and demands our affection, vv. 15–17, also determines our destiny, vv. 18–25.

We cannot know the contents of the infinitude of books that could be written about that Holy Life, v. 25, but the Father knows, forming treasured memories to eternal ages.

Introducing The Acts of the Apostles

AUTHOR: Identified with the writer of the third Gospel, Luke 1. 1–4; Acts 1. 1–2, the author is three times personally present during the events he narrates, 16. 10–17; 20. 5 to 21. 25; 27.1 to 28. 16. We can safely see him as "the beloved physician" mentioned by Paul, Col. 4. 14; 2 Tim. 4. 11.

DATE: Probably written between 60 and 67 A.D., the book covers the 30 years from Pentecost to Paul's arrival in Rome.

STRUCTURE: The key-verse is 1. 8 which outlines the geographical progress of the gospel: Jerusalem, chs. 1–7; Judaea, 8. 1–4; Samaria, 8. 5–25; and the world, 8. 26 to the end.

The two major sections of the book are:

Chapters 1–12. Centred on Jerusalem and Peter.

Chapters 13–28. Centred on Antioch and Paul.

Notice Luke's occasional summary verses, marking the growth of assemblies: 6. 7; 9. 31; 12. 24; 16. 5; 19. 20; 28. 31.

THEMES: 1. *Continuation.* Luke aims to show that the ascended Lord Jesus continues to work through His people on earth. Thus the book neither begins at its beginning (for it refers back to the Gospel, 1. 1) nor finishes at the end (for it leaves Paul still preaching, 28. 31). In a sense it is *still* continuing, for the work of evangelism is yet incomplete.

2. *Glorification.* The prime features of Acts are (i) the presence of a glorified Man in heaven, 1. 2, and (ii) the power of the Holy Spirit on earth, 2. 4. The resurrection and exaltation of the Saviour form the core of apostolic preaching, cf. 2. 36; 3. 15–16; 4. 10–11; 5. 30–31, etc.

3. *Transformation.* The outpoured Spirit of God gives power to weak disciples, 1. 8. Thus violent enemies like Paul are transformed into messengers of the cross.

4. *Initiation.* Luke documents the origin of the church and the growth of local assemblies wherever the gospel is spread, 2. 47. The gradual transition between Judaism and full Christianity takes in most of the book and creates many of the unusual problems encountered.

5. *Proclamation.* A handbook of gospel preaching, Acts includes some 18 addresses directed to a variety of audiences. All evangelists and teachers should study these carefully.

May 5th

READING : **Acts 1. 1-26**

THE LORD'S ASCENSION

VOLUME TWO of Luke's history of Christian beginnings starts with the climax of the Lord's earthly ministry, vv. 1–9. This is the foundation for all that follows and the inspired author aims to make clear, as in his "former treatise", Luke 1. 1–4, that the Faith is built on the rock of historical certainty. How reassuring for Theophilus to know that he has not "followed cunningly devised fables", 2 Pet. 1. 16, in trusting the Lord Jesus Christ! Thus Luke summarizes the events of the "forty days" between the resurrection and ascension, events which guarantee the genuineness of the former, Acts 1. 3, and prepare the disciples for the latter by means of teaching and gospel commission, vv. 3, 7, 8. Though the Lord Jesus had laid the perfect foundation in the finished work of Calvary, there was still the task of spreading the message of salvation to a lost world stretching from pious Jerusalem to pagan Rome, v. 8. And that unfinished work was entrusted to a few feeble disciples among whom were Peter the denier and Thomas the doubter. How could they possibly manage ?

The answer lies in the truth that whenever the Lord *entrusts* His people with a task He also *empowers* them. Luke is unique in telling us that the Saviour gave commandments "through the Holy Ghost", v. 2, introducing his special emphasis on the work of the Spirit in Acts. The Holy Spirit provides teaching, v. 2, John 16. 3; is involved in that baptism which incorporates all believers into the Body of Christ, Acts 1. 5; 1 Cor. 12. 13; gives needed power for witness, Acts 1. 8; and inspires the Scriptures, v. 16.

Through these Spirit-inspired Scriptures the believer today finds guidance, as did the early disciples, vv. 15–26. Peter's use of Psalms 69 and 109 indicates trust in the infallibility of God's Word, "this scripture must needs have been fulfilled", v. 16. Its intention, he shows, is to provide comfort (in that Judas' defection was foreknown) and counsel (in that a replacement is authorized, vv. 20, 21).

Let us take encouragement from the fact that we can proclaim the same historic message of the gospel, experience the same dynamic power of the Spirit, and rest on the same solid authority of God's Word.

May 6th

READING : **Acts 2. 1-47**

THE BIRTH OF THE CHURCH

A BIRTHDAY is always a special occasion, and the Church's birthday was no exception. On the day of Pentecost, through the descent and baptism in the Holy Spirit, all living believerss were incorporated into the Church, the Body of Christ, through which the absent Lord Jesus continues His work in the world. That day was marked by miraculous *signs*, vv. 1–13, an explanatory *sermon* by Peter, vv. 14–40, and the *salvation* of some 3000 people, vv. 41–47. Truly God was drawing attention to the beginning of something new as He had earlier demonstrated the uniqueness of Calvary, Matt. 27. 50–54.

Like the cross and resurrection, Pentecost is unrepeatable: as the Saviour's atoning work is once and for all, so is His gift of the Spirit. Thus the Spirit of God *has* come, and graciously takes up His permanent home today in all who trust the Saviour, at the moment of conversion, Rom. 8. 9; Gal. 3. 14; John 7. 37–39. From those special Pentecostal signs we can learn more of His ministry. The wind speaks of His unseen power, Acts 2. 2; John 3. 8, the fire suggests His essential holiness, Acts 2. 3; Heb. 12. 29, and the spoken languages underline His purpose of aiding our testimony to Christ, Acts 2. 4; Luke 24. 46–49. The signs have passed, but the reality remains—the indwelling presence of an unseen holy Person who longs to use us in glorifying the Lord Jesus.

Peter's sermon provides a notable pattern for all who proclaim the gospel. He explains what has happened by quoting Joel's prediction of the Spirit's outpouring, vv. 14–21, briefly rehearses the historical facts about the Lord Jesus, vv. 22–24, proves from the Old Testament that the Messiah would both rise from the dead and ascend to heaven, vv. 25–35, and deduces from this that the crucified One is therefore all He claimed to be, vv. 33, 36. His method is worthy of imitation: he is topical, vv. 14–16, Scriptural (11 out of 23 verses are O.T. quotations!), personal in his challenge, vv. 36, 38–40, and thoroughly logical in presentation. Above all, his message is Christ-centred.

Such spiritual preaching produces conviction, v. 37, and genuine conversion, v. 41, which is marked by continuance in the things of God, vv. 42–47. The pattern still applies today!

May 7th

READING : **Acts 3. 1-26**

A LAME MAN HEALED

AT PENTECOST, the Lord had demonstrated His concern for the nation of Israel. Now He manifests, through the apostles, His compassion on the individual. The incident is presented in two sections: the miracle, vv. 1–11, and the message, vv. 12–26.

The miracle itself has a threefold significance. First, it authenticates the apostles, and sets the seal of divine approval on their testimony to the Lord Jesus. The Saviour Himself had appealed to His works as a proof of who He was, John 5. 36, and likewise His apostles could point to "wonders and signs", Acts 2. 43, as their credentials.

Secondly, it brings glory to the Lord Jesus, vv. 13–16, for Peter points out that the apostles had no power in themselves, v. 12. Herein lies the difference between miracles in the Gospels and those in Acts: the Saviour worked them of Himself, Mark 2. 10–11, but the apostles perform them in His Name, Acts 3. 16; 4. 10. Thus all the praise goes to the ascended Lord. In his sermon, Peter underlines the contrast between man's estimate of Jesus and God's. Men delivered up and denied the perfect Servant, but God glorified Him, v. 13 R.V. Men preferred a murderer to the Holy and Just One, v. 14, and killed the very Author of Life, v. 15. God, however, reversed their verdict by raising Him from the dead, a fact proved by the apostles' eyewitness testimony and the miracle done in His Name, vv. 15, 16. Further, the Saviour is the focus of Old Testament prophecy, v. 18, the source of Messianic blessings, vv. 19–21, and the prophet like Moses, vv. 22–23. In short, He is the long-awaited Messiah sent to deal with sin, vv. 25, 26. How fitting that all this should happen in Solomon's porch, where the Jews had earlier demanded evidence of the Lord's Messiahship, John 10. 23–25. The evidence, a healed man, was now plain for all to see!

Finally, the miracle illustrates salvation. The lame man had been helpless from birth, v. 2; and his cure is instant, v. 7; perfect, v. 16; through the power of Christ, v. 6; appropriated by faith, v. 16. Such a deliverance naturally produces joy and worship, v. 8. Should not we, who have been rescued from sin, be all the more eager to praise the Saviour?

May 8th

READING : **Acts 4. 1-37**

OFFICIAL OPPOSITION

TRUE GOSPEL preaching always provokes two reactions: the response of faith, v. 4, and the opposition of unbelievers, v. 18. The miracle of chapter 3 with all its implications could not long remain unnoticed by the religious authorities, especially since the anti-supernaturalist Sadducees were now the dominant party, Acts 4. 1–2; 5. 17. Nevertheless the most striking feature of the chapter is not the fact of Jewish antagonism towards the apostles, vv. 1–22, but the way in which the believers responded to it, vv. 23–37.

Peter, only a few months before, had collapsed in the face of the most unofficial questioning, John 18. 17, but now demonstrates what a difference the coming of the Holy Spirit makes. Boldly he states his convictions as to who the Lord Jesus is, Acts 4. 8–12. When brusquely commanded to stop preaching he replies with the unanswerable assertion that God's authority overrules all others, vv. 19–20. The lesson is clear: the believer under attack can hold his ground with the help of the Spirit, v. 8; Luke 21. 12–15.

Then Peter and John return to "their own company" and share with them all that has happened, v. 23. What a suggestive comment on the value of assembly fellowship! The believers immediatly turn to the divine provision for all situations, prayer, vv. 24–30, for there can be no power in evangelism, no growth in the assembly, no true blessing, without this communion with God. There is no element of ritualism in their prayer: it is as fresh, Scriptural and spiritual as Peter's testimony before the Jewish leaders. Nor is it a request that the opposition be silenced or that the disciples be sheltered from their threats. Rather it is a spontaneous outburst of praise to the creator God, v. 24, the all-knowing God (for had not David prophesied the Messiah's rejection in advance?), vv. 25–27, and the sovereign God whose plans can never fail, v. 28. Their plea for boldness, vv. 29–30, is gloriously granted, v. 31, for ours is a God who delights to answer His people's prayers. May we learn to say "Lord, thou art God", v. 24, and, like those early disciples, enjoy the peace He gives to all who lean in faith on Him, Phil. 4. 6–7.

May 9th

READING : **Acts 5. 1-42**

THE ENEMY ATTACKS

LET US never forget that we have a subtle enemy to contend with. This chapter contains the first reference in Acts to Satan, v. 3, for wherever God is working, there the devil plants seeds of hatred, division, and antagonism to the truth. In chapter 4 he unsuccessfully attempted to discourage the apostles through official intimidation, 4. 18–20. Now he tries two new tactics: corruption from within the Church, Acts 5. 1–16, and persecution from outside, vv. 17–42.

Luke occasionally breaks his narrative with a challenging summary of early Church practices, as in 2. 41–47 and 4. 32–37. In the latter of these we learn that fellowship in the Jerusalem assembly was taken so seriously that some believers sold property and gave the proceeds to a common fund for the aid of poorer saints. This unconstrained exhibition of Christian love becomes the devil's target. Barnabas's selfless action, 4. 36–37, provokes a Satanically-inspired imitation by Ananias and Sapphira. Their sin is calculated deception: an attempt to gain credit for being more generous than they really are. Judgment is swift and sure, for God must show that His Church, so lately begun, is a *holy* company of people where sin cannot be tolerated, 1 Cor. 3. 17. Scriptural discipline characterizes the assembly where the Lord's Name is honoured. The solemn example of Ananias and Sapphira should remind us that fellowship is a sacred privilege not to be taken lightly.

The second line of attack involves physical punishment, v. 40. But violence cannot stop the apostles; after all, they have experienced so much divine corroboration of their message in miraculous signs, vv. 12–16, angelic deliverance, vv. 19–20, and the personal help of the Holy Spirit, v. 32. Despite their beating therefore, they witness with an even greater joy and vigour, vv. 41–42. Are we as gladly determined in our evangelism?

Each of Satan's assaults is turned into blessing by the God who is in complete control. The attempt to corrupt the assembly leads to a lesson in holiness and an increase in numbers, vv. 11–14. The attempt to stifle the Lord's messengers results in joyful rededication to the work, vv. 41–42. "If God be for us, who can be against us?", Rom. 8. 31.

May 10th

READING : **Acts 6. 1-15**

THE TRUE SERVANT

ACTS IS compulsory reading for anyone who thinks the early church was free from troubles! Yesterday we read of Satan's double attack on the Jerusalem assembly, and now comes a further difficulty arising from the suspicions that existed between Greek-speaking and Hebrew-speaking Jews in the company, v. 1. Yet the God who was equal to earlier emergencies can bring blessing out of this new, potentially divisive situation. Thus we find a crisis solved, vv. 1–7, and a Christ-like servant, vv. 8–15.

Wise apostolic leadership averts the danger of a rift in the assembly, vv. 2–6, and brings to the fore one who beautifully exemplifies some of the characteristics of the Christian servant. What can we learn from Stephen? First, he is divinely provided, vv. 1–3. Although the saints chose and the apostles appointed him, we can sense a divine hand in it all, for God always raises up men for Himself in the midst of difficulties. Moses arose from the oppression of Egypt, Saul will shortly emerge out of the enemy's ranks as a champion of the faith, and Stephen is brought forth out of an internal assembly crisis. Let us rejoice that it is the ascended Lord Himself who bestows gifted men on His Church, Eph. 4. 8–13. Second, he is a man "of honest report", Acts 6. 3. There can be no real service for the Master unless our lives conform to our profession of faith in Him.

Furthermore, Stephen is no empty vessel but a man *full* of the Holy Spirit and wisdom, v. 3, full of faith, v. 5, full of grace and power, v. 8 R.V. No wonder he did great things for God! He has nothing to give who is not first filled by the Lord. Again, this servant is humble enough to start with the small responsibility of minding practical assembly affairs. Faithfulness in a minor sphere opens up a wider area of opportunity, vv. 8–10. Perhaps it is because we have been unfaithful in little things that God does not award us greater service for Him, Luke 19. 12–27.

Finally, Stephen is like the Perfect Servant, the Lord Jesus, in faithfulness, blamelessness, and suffering, vv. 11–14; Matt. 26. 60. The true servant will gladly go the way of his Master, John 15. 18–20.

May 11th

READING : **Acts 7. 1-60**

STEPHEN'S DEFENCE

EACH BELIEVER should be "ready always to give an answer to every man that asketh you a reason of the hope that is in you", 1 Pet. 3. 15. Stephen certainly was. His speech is not a defence of himself but of the gospel he proclaimed.

There is much to learn from his handling of the Old Testament Scriptures. First, he accepts them as historically reliable, and speaks confidently of the persons, places and time-periods they mention. In the face of modern scepticism let us reaffirm our trust in the "word of truth", 2 Tim. 2. 15, given by the One who "cannot lie", Titus 1. 2. These authoritative Scriptures prophetically anticipate the coming of the Messiah, Acts 7. 37, 52; 3. 22–26. With Jewish audiences the early Christians were particularly keen to show that the gospel of the Lord Jesus is not opposed to Old Testament teaching; rather it is the divinely-planned fulfilment of all the ancient promises and ceremonies given to Israel. Stephen's attention to Joseph and Moses highlights the typical aspect of the Old Testament: not only does it *predict* the Messiah's coming, it contains *pictures* of Him for our instruction. For example, Joseph, rejected by his brothers, was accepted by God and elevated to great honour, vv. 9–13. Was this not exactly what happened to the Son of God in His crucifixion and resurrection, Acts 2. 36? Moses was sent to deliver his unwilling people from Egyptian bondage, vv. 25–28, 34–36, just as the Lord Jesus came to "save his people from their sins", Matt. 1. 21. How expressively the Old Testament witnesses to the pre-eminence of God's beloved Son! And how honestly it testifies to man's rebelliousness! Even the chosen nation persistently rejected divine messengers from Joseph up until Stephen himself, Acts 7. 51–53; 2 Chron. 36. 16.

The outcome of Stephen's address is a dramatic study in contrasts and a display of God's mercy, vv. 54–60. Surrounded by an enraged mob guilty of resisting the very Spirit who filled him, the servant stands serenely confident in his Lord. Like his Master he is gracious to the last, and ends his task by commending his spirit to the Lord, v. 59; Luke 23. 46, and praying for his murderers, Acts 7. 60; Luke 23. 34. May our message be as true and our manner as compassionate as Stephen's.

May 12th

READING : **Acts 8. 1-40**

EVANGELISTIC EXPANSION

THIS CHAPTER, all about preaching, is also about divine planning, for we get a glimpse of the omnipotent God working "all things after the counsel of his own will", Eph. 1. 11. In persecution, Acts 8. 1–4, in Samaria, vv. 5–25, and in the desert, vv. 26–40, God has a purpose for His people.

Stephen's murder signals the outbreak of a vicious attack which scatters the Jerusalem saints throughout Judaea and Samaria, v. 1. Yet the God who specializes in bringing triumph out of tragedy uses this means to accomplish His plans. When the risen Saviour laid the ground plan of Acts, He commissioned His disciples to preach in those very places, 1. 8. Thus far they had evangelized Jerusalem only. Now the fierce winds of persecution drive them to their new spheres of labour, 8. 4, and the message is gradually spread beyond the confines of Judaism.

Philip, one of the "seven" in Acts 6. 5, bears the good news to Samaria, whose half-breed religion was despised by the Jews, John 4. 9. It was in part to destroy these prejudices that the Lord Himself had passed that way and predicted future blessing, 4. 35–38. How perfect is the programme of an all-wise God! The Saviour's sowing produces an abundant harvest as Samaria gladly responds to the gospel, Acts 8. 5–8, and believers submit themselves to the Lord in baptism, v. 12. If the chapter teaches the importance of baptism, it also shows that the symbol cannot save, for Simon, though immersed, is "not right in the sight of God", vv. 21, 23. Let us beware of substituting a ceremony, however correct, for the reality of a personal relationship with the Lord Jesus.

Then, in the midst of the Samaritan revival, comes that strange call into the desert, v. 26. Philip's prompt and unquestioning obedience in this whole episode is a challenge to all disciples, vv. 26–27, 29–30. As ever, the divine design is proved to be flawless; the willing servant meets a man studying Isaiah 53 (and what better passage could have been chosen?), receptive to instruction, and, once saved, eager to obey his Lord, vv. 34–39. Those today who share the Ethiopian's zeal to honour God's Word will assuredly share his joy, v. 39.

May 13th

READING : **Acts 9. 1-22**

PAUL'S CONVERSION

THE MIRACLE of grace on the Damascus road is a turning point, not merely in Paul's life, 1 Tim. 1. 12–15, but also in Acts itself, for it marks the calling and preparation of God's special envoy to the Gentiles. Since he is later to be the apostle to whom the truth about the Church is uniquely committed, Eph. 3. 3–9, it is fitting that his conversion should be combined with some elementary lessons on that subject.

Lesson number one involves the person of Christ, the living Lord of the Church, vv. 3–5, 20, 22. He who has hounded Christians for worshipping the Nazarene discovered with a shock that he had been wrong: that Speaker from the heavenly glory, clearly Jehovah Himself, is identified as the Jesus whom Paul hated! On the basis of this experience, Paul lists himself as the last of the resurrection witnesses, 1 Cor. 15. 8, itself a proof of his genuine apostleship, 9. 1. But if Paul sees the Lord's glory, he also learns about his responsibility, for the lot of the Church on earth is serving and suffering, Acts 9. 15–16. His change of sides means that he too will share the reproach of Christ: just as the Master's path was one of suffering followed by glory, so is the servant's, 1 Pet. 1. 11; 4. 13; Rom. 8. 18. Yet this grave truth is made bearable by another, the oneness of Christ and His people. The life of the Church is the life of the Lord Jesus Himself, and therefore to persecute believers on earth is to touch Christ in heaven, for every child of God is a member of His body, Acts 9. 4; Eph. 5. 29–30. How comforting that we can know the tender sympathy of the Lord with all that we may endure for Him!

Last but not least, Paul receives a practical lesson on the love of the Church, vv. 6, 17–19. Although the Lord could have instructed Paul further at the roadside, He chooses instead to use a humble believer from Damascus, Ananias, vv. 10–12. The binding power of Christian love is thereby underlined, for Paul is graciously healed and served by one of those he came to destroy. Is it then surprising that he hastens to identify himself with the assembly in Damascus, v. 19? Were we as loving in our concern for fellow believers then our assembly would flourish too.

May 14th

READING: **Acts 9. 23-43**

THE SECRET OF A HEALTHY CHURCH

WHAT MAKES for assembly prosperity? Our passage can help us, for its spiritual heart is one of Luke's summary verses, v. 31, a recipe for assembly growth which still works.

Those early local churches were first of all characterized by "peace", v. 31 R.V., not necessarily because there was no persecution, but because they had learned to rest in the living God. Edification comes next, for sound teaching is a vital feature of any assembly that would honour the truth. Further, they were known for reverence, "walking in the fear of the Lord"; in a day of superficial "decisions" we need a deeper appreciation of our God's greatness. They experienced the comfort or counsel of the Holy Spirit, the only One who can direct the saints in worship and testimony to the Lord Jesus. Finally—and as a consequence—they were multiplied. Can it be doubted that if God's work is done in God's way there will be real and lasting blessing? A shallow Christianity in the assembly may draw crowds but it cannot change lives.

Of course, if these things are to be true of my local church they must first of all be true of me! Luke tells us what all believers ought to be: "disciples", vv. 25, 26, 36, 38, "brethren", v. 30, and "saints", v. 32. The first title emphasizes the disciplined life, for the disciple must be a constant and obedient follower of the Master, John 8. 31. "Brethren" suggests the devotion believers feel for each other as members of one divine family, Acts 9. 17. We can see it in the Jerusalem assembly's concern for Paul, vv. 29–30. The third title indicates distinctiveness: "saints" are set apart for God and marked out as different from the world.

But that is not all. Three believers exemplify the way in which each Christian has a work to do in his assembly. Barnabas lives up to his name, "son of encouragement", 4. 36, by supporting Paul in his desire to join the disciples, v. 27. Dorcas is "full of good works", vv. 36, 39, a touching example of the ministry available to godly women. Simon opens his home to the apostle Peter, v. 43, and demonstrates the value of Christian hospitality. If we pull our weight in the assembly where God has placed us, then blessing will surely follow.

May 15th

READING : **Acts 10. 1-48**

PETER AT CAESAREA

PREJUDICE IS a hard thing to overcome, especially if it is based on divine revelation. This explains Peter's dilemma. Reared on Judaism, acutely conscious of the ceremonial taboos, v. 14, and the traditional separatism of his people, v. 28, he is the one chosen to declare that Gentiles as well as Jews now have a right to the full blessings of the gospel, v. 43.

How can the ingrained prejudice of a strict Jew be broken down? God's method, gradual and gentle, is instructive. First of all, the events of Acts 8 have made it clear that Samaritan believers are in no way inferior to Jewish disciples. Then the providence of God has led Peter to stay with a tanner, whose occupation was an offence to Jews because it involved contact with animal carcasses, v. 6. That in itself is a step away from rigid Judaism. Next comes the thrice-repeated vision, vv. 9–16. Let us note that both visions in the chapter occur during times of prayer, vv. 9, 30. The mind of God is only revealed to the believer who spends much time alone with his Lord. Peter's vision symbolizes the end of the Jew-Gentile division, but it also suggests some grand features of the Church. The sheet gathers together clean and unclean, v. 12, even as all believers, regardless of race, are one in Christ Jesus, Gal. 3. 28. This is made possible by a divine cleansing, Acts 10. 15, for it is only on the basis of Calvary that we receive forgiveness and acceptance, Titus 3. 5–6. The source of the sheet, Acts 10, 11, 16, reminds us that the Church is of divine origin and awaits a glorious rapture to its heavenly home, Phil. 3. 20.

All these things, combined with the timely arrival of the messengers, vv. 17–22, and the account of Cornelius's vision, vv. 30–33, convince Peter that the Lord is at work. Therefore he unreservedly proclaims the good news to an eager audience, emphasizing God's impartiality, vv. 34–35, the universal lordship of Christ, v. 36, and the thrilling "whosoever" of the gospel, v. 43. God interrupts the meeting to set His approval on Peter's faithful action, v. 44. May He who is "Lord of all" preserve us from unscriptural prejudices through the aid of His Spirit, and allow us, like Peter, to see refreshingly evident blessing on our testimony for Him.

May 16th

READING : **Acts 11. 1-30**

FROM JERUSALEM TO ANTIOCH

THIS CHAPTER marks the great shift of Christian activity from Jerusalem to Antioch, from the heart of Judaism to the third city of the Roman empire, from the leadership of Peter to that of Paul. We have seen evidence of this transition over the past three chapters, with the conversion of the Samaritans, the calling of Paul, and the salvation of Cornelius. From now on, Luke's focus moves westwards as the gospel spreads out of Judaea into Europe. We progress, then, from a full account of Peter's report at Jerusalem, vv. 1–18, to the revival among Gentiles in Antioch, vv. 19–30.

Peter, not surprisingly, needs to explain his actions to Jewish believers who are as zealous for the law as he used to be, v. 3; 10. 14. His account is a model missionary report, clear, concise, and challenging. The man who is in the will of God need not be afraid to say what he has done. His orderly presentation of the facts, v. 4, emphasizes the most significant events of his experience: the vision, v. 9, the providential arrival of Cornelius's men, v. 11, and the out-pouring of the Spirit, vv. 15–16. After this, the conclusion is irresistible, vv. 17–18. It is good to learn that our God is so much bigger than the limited vision of His people. When He chooses to work in a way we had not thought possible, let us be sure to give Him all the praise.

Meanwhile, there is revival among the Greeks of Antioch, v. 20 R.V. These believers form an autonomous assembly responsible to the Lord Jesus alone, the One to whom they have turned, vv. 21, 26. How carefully the Holy Spirit guards the Lord's pre-eminence! Salvation is found neither in sect, nor society, nor assembly, but in the Person of Christ. Therefore Barnabas urges them "with purpose of heart" to "cleave unto the Lord", v. 23. But though this gathering is independent of the church in Jerusalem, there is a beautiful fellowship between them: Jerusalem sends Barnabas to encourage the new Christians, vv. 22–23, and Antioch sends back gifts to aid the hard-pressed saints of Judaea, vv. 29–30. Such a striking example of spiritual and material concern should challenge the relationship between assemblies today.

May 17th

READING : **Acts 12. 1-25**

PETER IN PRISON

WHY DOES God allow one of His children to die and another to live? Our chapter implicitly asks this question, because it records both the martyrdom of James and the supernatural rescue of Peter. The answer lies in the wonderful truth that our God makes no mistakes; He is glorified by His people in life and in death, Phil 1. 20–21. Our part is to trust that He knows best.

Peter's story, vv. 1–19, teaches us about faith, responsibility and prayer. Here is a man, guarded by sixteen soldiers, bound with chains, awaiting the dawn of his execution day, vv. 4–6. Yet Peter is sleeping so soundly that the angel has to strike him to wake him up, v. 7! Only a man resting in the goodness of God can sleep under such circumstances, Psa. 4. 8. There is serenity under pressure for all who fulfil the conditions laid down in Philippians 4. 6-7.

The manner of deliverance illustrates a principle that runs throughout Scripture. The angel snaps the chains and opens locked doors, but Peter has to dress himself and find his way home, vv. 7–12. God will do the impossible, but He leaves the rest to us. In our Christian service let us do the very best we can, trusting Him for the results.

Then comes a lesson in prayer, v. 5. Perhaps the disciples expect only death for Peter, and ask God to strengthen him; certainly they are not prepared for a miraculous escape, vv. 15–16. Nevertheless, God is pleased to honour prayer in an unforeseen way for He reserves the right to give us better things than we can ever imagine. It is reassuring to know that answers to prayer depend ultimately not on our *faith* but on his *faithfulness*.

While James's death and Peter's escape fulfil the Lord's gracious purpose, the judgment of Herod vindicates His honour, for this man "gave not God the glory", v. 23. Here is a stark contrast to the Lord Jesus. The proud blasphemer dies to prove he is merely a man, vv. 22–23; the Saviour, ever humble in His earthly pathway, is raised from the dead to prove He is God, 1 Pet. 1. 21; Rom. 1. 4. And because He is the ever-living One, His Word continues to grow and multiply.

MAP ILLUSTRATING THE ACTS

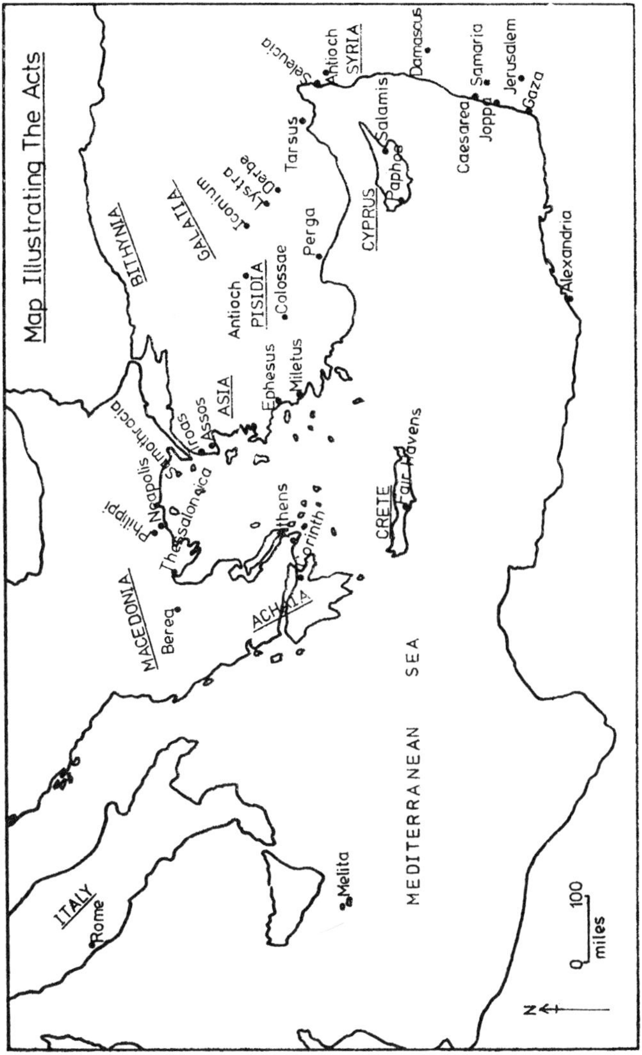

Survey of Peter's and Paul's Spheres of Service

IT IS obvious that the beginning of chapter 13 represents the next stage in God's plan for the world. In Mark 16. 15 the Lord had said, "Go ye into all the world", but in Acts 1. 8 this was to be accomplished in stages: firstly, local evangelization out to Samaria; secondly, far distant work "unto the uttermost part of the earth". Peter and others were the local evangelists; they worked where the Lord called them, "as the Lord hath called every one, so let him walk", 1 Cor. 7. 17, 20. Indeed Peter was the apostle to the Jews, Gal. 2. 8; this was the essential sphere of his ministry, "to the Jew first", Rom. 1. 16. It was not his own choice that through him "God . . . did visit the Gentiles, to take out of them a people for his name", Acts 15. 14. God Himself arranged all the circumstances for Peter to visit Caesarea, thereby giving him the second key, Matt. 16. 19, when the Holy Spirit was poured out on the Gentiles, Cornelius and his friends, Acts 10. 24, 45. Peter almost disappears from the record after Acts 12, except in Acts 15. 7; Galatians 2. 7–17, and in his two letters.

The reason is that the sphere "the uttermost part of the earth" was reserved for another servant of God, the apostle Paul: "the gospel of the uncircumcision was committed unto me . . . toward the Gentiles", Gal. 2. 7–8. This special work did not open up immediately Paul (as Saul) was converted. He was prepared (still as Saul) in Damascus, Jerusalem, Caesarea, Tarsus and Antioch, Acts 9. 22, 26, 30; 11. 26, but all this was not Gentile-ministry. The Lord had stated that he would bear His Name "before the Gentiles", 9. 15; "I will send thee far hence unto the Gentiles", 22. 21; "the Gentiles, unto whom now I *send* thee", 26. 17. It is from this particular Greek word "send" (but there are others) that the word "apostle" is derived. Thus Paul (as Saul) was an apostle *by calling* from his early experiences of Christ, but *in practice* his apostleship was manifested when he was "sent forth by the Holy Spirit", 13. 4, to the Gentiles. He now first acquired his new name "Paul", 13. 9. He recognized that "Christ sent me", 1 Cor. 1. 17. He carried this designation "apostle" only after the start of this first journey, Acts 14. 4, a title which he carried to the end, 2 Tim. 1. 1. (Contributed by J. Heading.)

May 18th

READING : **Acts 13. 1-13**

A MODEL CHURCH

THE SECOND half of Acts traces the spread of the Christian faith into the Gentile world. Thus we read of the commendation of Paul and Barnabas to the work, vv. 1–3, and the commencement of the first missionary journey, vv. 4–13. But let us not overlook the qualities of the church they leave behind them.

"The church which was at Antioch", v. 1, is clearly a distinct company of people distinguished from the rest of the city, just as the assembly today must be different from the world around. It is also a gifted company. We learned the importance of edification in 9. 31, and here we find its human source in "prophets and teachers". While the prophet *spoke* the Word of God before the completion of the New Testament, the teacher *explained* it. Obviously this is neither a one-man nor an everyman teaching ministry; God provides *several* gifted instructors to build up His church. Do we recognize and respect the gift in our assembly? Notice their warm-heartedness. Among the teachers are a Levite, a black man, a North African, a nobleman, and a Pharisee, v. 1. Such distinctions of race, colour, social class and education cannot harm a fellowship enjoying oneness in Christ Jesus!

Further, the church recognizes the liberty of the Holy Spirit to guide its affairs, vv. 2–3. In our passage the Spirit of God speaks, v. 2, sends, v. 4, and strengthens, v. 9; only as an assembly allows Him freedom will there be real progress. Finally, we observe a genuine concern for men who have been called by God to full-time service. Identification with those who serve the Lord in special ways, v. 3, involves a continuing responsibility to share in their spiritual and material needs. Do we truly exhibit a commitment to our missionary brethren and sisters?

As Paul and Barnabas start their work, there is a gradual shift of leadership from the older to the younger man. Hitherto the designation has been "Barnabas and Saul", v. 2, but now we begin to read of "Paul and Barnabas", vv. 13, 50. The one who so graciously encouraged Paul in the past, 9. 27 and 11. 25–26, now teaches us all a lesson in humility by taking the back place.

May 21st

READING : **Acts 15. 1-41**

THE JERUSALEM CONFERENCE

THE SPREAD of the gospel to Gentiles, 13. 48, soon arouses Satanic animosity, just as did the apostles' preaching in the days after Pentecost. First comes pressure from outside, 14. 2, 19; and when that fails (for the churches of God have always thrived on persecution) the enemy resorts to wilier tactics, infiltrating and corrupting from within, 15. 1, 2, 5. A doctrinal problem, vv. 1–5, and a Scriptural resolution, vv. 6–35, lead into Paul's second missionary journey to the Gentiles. vv. 36–41, proof in itself that the attempt to divide the Body of Christ has been foiled, Eph. 3. 6.

One of the fundamental teachings of God's Word is that salvation is by grace, through faith, *plus nothing*, Eph. 2. 8–9. This precious truth, which strikes the death-blow to all human self-effort and pride, is the devil's special target. To compromise it is to destroy that feature of the gospel which so plainly magnifies God's glory. But error is always subtle. The believing Pharisees, v. 5, do not deny that salvation is found in Christ, nor do they oppose the conversion of Gentiles. Their contention is that a Gentile must become a Jew to become a real Christian. In other words, faith in the Saviour is not enough! To be saved, they taught that one needs Christ *and* the law. How strictly we must guard against adding to the perfect Word of God, Prov. 30. 6!

The omnipotent Lord, however, is well able to preserve His truth. Notice how the error is checked. It is dealt with at its source, Jerusalem, as all evil must be, vv. 1–2. Respected and godly men speak out. Peter proves that Cornelius was saved as conclusively as anyone at Pentecost, vv. 8–9, and magnanimously places Gentiles in front of Jews, v. 11. Paul and Barnabas declare that God is continuing to save non-Jews v. 12. And James, the Lord's brother, concludes by showing that all this accords with the Old Testament kingdom prophecies of blessing on the Gentiles, vv. 13–18. Thus the Judaizers' misuse of Scripture is countered by a clear, orderly and charitable exposition of the Word.

Chapter 15 teaches that God's truth *must* be upheld whatever the cost. When false teaching enters the assembly it must be answered, graciously and cogently, from Scripture.

May 22nd

READING : **Acts 16. 1-40**

PAUL AT PHILIPPI

PAUL'S SECOND missionary journey, 15. 36 to 18. 22, is blessed by the addition of new helpers. The return visit to Lystra, vv. 1–5, introduces us to Timothy, later a beloved fellow-labourer, while the Macedonian call, vv. 6-11, marks Luke's arrival, v. 10. More significantly, we can note the sovereign right of the greatest Helper, the Holy Spirit, to direct His servants wherever He pleases, vv. 6–7. When God shuts some doors, He always opens others for those who have the faith and patience to wait on His will, v. 9.

The rest of the chapter concerns Philippi, vv. 12–40, and shows how varied and fitting are God's ways with souls. Lydia, already a devout worshipper of the God of Israel, is saved while Paul is speaking, v. 14, and demonstrates the reality of her faith in baptism and hospitality, v. 15. A devoted woman was the first witness of the Risen Lord Jesus, and now a woman is the first disciple of Paul's European venture. How quietly and tenderly the Lord works in her, opening her heart to His gospel! The Roman jailor, on the other hand, requires an earthquake! That sturdy veteran soldier receives a supreme display of divine power which convicts him of his deep need, v. 30. And, of course, the Lord has planned it all. The demon-possessed girl's testimony and miraculous deliverance, vv. 17–18, the remarkable demeanour of Paul and Silas in prison, v. 25, and an earthquake which looses prisoners but causes no harm, v. 26, combine to authenticate Paul's message, v. 31. It is delightful for the Christian to look back and see how carefully God led him to the moment of his conversion. As with Lydia the work of grace is proved by baptism, love and joy, vv. 33–34, for true faith *always* manifests itself in happy obedience.

The disciples' behaviour in the jail beautifully illustrates the correct response to unjust suffering, 1 Pet. 2. 20–21. Far from bemoaning their lot, as we are so prone to do, these dear men remain where God has placed them—and rejoice, Acts 16. 25. Instead of seizing the first chance to escape, they stay in prison to reach the jailor, v. 28. Let us likewise look for the Lord's hand in our circumstances, however difficult, and submit to His gracious purposes for us.

May 23rd

READING : **Acts 17. 1-34**

PAUL AT ATHENS

CAN THE gospel of Jesus Christ deal with the intellectual as powerfully and effectively as it has already met the needs of others? Paul proves that it can. Having passed through Thessalonica, vv. 1–9, and Berea, vv. 10–15, he arrives at the centre of ancient culture and learning, Athens, vv. 16–34. There he demonstrates that although the message cannot be compromised, its presentation can be altered to suit a particular audience. Thus, while he proclaims the Risen Lord Jesus both in the synagogue, vv. 2–3, and on the Areopagus, vv. 18, 31, he approaches this great truth by different routes.

In each case, Paul starts from where his hearers are. The Jews accept the authority of the Old Testament; to them, therefore, he argues in detail from Scripture, vv. 2, 3, 11, showing that the One so recently crucified and raised fulfils all God's promises about the Messiah. Any teaching that claims to be based on God's Word must be carefully scrutinized, and the Bereans are a challenging example of how it should be done, v. 11; 1 Thess. 5. 20–21. May we reject error and receive truth with equal whole-heartedness.

The Greeks, however, are indifferent to Jewish Scriptures and the concept of a Messiah. Back in Lystra, Paul and Barnabas had confronted superstitious pagans with three grand truths about the Living God: His greatness, grace and goodness, 14. 15–17. With the educated Athenians he starts from their religious inclinations, vv. 22–23, and moves into a forthright declaration of who God is, vv. 24–29. Our society, so influenced by an evolutionary humanism which rejects God and exalts man, needs to hear again the vital truth that God is Creator, v. 24, Preserver, vv. 25–26, and Judge, v. 31. Then comes the majestic conclusion, summed up in three words: *righteousness* (the character of God), *resurrection* (the guarantee of future judgment), and *repentance* (God's demand of man), vv. 30–31. Here is no sentimental appeal, but a clear command from the Sovereign Lord of all.

Gloriously, some are saved, vv. 32–34. Let us rejoice that the gospel is not limited by the boundaries of culture and education; it is for *all* who will believe in the victorious Lord of Calvary.

May 24th

READING : **Acts 18. 1-28**

AQUILA AND PRISCILLA

FROM A centre of world culture Paul now travels to a city sunk deep in sin. The moral state of the notorious Corinth is described by the apostle himself in 1 Corinthians 6. 9–11. Yet the grace of God can save to the uttermost all who turn to the Lord Jesus, be they philosophers or prostitutes, v. 11! This missionary journey has already demonstrated varied reactions to the gospel among Gentiles, and, despite all the difficulties, precious souls continue to be saved, 16. 5, 14, 34; 17. 4, 12, 34; 18. 8.

Rather strangely, it is in the midst of immoral Corinth that the Spirit of God gives us a glimpse of a real Christian marriage at work in Aquila and Priscilla, vv. 1–3, 18–19, 26–28. How brightly they shine against such a dark background! It is noteworthy that they are always *mentioned together* in Scripture; never do we read of one without the other. This in itself testifies to the divine ideal. Just as Eve was made out of Adam and for Adam, Gen. 2. 21–24, so Priscilla is perfectly suited to the needs of Aquila. In the same way, Aquila brings to his wife qualities which she would otherwise lack. The Bible's teaching about the sexes is that they are distinct but complementary, and nowhere is this better illustrated than in a God-planned marriage.

Furthermore, we find that this couple *minister together*. They are first seen opening their home to the Lord's people, vv. 2–3, and that good habit is continued, for twice Paul mentions the church that meets in their house, Rom. 16. 3–5; 1 Cor. 16. 19. Can we doubt that such sacrificial kindness gained the Lord's approval and the reward promised those who show hospitality to the saints, Heb. 6. 10? Certainly they learn much from Paul's stay with them, for both are able to encourage and instruct Apollos when he arrives in Ephesus, Acts 18. 26. It takes time, effort and patience to promote the spiritual and physical welfare of a young believer, but we can imagine the joy with which they watch his progress and hear of his ministry in Achaia, vv. 27–28.

Our world and our assembly badly need godly couples like Aquila and Priscilla, prepared unselfishly and unsparingly to care for the needs of folk around them.

May 25th

READING : **Acts 19. 1-41**

PAUL AT EPHESUS

PAUL'S CAREFULLY conditioned promise to return to Ephesus, 18. 20–21, is fulfilled in the course of his third missionary journey, 18. 23 to 21. 17. Luke provides much detail about the apostle's lengthy stay in this city of magic and superstition, vv. 8, 10, and, in so doing, helpfully illustrates the characteristics of those who truly respond to the gospel.

A Christian, we learn, is one who has *received* the Holy Spirit, vv. 1–7. These unusual disciples are not Christians in the full New Testament sense; they are followers of John Baptist. When Paul completes John's message and points them to Christ, they believe, v. 4, are baptized, v. 5, and receive the Spirit, v. 6. Like earlier events at Jerusalem, Samaria, and Caesarea, this is wholly exceptional and unrepeatable, for all now receive the Spirit the minute they trust the Saviour, v. 2 R.V.; Gal. 3. 2; John 7. 39.

Second, a Christian is a *receptacle* of divine power, vv. 8–12. Mentioned after his preaching, Paul's miracles are clearly secondary to his main purpose of evangelism. Now that authenticating signs have ceased, the Lord's power is manifested in the believer's life and testimony.

Third, a believer *reverences* the Name of the Lord Jesus, vv. 13–17. While both the fake exorcists and the demon speak casually of "Jesus", vv. 13, 15, the inspired historian carefully guards His Lordship, vv. 13, 17. Those who submit to His authority will gladly own it in their speech, for it delights God's heart to hear His children refer reverently and lovingly to "the Lord Jesus", Heb. 13. 15; Phil. 2. 11.

A Christian has been *redeemed* from his old ways, vv. 18–20; 1 Pet. 1. 18–19. Because they now belong to the Lord, these Ephesian disciples are prepared to make a clear and costly break with past evil practices. Are we?

Finally, because a believer *rejects* the false values of society, he must expect to suffer, vv. 21–41, for the world cannot bear folk who will not bow to its idols of materialism and religion, vv. 25-27. People of the way inevitably encounter hostility from those on the broad road to destruction, vv. 9, 23; Matt. 7. 13. But let us rejoice that God is able to keep His own, Acts 19. 30–31, 35–41.

May 26th

READING : **Acts 20. 1-38**

A CHALLENGE TO ELDERS

PROBABLY THE most moving episode of Paul's life is his tender farewell to the Ephesian elders, the climax to a chapter that finds him hastening towards Jerusalem. After the riot in the theatre, the apostle revisits the Macedonian believers, returning by way of Troas, vv. 1–6. There he meets with the local church, vv. 7–12, and passes on to Miletus, vv. 13–16, where he gives timeless instruction to the elders of the Ephesus assembly, vv. 17–38.

The brief mention of his week's stay in Troas indicates Paul's deep appreciation not only of Christian fellowship but also of the Lord's Supper. It seems clear that he deliberately delays his journey so as to join the saints in remembering the Lord Jesus, v. 7. If an apostle in such a hurry to reach Jerusalem can find time for worship, there is no excuse for us to miss this precious Lord's day gathering.

But it is the concluding address to the elders that must grip our attention. How many of us are consistently good examples to the Lord's people? Paul, however, is a gracious illustration of the very truths he has taught, v. 18; 1 Cor. 4. 16; 11. 1. His manner was ever humble, v. 19, as befits a man conscious of the depths from which grace has snatched him, 1 Tim. 1. 15. His service was fearless, despite the persistent and fanatical hostility of the Jews, vv. 19, 23–24, for he was a messenger from the King of kings. His teaching was comprehensive, for it covered "all the counsel of God", vv. 20, 27. No wonder he ministered "night and day with tears", v. 31, being entrusted with such a curriculum! His teaching was also profitable, neither avoiding difficult portions of the Word nor insisting on matters inconsequential, v. 20. Again, his activities were not characterized by secrecy or shame; he preached openly and publicly, v. 20. Yet this did not impede a personal ministry among the saints, the demonstration of a pastor's care for the individual, v. 20. Finally, his gospel was universal, v. 21, and without charge, vv. 33–35, for, having received freely from the Lord, the worker gladly spends himself in the Master's service.

With elders of this calibre the flock of God will surely be protected, fed and increased.

May 27th

READING : **Acts 21. 1-40**

PAUL AT JERUSALEM

It is a sad thing that most Christians possess a lively talent for criticism, especially in matters which are not clearly revealed in Scripture. Paul's visit to Jerusalem is a case in point because it confronts us with the champion of grace agreeing to a compromise with Judaism, vv. 23–26. However, rather than apportion praise or blame according to our judgment of the great apostle, let us simply note some facts worthy of our attention.

First, apostolic infallibility extends *only* to the Scriptures they write, and not to every aspect of their conduct, for even apostles could make mistakes, 23. 1–5; Gal. 2. 11. In sovereign grace, God chose weak human instruments through whom to communicate His flawless Word. Second, Acts is historical rather than doctrinal, and is therefore not meant to provide a totally unchanging code of behaviour; it just records the history of the young church. Further, Acts covers a unique period of transition from Judaism to full New Testament Christianity which accounts for many of its problems. Finally, and most importantly, God's Word is always accurate, as witnessed by the fulfilment of Agabus's prophecy, vv. 11, 33.

More encouraging than the events in Jerusalem itself is the journey, vv. 1–17, which shows once again Paul's interest in the assemblies along his route, vv. 4, 7. Verse 4 suggests that he deliberately sought out the believers in Tyre, and the warmth of their fellowship is seen in the fond farewell he is given after only seven days' acquaintance, vv. 5–6. At Caesarea, Philip the evangelist opens his home and reveals not only that he has continued steadily in the faith, but also that he has raised up a family in the fear of God, vv. 8–9. The possession of notable spiritual gifts does not relieve the Christian man of a special responsibility towards his dependants; Philip is a good father as well as a good preacher.

There is nothing in the world like the family affection that exists among Christians. It is in itself a testimony to the grace of God, John 13. 35. May we cherish and display it in our home and our assembly.

Even when Paul was a prisoner, this fellowship continued, Acts 27. 3; 28. 14, 15, 30; Phil. 2. 25; 4. 18.

May 28th

READING : **Acts 22. 1-30**

WITNESSING TO A MOB

IT IS no easy matter to face a hostile crowd and speak out for the Master. Paul can, because he possesses the indwelling Holy Spirit with all His enabling power for testimony in the most difficult of circumstances. Thus he delivers the first recorded public account of his conversion, vv. 1–21, a fine model testimony despite its rejection by the Jews, vv. 22–30.

Paul is first of all *concise*. His whole talk lasts only a few minutes, but contains so much. He rehearses his past life, vv. 3–5, the actual moment of his encounter with the Risen Lord Jesus, vv. 6–11, and the dramatic change this has caused in him, vv. 12–21. His view of the Saviour alters when he discovers Him to be the Lord and the "Just One", vv. 8, 14. His attitude towards Christians alters from murderous hatred, v. 4, to brotherly love, kindled by the kindness of Ananias, vv. 12–13. From being a zealous upholder of the law, he becomes the specially commissioned envoy of the Lord Jesus to the Gentiles, vv. 14–15, 21. The complete transformation of such a man is an unanswerable validation of his message; only a supernatural intervention could have converted this arch-Pharisee, Phil. 3. 4–7. Perhaps we can learn to be as incisive when we say what the Lord has done for us.

Second, he is *honest*. Paul fully admits the extent of his earlier opposition to the gospel, vv. 3–5, yet does not dwell on it in an unseem.y way. The Christian has no mandate either to conceal or exaggerate his unregenerate experience, for the purpose of God is not served by misrepresentation, however well-intended. Any temptation to glory in the sins from which we have been rescued must be countered by a recognition that the aim of all witness is to exalt the Lord Jesus and no one else, v. 15.

Third, Paul is utterly *serene*. Despite the tension of the situation, he can speak calmly and clearly of his Lord. Further, there is no burden of guilt overshadowing his talk, for, having been cleansed through the precious blood of Christ, he has "no more conscience of sins", Heb. 10. 2. May the inner peace that underlies Paul's preaching and proves him to be a forgiven sinner also characterize our testimony to the Saviour.

May 29th

READING : **Acts 23. 1-35**

FROM JERUSALEM TO CAESAREA

PAUL'S STAND for Christ in Jerusalem seems to produce nothing but uproar. On the stairway to the Fortress Antonia he was given a hearing until he mentioned his special mission to the Gentiles, 22. 22. Now, his defence before an informal gathering of the Sanhedrin ends in violent conflict between the rival Pharisees and Sadducees, 23. 6–10. Such antagonism towards the great apostle only underlines Israel's continued rejection of her Messiah and His messengers, John 19. 15; Acts 5. 40, and confirms Paul's determination to turn to the Gentiles, 13. 46–47. Therefore the two sections of the chapter, the council, vv. 1–10, and the conspiracy, vv. 11–35, mark a movement away from Jerusalem towards Rome.

There is a sharp *contrast* between Paul's behaviour before the council, and his Master's. The best of men can only react to the high priest's unjust assault with a flash of righteous anger and a subsequent apology, vv. 2–5, whereas the Son of God maintained a dignified silence under greater provocation, Matt. 26. 57–68. In His divine meekness the moral perfection of the Lord Jesus is displayed to the uttermost, Isa. 53. 7. May we strive to follow His example.

At the same time Paul firmly proclaims the *centrality* of the resurrection, v. 6. His testimony has consistently been to a crucified, risen and glorified Lord without whom there can be no salvation, 1 Cor. 15. 17. More than ever this truth needs emphasis in the face of modern unbelief.

After the riot we can imagine that Paul would be tired, disappointed and lonely. His message has been spurned by his own people and there is no evident fruit for his work. But the Lord alone knows His servant's sorrows. He therefore supplies *comfort* with His presence, His praise, and His promise, v. 11. Whatever we may think about the apostle's activities in Jerusalem, his Master offers only commendation and encouragement. It is good to know that the omniscient God appreciates fully all that His people seek to do for Him, however weak and imperfect it may be. And His promise of service in Rome is timely for it dispels any anxiety Paul may feel on hearing of the Jewish plot, vv. 12–17. Do *we* enjoy the nearness of this compassionate God?

May 30th

READING : **Acts 24. 1-27**

PAUL BEFORE FELIX

PAUL'S PRELIMINARY hearing before the governor of Judaea is remarkably similar to the trial of the Lord Jesus. An innocent man stands before a corrupt judge, vv. 26–27, accused by false witnesses, vv. 9, 12–13. Did Paul realize that he was treading the Saviour's pathway in enduring such a travesty of justice? How comforting to know that the Lord in heaven sympathizes with His people in that He has suffered the same, 1 Pet. 4. 12–16. As judge and prisoner face each other, let us highlight their contrasting hopes, consciences, and knowledge.

Paul's sure hope is in the fact of resurrection, v. 15, an Old Testament truth that is ratified in the New; Felix places his hope in temporal riches, v. 26. What a difference between heavenly aspiration and earthly lust! The Lord Jesus taught that our heart is where our treasure is, Matt. 6. 19–21. Thus the man with a home in glory can enjoy divine peace even in the midst of adversity. May our lives be encouraged by the "blessed hope" of the Saviour's soon return to take us, not *from* our riches, but *to* them, Titus 2. 13.

While the apostle's conscience is "void of offence", v. 16, the governor's is troubled beyond measure, vv. 24–25. Normally we expect a prisoner to tremble before a judge, but here is exactly the reverse! Divine truth which consoles the believer also convicts the sinner. Paul preaches of righteousness, self-control, and judgment; Felix, so lacking in the first two, is bound to fear the third. But the Christian can hear of these things with joy, because there is "no condemnation to them which are in Christ Jesus", Rom. 8. 1. Judgment is past for the Saviour has died.

The final contrast is between Felix's merely intellectual acquaintance with Christianity, v. 22, and Paul's personal experience of the Living Way, John 14. 6. A true knowledge of the Lord Jesus will grip the heart and mould the life, for our God demands reality. Paul's genuine love for the Saviour results in Scriptural worship, Acts 24. 14, and a daily walk sustained by his future hope, vv. 15–16. Let each believer make sure he is worshipping according to the Word, and living in the light of the coming glory.

May 31st

READING : **Acts 25. 1-27**

PAUL BEFORE FESTUS

PAUL'S TWO years of imprisonment at Caesarea, and the failure of both Felix and Festus to deal justly with him, serve to prove two things: the unchanging sinfulness of man and the unwavering faith of the apostle.

Hatred for the gospel that Paul preached has not abated in the least; men are still murderous and deceitful, v. 3, untruthful, v. 7, corrupt, v. 9, and inordinately proud, v. 23. Nor is man any better today, despite the wishful thinking of evolutionary philosophy. Education and culture may put a cosmetic on the cancer of sin, but they cannot heal it. Never let us forget that *all* men and women desperately need the Saviour of the world, and that God has appointed believers as the means of reaching them.

By contrast, Paul, always so much more upright and fearless than his judges, displays neither bitterness nor cynicism, vv. 8–12. What was his secret? Surely he was learning to enjoy that inner peace which depends not on earthly circumstances but on the unerring purposes of a loving God, Phil. 4. 11–13. Over two years earlier, the Lord graciously revealed part of His plan for Paul, Acts 23. 11, and, even though nothing seemed to have happened in the meantime, Paul has not lost his confidence in God's Word. The lesson is clear: "never doubt in the darkness what God has shown you in the light". The very fact that we are alive is evidence that God has a work for us to do; like Paul, then, let us cling patiently to the divine promises of God's Word, knowing that He can never fail.

Because of his confidence in God, Paul has no fear of death, v. 11. Whatever else the Christian may or may not know, this much is sure: when he leaves his earthly body he goes immediately and consciously to be with the Lord Jesus Christ, Phil. 1. 23; 2 Cor. 5. 8. No wonder we need not be afraid! Even Festus understands that the basic gospel message centres on the death and resurrection of the Lord Jesus, v. 19. A risen and glorified Christ means that, for the believer, death has been for ever defeated. Whether we be alive or asleep when the Lord returns, we shall go to be for ever with Him. And *that* compensates for everything, Rom. 8. 18.

June 1st

READING : **Acts 26. 1-32**

A CHALLENGE TO A KING

OUR GOD never makes mistakes. From the human viewpoint, Paul's return to Jerusalem has been a disaster; his missionary work has ceased, the Jews have rejected him, and he seems at the end of his career. Yet God has enabled him to preach before audiences ranging from a mob to a monarch, each time exalting the Lord Jesus Christ. This final testimony is a magnificent assertion of Christian truth revealing the character of God in salvation.

Verses 16 to 19 form the heart of Paul's talk: his special apostolic commission on the Damascus Road. We note the *plan* of God, in that he was delivered (or, better, taken out) "from the people, and from the Gentiles", v. 17. Salvation places the believer in that company wherein is neither Jew nor Gentile, for all are one in Christ Jesus, Gal. 3. 28. How much do we appreciate the divine plan for God's masterpiece, the Church? Salvation also means the granting of spiritual sight, v. 18. Here is the *grace* of God at work. All Paul's religious observance, however sincere, was done in utter blindness, and thus he would have continued had not God opened his eyes. Let us be thankful that free grace has opened our understanding to the gospel.

Then comes the *holiness* of the God who turns people "from darkness to light", v. 18. The dazzling light that struck Paul confronted him with One who demands a radical change of life from believers, vv. 12–14. Are we seeking to walk in the light, 1 John 1. 5–7? God's *power* is manifest in deliverance from Satan's bondage, Acts 26. 18, and, rescued from such slavery, we can be confident that our Deliverer will keep us safe for eternity. The *love* of God is seen in "forgiveness of sins", v. 18, specially cherished by one who had so grievously assaulted the Lord's people, vv. 9–11. Last comes the divine *purpose*: the inheritance awaiting the saints, v. 18, With Paul, let us look for the climax of our salvation in the return of the Lord Jesus.

Festus dismisses this grand teaching as madness, v. 24, and Agrippa conceals his embarrassment with a jest, v. 28. Paul alone exemplifies the correct response of simple obedience, v. 19. May we model ourselves on him.

June 2nd

READING : **Acts 27. 1-44**

THE VOYAGE TO ROME

ONE THING stands out in this exciting story: God is able to protect His own! His invisible hand is ever guiding and guarding those who belong to Him, for nothing befalls them without His permission. Luke's technically superb account of the voyage is more than just a graphic description of storms and shipwreck; it highlights the providence of God in His preservation of Paul, vv. 24, 42-44. Furthermore, it illustrates the accuracy of Scripture (in its expert use of nautical jargon, vv. 27–32, 39–41), the kindness of God (in the deliverance of all on board the ship, vv. 24–26, 34, 37, 43–44), and the apostle's faith (in that he maintains his confidence in the Lord despite the threat of imminent death, vv. 20–26). What can we learn about Paul's faith?

It is a faith based on *revelation*, vv. 23–25. Paul does not simply accept God's existence; he believes a God who has spoken, v. 25. Real Christianity argues that the Almighty Creator has graciously revealed Himself to man through His written Word and through the Person of His Son, Heb. 1. 1–2. If we are resting in His Word, we too can confess Him as the One "whose I am, and whom I serve", Acts 27. 23.

It is a faith that issues in *rejoicing* even in the midst of the most adverse circumstances, vv. 22, 25, 36. Those redeemed by Christ have every reason for happiness because of the blessings which grace has bestowed upon them, Rom. 5. 11. Paul's joy, manifest in a calm assurance, spreads to his companions, Acts 27. 25, 35–36. May ours be just as infectious.

It is a faith that involves *responsibility*, vv. 21–26. Far from hiding his knowledge of God, Paul informs the entire ship. Indeed, verse 24 suggests that he has been praying for their safety. The gospel is not a treasure to be hoarded; it is a seed to be sown in faith and watered with prayer.

It is a faith that enjoys *recognition*, vv. 3, 31–32, 36, 43. There is something attractive and convincing about Paul's demeanour, for it is in the tempests of life that the Christian's faith shines most brightly. As a result, God gives him favour with the centurion, thus ensuring fellowship at Sidon, v. 3, and safety at Malta, vv. 42–43. Does *our* faith make people take notice?

June 3rd

READING : **Acts 28. 1-31**

THE END OF THE JOURNEY

PAUL'S ENTRY into Rome is not accompanied by pomp or ceremony; on the contrary, the apostle to the Gentiles arrives as a prisoner. Yet all the events of this final chapter of Acts are a striking testimony to the reliability of God's Word and the culmination of His purposes for Paul's life.

The miracles in Malta, vv. 1–10, fulfil the Saviour's pledge in Mark 16. 18, and serve as signs to draw attention to Paul's message. The arrival at Rome, vv. 11–16, vindicates His promise that Paul should witness there, 23. 11. Mixed Jewish reaction to the gospel proclamation, vv. 17–29, not only fulfils an earlier warning that the nation would refuse the truth, 22. 18, but also confirms Old Testament prophecies of judgment on an unresponsive Israel, Isa. 6. 9–10. Finally, the apostle's continual preaching, Acts 28. 30–31, is an evidence both of his love for souls and his zealous desire to obey the Lord's command in Matthew 28. 18–20. How very encouraging it is to see that God's Word is so unquestionably worthy of our trust and obedience!

As we saw yesterday, the Master delights to watch over His servants in their labours for Him. God's goodness is here displayed in the uncommon kindness of the Maltese people, v. 2, and the supernatural protection afforded Paul, vv. 3–6. Then there is the opportunity for fellowship with believers along the road to Rome, vv. 14–15. These Christians think nothing of walking some thirty or forty miles to meet a brother in Christ; it is no wonder Paul thanks God for the encouragement. Are we prepared to inconvenience ourselves to benefit other believers, and show appreciation for those who minister the Word to us? Let us rejoice in a God who has provided all the Christian companionship and help that we need by placing us in a local church of His people.

But Acts leaves us not just with an awareness of God's goodness; it shows how fully committed Paul is to the gospel. Always prepared to serve even in a lowly capacity, v. 3, Paul's great mission in life is to honour his Lord by teaching His Word, vv. 23, 30–31. As we finish this great book, let us make sure that its concluding verse is true of us. May *we* be found thus working when the Saviour returns.

June 5th

READING : **Romans 1. 18-32**

JUSTIFICATION IMPERATIVE

ALTHOUGH GOD offers to justify the ungodly (i.e. to account him righteous), sinful man is not by nature concerned about being right with God. He must therefore be aroused as to his desperate need and dire peril by the dread alternative—the wrath of God, v. 18. All mankind is involved, but Paul deals first with the case of the depraved pagan. Although this is an appalling picture of the heathen world as Paul saw it in his journeys, he shows that this was not peculiar to his day—he traces the long history of decline. Mankind once knew God but they did not glorify Him as God, v. 21. Instead of thanking God for His innumerable benefits they dishonoured Him, v. 23. The next step was to exchange the truth of God for a lie, v. 25 R.V.; cf. 2 Thess. 2. 10. From disliking the knowledge of God they became God-haters, Rom. 1. 30, and eventually defied Him, v. 32. Having refused to obey the truth they knew they held it down, v. 18 R.V., suppressed it and smothered the voice of conscience. Inevitably they had to reap the fruit of their own way, v. 27; Gal. 6. 7. Since they refused to be restrained God gave them up to their own devices, Rom. 1. 24, 26, 28.

But the description holds good in our own day, and not only in the dark places of the earth—we need only to look behind the scenes in the cities and sea-ports of lands long blessed with the light of the Gospel. In such a situation some seem to think they can serve the cause of Christ by attempting to accommodate Christian teaching to contemporary attitudes, and in this permissive society we are asked to accept the verdict of sociologists and trim the Scriptures to suit. Seeing that God loved even the world Paul described, we should cultivate a spirit of compassion but without compromising the truth, Jude 22–23. How important it is to cherish all we know of God, to make His glory our aim, and ever be thankful lest we start on the downward path which gets more slippery with every step. So deceitful are our own hearts that, apart from grace, we are capable of doing what others have done. If we think we stand we should take heed lest we fall, 1 Cor. 10. 12. Let us praise Him who is able to keep us from falling and to present us faultless before the presence of His glory with exceeding joy, Jude 24.

June 6th

READING : **Romans 2. 1-29**

JEWS NO BETTER THAN GENTILES

THE APOSTLE now anticipates the likely reaction of the cultured Gentile to his indictment of the pagan world: "This is all true enough of the depraved barbarian. He may need to be saved—but not me!". Since human nature does not change, the same attitude is common today. Cultured people can imagine themselves seated on the bench with the Judge, when in fact they stand in the dock with the accused and exposed to the same wrath, v. 5. Enlightenment should lead to self-judgment and not to condemnation of others, Matt. 7. 1; 1 Cor. 11. 31. Judgment is God's prerogative.

What was Paul's reply to such objectors? They certainly had greater blessings but they were not better in heart, v. 5, and God is concerned with the heart. He will judge the secrets of men. They will not escape the judgment of God, unless they respond to His goodness that leads them to repentance, v. 4.

Verses 9–11 prepare the way for Paul's more specific treatment of the case of the Jews, which he reaches in verse 17. His Jewish opponents would say, "We agree with you about the Gentiles, but we are a people apart, the objects of God's special favour". Highly privileged they certainly were, but this increased their responsibility. Some Jews would make their boast of knowing God's will, when their lives were no better for all their superior knowledge. In fact, Jews were sometimes worse than those they despised and presumed to judge, so these latter were better fitted to judge such Jews. The sad result was that the name of God was blasphemed among Gentiles because of the very people who had been called of God to be His witnesses to the nations, v. 24. How intensely distressing and frustrating this must have been to the apostle as he sought to evangelize the Gentiles. If we know more, then more is to be expected of us; yet if deeper knowledge is not producing Christ-likeness in our lives, we could be doing more harm than good. Let us allow the grace of God to humble us and so save us from the humiliation suffered by the patriarch, Abraham. When out of touch with God, he was shamed by the higher standards of the heathen monarch he misjudged—a sad blunder that he repeated even after hi name was changed to Abraham, Gen. 12. 18–20; 20. 9–11.

June 7th

READING : **Romans 3. 1-31**

THE PRINCIPLE OF JUSTIFICATION

THE FOREGOING arguments as to human guilt are now summed up in verse 9, "both Jews and Gentiles . . . all under sin", and in verse 19, "all the world . . . guilty before God". How then can a man be justified? Paul picks up the theme of 1. 16–17 in verse 21, "the righteousness of God without the law is manifested". This "righteousness" is imputed on the condition of faith, but not of works. Notice the constant emphasis on faith and belief in verses 22–31. Faith is not the procuring cause—it is the empty hand which accepts the gift offered in grace. And not only in grace, but freely, suggesting not simply the absence of price to the receiver, but the generous wholehearted attitude of God without any cause outside Himself. But it is not without infinite cost to God. He set forth Christ as the propitiation who, through the redemption effected by His own blood, enables God to be just (as He must be), and yet the justifier of the one who believes in Jesus. God is not acting simply in mercy, but in righteousness.

Note the conclusion in verse 28, "a man is justified by faith without the deeds of the law". The law is not invalidated, v. 31; its awesome function and authority are recognized, and Christ has acknowledged its majesty by paying the penalty of man's sin in His own death. Thus God was able righteously to remit the sins of Old Testament saints because the cross-work of Christ was all part of God's great plan of redemption not only before the law was given but before the foundation of the world, 1 Pet. 1. 19–20. Then God could act in the most absolute confidence that the debt would be paid.

Sadly some Christians do not enter into the joy which these saints of old found in their salvation, because they do not really understand their Father God. Subconsciously they harbour the idea that Christ by His sacrifice obliged an unwilling God to offer grudging remission, when in fact He embraces the sinner who comes in faith, as the returning prodigal was welcomed with joy and rejoicing, Luke 15. 24.

The elder brother, the self-righteous Jew, would reject this doctrine as novel and suspect. In v. 21 Paul prepared his readers for his fuller answer in the next chapter; it was "witnessed by the law and the prophets".

June 8th

READING : **Romans 4. 1-8**

THE PRECEDENTS FOR JUSTIFICATION BY FAITH

In 1. 17 and 3. 21 Paul anticipated the objection that his doctrine of justification by faith was an innovation; now he turns to two notable Old Testament examples.

Abraham, the illustrious founder of their chosen race, captivated the imagination of Jews whose breasts would swell with pride as they uttered such words as we find in John 8. 33. They would never dream of questioning whether he was in a right relationship with God. Well—what are we to learn from his experience?, Rom. 4. 1. Was he justified by works? As if to sweep aside all bickering, he makes the one appeal no serious Jew could ignore—"What saith the scripture?". "Abraham believed God, and it was counted unto him for righteousness." So it is written in Holy Scripture—may the Spirit of God write it on our hearts.

Next, the case of David is taken up—a figure almost as illustrious as Abraham. An obstinate Jewish objector might still plead that Abraham's walk before God must nevertheless have had something to do with his justification. What about David then? He had to confess to particularly outrageous adultery which he attempted to cover by murder by proxy, giving great occasion to the enemies of God to blaspheme, 2 Sam. 12. 14. Yet David could speak of the blessedness of the man to whom the Lord, instead of imputing sin, imputes righteousness. Could this have been on account of David's merit? Obviously not—it was without (apart from, R.V.) works.

Nevertheless it is well to bear in mind that, though the Lord's forgiveness was full and free, David found that sin was a costly thing. Psalm 32, from which Paul quotes, and Psalm 51 give an insight into the deep soul exercise through which David passed. Though he tasted the sweetness of forgiveness, his sin left a heritage of sorrow for himself and his family. Howbeit, in the exquisite wisdom and ineffable grace of our adorable God, this inspired record of His tender dealing with poor David has, down the generations since, saved from dark despair many guilt-burdened but penitent souls, enabling them thereafter to walk humbly with a pardoning God.

June 9th

READING : **Romans 4. 9-25**

THE FAITH OF ABRAHAM

PAUL, WHO understood self-righteous Jews so well (Luke 18. 11–12; Rom. 10. 3; Phil. 3. 4–7), knew they would make a further effort to resist his doctrine by stress on circumcision as though that in itself imparted some merit. His answer is that Abraham was justified by faith long before he was circumcised, and that by the same token justification by faith is available to Jew and Gentile alike. This again was a sore point with fiercely fanatical Jews, Acts 22. 21–22.

We now confine our thoughts to two truths vital to the understanding of the working out of God's purposes in Christ: (i) God "quickeneth the dead", and (ii) "calleth those things which be not as though they were", v. 17.

(i) Although Abraham had never known such a thing to happen, he believed that God could and would revitalize bodies which were as good as dead. However, true faith must have its proper foundation—the promise of God, vv. 19–20; 10. 17. The fulfilment of that promise developed his faith until eventually he could act in the confidence that God would restore to life a body he expected to see reduced as a burnt offering to ashes and scattered by the mountain breeze, Gen. 22. 2; Heb. 11. 19. God is the God of resurrection—of life out of death. The resurrection of Christ is the irrefutable proof that His sacrifice perfectly accomplished (among other purposes of God) our redemption, Rom. 4. 25. Everything stands or falls by this, 1 Cor. 15. 12–22. We exult afresh in this glorious truth—Christ is risen, and all the purposes of God will work out on that basis. We do not see this yet, but "we see Jesus . . . crowned with glory and honour", Heb. 2. 9, and all else will follow.

(ii) God calls those things which are not as though they were. When God pronounces any purpose of His, that thing is virtually done. When God expressed what was in His mind, creation sprang into being. "The worlds were framed by the (spoken—*rhēma*) word of God", Heb. 11. 3. Thus God speaks of the believer as already glorified, Rom. 8. 30, even though we wait for the redemption of our body, 8. 23. How closely do we walk in the steps of the man who believed that when God spoke the word it was as good as done?, 4. 12.

June 10th

READING : **Romans 5. 1-11**

THE STANDING OF THE JUSTIFIED

THE DOCTRINE of Justification by Faith now gives place to its wonderful implications for believers so justified. True peace must rest on righteousness, Psa. 85. 10; Isa. 32. 17; Rom. 14. 17; Heb. 7. 2; but divine righteousness having been satisfied we can enter into the enjoyment of peace with God, Rom. 5. 1. Contrary to popular theology, the believer's security and peace rest not so much on God's marvellous mercy as on His inflexible righteousness.

Not until now has the love of God been mentioned, v. 5. Hitherto the predominant themes have been righteousness, judgment and wrath. Has undue emphasis on the love of God in modern preaching encouraged apathy in the unsaved? It was not mentioned in apostolic gospel preaching, but it should be experienced by the believer into whose heart it is poured by the Holy Spirit, v. 5. Nevertheless the ultimate proof of the love of God lies not in subjective experience but in objective *fact*. God commends (demonstrates beyond question) His love for us in that even when we were ungodly, sinners and enemies, Christ died for us, v. 8; cf. Eph. 2. 4–5.

Three reasons for rejoicing are mentioned. (i) *The hope of the glory of God*, v. 2. As to ourselves the glory is the promised conformity to the image of His Son, 8. 29; John 17. 22, but surely we look beyond our own blessedness to God's pleasure in the fulfilment of His purposes in us, Eph. 1. 6. (ii) *Tribulation!*, Rom. 5. 3. We should note that James 1. 2 encourages the same reaction to trials and gives substantially the same reason —that trials are designed to develop character. It helps to explain much in life if we see that this is God's great object. What we are, and are becoming, is more important to God than what we are doing, however good in itself, 1 Thess. 1. 6; 1 Pet. 1. 7. (iii) *God Himself*, Rom. 5. 11. We rejoice in what God has done, but the whole wondrous scheme of redemption so beautifully illuminates the character of God that we rejoice in what He is. The Psalms overflow with causes for joy and gladness, but the ultimate for the Psalmist, as for us, is "God my exceeding joy", Psa. 43. 4. But as with peace, so with our joy, all is "through our Lord Jesus Christ", Rom. 5. 1, 11.

June 11th

READING : **Romans 5. 12-21**

THE FIRST ADAM AND THE LAST ADAM

SINS WHICH destroy society and expose mankind to the wrath of God are now traced to the root of sin in our fallen nature. Our pedigree goes back in a long but direct line to the first Adam, so that our natural life is virtually the perpetuation of his life. Just as Levi was "in the loins" of his great-grandfather and could be regarded as implicated in the latter's action, Heb. 7. 9–10, so we were in the loins of Adam. In this sense his sin implicated the whole of his posterity so that all sinned in him, Rom. 5. 12 R.V. Moreover his sin-corrupted nature has been transmitted so that succeeding generations pay the penalty in universal death, vv. 12, 17. As the fountain head of the human race he is a figure of the Last Adam, but there the similarity ends. All else is by way of contrast—hence the repeated "not" in verses 15–16.

Adam's one and crucial act of disobedience (leading to a life of sin) rendered his posterity sinners (the many in contrast to the one). In the reverse order, Christ's life of perfect obedience led up to the one supreme act of obedience to His Father in voluntary acceptance of such a death as the death of the cross by which the many (in contrast to the One) were constituted righteous, vv. 18–19 R.V. In virtue of this culminating act of righteousness, He became in resurrection the head of a new humanity—all who are united to Him derive their new eternal life from Him. Death reigned through the first Adam's one act of unrighteousness—abounding grace now reigns through the Last Adam's one supreme act of righteousness, and they who receive this abundance of grace shall reign in life instead of being under the tyranny of death. Indeed death is now among the "all things" which are ours, 1 Cor. 3. 22; it becomes our servant to usher us into the immediate presence of the Lord, Phil. 1. 21.

Careful, as always, to attribute glory to his Lord, Paul stresses again and again that all this comes through Him. The phrase "through Jesus Christ our Lord", though constantly repeated in his writings, never became a mere formality. Our hearts may well bow in worship when we take the phrase upon our lips.

June 12th

READING: **Romans 6. 1–6**

THE BELIEVER'S RELATION TO SIN (1)

THIS CHAPTER deals with the justified sinner's relation to sin, not by a sustained line of argument but by a series of illustrations, somewhat intertwined because no analogy from human life can adequately set forth spiritual realities.

(1) *Baptism.* We are by nature identified with Adam, and under penalty of death. God in grace identifies us with Christ. When Christ died God reckoned us dead with Him. When Christ was buried God saw us as buried with Him. The "old man" is finished with, as far as God is concerned. But here the miracle of resurrection introduces a completely new situation, 5. 17. When Christ was raised, God saw us raised with Him in a new life. (Trace the word "with" in Col. 2. 12 to 3. 4). The believer who intelligently submits to the ordinance of baptism thereby signifies his acceptance of the situation from God's standpoint. Since a dead man responds no more to his old surroundings, the believer ideally makes no response to the solicitations of sin. Instead, being alive to God, he responds to the will of God, and walks in newness of life. Paul (as Saul) was exhorted to be baptized, to "wash away thy sins", Acts 22. 16, a phrase that must be interpreted in the light of our remarks.

(2) *Crucifixion.* Within this section a different aspect of death is inserted, to bring out a point not illustrated by baptism. Christ was crucified, and in God's reckoning we were crucified with him. Death by crucifixion is normally a long drawn-out process. Pilate was amazed that Christ had died so quickly, Mark 15. 44. Yet, though a felon's life could linger on for days, the body in which he had carried out his crime was "destroyed"; crucifixion rendered it ineffective. He could do nothing. His heart could be unchanged, but his activities were over. It is said, however, that accomplices, whose tool a crucified man had been, have been known to take him down from the cross and revive him so as to resume his old ways in their service. We are to regard our old nature, which cannot be reformed, as crucified with Christ. Just as the "old man" from one standpoint should be left in the grave, so from this other standpoint he should be kept on the cross despite efforts sin will make to reclaim him as its servant, its slave.

June 13th

READING: **Romans 6. 7–23**

THE BELIEVER'S RELATION TO SIN (2)

OTHER ASPECTS of the believer's relation to sin are now illustrated:

(3) *Warfare*, v. 13. The word translated "instruments" means "weapons" and is so translated in John 18. 3; 2 Cor. 10. 4. The members of our bodies (and the tongue is a member! James 3. 5) can be wielded by sin in warfare against God. On the other hand they can be yielded to God in war against evil. The Egyptian, abandoned by his wicked Amalekite master and left to die when no longer of use to him, was forgiven by the noble David whom he had wronged, and then enlisted in a better service enabling him to undo some of the evil he had done, 1 Sam. 30. 11–15.

(4) *Slavery*, vv. 14–16. The word "servants" should be "slaves". Slavery involves being at the absolute disposal of another. We became slaves of sin by our voluntary abdication. But we have been purchased by God, as it were, out of the slave market. Though now His rightful property, we are free to choose the happy slavery to righteousness. But sin, impudent in defiance of the change of ownership, will attempt to re-assert itself, but we can defy its claim to dominion, v. 14.

(5) *A mould*, v. 17. The truth is here likened to a form or mould. The response of our hearts is like being poured into this mould which then shapes our minds and wills into conformity with the will of God.

(6) *Profit and loss*, vv. 21–23. What fruit, i.e. profit, did we gain from our slavery to sin? Ironically it is said that we get our wages, in other words, what we have earned. The pay is death to all that is finest in life now, and eternal ruin hereafter. Where then is the sense of taking up this slavery again? We have been freed from sin to take up voluntary and devoted slavery to God. As there is no merit in this, we do not receive wages, but our gracious God gives us the undeserved bounty of eternal life to be enjoyed now whilst awaiting its fulness hereafter.

Once again Paul employs his favourite phrase "through Jesus Christ our Lord" to safeguard against the danger of forgetting that all this, and a great deal more, reaches us from the heart of God by this one and only channel.

June 14th

READING : **Romans 7. 1-25**

THE STRUGGLE OF THE JUSTIFIED

THE FIRST six verses continue the theme of chapter 6 with a further illustration of the believer's deliverance from the authority of the law and the power of sin. Our obligation to the stern and unyielding law is likened to the irksome bondage of a loveless and barren marriage which being dissolved by death, allows of a new union. No illustration from human life can fully portray the wonders of God's ways, and this analogy breaks down because the law does not die. In our case the claims of the law are dissolved by our death with Christ and our new life in union with Him.

The remainder of the chapter is a penetrating analysis of the inner struggle of one strongly attracted by the vision of a new life after God's mind; constantly frustrated by the irresistible downward pull of the old nature, yet he is determined to achieve victory in his own strength. Notice the constant recurrence of "I", "me" and "my", and the equally remarkable omission of any reference to the Holy Spirit or of Christ—indeed the absence of any relevant mention of God—until verse 24 where the struggler is forced to admit wretched defeat, realizing at last that deliverance can come only from God through our Lord Jesus Christ. The next chapter enlarges on this theme.

The struggle had at least this merit—it taught the struggler (and surely it was Paul himself) that in him, in his flesh, dwelt no good thing. Paul's intensity meant that he learned the lesson quickly. Most of us learn it very slowly—some never. Healthy self-examination is good, but morbid introspection often conceals pride that still hopes to find some good in ourselves. It is one of the many paradoxes of the Christian life that victory begins when defeat is accepted. The greater the desire the more frustrating the futility of self-effort. Only the indifferent escape the struggle.

They who fain would serve Thee best
Are conscious most of wrong within.

Since Christ says "My strength is made perfect in weakness", we can say "When I am weak, then am I strong", 2 Cor. 12. 9–10.

June 15th

READING : **Romans 8. 1-17**

THE VICTORY OF THE JUSTIFIED

PAUL USES the word "law" not only for the law of God but also in the sense of a principle, or a uniform mode of operation. His new nature delighted in the law of God, but he saw a contrary law (principle) operating in his members in such a way that, when he would do good, evil was present with him, 7. 21-23.

Chapter 8 turns defeat into victory. "O wretched man that I am!" is changed into "We are more than conquerors", 7. 24; 8. 37. "I", "me" and "my" almost disappear along with the self-occupation they indicated, and now God the Father, the Lord Jesus Christ (little noticed in Chapter 7) and the Holy Spirit (not noticed at all) become the dominant theme. The anguished question, "who shall deliver me?", is replaced with ". . . free from the law of sin and death", 7. 24; 8. 2. But how? Paul could not resist anticipating the solution in 7. 25 on which he now elaborates.

He has discovered yet another law—the law (principle) of the Spirit—that is, the basis on which the Holy Spirit operates in the believer. That basis is "life in Christ Jesus", and by it he is freed from the gravitational pull of sin.

The indwelling of the Holy Spirit is equivalent to the indwelling of Christ, vv. 9-10. Some one has said that no one but Christ can live the Christian life, but that He is willing to live it in and through the believer, Gal. 2. 20; 2 Cor. 4. 10-11; Phil. 4. 13.

In the reckoning of God, the old man has been crucified with Christ. The power of an ungrieved Spirit can enable a yielded believer to put this into effect by mortifying (putting to death as in crucifixion) the deeds of the body; cf. 6. 6 with Gal. 5. 24. What that yielding involves is explained—walking after the Spirit, minding the things of the Spirit, and being led by the Spirit. The soul's bondage from fear of the law gives place to the gracious influence of the Spirit of adoption. He makes real to us the fact that we are the children of God, and prompts the glad response of grateful hearts spell-bound with the tremendous privilege of breathing out "Abba, Father" to the One who has stooped to ask the love of our poor hearts.

June 16th

READING : **Romans 8. 18-39**

ALL THINGS WORK TOGETHER FOR GOOD

IF WE are the children of an almighty and loving heavenly Father, may we expect a smooth and comfortable passage on our way to our eternal home? Scripture gives ample warning that such false expectations will be disappointed. We are not exempt from the ills and frustrations common to mankind in a world marred by sin, vv. 22–33. Indeed, loyalty to Christ may well involve us in privations above the normal lot of man, to say nothing of persecution, v. 35.

True we have the Spirit of adoption, but His gracious operations in us are not aimed at removing difficulties, but enabling us to surmount them in the spirit of sonship. These are, however, only the firstfruits of the Spirit—we shall not enter into all that adoption means until our bodies are redeemed at the coming of Christ. We are assured that all things work together for good, v. 28, but "good" in God's eyes does not mean material prosperity and comfort but development of character. Even so, life poses many insoluble problems, and faith is often perplexed, 2 Cor. 4. 8. "What shall we then say to these things?", Rom. 8. 31. No detailed answers are provided, but if we ask "Is God for us?" ample evidence is offered. He purposed our blessing before the world began, v. 29, and when in due time the implementation of that purpose required the sacrifice of His own Son, He delivered Him up for us all.

He spared not His Son!
'Tis this that silences each rising fear,
'Tis this that bids the hard thought disappear,
He spared not His Son.

We now have the help and intercession of the Holy Spirit within, the intercession of the Risen Christ on high, and the certainty of future glory. Well—if God be for us, who can be effectively against us? In effect the answer of verses 38–39 is "Nothing and no one". Persecutors may oppress us, principalities may scheme against us, but nothing shall separate us from the love of God which is in Christ Jesus our Lord. In all these things we are more than conquerors through Him who loved us.

Survey of Romans 9–11

THESE CHAPTERS are sometimes regarded almost as a digression, that Paul's ever-present burden for Israel, 9. 1–5, had suddenly swept him into a somewhat irrelevant discussion of the mystery of Israel's fall, resuming at 12. 1 the theme he had dropped at the end of chapter 8. On this view the "mercies of God", on which he bases his appeal for complete surrender, refer to the assurance of 8. 38–39 that nothing shall separate the believer from the love of God.

But it is this very subject of the love of God which led Paul to take up the case of Israel. Sensitive as always to the possible reactions to his teaching, he realized that God's action in setting aside a nation for whom He had declared His love, Deut. 7. 7–8; Mal. 1. 2, might seem to conflict with this assurance. It is difficult for twentieth century Christians to realize how grave a problem this was.

The following brief meditations can do no more than touch on Paul's treatment of the problem, but it will help if we first look at his summing up in 11. 25–36. Israel's blindness will be removed when God's present purpose for the Gentiles has been fulfilled. God has not forgotten His covenant, and Israel is still beloved. If their unbelief has opened the door of mercy to Gentiles so, in turn, will Israel find mercy. It is true that God included Jew and Gentile alike in condemnation, but this was in order that He might have mercy on both. The theme of mercy has already been stressed, 9. 15–16, 18, 23, but Paul evidently wishes to impress it upon his readers, and he returns to it later in 15. 8–9.

It is clear therefore that 12. 1 is not taking up a theme dropped at the end of chapter 8, but flows naturally on from the end of chapter 11.

Paul's exploration of the profound issues involved in God's master plan spanning the ages causes him to wonder afresh at the depth of the wisdom and knowledge of God. God will yet be vindicated in the eyes of the universe in all His ways. He is the source of all, He is the effective cause of all and all will glorify Him. We may rest there even when His ways are to us, at present, "past finding out".

June 17th

READING: **Romans 9. 1–33**

THE ELECT OF ISRAEL

IF ANY of Paul's readers were tempted to think that the bitter persecution by his fellow Jews had embittered him and alienated his sympathies, then his affecting assurances should have sufficed to dispel such false impressions. His love for his kinsmen according to the flesh was unabated, and his confidence in the promised future for the true Israel unshaken.

We can now touch on only two of the problems raised.

(1) *Israel.* Although it was God's purpose that the nation should be a kingdom of priests and a holy nation, Exod. 19. 6, the people as a whole failed. The true Israel was the believing element in the nation. In the present age, believing Jews are incorporated in the Church on equal terms with believing Gentiles—they are a remnant according to the election of grace, Rom. 11. 5. But God's promises to the true Israel stand. In a future day among the regathered Jews there will be a mighty sifting by the Spirit of God, and from it will emerge a literal but spiritual nation in whom these promises will be fulfilled, 9. 27; 11. 26; Zech. 13. 9.

(2) *Election.* All attempts to explain this problem to the satisfaction of mere human intellect are futile. The true Israel has been chosen by God. His sovereignty in election is boldly and unequivocally asserted, and any questioning of His absolute right to make His own choice is dismissed as daring impertinence. Nevertheless, the parallel truth of human opportunity and responsibility is safeguarded in verses 22 and 32, and more fully later in 10. 13, 16, 21; 11. 14. The vessels of wrath were fitted to destruction, but it is not said that God fitted them. The use of the Greek middle voice suggests that they fitted themselves. Pharaoh is an example—he hardened his heart repeatedly before God finally hardened his heart; see 2 Thess. 2. 11–12. The solemnity of this enhances the wonder of God preparing the vessels of mercy unto glory.

Although we cannot now see how these two lines of truth are reconciled, we must hold both in balance, 1 Tim. 2. 4; 2 Tim. 1. 9. When modern astronomers have to accept that the physical universe is stranger than we can imagine, it should not surprise us if we must wait for the light of eternity to illuminate the perfection of all God's ways.

June 18th

READING: **Romans 10. 1–21**

SENT WITH THE GOOD TIDINGS

PAUL SEES in Israel's spiritual state a reflection of his own pre-conversion condition. Compare his references to zeal, ignorance and righteousness in verses 1–4 with Phil. 3. 5–6; 1 Tim. 1. 13. Human pride closed their minds to the implications of familiar Scriptures, and deluded them into thinking that the divine ideal could be attained by self-effort.

Bigoted zeal can go to terrible lengths. Paul was an example of the Lord's warning that some would think they were serving God in killing His disciples. He genuinely thought it was his duty to do many things contrary to the name of Jesus of Nazareth. The stoning of Stephen was not the only instance of implication in the death of believers, Acts 26. 9–10. What a shock it was to discover that this Jesus of Nazareth was indeed the exalted Messiah! Paul never ceased to wonder at the mercy of God shown to him because he had acted ignorantly in unbelief, 1 Tim. 1. 13. Encouraged by the grace of God to him, he could long and pray for Israel's salvation, Rom. 10. 1. He certainly held in proper balance the twin truths of election and human response.

In verses 8, 14, 15(a) the idea is that of being a herald—one who could proclaim his sovereign's will with a note of authority in the conviction of having been sent. Men who go unsent are often more of an embarrassment than a help to their fellow-workers, 2 Kings 4. 39. An extreme case is Jeremiah 14. 14. Isaiah, responding to the voice of the Lord "Whom shall I send" with "Here am I; send me", received his commission "Go". Yet he was told that his "good tidings" (i.e., gospel, Isa. 40. 9; 41. 27; 52. 7; 61. 1) would not receive general acceptance, and later he had to lament "Who hath believed our report?", 53. 1; Rom. 10. 16. On the other hand, he could speak of those being found of God who had not sought him, i.e. Gentiles, Isa. 65. 1; Rom. 10. 20.

Paul's experience was similar. He was very conscious of his divine call as an apostle (i.e. a sent one) of Jesus Christ with a definite commission, Acts 26. 15–18. On the whole, God's chosen "people", who might have been expected to respond, resisted the message, whereas multitudes of Gentiles responded gladly, 13. 46–48.

June 19th

READING: **Romans 11. 1-36**

FUTURE OF JEWISH AND GENTILE NATIONS

IN VIEW of verse 33, we must expect problems, but we only add to them unless we accept that God, as in O.T. times, is still concerned with nations, Acts 17. 26–27.

To many the chief problem is in verses 21–22 which they see as jeopardizing the security of the believer, but surely this would contradict the tenor of Scripture and Paul's main theme in this section—the faithfulness of God to His promises. Because of space limitation only a few brief comments can be offered.

At least two considerations would indicate that the believer is not in view:

(1) The fall of Israel is said to result in the riches of the world, the riches of the Gentiles and the reconciling of the world. These expressions can hardly be equated with what is said in Colossians 1. 21 and Ephesians 3. 8 about the reconciliation of believers and the unsearchable riches of Christ.

(2) Verses 12 and 15 clearly imply that the restoration of Israel will mean even greater blessings for the Gentiles, but it is difficult to see how this restoration will enhance the believer's portion in Christ—all spiritual blessings in heavenly places, Eph. 1. 3.

Is not Paul saying that the putting aside of Israel has brought Gentiles into the place of privilege and opportunity?, Acts 11. 18; 14. 27. If, like Israel, they do not respond, judgment will fall on them. We know that the response has been marginal, and that at the end of the age there will be rebellion against God and the guilty will be destroyed, 2 Thess. 2. 8–12; Rev. 19. 19–21. The residue will enter into kingdom blessings as saved nations, with restored Israel at the head, Matt. 25. 31–34; Rev. 21. 24–26.

This view is in accord with Acts 15. 13–18. God is now visiting the Gentiles and calling out a people for His name. After this (when the fulness of the Gentiles has come in, Rom. 11. 25) the ruins of Israel will be rebuilt. Then the remnant of men and all the Gentiles upon whom God's name is called (the survivors of God's judgment on the nations) will enter into blessing.

June 20th

READING: **Romans 12. 1–2**

PRESENT YOUR BODIES A LIVING SACRIFICE

"PRESENT" (YIELD) is an echo of 6. 13, 16, 19. Although a voluntary act, it is not a gift but simply a proper recognition of God's rights, 1 Cor. 6. 20. His purchase of us has given Him the title to us—our yielding gives Him possession. The tense signifies a crucial once-for-all decision (like a soldier's oath of allegiance), the future implications being accepted even if unforeseen. A sacrifice at the altar died and all was over, but ours is to be a living sacrifice perpetuated day by day. Sacrifices made grudgingly were an insult to God and quite unacceptable, Mal. 1. 8, but the godly offered with joy, Psa. 27. 6; 51. 17–19. Have we less cause than they for gratitude and joy?, Heb. 13. 15–16.

"Reasonable" indicates that our sacrifice is to be intelligent. There is nothing so senseless as sin, and nothing so wise as the will of God. The service is spiritual: "serve with my spirit", 1. 9; "divine service", Heb. 9. 1. Tabernacle services were attended by ornate ceremonial, and the religionist still loves ritual. Here is a beautiful "ritual" for us—the daily renewal of our original vow.

But if yielding is to be a crucial act, both the conformity against which we are warned and the transformation advocated are continuing processes. Though shunning the worldling's haunts, it is possible to be conforming to the world's spirit and its current trends. It is all superficial like dressing up for a fancy dress ball. But the transformation (namely, transfiguration, as in Matt. 17. 2; 2 Cor. 3. 18) is the outshining of inner reality. It is not enough to be unlike the world; this is something positive—being like Christ.

The renewing of the mind is also a constantly recurring process, the mind being re-invigorated and re-adjusted daily by prayer and meditation, Rom. 8. 6. Thus we shall be able to prove in happy experience that the will of God, from which the carnal mind recoils, is *good*, designed for the glory of God and our blessing, increasingly *acceptable* to us as experience grows, and *perfect* because it cannot be improved upon, nor its possibilities exhausted.

June 21st

READING: **Romans 12. 3–21**

THE BELIEVER'S CONDUCT

The believer's proper attitude to himself, v. 3, implies sober thinking which will avoid two extremes. Exaggerated ideas of our importance will deceive no one but ourselves; God will be dishonoured if we think ourselves useless when He has fitted us to be useful. Sober thinking recognizes limitations, and accepts thankfully any God-given ability to serve others. Compare "measure of faith" with Ephesians 3. 8; 4. 7.

The believer's proper attitude to fellow-believers, vv. 4–13. We are all members of the one body and each has a part to play in the well being of the whole, whilst willing to yield the place of honour to others. The figure of the human body to illustrate the relationship between Christ and His people opens up several avenues of thought. We select one. Every human being has the same *kind* of life, but each individual has his own separate life independent of all others. This one life permeates his whole body and activates every member. It is this, rather than the connection of the parts, which makes the body the wonderful unity it is. But in the case of believers as members of the body of Christ, it is not merely that we have the same *kind* of spiritual life—all share in one identical life, the life of Christ. The unity is invisible but none the less real. The bearing of this truth on our present passage is obvious.

The believer's proper attitude to persecutors, vv. 14–21. This same truth has its implications here. In fact it seems highly probable that the seed of this truth germinated in the mind of the persecuting Saul as he pondered the significance of the first words he ever heard from the lips of Christ—"why persecutest thou me?". The fact that blows struck at members of Christ's body on earth were struck at their exalted Head in heaven undoubtedly coloured a lot of Paul's subsequent thinking. The wonderful thing is that through His members still on earth the Lord Jesus can still take toward persecutors the attitude that He took when on earth, 1 Pet. 2. 20–23. Evil will be judged—but that is the prerogative of God which we dare not usurp. To meet evil with evil gives the devil the victory. To meet evil with good makes the sufferer the victor.

June 22nd

READING: **Romans 13. 1–14**

THE BELIEVER'S ATTITUDE TO OTHERS

The believer's proper attitude to authority. God is concerned with order, not only in the church, 1 Cor. 11. 34; 14. 40; 16. 1; Col. 2. 5, but also in society, Titus 3. 1; 1 Pet. 2. 13–17; the Christian has responsibilities in both spheres. In 1 Timothy 2. 1–3, where God's desire for quiet and peace is indicated, the importance of prayer is stressed. In this connection it is well to remember that Abraham praying on the mountain had greater influence on the affairs of Sodom than had Lot in the city. Our passage stresses the duty of submission to lawful authority, which in this case meant the tyrant Nero and his officers.

Retribution is God's prerogative, so the Christian in his personal capacity should give place to wrath, but God has delegated authority to appointed rulers who are commissioned to administer justice in the interests of public order. Because rulers are appointed by God, it does not necessarily follow that they rule in accord with God's mind, but even so, rule is preferable to anarchy. When rulers from self-will (and in some cases activated by Satan) exceed their implied mandate, God overrules their misrule for His own purposes, in due course chastening the offenders. It is true that we have to go to the Old Testament with its long historical perspective for specific examples of this principle, particularly where the fortunes of Israel are involved, but it is not difficult to see the wheels of God grinding in modern history.

The believer's proper attitude to neighbours. Advocates of the permissive society have seized upon the expression "love is the fulfilling of the law", and perverted it to justify the idea that the only criterion conduct has to satisfy is its sentimental or emotional value. Love is the fulfilling of the law because love makes the true good of others its unselfish aim. In this connection it seems remarkable that in verse 9 the order of the commandments in Exodus 20. 13–14 is reversed, so as to put adultery first in the list of things inconsistent with love for one's neighbour. Our modern situation is the same as that of first-century Christians, who lived in a society which ridiculed their standards as out of date!

June 23rd

READING: **Romans 14. 1–23**

STRONG AND WEAK BELIEVERS

The believer's proper attitude to the over-scrupulous. Some believing it wrong to eat flesh ate only vegetables. Others felt it obligatory to attach special sanctity to certain days. They were "weak in the faith", not having that robust enjoyment of their new life in Christ which would have delivered them from the false notion that slavish observance of rules and regulations was pleasing to the Lord. The "strong", however, with a firm grasp of their liberty in Christ, would not be hampered with needless restrictions. Human nature being what it is, the weak brother was apt to judge the other for being, as he thought, unspiritual, whereas the strong was inclined to despise what he regarded as childish scruples. Here were the ingredients of disharmony so destructive of true fellowship and effective witness. But this could be avoided if each were willing to recognize sincerity in his fellow. If the weak brother had a genuine conscience in the matter, it was wrong to go against his conscience even if mistaken. The strong must therefore respect this. On the other hand the scrupulous must resist the temptation to suppose himself more spiritual and condemn what he may regard as laxity.

Times change, but these problems continue to crop up in other forms. Some Christians seem to be cast in a mould which inclines them to regulate their lives and service by certain rigid rules, quite convinced they are on scriptural ground. Of course, we must bow to the authority of Scripture, at the same time guarding against putting our ideas *into* Scripture instead of getting our ideas *from* it. Other Christians are able to serve the Lord in a free and happy spirit, depending on Him for guidance and discernment in applying the changeless principles of God's Word in the ever changing circumstances, instead of taking what is in some respects the simpler and easier path. But they have other responsibilities. If they can with understanding and grace help the weak to a better appreciation of liberty in Christ, so much the better, but they must be ready to sacrifice some of their personal liberty, rather than risk wounding sensitive consciences and endangering their spiritual welfare. This would be sin against Christ, 1 Cor. 8. 12.

June 24th

READING: **Romans 15. 1–33**

PAUL AND ROME

THE FOREGOING plea for unselfish concern for the good of others is now reinforced by the example of Christ who pleased not Himself. The unity of the Spirit should be maintained in a practical way, but this can never be achieved by mere organization—it calls for like-mindedness.

To fortify his implied appeal for this unity between Jew and Gentile believers, Paul soars almost to sublimity in a fresh if condensed review of the grand sweep of God's plan for the blessing of both. He glories in his vast privileges in being chosen as a minister of Jesus Christ to preach among the Gentiles His unsearchable riches; cf. vv. 15–16 with Eph. 3. 8. From this lofty theme he smoothly and gracefully descends to an outline of his intended itineraries. Was there ever a man with a greater capacity for resolutely setting his mind on things above whilst keeping his feet firmly on the earth!, Col. 3. 2. For the sanctified imagination there is here a wonderful insight into the exercises of the great servant of Christ. We venture to think that he dearly wished to reach the uttermost part of the Roman empire, Acts 1. 8. Clearly he had for some years cherished the idea of visiting Spain. We do not know whether he was ever allowed to carry out his plan. Maybe, even an apostle had to suffer personal disappointments. He likewise had a great desire to preach the gospel in the Imperial City and had long prayed for a prosperous journey there, Rom. 1. 10. It is unlikely that he imagined that this prayer would be answered by his arriving at Rome as a prisoner after a disastrous sea voyage. Quite possibly he thought it a prosperous journey in spiritual terms, Acts 28. 31; Phil 1. 12–13. For the present his plans had to yield to the necessity of conveying the bounty of Gentile churches to the saints at Jerusalem at considerable risk, Rom. 15. 31. A mighty apostle, highly privileged, utterly devoted to Christ, an eminently successful missionary, an outstanding pastor, an agent of the Holy Spirit in inspired Epistles, but charmingly natural and unaffected. How real it makes him to us. And how small it makes us feel!

But looming behind the apostle is his Master. "Be ye followers of me, even as I also am of Christ", 1 Cor. 11. 1.

June 25th

READING: **Romans 16. 1–27**

GREETINGS, DIVISIONS, WORSHIP

A LONG list of personal greetings brings into sharp focus what is implicit in other letters of Paul—his amazing capacity for keeping people, not merely in his memory, but also in his heart, Phil. 1. 7–8. A study of the many names would prompt helpful reflections, but we cannot now do more than point out how effectively the charge of prejudice against women is refuted by the kindly mention of something like a dozen sisters most of whom come in for some special commendation; cf. Phil. 4. 3.

Little did these folk dream that their names would have an honourable place in Holy Scripture and in the regard of succeeding generations. Let us reflect that there is another record being kept on high in which all our names appear. If we could choose for ourselves one of the many commendations in this delightful list, which would it be?

The apostle had also to speak of those who were liable to cause divisions and offences. A man who could be as gentle as a nursing mother, 1 Thess. 2. 7, could wax indignant when such things prejudiced the cause of Christ and the welfare of the saints. Division-makers can be so adroit with gullible people that those who have always sought to maintain unity and harmony are made to appear as the cause of the trouble! Absalom in his rebellion made David look like the culprit. Some who knew the facts were disloyal, but others were taken in and followed Absalom in their simplicity, 2 Sam. 15. 11–12; 17. 1. So it has often been, Col. 2. 4; Titus 1. 10. Nevertheless Paul was glad to commend the saints as a whole for their well-known obedience to the truth, Rom. 16. 19.

His experience was a mixture of joy and sorrow and, not being super-human, he even felt depressed and disheartened at times, 2 Cor. 1. 8; 2. 13; 4. 8; 1 Thess. 3. 5. Yet as he closes this noble Epistle, his worshipping spirit soars as he glorifies the eternal God for the invincible progress of His purposes, which like a resistless incoming tide advance, steadily wave by wave whatever the conditions; cf. Eph. 1. 10; 1 Tim. 6. 15. "To God only wise, be glory through Jesus Christ for ever. Amen."

Introducing 1 Corinthians

THIS EPISTLE to the Corinthians forms part of Paul's first cycle of letters commonly referred to as his Missionary Epistles, comprising 1 and 2 Thessalonians, 1 and 2 Corinthians, Romans and Galatians. In these Paul deals mainly with basic doctrinal issues. In 1 Corinthians, he is writing to a church which he established some three years before during a stay of some eighteen months, Acts 18. 11.

Corinth had two outstanding features. It was a city known for its seeking "after wisdom". There was a phrase of the time "to speak as they do at Corinth", which implied their speech was with accuracy and artistic beauty. It was the centre of intellectualism. On the contrary it was noted for its extreme corruption. Lasciviousness so ruled its life that it was the New Testament Sodom. Hence to "Corinthianize" was a term used proverbially for an immoral life. Thus two extremes walked arm in arm. In such an atmosphere the church lived its life.

The Epistle was occasioned by two factors. Firstly, reports had reached Paul through the "household of Chloe", 1. 11, as to conditions prevailing in the assembly. These matters he proceeds to deal with in chapters 1–6. In addition, a letter had been sent him by the church posing certain queries, and these he continues to answer from chapter 7 onwards (note verse 1).

In approaching this letter, it must be borne in mind that whilst its substance is dealing with matters current in Corinth, its ministry has an intended wider sweep. Paul with one "Sosthenes our brother", whilst writing to the church of God in Corinth, also addresses "all that call upon the name of our Lord Jesus Christ *in every place*" R.V. Since this is so, then the message of this Epistle applies not only to every place but for all church times, and therefore is applicable to our day and age. We dare not say that any part of it is merely local and does not apply to us in principle today. Jesus Christ is Lord, not only of the Corinthian believers but of all His people in every place and throughout all time, v. 2; therefore His will is common to all. To such Paul sends greetings of grace and peace.

June 26th

READING : **1 Corinthians 1. 1-31**

THE RICHES AND RESPONSIBILITIES OF THE REDEEMED

PAUL COMMENCES his corrective letter with words of encouragement. How like his Lord he is, giving commendation before censure; cf. Rev. 2–3. He writes of four things.

The Believer's *Condition*, vv. 4-9. Here is a munificence for thanksgiving. Notice the cluster of good things: "in everything enriched"; "ye come behind in no gift"; "confirm you unto the end . . . blameless"; "called unto the fellowship of his Son". We observe these blessings to be bestowed by God's grace, v. 4, and guaranteed by His faithfulness, v. 9.

The Believer's *Concord*, vv. 10–16. Here is a matter for concern. Called into such a fellowship demands unity amongst the members. This unity must be expressed by act and attitude, v. 10. There must be an absence of partisanship, v. 12. Where such abounds it bespeaks a divided Christ and an over-exalted leader, vv. 13–16.

The Believer's *Communication*, vv. 17–25. Here is a message for emphasis. This message will only be effective where concord reigns. Paul's target was always to "preach the gospel". Is this ours? Its *Subject* was always the good news of Christ crucified—the word of the cross. Its *Style* was not by the intellectual use of worldly wisdom for such will nullify it, v. 17, and such is disapproved by God, vv. 19-20. Its *Substance* is the power of God to save and keep saving, v. 18.

The Believer's *Calling*, vv. 26–31. Here is a mercy for recollection. It is altogether unworldly. Note the call itself, "by the foolishness of preaching (or the thing preached)"; the called, "the foolish things of the world", v. 27; the entire accomplishment being the product of "the foolishness of God", v. 25. How contrary to the ways of men is this! Truly God's ways are not our ways. Our calling was never on the grounds of our greatness, v. 29, but solely on the grounds of divine grace. In salvation, as in all other things, God will ever be "all in all". Where the mercy of our call grips the heart, and our spiritual condition through Christ thrills the soul, then concord will be realized and the message preached.

Lesson. Let us *wonder* at our richness, *work* at our oneness, *witness* by our faithfulness and *worship* at His graciousness.

June 27th

READING : **1 Corinthians 2. 1-16**

A BLOW TO INTELLECTUALISM

GOD HAS graciously prepared manifold blessings for those who love Him. Human eye has never seen their like; human ear has never heard such rapturous news; the human heart has never conceived such unprecedented bounties, v. 9, yet God has made them known, v. 10. How are they made known, and how can such be known when so beyond the imagination and conception of man's mind?

For this communication, the wisdom of Corinth, however assiduously pursued, was totally inadequate. Paul, the great testimony-bearer of these things to Corinth, did not make his declaration to them with skill of speech or wisdom, v. 1. He refused the use of persuasive words of human understanding. Why? He knew the inadequacy of such as a means of communication. He knew God had utterly rejected it, 1. 19–20. If this was true where intellectualism reigned and where a skilled and learned apostle was present, how dare we revert to it today? It is still true that the world by wisdom knows neither God nor the things of God.

Then how are these things made known? Firstly, they are altogether bound up in the preaching and knowledge of Christ and Him crucified. Christ and His crosswork form the sole foundation of all God's blessings for man. To reject such is to be alienated from His gifts. Because of this Paul manifests concern about his ministry, 2. 3. This fearing and trembling (a Pauline expression) was not because of personal danger but an anxiety correctly to perform a holy duty. Secondly, the revelation of these things does require a wisdom, v. 6, yet not of this world which is impermanent, but a wisdom which is of God, v. 7, hidden from human intellect and eternally enduring, v. 8. Thirdly it is a communication only made possible by the Spirit of God. Only by Him is the divine revelation all-embracive, vv. 10b, 11, and consequently adequate. This all-knowing Spirit is God's gift to them that love Him.

Paul concludes that spiritual men cannot discern spiritual things by natural means, neither can the natural man understand the things of the Spirit by the employment of his own capacities. Having the Spirit, we have the mind of Christ.

Lesson. Ask for wisdom, James 1. 5, and attend to the Spirit.

June 28th

READING : **1 Corinthians 3. 1-23**

SPIRITUAL CAPACITY AND CONSTRUCTION

AFTER THREE years they were still infants needing milk. Their capacity was faulty; and they were found to be carnal by strife and division, so they were faulty in their construction.

As God's husbandry (tilled field) growth was expected, but this was not in evidence. It was stunted because of a party-spirit. The men they preferred were only instruments for planting and watering, whereas only God could give growth—He makes the seed to grow! The type of spiritual food assimilated determines the degree of growth, and party-spirit but manifests it. Let us lament the absence of spiritual appetite for the deep things of God, as often displayed these days, and the manifest lack of spiritual development which accompanies it. Let us pray for robust appetites for God's "strong meat" that, moving on from spiritual minorities, we may become men and women of God.

We are not only babes in a family being watched for growth, we are also builders in an assembly employed for industry. "Ye are God's building", v. 9, and are expected to build, v. 10b. Hence whether as husbandry or building growth is expected, one passive and one active. There is but one foundation, viz., Jesus Christ, Matt. 16. 16–18, already potentially laid, and at Corinth locally laid by Paul, who now instructs the builders. If as a believer God carefully watches my spiritual development, as a builder I must carefully watch my service development. Whatever be our capacity or place in the assembly, we are responsible for the building progress. Our materials must be carefully selected. Note the "*what* he builds", v. 10b R.V. Are our materials costly, demanding sacrifice and concentration and enduring (gold, silver, precious stones), or cheap and shoddy, reared with small effort and unenduring (wood, hay, stubble)? Am I building as the ancients, a temple worthy of God, or is my contribution like modern jerry building? The great Clerk of works will one day scrutinize it and test it by fire. A thousand pities: it will be for the builder to be saved as it were through the flames, seeing a life's work in ashes! We are a holy temple—mar it, and be marred!

Lesson. Live in the light of the judgment seat !

June 29th

READING : **1 Corinthians 4. 1-21**

APOSTOLIC AUTHORITY QUESTIONED

PAUL'S RIGHT to direct was still being questioned by many. He defends his divinely delegated authority in four ways.

He acquaints the church with what Apollos and he were. In 3. 5 he asks, *What* after all is Apollos? and *what* is Paul, (not so much "who"). They were servants (*under-rowers* is the word) of Christ, and thus they must render obedience. Also they were stewards and must consequently show faithfulness, 4. 1–2. As such, he says, men ought mindfully to regard them.

He instructs them as to the court to which they are solely answerable. Not the courts of men, however ecclesiastical; not even the court of his own conscience, for though clear it would be no criterion. He is answerable to his Lord. Judgment of others must, therefore, await the judgment seat. Only He who will sit thereon can correctly expose motives and weigh evidence, vv. 3–5.

He refers them to what he knows the apostles are: not usurpers of authority, seeking to head the procession, but rather seen at the rear (as if the plunder of war), condemned to death and a spectacle to all as scum and refuse, v. 9.

He then reminds them of what he was to them: not just a guardian amongst many but a father who had begotten them through the gospel. Does this not call for respect and a readiness to follow his words, rather than rejection?, vv. 14–16. Does all this require confirmation? Timothy will supply it, v. 17.

But Paul *had* authority! Listen to its voice. What irony he can use, vv. 8–10. Listen again to it. What righteous indignation, vv. 18–21. Yet what fatherly concern, v. 14.

How this party spirit was rocking the assembly, cf. 1. 10–13; 3. 3–4; 4. 6–7. Indeed how this works havoc today. How do we view the servants of the Lord who speak to us the word of life? Disparagingly? Selectively? With party spirit? Or as those who bring to us the good word of God? How do we value the ministry of the apostle Paul? Do we read with discrimination, with belittlement, relegating much he says to the past? Or do we listen to him as unto "the commandments of the Lord"?, 14. 37.

Lesson. Lord, help us not to be choosers, but listeners.

June 30th

READING : **1 Corinthians 5. 1-13**

CONDEMNED CONDUCT IN THE CHURCH

HERE IS a sad reading for today, and we pursue it with careful attention. We remember that our God is not only love but also light, and in Him is no darkness at all. How faithful is the Holy Book, hiding nothing but dealing with sins in the open. Paul hastens to deal with a situation which is begriming the church's record and marring its testimony. Incest is reported, v. 1. In such a place as Corinth how easily could young saints be taken unawares! Yet it has outmatched the city for enormity, v. 1. Hence the need to "Watch", 16. 13. How the flesh can reach greater depths of shame than the unregenerate!

An attitude which was deplorable, v. 2. There was no concern amongst the believers, v. 6a. They were content to have the guilty one amongst them. Similarly today, there are matters in assemblies which create no concern.

An action which was decisive, vv. 3–5. Paul is on the alert. Though absent he judges the matter, and delivers the wrongdoer to Satan for the destruction of the flesh and for the saving of the spirit.

An accompaniment that must be defeated, v. 6. If the guilty one is not put away the leaven will affect the whole. The cancer must be excised or the limb will be lost.

An activity which was determined, v. 7–8. They must purge out the old leaven remembering Christ our Passover sacrificed for them, and as unleavened keep the feast of unleavened bread, i.e., keep their resultant redeemed lives with sincerity and truth. Israel had to put away leaven on the very first day.

An advice that was delivered, vv. 9–13. There must be refusal to company or even eat with such as walk and behave shamefully. This is no authority for ostracising those who, though faultless in life, do not pronounce our particular shibboleths to our self-conceived satisfaction. But the Word instructs us to withdraw from those within our own fellowship who are defaming the testimony. The wicked person must be put away entirely, with a view, of course, to his restoration. He must be "put away from among yourselves", v. 13. It is an act of discipline by the whole assembly; note vv. 4–5.

Lesson. As we see such a one retreating into excommunication, we reflect, "there, but for the grace of God, go I".

July 1st

READING : **1 Corinthians 6. 1-11**

THE CHRISTIAN AND THE COURTS

CONFLICTS CAN and do arise between brethren. How must they be settled? Let us bear in mind that this section of our chapter deals exclusively with matters arising between fellow-believers. It is evident that the Corinthians were going to law with each other, vv. 6–7, and Paul expresses surprise at their lack of knowledge, v. 2a. In the light of greater responsibilities ahead, vv. 2–3, theirs must be the ability and right to judge their own internal matters. How does Paul describe the tribunals of men? "The unjust", v. 1; and "unbelievers", v. 6. To have our disputes settled before the courts of men, Paul says is unjustified, v. 1, a shame, v. 5, and a manifest defect, v. 7.

He states the right way. Surely there is at least one wise man in the assembly with ability to arbitrate, v. 5.

He suggests a better way. Why not rather take wrong and suffer, being defrauded? Instead of seeking vindication, would not this be a better display of the law of Christ? "Ye have heard that it hath been said, An eye for an eye, and a tooth for a tooth; but I say unto you, That ye resist not evil; but whosoever shall smite thee on thy right cheek, turn to him the other also", Matt. 5. 38–39. "Pray for them which despitefully use you", v. 44. "Blessed are the merciful", v. 7, viz., those who do not press their rights, for they shall obtain mercy. Testimonies have been marred by lawsuits.

He now exposes the truth of the matter. Ye yourselves do wrong and defraud, and that your brethren. Verses 9 and 10 certainly bring us up with a start! Such as these *were* some of you, but not *now*, Paul reminds them. They had been changed by the transforming grace of God, v. 11. They had been washed from sin's defilement (in fact Paul employs the active tense here), and so set themselves apart from others for God. Thus they were for ever separated from what they were, to what they had become; and they had been fully justified before God in the name of the Lord Jesus Christ and in the Spirit of our God.

Lesson. We are not what we were, so our behaviour must not be what it was.

July 2nd

READING : **1 Corinthians 6. 12-20**

THE BELIEVER'S BODY

IF THE SOUL is a subject of interest with Peter, the body is with Paul. Had he heard from the house of Chloe that the truth concerning the believer's body was still very distorted in the minds of some in the church, and that Corinthian practices continued to defile the assembly of God? He begins by explaining the law of Christian liberty. It is not licence. "All things are lawful unto me" (was he repeating one of their oft spoken slogans?), but not necessarily expedient. As motorists we have the right of the road. Our road tax and driving licence give us that, but we have no right to drive on any side we like. Such would be very inexpedient. Furthermore, whilst we may have every right to do a thing, Christian freedom should lift us beyond such petty bondage, v. 12b. Paul illustrates in verse 13a. This link brings the realm of the body into focus. He would teach us that:

The body is not for *Self-gratification*, vv. 13b-14. Liberty but not licence (fornication). Its functions must be Godward not selfward. It is purposefully for the Lord and contrariwise, the Lord is for the body, its Proprietor and Controller.

The body has *Sacred privilege*, vv. 15-18. It is a member of Christ! What holy association! This body of mine, this tangible fleshy frame is one of His members! Dare I desecrate it? Shall I take that thing made sacred, and make it one flesh with harlotry? I am one spirit with *Him*. Flee it!

The body has *Sanctity*, vv. 19–20. It has a holy Resident. By grace it has become the residence of the Spirit of God—His holy *naos*, His holy of holies! If unholy hands dared not touch the mount on which divine holiness temporarily rested, should anything defiling touch this body in which the Spirit of holiness permanently dwells? This holy Presence confirms we are not our own to please, and the body of the believer bears the notice "Sold". It has become the possession of Another at a very great price, v. 20a. Purchased for a dwelling place!

Lesson. May the motto of our bodies, today and every day be, "to Him be the glory for ever, Amen".

July 3rd

READING : **1 Corinthians 7. 1-40**

THE CHRISTIAN AND MARRIAGE

IN VIEW of moral conditions in Corinth it is not surprising that this subject has a place in this letter. There must have been concern about it in the assembly, v. 1. In his reply, Paul is permitted to mingle divine commands with his own apostolic judgment; cf. vv. 6, 25, 40. In seeking to summarize the content of this lengthy chapter, let us consider four loyalties it presents.

Loyalty to the Marriage Bond, vv. 1-9. Paul states that marriage is not for all, vv. 1b, 7-8, yet morally advisable v. 2; howbeit this estate must not be bigamous; note v. 2b. The bond must be mutually recognized, both morally, v. 3, and physically, vv. 4–5. Upon marriage the two become "one flesh" and this union must be constantly honoured.

Loyalty to the Marriage Partner, vv. 10–24. The bond must not only be honoured, but never broken, vv. 10–11. If, however, one partner depart, reconciliation is advised and remarriage is not permitted. Another situation is contemplated which must have often been the case at Corinth, where one partner was converted and the other not, v. 12. This should become no ground for separation, vv. 12–13. Even though a house was spiritually divided, where there was contentment there must still be loyalty to the unsaved partner for domestic and family reasons, v. 14. Should the unbelieving one depart, so be it, but otherwise, by remaining together the one may become the means of the other's conversion, vv. 15–16. So in all circumstances the rule is, "let every man, wherein he is called, therein abide with God", v. 24.

Loyalty to the Lord, vv. 25–38. He now considers the matter of the yet unmarried man or woman. Some set of conditions then and there prevailing, but not disclosed to us, vv. 26–32a, causes Paul to advise non-marriage, and he refers to a greater loyalty, vv. 32b–35. How carefully marriage must be considered. Will it promote or prevent my devotion to the Lord? However, each must be convinced in his own mind, vv. 36–37.

Loyalty to the Marriage Law, vv. 39–40. This pointed passage utterly discountenances divorce, v. 39a; permits re-marriage only after the death of one, and that "in the Lord".

Lesson. The demand of the hour is loyalty to these principles.

July 4th

READING : **1 Corinthians 8. 1-13**

CONCERN FOR THE ONE-TIME IDOLATER

THE CORINTHIAN believers had been idolaters, but the gospel had set them free. Nevertheless, after generations of such servitude and the constant presence of idolatrous practices, it is to be understood that there would be many lingering difficulties to be faced. Many today who have known deliverance from lives of debauchery and immorality, and from the power of heretical religion, often struggle with evil tendencies. With such believers sympathy and tender care must be shown, Paul advises.

Here it is a matter of eating things offered to idols. This would be a difficulty in Corinth, where what was sold in the shambles had thus been ceremonially offered. Daniel refused to defile himself with such. Now, says Paul, we know we all have knowledge, but this merely puffs up whereas love builds up. Merely to think that we know is to reveal our lack of knowledge. Paul says we know that the idol is nothing—just a piece of wood or stone—and that there is but one God and Father, and one Lord, Jesus Christ, but all have not this knowledge. Some, long used to the idol, consider eating such meat to be equal to having vital contact with it, and hence their weak consciences are defiled, but we know that meat has nothing to do with our acceptance, v. 8.

What, then, should the attitude be of those who "have knowledge"? Act according to it? "Take heed lest by any means this liberty of yours become a stumblingblock to the weak". Destroy not with thy meat him for whom Christ died, says Paul, Rom. 14. 15. My practice must be geared to my weaker brother's conscience, 1 Cor. 8. 11. How important the use of my liberty is seen to be when its misuse will stumble my weaker brother. Such is sinning "against Christ", v. 12.

Whilst such eating of meat offered to idols may be irrelevant in many lands today, the principle holds good. Are there matters of behaviour and practice which are lawful to me because of my enlightened understanding, but likely to be stumblingstones to some of my brethren? Then I must seek grace to desist therefrom.

Lesson. Does Paul's decision, v. 13, also rule my behaviour? Is it knowledge or love that decides?

July 5th

READING : **1 Corinthians 9. 1-27**

APOSTLESHIP CALLED IN QUESTION

WERE SOME in the city questioning Paul's apostolic authority and so attempting to undermine his work? This must be considered and resolved here and now, or of what effect shall this letter be? Paul deals with the problem in three ways.

He establishes the *Rights of his life and service*, vv. 1–15. He reminds them that he should have no need to certify his apostleship. They themselves were the seal of his calling, being the fruits of his ministry, vv. 1–2. Furthermore, was it essential to have seen the Lord to be an apostle? I have seen Him, he says. He never forgot the Damascus road! So he proceeds to the defence of his apostolic liberty. Do they question his physical, marital and employment rights?, vv. 4–6. He will advance mundane arguments. Do not soldiers serve for wages, vinedressers eat of the fruit, and shepherds live of the flock? He advances scriptural precedents, quoting the law of the threshing ox, the plowman and the priest, v. 9–13. So does not labour in the spiritual sphere deserve recompence in the material? Has he not his Lord's own authority for this?, v. 14. On a threefold ground he bases his rights—the ways of life; the witness of Scripture; the Word of the Lord. Rights he had, but he waived them for the gospel's sake.

He proceeds to speak of his *Responsibilities*, vv. 16–23. The gospel was his life's burden, and for it all must be sacrificed. Concerning it necessity was laid upon him. He had a stewardship entrusted to him, and did all things for the gospel's sake. This he discharged freely. Though he may live of the gospel, he lives by tentmaking. His dedication is to all, seeking only their salvation.

He then states his *Resolve*, vv. 24–27. This sacrifices his rights and sustains his responsibility. In the race as runner he will concentrate on the goal; in the games as the contestant he will consecrate all for the crown; in the ring as the boxer he will contend with himself for the commendation of his Lord. He will "so run", disdain intemperance and scorn shadow-boxing, so controlling and curbing personal appetites lest he should be rejected. He possesses a charge, respects a confidence, and fulfills a commission.

Lesson. What does my work and witness cost me?

July 6th

READING : **1 Corinthians 10. 1-33**

ON TAKING HEED LEST WE FALL

AN *illustration* is advanced, vv. 1–5. Note the contrasted and repeated "all" with the "many" in verse 5. Hence from Israel's history we learn that mutual privilege gave no immunity from failure and judgment. Enjoyment of Christian privileges and blessings in themselves, is no guarantee of escape from discipline.

An *application* is enforced, vv. 6–12. Israel is thus seen as being the great example for the Christian Church. Do not ignore your Old Testament! Do we lust, harbour idols in the heart, commit fornication, tempt the Lord or murmur? Beware! History can and does repeat itself. God has not changed.

An *inspiration* is provided, v. 13. It is the encouragement of the revealed and operative faithfulness of God.

Paul now begins a new paragraph and settles down to deal with a trouble spot at Corinth, v. 14, viz, idolatry. They had turned to God from it. They must persistently flee from it. He has dealt with eating things offered to idols in chapter 8, and now deals with association with the idolatrous. Has this section a voice for us? Yes says John, "Little children, keep yourselves from idols", 1 John 5. 21. The believer has been given a place at the Lord's table at which he is privileged to sit and eat continually as one of the king's sons like Mephibosheth. It is a table of spiritual provision for every day and all day, 1 Cor. 10. 21. This holy privilege must be guarded and practised by us. It brings us into holy communion with the blood and body of Christ; thus it debars us from tables that are idolatrous because devilish, vv. 20–21. Dare we provoke the Lord by seeking satisfaction from His board and theirs? Again he quotes their slogan. Are all things lawful? Yes but not necessarily expedient or edifying. In such we must consider our neighbour's good. Another's conscience must be respected, so once the nature of the food is known, we refuse it for the other's good, vv. 28–29. Partaking of what we know to be alien to the Lord's table is to provoke the Lord to jealousy, and to stumble others whether saved or unsaved, v. 32.

Lesson. At which table am I seen feasting? Note 11. 1.

July 7th

READING : **1 Corinthians 11. 1-16**

THE RECOGNITION OF HEADSHIP

WE MUST commence our meditation today with our last verse, so that we may learn what Paul has been saying in the previous verses was not applicable to Corinth only. It would appear such was Paul's teaching wherever he went, and the significant "we" indicates that he was not alone in this matter. Let us observe how J. B. Phillips expresses it in his paraphrase. "If anyone wants to be argumentative about it, I can only say that we and the churches of God generally hold this ruling on the matter". In our passage we find firstly:

Headship expounded, vv. 2–3. Many things at Corinth called forth Paul's praise but one thing required correction, and this was involved with headship. Every man has a head—Christ; every woman ("the woman" of verse 3 must mean every woman as v. 15) has a head—the man; Christ has a Head—God. This is divinely ordered, not apostolically conceived. This truth is presently ignored by a sex-equalizing age. Paul then proceeds to deal with

Headship applied, vv. 4–15. Where male and female faithfully recognize their respective head this will be manifestly shown, not only by general behaviour but by a simple sign. In the matter of spiritual exercises, the man will uncover his head (not even have his hair long, v. 14) in recognition and honour of his Head, v. 4. The woman, on the contrary, will veil her head (having her hair unshorn, for this is a second covering, v. 15) in recognition and honour of the man, viz., the male species, vv. 5, 13. The praying and prophesying of verse 5 cannot authorize public activity, for Paul deals with this in chapter 14. He says for a woman wilfully to ignore and disobey this she might as well have her hair totally removed, vv. 5b–6. It would seem that the emancipation of women by the gospel had led to licence in the assembly, and this needed controlling by the apostle. In vv. 8–12 he lays down the need for the relative positions of the sexes to be recognized. Angels, who ever hearken to the voice of His word, are watching our behaviour and hence the need for the sign of authority, v. 10.

Lesson. As Christ ever recognized and pleased His Head, may we ours, that God may be glorified thereby.

July 8th

READING : **1 Corinthians 11. 17-34**

DISORDER IN THE GATHERINGS OF THE SAINTS

OUR OPENING verse would teach us that the substance of yesterday's reading had been causing, in part, the disorders of the assembly. There was another cause. Divisions and schisms were in evidence, and this was so during their gathering to remember the Lord. In those days the gathering commenced with a "love feast", but this was developing into a drinking and feasting orgy as the rich brought in abundance and the poor remained hungry and embarrassed, vv. 21–22. This was rendering unholy the sacred feast of remembrance they had come to celebrate, v. 20. Hence, in writing to correct such disorders, Paul seeks to promote orderliness. He would instruct the saints that the feast of remembrance must be:

Governed by the Lordship of Christ. Note the sevenfold mention of "Lord" in today's section. As such He must dominate our gatherings and thus the schismatic tendency will be curbed.

Guided by the remembrance of His sufferings and death. As remembering Him, we shall forget ourselves and our priorities, vv. 24–26.

Graced by simplicity. How beautifully simple is the feast seen to be in verses 23–25, and how man has marred it by invented embellishments and unauthorized legalism. Also it should

Gender expectation, for it is only "till he come". How these four things are calculated to remove self from the gatherings of the church.

With such in mind with what preparation of heart and carefulness of behaviour should we wend our way to the communal remembrance of our Lord, vv. 27–29. To attend otherwise may incur the discipline of the Lord, v. 30. Sometimes may ill-health and even death be the result of the disobedience of this chapter? When we gather to break bread we must not only reverently remember our Lord but have respect to our fellowmembers of the great body of Christ, vv. 29, 33, for "ye are one loaf", 10. 17. How needful it is, and wise, to judge ourselves and that we be not judged by Him.

Lesson. Lord, teach me how to behave myself in the house of God!, 1 Tim. 3. 15.

July 9th

READING : **1 Corinthians 12. 1-11**

CONCERNING SPIRITUALS

PAUL WOULD remind his readers of their former days. As members of nations so different from Israel, they had been carried away in their religion to worship idols which Paul describes as dumb. They were unable to hear or speak, and could therefore not reveal themselves. Now, however, they had "turned . . . to serve the living and true God". This God hears and speaks and makes Himself known to men, and He has sent His Spirit into our hearts. Under His influence, no one would ever curse Jesus but rather crown Jesus. The Holy Spirit is therefore the great Preventive in my life and the great Promoter. Cursing Jesus is proof that the Spirit is foreign to me, whereas crowning Jesus as Lord is exclusively the result of the Spirit operating in my life, vv. 1–3.

This Holy Spirit who prompts me to recognize and own Christ's Lordship, links me with His service. Owning His Lordship I become His glad vassal, that through me the ministries of God may speak. Thus in our passage we read of the Spirit and His gifts; the Lord (Jesus) and His ministrations; God (the Father) and His workings. The *potentials* for service are at the disposal of the Spirit, vv. 7–11; the *place* and *practice* of them is the choice of the Lord of the servant; the *power* (energy or working) for ministry is of God. There is no dumbness about our God! We observe that the gifts, ministrations and workings are all manifold in their diversity yet coming each from its own unchanging source.

As those who are able to call Jesus Lord, to "each one" (not some) the Holy Spirit gives His manifestation for profiting. It is for "trading", cf. Luke 19. 13, 15, in the Master's interests. Note the diverse character of these gifts, vv. 8–10, yet all the bestowment of the Spirit. None is achieved personally. These are all and equally ours "through" or "according to the Spirit", v. 8, and become effectively operative "in" the Spirit, v. 9. None is achieved or exercised merely by the intellect, v. 11a, neither are they self-selected; they are distributed to each, severally as the Spirit wills. I serve neither in any capacity nor sphere as I choose, but as He desires.

Lesson. What is *my* gift; *my* sphere; and whence *my* power?

July 10th

READING : **1 Corinthians 12. 12-31**

THE BODY OF THE CHRIST

WRITING TO the Corinthian believers, Paul says "ye are the body of Christ and members in particular", v. 27. To the Ephesians he writes, "there is one body", Eph. 4. 4. We therefore conclude this phrase "body of Christ" has local and universal expression, being made up in each case of every born again believer. The *illustration* of it is in verse 12, the human body, many members but one whole. The *inception* of it is in verse 13. The many members become one body by baptism *in* the Spirit. No one in the church at Corinth was without this baptism (note, we were "*all* baptized", and thus Paul includes himself and every other believer). No Christian should be asked "have you had the baptism of the Spirit", for if not he is no Christian. This baptism was historically actual at Pentecost, Acts 1. 5; 2. 4, and is spiritually actual at conversion. The *inclusiveness* of the body is in verses 14–19. There is diversity in the body, but all members are alike essential. We must not complain if we feel we are an inferior member of it, for we are what we are and where we are in it by the choice of God, v. 18. Not one of us has been positioned in it by chance or caprice but by divine design. If all were one member the body would be a caricature and abnormal. We are vitally required to be what and where we are. We now see the *indispensability* of the members, vv. 21–24. If each is indispensable to the Designer, v. 18, then each is also indispensable to its fellow. How necessary it is then that all play their own part and attend to their own function. The encouraging factor is that the members seemingly of least importance have abundant honour conferred upon them by God, v. 24. A great toe may be much out of sight, but without it the body loses poise.

These truths prevent inconsideration among members, vv. 25–27. Note the phrases "no schism", "same care", "all the members suffer" or "rejoice". We promote unity by fellow-concern, fellow-sympathy, fellow-appreciation. So Paul concludes by interpreting the meaning of the members, vv. 28–30. As well as divine emplacement, v. 18, there seems room for personal exercise, v. 31a—yet a more excellent way, v. 31b.

Lesson. Am I prejudicing or perfecting the body?

July 13th

READING : **1 Corinthians 14. 26-40**

WHEN THE CHURCH GATHERS

TWO THINGS must mark our assemblings: (1) Edification, "Let all things be done unto edification", v. 26; and (2) Dignity, "Let all things be done decently and in order", v. 40. So the gatherings of the saints are (*a*) to promote mutual advancement, and (*b*) to preserve spiritual arrangement. At such gatherings, obviously, the tongue is the operative factor. In view of this, Paul says the tongue should be in control, vv. 26–33, and under restraint, vv. 34–36.

(i) *The tongue in control.* In church exercise, all the gifts are not confined to one member, v. 26; all may contribute according to their several ability. Seeing those were days when the gift of tongues was exercised, Paul says its exercise must be controlled; it must be limited. The gathering must not become confused, for each must minister "in turn", or "by course". One must interpret else the speaker in a tongue must be silent, vv. 27–28. Prophesying, too, must be under control, vv. 29–31, and its substance must be attended to and discerned by the hearers. It is important to observe, "the spirits of the prophets are subject to the prophets", v. 32, and also to remember that our God is not a God of confusion but of peace, v. 33. What do I contribute when I am present? Am I ever exercised before God? Verse 26 would not authorize my saying the first thing that comes to my mind, but rather the need for soul-preparation.

(ii) *The tongue under restraint.* This pertains to female members. What does "keeping silence" mean? Let the previous passage interpret. When one who spoke in a tongue must keep silent, it obviously means he refrains from his ministry, v. 28. Hence, to keep silence (the same Greek word) does not mean here that they must stop conversing with each other, but must not engage in any public ministry. Their place is one of subjection, as also says the law. So this was not a Pauline innovation. For sisters to take part in church gatherings is rebellious, v. 34, and shameful, v. 35. Does Paul detect opposition in these matters? Were they the originators of the divine word or the sole proprietors thereof?, v. 36. True spirituality recognizes Paul's words as being the Lord's.

How do I personally react to this chapter?

July 14th

READING : **1 Corinthians 15. 1-11**

THE GROUND AND GLORY OF THE GOSPEL

WE PAUSE to reconsider the message which brings salvation.

Firstly, its *Communication.* It is a message to be preached, v. 1a. Paul preached it and they received it. It demands response, v. 1b. It must be permanently embraced becoming the anchorage of the soul, "wherein ye stand", v. 1c. Through its message we are saved, if we grasp it with real conviction, "hold it fast", and if our faith is genuine, not being an empty assent, v. 2c. In its transmission from age to age it remains unalterable, for Paul states *now* what he preached *then.* He is making a re-statement not an amendment. He is meticulous about its very expression saying, "I make known, I say, in what words I preached it unto you", v. 2 R.V. Are we, too, careful in our terminology? Paul was a steward of the gospel, "I received it", and I "delivered" it. The gospel is not Pauline but divine.

Secondly its *Content.* We learn from verses 3b-5a that the gospel is a historic faith, not a philosophy, an ideal, a theory or mental conception. The gospel happened! It is based on historic events which took place on this earth in the sight and in the hearing of men. It has four *historic factors*: Christ died; Christ was buried; Christ was raised; and Christ was seen. Note where the gospel begins: not with His birth, life or ministry, but with His death! Note, too, by what it is consummated: Christ raised again. Of these, there are two *fundamental factors*: Christ died and Christ was raised, both qualified by "according to the scriptures". Neither was an afterthought; both were foreordained and promised in the Old Testament. There are two *establishing factors*: Christ was buried (signifying He had died), and, He was seen (proving His physical rising). Paul calls his witnesses, and among the striking array are above 500 brethren who all saw Him at one and the same time. Do some disbelieve? At Jerusalem one would have contacted many who would have gladly supplied evidence. There is one *potent factor.* Christ died for our sins! Again, this was "according to the scriptures", and, in view of our desperate need, it was by the love and grace of God. This grace wrought in us; let it work through us, vv. 9–11.

Lesson. Woe is me if I preach not the gospel, *this* gospel!

July 15th

READING : **1 Corinthians 15. 12-58**

CHRIST RISEN, RETURNING, RAISING, REIGNING

THE OPEN tomb focuses on great prospects. Christ's resurrection is the guarantee of great issues. The present passage hinges on two important assertions, (1) "But now is Christ risen from the dead", and (2) "at his coming". Because Christ has been raised, our resurrection is assured; and because He is coming again, it will be achieved.

Christ's resurrection and ours are inextricably involved, vv. 12–13. The one demands the other; the one rests on the other. The importance of Christ's rising is seen in that, if it be not factual, apostolic preaching is empty; faith is vain; sin remains; our trusting dear ones have perished; and we are most to be pitied. Christ being raised assures a great harvest to come, for just as the "all" in Adam died, so the "all" in Christ shall be made alive, each in his own order at the Lord's return to the air.

Having dealt with its *ground*, he now speaks of the *genuineness* of our resurrection. Is baptism a farce? We would only be baptized as dead ones, if the dead do not rise. Our living in danger for Christ is pointless, and our willingness to meet death for Him purposeless, if the dead are not raised. Were some denying this? He now deals with its *guise*, vv. 35–49. Paul uses the vegetable kingdom to illustrate: Our corruptible body is as seed sown in the earth; it will be raised incorruptible and for heaven, as it pleases God, vv. 38–42. Sown in corruption it will be raised beyond decay; sown in dishonour it will be raised radiant; see Matt. 13. 43. Sown in weakness it will be raised with new potential; sown a natural body it will be raised a spiritual body, unrestricted by time, space or matter. The *grandeur* of it all! It will be victory through our Risen and returning Lord.

Then the consummation, v. 24: the reigning Christ will have no contestant, and all adverse rule and power will be subdued; all His enemies will be subjected; death will be abolished, and He will render up the kingdom to God the Father. Then the death of Christ will be answered by the rule of Christ, leading to the final state when God shall be all in all.

Lesson. With such certain prospect may we all be "steadfast, unmovable, always abounding in the work of the Lord", v. 58.

July 16th

READING : **1 Corinthians 16. 1-24**

SUNDRY CONCLUSIONS

MAJOR MATTERS have been dealt with, difficulties answered and solved, and Paul now draws his letter to a close. He will end his Epistle with:

A reminder to remember, vv. 1–4. Important doctrinal issues must never becloud earthly needs of others; and matters of correctness of faith before God must always go hand in hand with our dutiful concern for our fellows. Note the priority given to this exercise. It was on the day of their remembrance of the Lord in His death when they must practically remember their suffering fellowsaints.

An intimation of his proposed stay with them, vv. 5–9. What interest in, and love for, them he shows despite his many censures, not desiring a fleeting visit but a prolonged stay.

A fatherly word of counsel, vv. 10–12. He will prepare for the wellbeing of Timothy if he visits them. He will seek to protect him, his true child in the faith, from any unpleasantness from the Corinthian believers, and will also explain the movements of Apollos. What care he shows for his fellow-workers. This man does not forget human niceties.

A directive to duty, vv. 13–14. He urges his readers to vigilance, faithfulness, readiness, fortitude and love. With what thrust this final pointed instruction would reach their ears.

A word of advice, vv. 15–18. He reminds them of some they know, and acquaints them with their ministries to him and of their service to them, and exhorts to suitable esteem and obedience.

A number of forwarded greetings, vv. 19–20. He now closes

With his own personal salutation, vv. 21–24. Though his letters may at times be written by the hand of an amanuensis, he must append his own signature as a sign of genuineness, v. 21. Then he gives his final warning and greeting. If any man love not the Lord (how he has stressed the Lordship of Christ in this Epistle) let him be accursed—the Lord cometh! The apostolic treatise, in parts so stern and corrective, so emphatic yet so encouraging, closes with strains of divine grace and the sweetness of his own love in Christ.

Lesson. Let us always be mindful of Christian courtesies.

Introducing 2 Corinthians

PAUL'S FIRST letter to the Corinthians had awakened the conscience of the majority, and had re-established the fear of God in their hearts and integrity in their walk. Paul was relieved. Whereas he describes his feeling before the arrival of Titus from Corinth with the words "our flesh had no relief", he is able to express his present situation as not a little comforted by the presence of Titus and by the news that he brought of the Corinthians, 7. 6, 7.

There were still some disturbing features. There seemed to be still a danger from immorality; thus his exhortation in 6.14. More personally painful was the strong opposition to himself of some at Corinth. What is so cruel as religious strife? To what depths will it go! The letter shows the depths to which it will be pursued by false brethren. They accused him of being fickle, 1. 17; egotistical, 3. 1; uncommended, 3. 1, 2; unbalanced, 5. 13; no apostle, 11. 5; 12. 12; dishonest, 12. 16–19; bombastic in writing but contemptible in person, 10. 10; cowardly, 11. 30–33; under God's displeasure, 12. 1–10; no preacher, 10. 10; crafty, 12. 16.

It was necessary to face his detractors. Paul was stung into self-defence, and he found it necessary to commend himself, 4. 2; 6. 4; 12. 11, and to talk about himself. Thus we have possibly the most personal as well as the most poignant of Paul's Epistles. He had been accused of walking "according to the flesh", 10. 2. He will challenge his accusers to stand side by side with him when it comes to the matter of allegiance to Christ, 10. 7. Contemptuously they said his bodily presence was weak. He will dare them to meet him when he comes, 10. 10–15. They posed as superlative apostles, 11. 5, and denied his apostleship. He will show them to be what they really are—"false apostles, deceitful workers, transforming themselves into the apostles of Christ", 11. 13. Arrogance marked them, but service and suffering marked Paul. He therefore found it necessary to talk about himself. It was distasteful to him; his preference would have been to magnify Christ directly. It was, however, necessary for them. If he had not done so, it would have been to leave the Corinthians open to their adversaries.

July 17th

READING : **2 Corinthians 1. 1-24**

THE GOD OF ALL COMFORT

IT SHOULD be remembered in considering the early verses of this chapter that there were those who were opposed to Paul. This makes more remarkable the beautiful tenderness of his greeting as he addresses them. He is going to tell them of his afflictions, and he starts with the word "Blessed". He has a comfort which he recognizes as coming from God. His sufferings have brought him a new revelation of God expressed in a new Name, a Name wonderful in its tenderness, "Father of mercies . . . God of all comfort", v. 3. God is the Originator of all mercies, the Source from which they flow, James 1. 17; Rom. 12. 1; Heb. 12. 9; Eph. 1. 17. If there is a mercy, God is the Father of that mercy, whatever it may be. He is "the God of all comfort", the tender cheer and comfort which love can give to the one beloved by meeting his inmost need. Paul mentions "mercies" and "comfort" before he speaks of "affliction", but on every occasion when he had been in affliction he had been sustained by the hand of God, and derived blessings from it. Blessings? Yes, not the least the ability to extend to others in their hour of need a sympathy born of divine sympathy he had himself received, v. 4. He had not only a new revelation of God, but a new power to comfort others. His trials added to his usefulness in the Lord's service.

It is only as Christ's reproach is willingly learned and borne that suffering is swallowed up by His comfort, v. 5. Yet whatever befell Paul in Christ's service was for their good, vv. 6, 7, and their afflictions were a testimony to him that they shared his comfort. He would not have them unaware of what he had suffered, because it enabled him to show how deeply he was interested in them. It had taught Paul an unshakeable confidence in God, vv. 9, 10. The God who could bring him through the affliction of verse 8 could bring him through anything!

As to his not having come to them, he was a man of clear conscience, vv. 12–14. Furthermore, he was a man of certain convictions, vv. 15–24. His decisions were not "according to the flesh" v. 17. His message was definite, vv. 19, 20. The reason he had not come to them he explains in verse 23. As always, his love for them governed his actions.

July 18th

READING : **2 Corinthians 2. 1-17**

THE TRIUMPHS OF THE LOVE OF CHRIST

PAUL HAD been consistent. His aim was the happiness of the saints, and he shrank from coming to Corinth with a rebuke that would have caused them grief. He used severity and rebuke very sparingly. If we rebuke far more than we praise, then our severity will lose its effect, being discounted because it is so frequent. When Paul did rebuke, he did so in love, v. 4. The only effective rebuke is the one which is given with an arm of love around the other person.

They had acted in discipline after his first letter, but were now guilty of extreme severity and sternness. Discipline had been exercised in order to restore the offender. Now they must be ready to forgive. The Christian should always be ready to forgive just as he has been forgiven by God. There were two dangers. Over-severity might drive the offender to despair, v. 7, or Satan might seize it as an opportunity to drive him from the fellowship of Christians, v. 11.

At Troas Paul had been faced with one of the most difficult decisions of his life—to serve sinners or saints?, souls saved or the interests of a carnal church? His was a twofold ministry, Col. 1. 23–25. He left Troas with its opportunities to attend to the needs of the Corinthian church. At that moment, it was of more importance to keep those who were called by the Name of Christ from disgracing Him, than to bring fresh souls to the knowledge of Him.

Titus had brought him the news of another triumph of the love of Christ at Corinth and Paul gave thanks to the One who always brought triumph. The metaphor of verse 14 derives from the triumphant generals of Rome. Paul's Almighty Conqueror was leading him about the world as an illustrious example of His power to subdue and save. The foe of Christ was now the servant of Christ. He was led in triumph, not merely as one triumphed over, but as one triumphing with God.

The apostolic preachers themselves were represented as an odour, their personality fragrant with Christ, their message well pleasing to God. They were wholly acceptable to God, though some of their listeners were on their way to destruction, whilst others were being saved, vv. 15, 16.

July 19th

READING : **2 Corinthians 3. 1-18**

EPISTLES AND COVENANTS

THE CORINTHIANS were Paul's "epistle", the fruit of his labours, v. 2. They were also an "epistle of Christ", v. 3. Just as God wrote on tables of stone for Israel, so now Christ is engraved on the hearts of His people. The life of the Christian is an epistle; it is a message of Christ to the world. The most powerful sermon in the world is a consistent Christian life. Is His message to men legible in our lives?

Paul disclaimed any credit for the change in their lives—it was God's work, vv. 4, 5. The same divine sufficiency made him an able minister of the new covenant. The old covenant was based on a written document, Exod. 24. 1–8, the new covenant on the power of a life-giving Spirit. The "old" told man what he ought to do; the "new" changed a man, giving him the power to obey. The "old" was a ministration of death because of man's inability to live by keeping it, and death was the penalty. It was born in glory, but its glory was transient. The new covenant ends in glory with a splendour which is eternal, 2 Cor. 3. 7, 8, 9. The glory of the old covenant was illustrated by the glory seen on Moses' face, neither intrinsic nor permanent. Hence he veiled his face so that the passing of the glory should not be seen by his people, v. 13. That veil also symbolized the veil on their mind when they read the Scriptures. They do not see that the glory of the old covenant is eclipsed by the brightness of the "new". The veil will be taken away when they turn to the Lord, v. 16.

Moses' aspiration had been to see God's glory, Exod. 33. 18. That aspiration is realized in the new covenant, 2 Cor. 3. 18. More, we are transfigured into that glory. How are we transformed? By "beholding"; by a steady, concentrated gazing on Christ as seen in His Word, and a confident relying on the Holy Spirit to effect the change. It will be progressive—"from glory to glory". An inward change is wrought in us by the Holy Spirit, a daily transformation into the image of our Lord. We behold in silent, adoring contemplation; He works into our lives what we see in Christ. "Beholding", we "are changed".

Note. In verse 17 the title is "the Spirit of the Lord", but in verse 18 it is "the Lord the Spirit", A.V. marg., R.V.

July 20th

READING : **2 Corinthians 4. 1-18**

CONTRASTS

HERE IS a chapter of contrasts. Light is contrasted with darkness, vv. 1–6, weakness with power, vv. 7–14, affliction with glory, vv. 14–18.

The gospel remains a secret even to many who hear it again and again. That it remains hidden from some is their condemnation, and marks them out as on their way to destruction. Satan has blinded their eyes, v. 4. To Paul the gospel was a very great thing. The light which comes from it is so dazzling that it is incredible that men do not see it. The power of evil that opposes it must have an immense malignity. Men's unbelief gives Satan the opportunity to blind their faculties of spiritual perception. The god of this world does his work of blinding; the true God called light out of darkness. In His light Paul saw the face of Jesus Christ, and knew that the glory that shone there was the glory of God, v. 6.

The knowledge of that glory was held in an earthen vessel—man's body with its weakness, his mind with its limitations. But therein lay a divine principle, which protected the truth that salvation was altogether of the Lord. God will always have His work done by men who are willing to recognize that the exceeding greatness of the power is His, not theirs. In the contrasts that follow Paul brings out both his weakness and God's power, vv. 8–10.

All was for their blessing and God's glory, v. 15. The declining powers of Paul's bodily life are contrasted with the progressive renewal of his spiritual life, v. 16. The veil of tired, suffering humanity held concealed beneath it, beating with immortality, the very life of Christ. The outward man was perishing, but the inward man was renewed day by day. Paul contrasts the present with the future. The affliction is light, passing, and tends to glory. The affliction is surpassed beyond measure ("excessively to excess", Greek) by the coming glory. Language is inadequate to describe it. Finally, the apostle contrasts the seen and the unseen. Things seen have their day and then cease to be; things unseen, things of glory, last forever. It all depends where our eyes are fixed; "while we look". Lift your eyes to heaven, and measure the present by the unseen and the eternal.

July 21st

READING : **2 Corinthians 5. 1-17**

A POSSIBILITY AND A CERTAINTY

WHAT IF our present body be dissolved by death? We have "a building from God", v. 1. The present tense expresses the certainty of our receiving a resurrection body, 1 Cor. 15. 42–49. Until then we "groan", Rom. 8. 23, under the body's weaknesses and our liability to sin, longing for the heavenly glory. Our glorious future is secure for we possess the promise of it in the earnest of the Spirit, and even now we are God's workmanship, 2 Cor. 5. 5. In the present we can enjoy the foretaste of the glory to follow. Of course, residence in the body now is exile from the Lord, absence from our true home, v. 6. Whilst the Lord is spiritually present with us all, He is physically absent. Paul had no doubt what would happen to him at death, v. 8. He would pass into the immediate presence of Christ; see Phil. 1. 23. For the present he was ambitious to be "accepted" in His sight, 2 Cor. 5. 9.

"We must all appear before the judgment seat of Christ", v. 10. This is not meant to cloud the believer's prospect of future bliss, but to act as a stimulus to his ambition to be well-pleasing to the Lord. Future events have a bearing on present Christian living. What we have done in the body will be manifested then. The Master who will preside at the scrutiny is the same Lord who loves us and who gave Himself for us. He will not be harsh; He will not be unfair. He will overlook no extenuating circumstances. He understands every difficulty we face.

Paul served as one who would have to give account, v. 11. He therefore persuaded men out of a deep reverence and fear of God. He was constrained by "the love of Christ", v. 14. The love which Christ exhibited for men when He died for them held the apostle fast in his allegiance to such a Saviour. That love impelled him, drove him, constrained him. Here is the unashamed testimony of a life that was commanded by a mighty and all-mastering motive; the ever-blessed enslavement of a life that was claimed, captured and controlled by this Prince of lovers, the Lord Jesus Christ. Well might Zinzendorf, the founder of the Moravian Mission, write, "I have one passion in life, Him".

July 22nd

READING : **2 Corinthians 5. 18-21**

THE MINISTRY OF RECONCILIATION

Reconciliation is the substitution of friendship for enmity, and points by implication to a friendship which had once existed and which had been subsequently lost. Man was made for fellowship with God. He fulfils his destiny when he is at one with God. But there is a disrupting influence—sin. Sin has come between man and God. Man's alienation from God, together with the active enmity against God which followed, was brought about by Adam's disobedience and sin. Disobedience to the will of God made fellowship between man and his Creator impossible. Communion was broken, and this consequence of Adam's sin continues even today.

Man needs to be made right with God, he needs to be reconciled. Any professed gospel must be tested here. It is a crucial test, for at the centre is the cross. God reconciled us to Himself by making Christ to be sin on our behalf. Christ was sinless; "He knew no sin". He was altogether holy. He was tempted in all points like as we are, but He was never tempted by inbred sin. It was, of course, unthinkable that He could ever sin, for He was "God . . . manifest in the flesh".

He was made sin. His sinlessness was the qualification which fitted Him in God's eyes to be the Agent of reconciliation. God identified Him, the Sinless One, with sin. That involved nothing less than the death of the cross. Christ not only "bore our sins in his own body on the tree", but He was "made sin". He stood charged with the entire question of sin. So long as sin remained in question, reconciliation was impossible. But Christ, being made sin, died and put it away for ever. Sin was laid on Him by God; His death is the execution of the divine sentence upon it. When He died, He put away sin; it no longer stands as a barrier. God has made peace by the transaction at Golgotha; He has accomplished reconciliation. Sin could be dealt with only by death. It required the death of Him who, being a Man, could die and, being God, could impart all the dignity, virtue, value and glory of His divine Person to the atoning sacrifice which He offered. "God was in Christ, reconciling the world unto himself". The Christian is an ambassador from the court of heaven, coming with the ministry of reconciliation to men from heaven's King.

July 23rd

READING : **2 Corinthians 6. 1-18**

RESTRICTED AFFECTIONS, LAX ASSOCIATIONS

WHY WERE the Corinthians so critical of Paul? The answer is that their love was not what it ought to have been, v. 12. They were constricted in their love. Heat expands, and the warmth of love will always expand a man's heart. In contrast to the Corinthians, Paul's mouth was "open" and his heart was "enlarged". He was utterly frank and he had the warmest love for them. The statement is the more wonderful on his lips, because the Corinthians had denied the truthfulness of his ministry—and what a ministry it was!, vv. 3–10. They had charged him with interested motives, sneered at his manner, and held up to scorn the meanness of his appearance. In the face of this his heart expanded! There was no constriction in the apostle. There was room in his heart for them all, but not in their hearts for him. His heart was sufficiently large for all his converts to be the objects of his affection. Yet they did not always find room in their hearts for him, v. 12. The Corinthians needed to be expanded, v. 13.

They also needed care in their associations. Where Christ is not before the heart, the world in one form or another will always ensnare. Excuses which cover unholy alliances escape detection, and His honour is soon compromised. Every evil connection is prohibited, vv. 14–18. We cannot accept both Christ's yoke, Matt. 11. 29, and that of the world which rejected and crucified Him. The text prohibits every kind of union in which the character of the Christian loses anything of its integrity and distinctiveness. We are to have no compromising fellowship with anything in the world that is alien to God. There are things in the world with which the Christian cannot and dare not associate himself. The Christian is therefore called to separation, v. 17. Yet his life is not one of barren renunciation, for he is separated from the world for no less a purpose than that he might enjoy fellowship with God. He receives us, that is, looks upon us with favour, and we enjoy the privilege of the sons and daughters of the living God.

Because of this separation, the marks of the true ministers of Christ stand out more clearly. Only they could sustain the 28 features given in verses 4-10, His servants having the definite objective, "that the ministry be not blamed", v. 3.

July 24th

READING : **2 Corinthians 7. 1-16**

GODLY SORROW

PAUL HAS the Corinthians in his heart, v. 3. He asks that they open their hearts sufficiently wide for him to become an ever-present object of their love, v. 2. And why not? He had not wronged them. Not only does he glory in them, but he was comforted by news of them, vv. 4–7. There is the question of the letter he had sent them, but he does not regret it because of its moral results, vv. 8, 9. It had produced repentance. He outlines the process by which it had done so, vv. 9, 10. There was the root of the matter—godly sorrow; then the stem—repentance; finally the fruit—salvation. Godly sorrow is to see sin as God sees it, not only in its consequences, but infinitely evil in itself. It is to concur in God's view of sin. From this sorrow there flows the abundant river of repentance. Repentance is a change of purpose in regard to that sin for which the person mourns. It is "repentance toward God", Acts 20. 21, the turning away from the sin to the Father, and this leads to salvation. It is the great power of Christ's love and sacrifice which will melt the heart into true repentance—"the goodness of God leadeth thee to repentance", Rom. 2. 4. God does not save a man whilst he is yet holding to his sin. Yet the work of Christ on the cross, and not repentance, is the ground of salvation.

Now what of the Corinthians? They had sorrowed over the offence committed among them. Instead of indifference, there had been an eagerness to clear themselves of the guilt in which they were involved, indignation at the shame it had brought upon them, fear of God's anger, a vehement desire to see Paul again, a zeal to promote his honour, a readiness to mete out to the offender the punishment he deserved. The teaching of verse 10 was confirmed in their own experience.

While Paul desires the punishment and reformation of the offender, his main object is that the fidelity and zeal of the church should be safeguarded—as it was, v. 14. He may say severe things to them, but he does not disparage nor malign them to other people, vv. 14–16. This, surely, is a good example to follow.

Note how Paul refers to the service of Titus throughout the Epistle: 2. 13; 7. 6, 13, 14; 8. 16-18, 23; 12. 18.

July 25th

READING : **2 Corinthians 8. 1-24**

THE RICHES OF LIBERALITY

PAUL HAD been gathering material help for the Jerusalem church. The Corinthians had been tardy in contributing. Paul now challenges them. His conception of Christian giving is a lofty one. It was a "grace", a ministry of the Holy Spirit inwrought in personal experience and outwrought in practical expression. Corinth abounded in everything else, but lacked here. Paul challenges them with two examples.

Firstly, the Macedonians, vv. 1–6. They were in deep poverty and had experienced affliction, yet there was unselfish devotedness, loving others better than themselves. Despite poverty they had shown liberality and had given spontaneously ("willing of themselves"). They had begged permission to help, and exceeded Paul's expectations, even "beyond their power", v. 3. Love does not calculate what it can spare, or what it can afford. What was the secret? "They first gave their own selves to the Lord", v. 5. Their giving was the outward expression of their inward devotion. First in importance they gave themselves to Him. If a man feels that he does not own himself, much less will he feel that his goods are his own. God wants us before our money. The Corinthians' giving was preceded by an act of complete self-surrender.

Secondly, Christ Himself, v. 9. The example of Christ and our gratitude to Him for His infinite condescension on our behalf, are the supreme motives for Christian giving. Paul speaks of Christ's mysterious and unique self-impoverishment. Who can conceive the riches which were His? Making Himself poor, making us rich; taking our cross, giving us a crown; taking our sin, giving us God's righteousness; taking our curse and giving us His blessing. He impoverished Himself that we might be enriched. Part of our response should be to sacrifice a portion of our worldly goods to meet the needs of others who are Christ's.

Now the Corinthians had begun earlier to prepare to give, but had stopped, vv. 6, 10. Paul wants them to start again with a willing mind, v. 11, according to their ability, v. 12, and with every confidence in his scrupulosity over the safe-keeping and stewardship of their contribution, vv. 16–24.

July 26th

READING : **2 Corinthians 9. 1-15**

CHRISTIAN GIVING

GIVING IS not a sacrifice purely and simply; it is a "sowing" and will be followed by a "reaping". You reap what you sow, v. 6. No man ever loses by being generous. The harvest reaped will be proportionate to the seed sown. Sow sparingly, reap sparingly. Sow abundantly, reap abundantly. Giving is not just a contribution; it is an investment.

Of course, giving must not have selfish ends in view. The motive must be right. The spirit of giving is more important than the gift, v. 7. Giving must spring out of a deliberate choice, "according as he purposeth in his heart". There must be neither constraint nor complaint, "not grudgingly". Everyone must be entirely free to decide what to give, "not . . . of necessity". Giving must be with cheerfulness. God loves the happy giver, as characterized by a spirit of real enjoyment in his giving which sweeps away all restraint.

Not only does God love a cheerful giver, but He is able in His grace to see that there shall always be the means to give, vv. 8, 9. God can give a man both the substance to give and the spirit in which to give it. The desire to be generous and the means to be generous both come from God. All our resources, great or small, come from God ultimately, 1 Chron. 29. 14, and God is able to increase those resources. Where the generous spirit exists, God will provide the means whereby it can be expressed. The result is that the Christian will have an "all sufficiency in all things", and the man with the bountiful heart will find that God always supplies him with something to bestow.

Furthermore, as we give to God, He meets our needs, v. 10, (compare Phil. 4. 11, 12, 19). But He does more than that. He multiplies our resources. Because He multiplies the seed sown, giving is not self-impoverishment, but self-enrichment. Giving brings opportunities for thanksgiving to God, 2 Cor. 9. 12, 13, 15. It inspires prayer, draws out praises from those who receive, and rouses them to earnest longing for those who manifest such grace. Christian giving therefore becomes a thanksgiving, a systematic act of gratitude to the God who so loved the world that He gave His gift beyond words, v. 15.

July 27th

READING : **2 Corinthians 10. 1-18**

THE MEEKNESS AND GENTLENESS OF CHRIST

"Now I Paul myself beseech you", v. 1, has a peculiar emphasis, indicating that Paul is not only the grammatical subject of the verse, but the subject under discussion. The chapter is full of references to the accusations made against him, and forms part of the apostle's vindication which continues into chapter 13. Some said he was "base", fainthearted, when with them and "bold" when not, v. 1. They claimed he "walked according to the flesh", vv. 2, 3, was prone to self-exaltation, v. 8, and used his letters to terrify them, v. 9. Some made fun of his undistinguished personal appearance, v. 10, and the lack of majesty in his manner. How does Paul address himself to the task of rebutting these accusations? Does he do it with justifiable indignation? No, he beseeches them by "the meekness and gentleness of Christ". These qualities were of great price in his eyes, though not in theirs. He remembers the Lord Jesus. He remembers how far He was from violence and passion when under the most hateful provocation; how far from that sinful self-assertion which cannot consider the claims of others. This is the spirit in which he approaches the situation. He is going to deal with it as Christ would have dealt with it. He displays the characteristics of his Master. He mentions these graces of Christ in particular because, on account of his imitation of them, he was despised.

Note that Paul's service was for edification, v. 8; 12. 19. "Let all things be done to edifying", 1 Cor. 14. 26.

There were, of course, some who were experts in comparing their labours with those of others, v. 12, and that to their own advantage. Paul makes the point that self-praise is always dangerous. Paul himself kept to the limits of labour God had appointed for him, and did not boast in other men's labours as if they were his own, vv. 14–16. He does not want it thought that he is engaging in self-praise, or that his achievements are due entirely to himself. His detractors glorify themselves, and by doing so disqualify themselves from receiving God's approbation. To have God's approval is Paul's sole desire. The only things in which we can truly glory are the things which God has already done through us. Concerning them we exclaim, "To God be the glory, great things He hath done".

July 28th

READING : **2 Corinthians 11. 1-33**

THE HEART OF A TRUE SERVANT

THE MOTIVE of a true servant of Christ is here revealed. Paul wishes to present the Corinthians as a chaste virgin to Christ, v. 1, as a people whose faith had not been contaminated by falsehood. He had espoused them to "one husband". Just as the marriage relationship is exclusive, so believers are pledged to an exclusive loyalty to Christ. The heart of the virgin is undivided. She ought not to have a thought for any but for the "one man" to whom she is betrothed. Here lay the problem. The Corinthians were having their attention diverted from their true Object by false teachers. They were being spiritually seduced, their hearts being won away from absolute loyalty to Christ. Paul's aim was to prepare the believers for Christ. His fear was that they might be diverted from single-hearted devotion to Him.

These teachers (superlative apostles, v. 5), who led them astray, gloried after the flesh, v. 18, enslaved them and were dictatorial and overbearing, vv. 19, 20. What then were the marks of a true servant of Christ?, vv. 23–28. What a catalogue of suffering we find in these verses! And the man who endured them was a man constantly suffering from ill health. Yet all these perils and travails were incidental things to the apostle. That which pressed upon him daily and from which he had no escape, that which constituted his central anxiety, was the care of all the churches. Daily these cares rose up as a crowd against him. He carried on his heart the churches which he had established and visited, with all their problems and differences. He laboured for them in prayer and in every other way possible. His "care" consisted in taking upon himself all the anxieties of every individual member of each flock. Two complementary aspects of his care are seen here—sympathy with the weak and an indignation at wrong, v. 29. Paul felt the weaknesses of the weak as though they were his own, and the injuries suffered as though they were done to himself. Sympathy is of the essence of Christian love. This was true Christian ministry.

Search the Epistles to find out the subject matter of Paul's daily prayers for the churches. He prayed "without ceasing", Rom. 1. 9; "always", 1 Cor. 1. 4; "I . . . cease not", Eph. 1. 16.

July 29th

READING : **2 Corinthians 12. 1-21**

THE THORN AND THE GRACE

ONE OF the cruellest insinuations made about Paul was that he was under the manifest displeasure of God. His attackers pointed to his thorn in the flesh, v. 7. It is not clear what this was, but the terms used are physical and the indications are that it was excruciating. Paul is forced to explain how it is that he has this disability, and in doing so he breaks a self-imposed silence of fourteen years. Fourteen years ago he, "a man in Christ", had a stupendous experience. He was caught up to the third heaven and saw things impossible to communicate in human language. Paul's amazing humility comes out in that he kept silent for so long about something which others would have shouted from the housetops. There had been a possibility of pride, and the Lord had taken effective steps.

Paul was given that which proved both painful and humbling. He prayed the Lord thrice for its removal, addressing Him who, in the days of His flesh, had thrice prayed the Father, "Take away this cup from me". The answer came, v. 9. The words "He said" imply that the answer was repeated and final. It was valid for the apostle's whole life. The thorn was not taken away, but then there are two methods of lightening a burden. Its actual weight can be lessened, or the strength of the shoulder that bears it can be increased. The latter was the Lord's way with Paul. Sufficient grace and strength was promised.

The promise is recorded in the present tense; it is ours today. His grace is still sufficient, and it corresponds to our needs; never too much, never too little; never too soon, never too late. "My grace", said the Lord. What grace was His! He was "full of grace and truth". And that grace is available to us today. Once Paul realized that the thorn was part of God's purpose for his life, his whole attitude changed. The thorn saved him from spiritual pride, made him conscious of his own weakness and made available to him new reservoirs of spiritual power. Through Paul's weakness, God's power, perfect in itself already, was perfected in its manifestations and operations. God's power still operates in conscious human weakness.

July 30th

READING : **2 Corinthians 13. 1–14**

THE BENEDICTION

PAUL'S NEXT visit to Corinth would be one of heart-searching, vv. 1, 2. They had accused him of weakness. He recalls that Christ was crucified in weakness. The Lord assumed human nature with all its weakness that He might be capable of submitting to the most ignominious death. As He hung on the cross it seemed He was completely at the mercy of sinners. Yet now He lives by the power of God. Paul has experienced in full measure what it meant to be weak in Christ, but he was no stranger to that power which is made perfect in weakness. Paul hoped the Corinthians would not be found wanting in this respect, vv. 7, 9. Significantly, his fullest form of benediction comes at the end of this, his severest, letter. Here is the overflowing of a loving heart; he wished blessing for all, critics as well! This is the measure of the apostle's heart; his love embraced them all.

The three Persons of the Trinity are invoked. The distinct personality of the Son, the Father and the Holy Spirit is here taken for granted. The passage is therefore a clear recognition of the doctrine of the Trinity. Each Person is invoked to vouchsafe His Presence according to His essential nature and the part which He plays in the divine work of salvation. The means of salvation is the grace of our Lord Jesus Christ. Grace belongs to the Father but is here ascribed especially to Christ, partly because through Him God's grace manifests itself and partly because of His act of grace, 8. 9. The fountain from which that grace flows is the love of God, who "is love", 1 John 4. 8, 16. It was through their participation in the Holy Spirit that the Corinthians had come to know the love of God and to experience the grace of Christ. He is the living Agent of fellowship both between believers and the Father (by the Spirit we cry "Abba, Father", Rom. 8. 15; Gal. 4. 6) and between believers and the Son, Rom. 8. 9. The Spirit is also the living personal bond of that fellowship amongst believers which is the communion of saints. The grace of the Son, the love of the Father, the fellowship of the Spirit—what richer blessings could be desired?

Shortly after writing this, Paul visited Corinth, Acts 20. 2, but we do not know how the church received him.

Introducing Galatians

WE KNOW not for certain when or where Paul wrote his letter to the churches of Galatia. It may also be impossible to tell exactly where those churches were which received it. Such information can, therefore, neither add to, nor take anything away from, its value. What matters is the letter itself; Acts 15. 1–31; 16. 1–7; 18. 23; and the references to Galatia and the Galatians in 1 Cor. 16. 1; 2 Tim. 4. 10 and 1 Pet. 1. 1; with the remainder of God's Word as our commentary.

In the course of an early "missionary" journey the apostle had suffered an ailment, or developed some bodily weakness, which became the immediate cause of his preaching the gospel to the Galatians. Superstitious idolaters, as they were, they could easily have despised and rejected him on account of it. But God, who invariably chooses for His ends what we would discard, and works the unexpected lest anyone should presume to have discovered the secret of His ways, used a little, contemptible man to turn many from darkness to light and from the power of Satan to Himself. Churches were planted, and with the Holy Spirit ever present to guide them into all truth, they flourished.

Before long, however, false Jewish brethren arrived, teaching perverse things; saying it was necessary to be circumcised to be saved, and that Paul was inferior to the twelve. The Galatians quickly fell under their bewitching spell, became disloyal to Christ, and virtually regarded Paul as an enemy. Paul made no attempt to conceal his passion; he was righteously incensed. Nothing less than the truth of the gospel was at stake. The threat must be met head-on. No compromise could be considered, else the power of the only message to deliver souls from the course of this evil world would have been broken for all time. Hence this letter.

Whenever true Christian liberty has been threatened by a form of works, be it Judaism, Romanism or Ritualism, Galatians has proved repeatedly the Spirit's complete answer. For Jew and Gentile alike there is but one gospel; one way of being justified; one way of receiving the Spirit; one way of becoming a son and heir of God: that way is, through grace, by faith in Christ alone.

July 31st

READING : **Galatians 1. 1-24**

THE GOSPEL

Is IT hard for us to capture the atmosphere in which Paul begins this letter? He writes to his "little children", 4. 19; to those whom he subsequently refers to repeatedly as "brethren" but his cool greeting, "unto the churches of Galatia", 1. 2, seems to belie a special relationship, and indicates a studied distance. Their relationship was, indeed, strained, as any relationship between Christians will be when either party is affected by error. Paul was in no mood to commend the Galatians for anything, or even to mention the place that they had in his prayers. So, with the simplest of greetings, he tersely makes reference to the work of Christ, by way of laying stress at the outset on the chief point of his gospel, vv. 1–5.

Paul's gospel, "the gospel which I preach among the Gentiles", 2. 2, through which God's call was heard then, and can still be heard today, is not one gospel among many. In 1. 6–12 this all important truth is set forth, and must be clearly understood. Failure to grasp its full significance exposed the Galatians to those who troubled them, and will also make us a prey to like wicked and religious people. The five facts to note are: (i) Any preacher, human or angelic, who does not preach the apostolic gospel, is fit to be damned. (ii) The message is not after man, that is, was not invented by man. (iii) It was not received from man. (iv) Neither was Paul taught it. (v) It came to him as a direct revelation from Jesus Christ. How pure and elevated all this is! The one and only gospel originating with God Himself, was revealed by Jesus Christ to Paul, making him equally an apostle with the twelve yet quite independent of them. Preachers take heed! Let all believers beware of the preacher who adds to, or takes away from, the gospel of Christ.

In verses 13–24 Paul contrasts his years as a persecutor of the church of God with the early years after his conversion, as a preacher of the faith. Such is the grace of God, that the chief of sinners became the foremost soul-winner.

The experiences of Paul described in verses 16-24 were preparatory to his later missionary work. He also spent time in his home city Tarsus, Acts 9. 30, and a year in the church at Antioch, 11. 25-26, to provide further adequate preparation.

Aug. 1st

READING : **Galatians 2. 1-21**

THE TRUTH OF THE GOSPEL

PAUL WAS personally unknown to the churches of Judaea, although he had paid a visit to Jerusalem three years after his conversion, to stay fifteen days with Peter, vv. 1–10. Fourteen years later, he went up again with Barnabas, and took Titus. Before going, Paul had received a direct communication from God to share his message with the leaders individually, and ascertain their spiritual reactions. It was important for him to know if his labours were in harmony with theirs. The happy outcome was that all readily admitted God had entrusted Paul with the gospel for the Gentiles, as much as he had Peter with the gospel for the Jews. Indeed, James, Cephas and John shook hands with Paul and Barnabas as a token of their full fellowship with their work. Thus the harmony which marks what is of God, and is so essential in the work of the Lord, was demonstrated; and the equality of opportunity and blessing for Jews and Gentiles was once for all acknowledged by those at the centre of Jewish testimony. Paul and his gospel were vindicated. The proof of this was seen in that Titus, an uncircumcised Greek, did not have to submit to the Jewish rite. No ritual, and no prescriptive practices whatsoever, adds anything to one who believes in Christ for salvation. How great, then, the liberty every believer in Christ should enjoy, and be ready to defend!

There was a sad sequel to the Jerusalem mission which serves to show how even the most honoured Christian can succumb to sinful acts devoid of faith, vv. 11–17. Peter paid Paul a visit at Antioch, the Gentile centre of testimony, and at first ate meals with his non-Jewish brothers in Christ, as was to be expected of him; see Acts 10. But Peter's religious bias stumbled him when Jewish believers came from James, and Paul had to oppose him to his face, yet not before others had been led away. The Galatians were in just the same danger, for they were not living by faith alone in the Son of God. In verses 18–21 Paul wrote one of the greatest statements of the gospel as his own testimony to its truth, to show them the only way to true spiritual freedom. Note: divine love to the *world*, John 3. 16; to the *individual*, Gal. 2. 20; to the *company*, John 13. 1; to the *church*, Eph. 5. 25, and to *the Son*, John 3. 35.

Aug. 2nd

READING : **Galatians 3. 1-14**

BLESSING NOT CURSING

PAUL NOW turns to explain the basic doctrines of his gospel, having told how he received it, how it was subsequently acknowledged by the other apostles in Jerusalem, and how, finally, it had triumphed over Peter's lapse at Antioch. But, before doing so, he stresses the truth that the gospel is no less than God's message of blessing for mankind. When this becomes plain, it is seen that the One, who man mistakenly thinks is against him, could not be more for him, nor have done more for his good. Indeed, what God has done in Christ for man is so complete that all man can do is to accept it by faith. Any other response would deny God's right, in keeping with His promise, to be gracious in a way that exhibits the whole range of His personal glories.

The lapse of the Galatians from the truth stirred the apostle to fire five questions, aimed at their consciences, to make them review their Christian experience, vv. 1–5. Who bewitched you? How did you receive the Spirit? Is the life begun in the Spirit completed by the flesh? Have you suffered as believers in Christ for nothing? Was it because you kept the law, or because you believed the gospel that God lavished His Spirit on you? We talk of their lapse, but perhaps many others lapse without being made aware of it. Let these questions, then, act as sharp probes to search our hearts and show us if our condition also is a sub-Christian one.

Nothing is more powerful than the Word of God, Heb. 4. 12, and no matter can be settled more effectively than by reference to it. Therefore, in verses 6–14, having opened their minds, Paul shows from the Scriptures how God's blessing is obtained. Abraham's faith in God was reckoned to him for righteousness, Gen. 15. 6. He also received the promise of blessing for believers of every nationality, Gen. 12. 3. There is no blessing for the law-breaker; only a curse, Deut. 27. 28. Justification comes not by the law, for Habakkuk 2. 4 says, "The just shall live by faith". Faith in Christ crucified, who was made a curse on the tree, is the only means by which redemption is obtained from the law's curse, Deut. 21. 23. Ponder these references, and remember, God still delights to bless.

Aug. 3rd

READING: **Galatians 3. 15–29**

THE PROMISES NOT THE LAW

As a rule to understanding an involved passage of Scripture, first look for what is written about Christ. When He is seen, and His place appreciated, the other parts usually fall into place quite quickly.

Yesterday we read that Christ had become the Jews' Redeemer from the curse of the law, and the One through whom the Spirit had been received by Gentile believers. Today we learn that God, in making promises to bless Abraham and his seed (not seeds), in effect made His promise to Christ. It is not Isaac, though himself a seed of promise, who is The Seed, but the One whom Isaac foreshadowed. When God had made His promises and confirmed them (cf. Heb. 6. 13-14), it was impossible that the law which He gave 430 years afterwards could set them aside, Gal. 3. 15-18.

Then why was the law given with such awe-inspiring signs?, v. 19. Is not the law contrary to the promises?, v. 21. Right answers to these questions were essential for the Galatians seeing they were making more of the law and less of Christ. They are important for us, too, if we are to stand firm in Christ's freedom, 5. 1. God gave the law to Israel, not to every nation, in order to accentuate that kind of sin called transgression; cf. Rom. 4. 15; 5. 14; James 2. 11. It was added after the promises, and came in, as it were, by the way to act as Israel's guardian until Christ, the promised Seed, should come. For that period it put them in the category of transgressors, who, with the rest of mankind waited for the faith that was still to be revealed. The law was in no way against the promises, for its purpose was not to give life. It served to show indirectly that life, righteousness, the inheritance, and all that had been promised could be obtained by faith in Jesus Christ alone, Gal. 3 19–26.

In a word, Paul's gospel was "Christ". As at the end of chapter 2, so he warms to it once again in verses 27–29. All who have been baptized into Christ have, like soldiers putting on their uniforms, put Christ on. Seen standing in Him all are one "corps", in which there are no natural, social or sexual distinctions. Since all belong to Him by faith, it follows that all are equally Abraham's seed and heirs of God.

Aug. 4th

READING: **Galatians 4. 1–20**

NOT SLAVES BUT SONS

It is one thing to have a title to inherit, but altogether another to be capable of realizing it. One might as well be an infant, or a slave, as boast the right to an inheritance one has no hope of obtaining and enjoying. The Jews blindly considered themselves to be solely in line to inherit the promises made to their fathers; but, as infants, they could not inherit anything of God's disposing until God's time arrived for doing so. On the other hand, the Gentiles, living in ignorance of the only true God and His promises, and bowing down to idols, were unaware of the possibilities of wealth and blessing open to them, vv. 1–3; 8–9.

The gospel discloses that God always had an appointed time for fulfilling His promises, and bringing His desired blessings to all mankind. It is called in verse 4, "the fulness of the time". It was the time when God, in order fully to display the glories of His incomparable grace to a totally unworthy world, would send forth His Son, v. 4; and, subsequently, would send forth the Spirit of His Son, v. 6. That time had come. God, through Christ, had provided redemption for those in bondage, and by the free gift of the Spirit of His Son had made possible for believers the status of fullgrown sons. Since this applies to all who obey the gospel, it is no wonder Paul says to his wayward children in the faith, "Wherefore thou art no more a servant, but a son; and if a son, then an heir of God through Christ", vv. 4–7.

Do we realize the intense seriousness, and grave consequences, of going back from so great liberty to such mean bondage? Whether we become slaves to sin, or to honoured, religious ceremonies, however gratifying both may be to the flesh, we have, nonetheless, become slaves again. Christ will be no use to us; we shall have fallen from grace, 5. 4.

Moved by a zeal which can seldom, if ever, have been seen in another servant of Christ, the apostle passionately reasons and pleads with them out of a heart still only full of love, 4. 11–20. He could not even bear being at a distance from them, and he felt that perhaps the tone of his voice was too severe. What an example for all those who have a love for souls, and a charge to care for the flock of God!

Aug. 5th

READING: **Galatians 4. 21 to 5. 12**

NOT OF THE FLESH BUT OF THE SPIRIT

PURSUING HIS passionate appeal to the Galatians so as to arrest them, and turn their steps into the path of truth, Paul further expounds his "Gospel of Christian Freedom" by means of a remarkable allegory, 4. 21–31. The background can be read in Genesis 16. 1–16; 21. 1–21, based on Abraham's family life. Beginning with the story of Abraham's "wives" and their two sons, and the way the question as to which one should be the heir was decided, he goes on to teach things beyond what is recorded, drawing out parallels which had a very real bearing on the situation in the Galatian churches.

The circumstances Paul was dealing with involved true and false brethren; those who were of the Spirit and those who were of the flesh; God's sons and heirs by faith and those who jealously persecuted them, making mockery of faith by teaching the need for circumcision. Said the apostle, Abraham's wife and handmaid represent two covenants; the one like Hagar the bondmaid produced slave-children after the flesh; the one like Sarah the freewoman produced children of promise who were free. Jerusalem on earth answered to Hagar, while Jerusalem above answered to Sarah. Just as he that was born after the flesh (Ishmael) persecuted him that was born after the Spirit (Isaac), so the Judaizers persecuted true believers in Christ. But, as Abraham put the bondmaid and her son out of his house without sentiment, so must believers absolutely reject those who practise a denial of the truth of the gospel. The apostle John, writing much later of those who were not continuing in the doctrine of Christ, said, "receive him not into your house, neither bid him God speed", 2 John 9–11.

The Galatians had but to stand firm in their freedom and let no one make slaves of them again. In Christ Jesus the flesh counts for nothing, nor even the most time-honoured item of religious ritual; faith acting in love alone counts, 5. 1–6. With feelings roused as high as anywhere else in all his writings, Paul contrasts their persuasion with his persecution, vv. 7–12. Though the cross is a stumbling block to many, the Lord's faithful servant will not deny Him who endured it and bore its curse; see 2. 20; 5. 24; 6. 12, 14.

Aug. 6th

READING: **Galatians 5. 13–26**

LIBERTY NOT LICENCE

IT HAS often been said, and with much truth, that man is a creature of extremes, swinging from one side to another like a pendulum. Under the law his tendency was to develop a code of conduct to regulate his every action and thereby to demonstrate the perfection of his obedience. Alas, in his punctilious attention to things not commanded, he altogether neglected the law's weightier matters, as the Lord Jesus pointed out in dealing with the scribes and Pharisees, Matt. 23. 23. When delivered from the law's yoke and curse, and set free to live a life in the power of the Spirit of God's Son, his tendency is to go to the opposite extreme and presume he is free to do as he pleases. Both attitudes are equally wrong, are inconsistent with the gospel, and are proof that the libertine, professing faith in Christ, is as much a man after the flesh as is a Pharisee under the law.

The great practical lesson the gospel teaches its converts is that the liberty, to which they are called, involves them in the obligation to live lives under the control of the Spirit. It is at this point in his letter that Paul indicates how such lives differ radically, and patently, from the lives of those who have no place or part in the kingdom of God. Firstly, walking in the Spirit will ensure that the believer does not live a life to gratify the desires of the flesh, Gal. 5. 16. Secondly, being led by the Spirit he will not be under the law, v. 18; he will, nevertheless, be subject to Christ. Thirdly, his life will be productive of every spiritual and moral quality, such as were perfectly displayed in all their beauty in the life of Christ Himself, vv. 22-23. Evidently, a believer not holding to the fundamental basis of the gospel cannot attain to this Christ-like display of character and conduct.

Earlier the apostle had written, "I am crucified with Christ: nevertheless I live; yet not I, but Christ liveth in me", 2. 20. Now he writes, "And they that are Christ's have crucified the flesh with the affections and lusts", 5. 24. So that, by means of the cross, in which Paul for one gloried, 6. 14, all the hideous works of man's incorrigible, fallen nature, 5. 19–21, are counted as crucified, and, instead, the believer's new life in Christ is seen in lowly, Christ-like service to others.

Aug. 7th

READING: **Galatians 6. 1–18**

THE FINAL WORD

IN THE concluding chapter of this weighty and powerful letter (see also 2 Cor. 10. 10), it is remarkable how the dynamic force of the preacher in Paul blends with the tender care of the pastor-teacher. The false brethren have been cut down. Those who merely boasted in the mutilation of the flesh of others have been shown to be ignorant of the truth concerning the cross of Christ. As the apostle was later to write, all believers in Christ "are circumcised with the circumcision made without hands, in putting off the body of the sins of the flesh by the circumcision of Christ", Col. 2. 11. In this letter he has once already said that neither circumcision nor uncircumcision counts for anything, Gal. 5. 6; and before he lays down his pen he will say it again, 6. 15.

Finally he will insist that doctrines are meant to affect practice. He thus applies his gospel to certain of the Galatians' personal attitudes and actions. So deftly is this done that, although we might not recognize his pen pictures, they must clearly have portrayed the lineaments of the Galatians' lives very accurately. There is the person who has been caught off his guard by some sin, and the "spiritual gentleman" intervening to restore, and, out of love for Christ, taking some of his load lest he stumble under it again, vv. 1–2. Then there is the self-seeking man who bores others with his achievements, who, being nothing, has only succeeded in deceiving himself. Such must learn to keep their boasting to themselves, vv. 3–5. There are those, too, who receive spiritual instruction, but feel no obligation to make any material recompense to their instructors. Such are warned that God is not hoodwinked, for what is spent on self is better given to others, especially to those of the household of faith, vv. 6–10. Lastly, there are those who were courting popularity with the world, and seeking to avoid the persecution which is the common lot of Christians, vv. 12–16.

Before his short benediction Paul's godly zeal flares up once more. His own hand had penned these words in large characters; his own body bore the marks of his sufferings with the gospel, proof of his bondservice to the Lord Jesus. He has had trouble enough. That is all.

Introducing Ephesians

THE LETTERS to the Ephesians, Philippians and Colossians, which the apostle Paul wrote from prison, stand out as a magnificent mountain range above his other inspired letters. In Ephesians he scales the highest peaks of all.

In his Epistle to the Romans, he wrote first of the appalling need of the sinner and then of the grace of God in meeting it. But in Ephesians Paul is free in spirit, despite his chains, to begin with a doxology revealing the counsels and gracious purposes of God for the blessing of man long before sin marred His fair creation.

It is not written to correct errors in any particular Christian assembly. It may have been a circular letter; there are no personal greetings, though Paul had laboured long at Ephesus. His thought is dominated by his lofty theme, the exceeding grace of God to man in Christ. Consider the triumphs of that grace in Ephesus in Acts 19. 18–20.

Ephesians presents truth not mentioned in the Gospels or earlier Epistles. It reveals the intention of God to unite everything in heaven and earth under the headship, the authority, of Christ. This is called a "mystery"—that is, a sacred secret previously hidden but now made known, Eph. 1. 9–10; 3. 5–6. This is the final form of the government of God as vested in the Man Christ Jesus prior to the eternal state where righteousness shall dwell and God shall be all in all.

Connected with this is another new revelation, that all believers, Jew and Gentile alike, have been made one, so as to form the body of Christ, who is the Head. Also this church, this assembly, the special object of His love and sacrifice, is to be presented to Him in glory as His bride, 2. 15; 5. 27.

The first part of the letter, chs. 1–3, is markedly doctrinal explaining the purpose of God toward us and our resultant privileges; "grace" and "in Christ" are keynotes; note their repetition. Chapters 4–6 are an exhortation to conduct ourselves worthily of our high calling; "walk" and "in the Lord" are keynotes. The first part deals with spiritual Wealth and spiritual Wisdom. The second deals with spiritual Walk and spiritual Warfare.

Aug. 8th

READING : **Ephesians 1. 1-14**

PRAISE FOR SPIRITUAL BLESSINGS

"BLESSED BE the Lord God, the God of Israel, who only doeth wondrous things. And blessed be his glorious name for ever." So sang David, Psa. 72. 18–19. We bless the same God, but now fully revealed as the God and Father of our Lord Jesus Christ. Paul bursts into praise for the wealth of blessings that God has lavished upon us in Christ. Surely praise becomes us, whether at the outset of the day or when beginning a letter; see Psa. 33. 1; 147. 1.

First, note the *cause* of our blessing. It is the sovereign will and activity of God Himself. It is according to the good pleasure which He purposed in Himself. How comforting is this! "The counsel of the Lord standeth for ever, the thoughts of his heart to all generations", Psa. 33. 11. And none can stay His hand; God has commanded the blessing of His people, and none can reverse it, Num. 23. 20. The eternal security of the believer is rooted in the eternal purpose of God. So are all our blessings.

Secondly, note the *character* of the blessings. Israel's blessings were earthly and material; ours are heavenly and spiritual. Israel lost theirs by their sin; ours are eternally secured in Christ. Paul's enjoyment of them was unaffected by the rigours of prison life, or by the threat of impending death. Do we really enjoy them too?

Thirdly, note the *cost* of such blessings. It is "through his blood". We can never forget that it is by the death of the Lord that we become such beneficiaries.

Finally, note the *purpose* of such undeserved favour. It is that we should be holy and without blemish before Him. To be holy is to be set apart for the service of God as were the holy vessels in the temple, that we should stand before Him as honoured servants in the presence of their monarch. Thrice we read that God's purpose is that we should be to the praise of His glory. His grand design is that now and in eternity men and angels should praise Him for His work in us, seen in what we are and do. Let us pray, "May this be true of me today!".

"*Every day will I bless thee; and I will praise thy name for ever and ever*", Psa. 145. 2.

Aug. 9th

READING : **Ephesians 1. 15-23**

PRAYER FOR SPIRITUAL WISDOM

GOD'S GRACE and the believers' response move Paul to thanksgiving and prayer. How much do we give thanks for all the saints? How much do we make mention of them by name, each with his particular need? Do we pray for their spiritual progress, or only for their temporal welfare? Do we pray for all, backslider and faithful servant, youngest and eldest? To do so takes time. Paul sets us an example, Col. 1. 3; Eph. 6. 18.

He prays to the Father of glory, the source whence all true glory radiates, that we may really come to know Him. We must diligently learn His will from the Scriptures, and get to know Him more, 2 Pet. 1. 5; Col. 1. 9; Phil. 3. 10. He wants the eyes of our heart enlightened to know, and to have an inward conviction about, three things.

Firstly, we must remember that attached to our calling is a hope, an anchor to the soul, sure and steadfast. We are saved in hope of eternal association with Christ in glory. To be looking forward to that day is to fortify ourselves for the trials of the present. To have our heart set, not only on the redemption of our bodies, but on being with Christ and like Him, will wean us from worldly pursuits.

Secondly, we must consider the wealth of glory that God has in His inheritance in the saints. Every true Israelite treasured dearly the inheritance allotted to him in Canaan. But God also has an inheritance. Moses said, "the Lord's portion is his people; Jacob is the lot of his inheritance", Deut. 32. 9. We must view our salvation, not primarily as a blessing for us, but as bringing pleasure and eternal glory to God. His glorious work in the material creation is eclipsed by His moral and spiritual triumphs in His people.

Thirdly, we need a firm conviction concerning the exceeding greatness of His power. This is the mighty strength exerted against all the powers of darkness when He raised Christ from the dead, and when He enthroned Him at His right hand far above all. This is the power available to us who trust Him, power that is available now.

"*As for me, God forbid that I should sin against the Lord in ceasing to pray for you*", 1 Sam. 12. 23.

Aug. 10th

READING : **Ephesians 2. 1-10**

NEW LIFE AND A NEW CREATION

WHAT A triumph is life from the dead! The mighty power of God wrought not only in Christ's resurrection, but in giving new life to us. For we were dead, dead towards God, wholly unresponsive to His claims upon us, Eph. 2. 1. We were certainly actively responding to the subtle Satanic suggestions that govern men in the world. This, says Paul, was true both of you Gentiles and of us Jews. We were all children marked by disobedience, and so we were all children arousing the wrath of God, 2. 2–3.

But God has acted. Consider His great love wherewith He loved us; contemplate the exceeding riches of His grace toward us. By grace, by the undeserved favour of God, we have been saved (R.V.). Salvation from our sins is a daily process as we watch and pray, and as our Lord intercedes for us, Heb. 7. 25. Salvation from the presence of sin is future, Rom. 13. 11. But already we have been saved from eternal judgment for sin. We can say that, not by our efforts, but "according to his mercy he saved us", Titus 3. 5.

God has so acted that in the ages to come He might display the incomparable riches of His grace towards us. We are His handiwork, a new creation. We dare not be secretly proud of, or satisfied with, any efforts of our own, Jer. 9. 23–24. Just as the praise for a work of art goes solely to the craftsman, so the praise for God's work in us is wholly His.

But God has a present purpose also. We are created anew to walk, moving step by step through life, in a path of good works. We exist now to make known the character of God who is good and who does good, to follow the steps of Him who went about doing good. We must *do* good to all men, and especially to the household of faith, Gal. 6. 10. And God has designed good works for us: giving to the poor, visiting the sick, showing hospitality. Let us pray that daily we may be ready for every good work; let us say with king David, "Is there not yet any . . . that I may show the kindness of God unto him?", 2 Sam. 9. 3; Titus 3. 1.

God has "*quickened us together with Christ . . . raised us up together, and made us sit together . . . in Christ*", Eph. 2. 5–6.

Aug. 11th

READING : **Ephesians 2. 11-22**

REMEMBER . . . BUT NOW . . . PEACE

"WHEREFORE REMEMBER." It is wholesome to remember how far we once were from God. We do well to look to the hole of the pit whence we were digged, Isa. 52. 1. She who has been forgiven much will love much; and who has not been forgiven much?, Luke 7.47. Every sinner is far from God, and salvation is like bringing up the poor and the beggar from the dunghill to sit among princes and to inherit the throne of glory. Gentiles could not even claim the promises of a Saviour that had been made to Israel, Rom. 9. 4. Moreover, the very commandments of God were designed to keep Israel pure from the idolatry and immorality of the nations. Yet this was misused to pander to Jewish pride and Gentile jealousy. Of the ingrained national prejudices and tribal hatreds that have plagued mankind, none was greater than those between Jew and Gentile. But the cross cancelled all this; now both have been reconciled to God. The result is peace with God and peace between man and man. Now we enjoy peace.

"How beautiful upon the mountains are the feet of him . . . that publisheth peace", Isa. 52. 7. How could the courier traversing the hills of Judaea bring good news of peace? Because the victory was won. So the message of the Lord after the victory of His cross was, "Peace be unto you", John 20. 19.

Now from Jew and Gentile Christ has made one body, completely new. We are all citizens of the heavenly city, all members of the same household, all children with access to the same Father, all built together as a building where God Himself has His dwelling by His Spirit.

Let us keep in remembrance the contrast, and the grace of God that has made such a difference. Once we were separated from Christ, excluded from the promises made to Israel, without a hope for the future, and utterly without God. Now we have been brought near. "So near, so very near to God, Nearer I could not be; For in the person of His Son, I am as near as He." "In Christ Jesus" we could not be nearer the heart of God; and "by the blood of Christ" that place is assured us for ever, Eph. 2. 13.

"All . . . fitly framed together . . . a holy temple in the Lord."

Aug. 12th

READING : **Ephesians 3. 1-13**

A PRISONER . . . FOR YOU

PAUL IS in prison. It is the result of bringing the Gospel to the Gentiles and arousing Jewish jealousy. But he speaks not of being Caesar's prisoner. He is the prisoner of Christ Jesus, still in the wise and loving hands of his Saviour. He recognizes that it is the will of our sovereign Lord for him. Later he asks for prayer, not for liberation from prison, but for grace to be faithful in it, Eph. 4. 1; 6. 18–20.

How many have suffered for us in declaring the whole counsel of God? How many have suffered at the stake so that we would have the Scriptures in our own language! How many are imprisoned today! Let us remember and pray for those who are in bonds.

The Lord takes us aside in various ways to reveal Himself and His will to us. Paul wonders at the favour given him of being chosen to make known secrets that had been hid for ages. The Old Testament taught that Gentiles would be blessed with Israel, Deut. 32. 43. But now, says Paul, both are brought into *one new body*. Whatever our pre-conversion background, we are joint-heirs of an eternal inheritance, joint-members of the body, and joint-sharers of God's promises, Eph. 3. 6. How honoured was Paul to preach the illimitable, untraceable, unsearchable riches of Christ, to preach not only Christ crucified, but Christ glorified! He has already called himself the least of the apostles, but now "less than the least of all saints". When we recall the barrenness of our unconverted days and the amazing goodness of God, how can we think anything of ourselves?

"O Lord, how manifold are thy works! in wisdom hast thou made them all"; this is praise of the first creation, Psa. 104. 24. But now God is displaying to unseen intelligences His manifold wisdom through the new creation that will never be marred by sin. It is His wisdom, multi-coloured and radiant as the rainbow, seen in the Church. The Church is the outcome of His eternal purpose and is destined for eternal glory. Therefore we faint not, Eph. 3. 13.

When you suffer for Christ's sake, "*Rejoice, and be exceeding glad: for great is your reward in heaven*", Matt. 5. 11–12.

Aug. 13th

READING : **Ephesians 3. 14-21**

KNOWING LOVE THAT SURPASSES KNOWLEDGE

HOW GRACIOUS of God to preserve for us the prayers of men of God like Nehemiah and Daniel! How valuable in the Psalms is the record of the private confessions and prayers of king David. By such scriptures we may learn to pray. For we are men of like passions, having to do with the same God. Here the apostle Paul records another of his prayers.

Prayer—How? Paul bows his knees to the Father. To fall on our knees is to express reverence, dependence and entreaty. In Gethsemane our Lord Himself kneeled down and prayed. At Miletus, Paul and the Ephesian elders knelt in prayer, Acts 20. 36. Daniel kneeled upon his knees three times a day and prayed and gave thanks to his God. The bodily attitude is the outcome of, and an aid to, our spiritual state.

Prayer—to Whom? Prayer today is to the Father of our Lord Jesus Christ. David and Daniel did not know Him as Father, but now the Son has made Him known, and the Holy Spirit is sent forth into our hearts crying, "Abba, Father", Gal. 4. 6. To Him, the Father of lights, the Father of spirits, we have access with confidence, Eph. 2. 18; 3. 12.

Prayer—for What? That Christ may make His permanent dwelling in our hearts, and that we may grasp the vast extent of the purpose and love of God in Him, John 14. 23. Mere intellectual study is insufficient. We need the enabling of the Holy Spirit to know the love that surpasses knowledge. How important therefore to confess our sins immediately we grieve the Holy Spirit. Moreover, it is a privilege open to us all; every fellow-believer has something to offer as we seek a full-orbed view of the love of our Lord. "Thou art coming to a King; Large petitions with thee bring. For His grace and power are such, None can ever ask too much."

To comprehend we must be rooted and grounded in love. The strength and beauty of a tree stem from the depth and spread of its roots. The stability of a building depends on the strength of its foundations. So the assurance and enjoyment of the love of Christ is the soil whence grows an increasing opening of the heart to Him.

"*Now unto him that is able to do exceeding abundantly above all that we ask or think . . . be glory*", Eph. 3. 20–21.

Aug. 14th

READING : **Ephesians 4. 1-16**

WALKING WORTHY OF OUR CALLING

HOW SHOULD we behave in view of the amazing grace of God toward us? First, we must be marked by lowliness, v. 2.

Humility is the key both to pleasing God and to all Christian progress. It is a rare plant in this world's jungle. It blossoms in the presence of God. It grows out of a sense of our utter dependence upon Him, out of a sense of our shortcomings and of His greatness. "Humble yourselves therefore", 1 Pet. 5. 6. Meekness was the spirit Moses showed when cruelly criticised by Miriam, Num. 12. 3. It is not lack of spirit, but having our spirit under control even when unjustly treated. Longsuffering is long patience with men such as God Himself has, 2 Pet. 3. 15. How different the history of the churches would have been if these commands had been obeyed! All tend to God's great objective of harmony and unity.

Unity. There is one body indwelt by one Spirit, and a common hope for every member. We all confess the same Lord, exercise the same faith, have the same faith to hold, and submit to the same baptism. The Spirit-made unity is cemented by our diligently pursuing peace. Ephesians 4. 1–3 shows the spirit that must direct us; 4. 4–7 emphasizes our unity; 4. 7–11 shows that in the various members of the one body there is a diversity of function.

Diversity. Gift and suitable grace are given to every member by our exalted, sovereign Lord. Apostles and prophets in the early church; evangelists, teachers and pastors today; each and all we must value as gifts from Him. How low He descended for us! How high He has ascended! He uses His triumph to enrich His church, giving far more lavishly than a Roman general enriching those who shared his victory. Each gift is for the building up of the whole body of Christ, though many gifts are exercised in local churches. Each one of us is responsible to help. Are we content to remain babes? If we are not concerned to grow we are in danger of being "carried about" like frail rudderless craft losing sight of our true objective in life. This is to attain to the spirit, character and behaviour of Christ Himself, to "grow up into him in all things".

"*Let us go on to perfection*", to full growth, Heb. 6. 1.

Aug. 15th

READING : **Ephesians 4. 17-32**

PUTTING ON THE NEW MAN

The Way of the World, Eph. 4. 17–19. Here is a solemn charge from the Lord Himself—to think and act differently from the world around. The shameless indecency and unbridled lust of the Roman world is increasingly seen in the world today. Men's minds are blinded and their hearts are hardened, insensitive to God and His Word. What a description of godless men! It emphasizes the corruption of the evil nature which we each inherit from Adam and still carry with us. It does not improve at our conversion, Eph. 4. 22 R.V. So we dare not just drift through life.

The Way of Christ, Eph. 4. 20–21. Thank God there is another way of life which was seen in Christ. We have not merely learned about Him, but have seen a life of perfect holiness embodied in the Man "Jesus". Truth is seen in Him.

The Way of Christ's Members, Eph. 4. 22–32. Each member of Christ's body is viewed by God as being "in Christ"; hence he must manifest the character of Christ. He is part of the "new creation"; hence he must habitually walk "in newness of life". We must be in practice what we are by calling, "saints". We are deliberately to put off the old habits, and also to don new ones, Eph. 4. 22, 24 with Rom. 13. 14.

The Holy Spirit alone can empower us to do this. He seals us as God's possession until our very bodies are redeemed, Rom. 8. 11, 23. He imparts and envigorates our new nature. But we may sadden or vex Him as Israel did, Eph. 4. 30; Isa. 63. 10. So all bitterness and all ill-will must be put away. Our attitude to others must be right. How often is speech mentioned! Because out of the fulness of the heart the mouth speaks, the Lord Jesus says, "by thy words thou shalt be justified" or "condemned", Matt. 12. 37. To adjust our speech we must first adjust our thinking; this determines behaviour. We need to be renewed in the spirit of our minds by humbly meditating on the Scriptures, Eph. 4. 23. Then, occupied with Christ, we shall walk even as He walked; and this is our joy. We gladly put off dirty old clothes so as to put on our "beautiful garments", Isa. 52. 1. Moved by God's love for us we become positively kind and freely forgiving.

"*Forgiving ... even as God also ... forgave you*", Eph. 4.32 R.V.

Aug. 16th

READING : **Ephesians 5. 1-21**

CHILDREN COPYING THEIR FATHER

Walking in Love, Eph. 5. 1–2. What a privilege!—bidden to be like God Himself, children imitating a loving Father; urged to live in love as Christ loved us, securing our forgiveness at unspeakable cost to Himself.

Walking in Purity, Eph. 5. 3–6. His self-sacrificing love is the opposite to what men often call love; so comes "a trumpet-call to purity". Avoid discussing the unbridled lusts of godless men, shameful things like sodomy which God condemns outright; they are better not named or thought of. Think rather of things of good report, Phil. 4. 8; Rom. 6. 21; 16. 19. Jesting often leads to a flippant attitude to the sacred bond of marriage, and also to things that shut men out of the kingdom of God and bring His wrath on them. Saints dare not share in defiling things. Beware worldly comedians!

Walking as Children of Light, Eph. 5. 7–14. We are not only in the light, but light itself, identified with our spiritual environment and with the nature of God our Father. Those who lie dead and those who lie asleep may not easily be distinguished. But shame on us if we are not different from children of disobedience, dead in their sins! We should be as different as light from darkness. Let us not then be careless. Men around us relax in ignorance of divine displeasure, but we must be wakeful and watchful.

Walking Wisely, Eph. 5. 15–21. The path of love, purity and light is also the path of wisdom. The wise count the present time too precious to waste on pastimes. The time is short for all. As one eagerly grasps a bargain in the market-place, so we must "redeem", buy up, every opportunity to serve God and men. How can we be frivolous in such evil days? The saint dare not indulge recklessly in anything, let alone intoxicating drink. Drunkenness leads to "riot", the folly of the prodigal son. Do we make full room for the *Holy* Spirit in our hearts? Only so shall we have true joy issuing in praise to God, James 5. 13. Then in everything we shall give thanks, and out of reverence for Christ develop a submissive spirit in our relations one with another.

"*Have no fellowship . . . but rather reprove them*", Eph. 5. 11.

Aug. 17th

READING : **Ephesians 5. 22-33**

THE SACRED BEAUTY OF MARRIAGE

THIS CHALLENGING passage is a call for mutual submission and affection; a call first for the submission of wives to husbands, then (in chapter 6) of children to parents and of servants to masters, with the duties also of husbands, parents and masters.

The natural man finds it irksome to submit to anyone. Yet the Lord of the universe Himself, when a child, was subject to His failing parents, and later to unjust rulers; He recognized that all authority stems from God, Luke 2. 51; John 19.11. Indeed, when all enemies are put under His feet He will, still in perfect glorified Manhood, subject Himself again to God, 1 Cor. 15. 28. Therefore no thought of personal inferiority is implied in submission. As man is the head of the woman her submission is to be as unto the Lord Himself. Further, it is to be as the Church is subject to Christ. This is not cringing obedience, but a glad response to a love that is worthy of it.

The charge to husbands is equally demanding, to love one's wife even as Christ loves His Church. This means sympathetic consideration and deliberate self-giving for one's wife. Surely, such exhortations should govern one's thoughts before choosing a life partner, and we must cultivate these virtues in all our relations with our fellow-men; whether married or unmarried, the spirit of Christ must mark us. Moreover, man and wife are one, so a man must care for his wife as for his own body. In considering the interests of his partner he is considering his own.

What a high estimate of the sacredness and preciousness of the marriage bond! It is likened to that between Christ and His Church, uniquely that for which He gave Himself. How privileged to be a member of such a community! The purpose of His sacrifice was to sanctify it, to set it apart for Himself, having cleansed it, just as each member is cleansed, by the spiritual purifying of the spoken word of God. Thus the Church is made suitable for her divine Lover as Eve was for Adam, to be presented glorious, with no defiling spot or disfiguring wrinkle, but "as a bride adorned for her husband", Rev. 21. 2.

"*Love . . . even as Christ also loved . . . and gave*", Eph. 5. 25.

Aug. 18th

READING : **Ephesians 6. 1-24**

FIGHT THE GOOD FIGHT OF FAITH

PARAGRAPH 6. 1–9 concludes the section of the letter urging us to behave as befits our high calling. In the home children must obey, and fathers must be considerate but firm. In daily work both servants and masters must act as under the eye of our Master in heaven.

The Wealth of our spiritual blessing is immense. But do we enjoy it? Have we lost our joy in the Lord, the Holy Spirit's guidance, and power to live as we ought? As Israel's enemies robbed them of their God-given inheritance in Canaan, so unseen spirit-forces try to rob us of ours. Here we are told how to withstand these foes.

The Warfare is not against human enemies. Men, used by Satan, may water down the truth or shake our faith in the Scriptures; false teachers may make us self-complacent. But the real battle is against spiritual foes who are mighty and cunning, 1 Tim. 4. 1. Yet God has provided us with complete armour; this we must take up resolutely.

The Weapons are spiritual, 2 Cor. 10. 4–5. Daily we must put on the belt of truth; we must know the truth and then apply it to our conduct, John 8. 31–32. We need a breastplate to meet the foe, assurance that we are really right with God and men. We must be ready to announce the gospel of peace; thus we carry the war into enemy territory. We tell men that victory was won at the cross, so that we and they may enjoy peace, Isa. 52. 7. Above all, faith in God and His Word is a wonderful protection like the great shield that covered Roman soldiers. With the hope of final salvation as a helmet, we take the sword of the Spirit which is the spoken Word of Christ. We must read, memorize and meditate upon the Scriptures "day and night", Josh. 1. 8. A humble dependence upon them will help us parry the attacks of Satan, as our Lord did when tempted in the wilderness, Psa. 1. 2; Matt. 4. 4, 7, 10.

Finally, at all seasons, in every crisis, we must draw near to God in earnest prayer; and not just for ourselves, because "all saints" need support, even a man like Paul. So the truth of the one Body recurs at the end of the letter.

"Grace be with all them that love our Lord Jesus Christ in sincerity", with uncorrupted, undying love, Eph. 6. 24.

Introducing Philippians

THE BACKGROUND to the Epistle is found in Acts 16, where we are told that Phillippi was a Roman colony. Colonists from Rome had settled there in the midst of an alien population. They were citizens of Rome and their customs, language, laws and dress were Roman. They owned their allegiance to the Roman Emperor, and their safety was guaranteed by Roman soldiers. However, a heavenly colony had been planted by the preaching of the Gospel, and the saints were to conduct themselves as citizens of Heaven, owning allegiance to Christ.

There seem to be two main reasons for the writing of the Epistle. It is written first of all to express Paul's gratitude for the gift sent by the assembly, Phil. 4. 10–20, and secondly to rectify disharmony that had come between two sisters, 4. 2–3. There was a grave danger of the saints at Philippi taking sides in the quarrel, causing strife and division; thus Paul exhorts the saints to oneness of mind and purpose, 1. 27; 2. 1–4, 14–16; 4. 2–3. In the Epistle Paul also warns the saints against the enemies of the assembly, 1. 28–30; 3. 2, 18–19.

The Epistle divides readily into the four chapters:

Chapter 1—Confidence in the Purpose of God.
Chapter 2—Conformity to the Pattern of Christ.
Chapter 3—Constant Progress in the Pursuit of Christ.
Chapter 4—Concern for the People of God.

In chapter 1 the apostle shows his confidence in the purpose of God despite the conditions in which he is found. Here the mind of Christ will give me a love for the Gospel and cause me to rejoice when it is preached. In chapter 2 Paul unfolds the Perfect Pattern of humility and seeking the interests of others, and exhorts the saints to be conformed to Christ. Here the mind of Christ will give me a love for the assembly and cause me to seek humbly the welfare of my fellow saints. In chapter 3 he shows the need for constant progress in the Christian pathway, with Christ as the goal. Here the mind of Christ will give me a love for the heavenly manner of life. In chapter 4 he shows his concern for the spiritual welfare of Euodias and Syntyche, and thus for all the saints. Here the mind of Christ will give me a love that will seek to heal every breach.

Aug. 19th

READING : **Philippians 1. 1-11**

THE PRAYER OF PAUL

THE APOSTLE writes as a bondslave of Jesus Christ, to show undivided allegiance to Christ and to stress the idea of humility and lowliness. Every believer has been bought with a price, 1 Cor. 6. 19–20, and should therefore manifest these characteristics. The word "saints" means "set apart ones", and this was to be demonstrated in lives set apart to and for God. Positionally they were in Christ but practically their lives were lived in Philippi. Their lives were to be fully in harmony with their position in Christ, and for this grace and peace were provided, vv. 1–2.

The apostle's remembrance of the saints was the basis of thanksgiving to God as he made request for them, vv. 3–4. Their past lives caused thanksgiving but there was a present need. Past achievement is not sufficient for the present testimony. Paul's thanksgiving is linked with their fellowship in the gospel, v. 5, and with his confidence in God, v. 6. How needful to be consistent in the Christian pathway, and how comforting to know that God will accomplish His purpose.

Conscious that God was witness, v. 8, Paul prays that certain characteristics be seen in the saints. *Increasing in love*, v. 9—as a river increasing in volume as it pursues its course, flowing between the banks of knowledge and judgment. Knowledge is that which has a practical effect upon the life. The word translated "judgment" only occurs here, and carries the idea of perception and sensitivity. Thus increasing in love is linked with the working out of the will of God and a perception of every situation, a sensitivity to the feelings of others. *Intelligent in discernment*, v. 10—approve things that differ (are excellent). The idea is of discerning what is of greater value. Spiritual things are more valuable than material, and the welfare of the assembly more important than personal ego. *Irreproachable in character and conduct*, v. 10—sincere and without offence. Sincere means to be pure, unalloyed, and shows there is to be no veneer. Without offence is conduct that does not cause another to stumble. Only as these characteristics mark us shall we be serving the glory and praise of God by a fruitfulness that carries with it the fragrance of Christ, v. 11.

Aug. 20th

READING : **Philippians 1. 12-30**

THE PURPOSE OF LIFE

THE INTERESTS of Christ are advanced by the preaching of the Gospel, vv. 12–18; the presenting of Christ in a believer's life, vv. 19–26; and the protecting of the testimony, vv. 27–30.

What seemed to be a set-back to the spread of the Gospel was in fact a help, v. 12, and thus the apostle rejoices that Christ is preached, v. 18. In the preaching of the Gospel the interests of Christ were furthered and this caused Paul to rejoice. He was not taken up with his circumstances but with the preaching of Christ. Thus he expresses his confidence, that he would be saved from despairing and becoming ashamed, and this through the *preaching of Christ*, v. 18, *the prayers of the saints* and *the provision of the Spirit*, v. 19.

The magnifying of Christ in the apostle's body was all important, and he was prepared to live or die as long as life or death served that purpose, v. 20. The whole purpose of his life was "Christ". "For to me to live is Christ", v. 21. Life is the opportunity to further the interests of Christ, to tell the gospel, to be of help to the people of God, and to stand for Christ in a world that rejects Him. One passion should fill the heart—affection to Christ, and one purpose should fill the life —to live for Christ. Death was gain, very far better, but Paul in true bondservant-character was prepared to remain for the benefit of others, vv. 23–25.

Life, to Paul, was only of value if it served the glory of Christ, and so he sought not his own welfare but the welfare of others. If this purpose of life characterized each one in the assembly, then the testimony would be maintained despite the attacks of the enemy. Such purpose of life would govern behaviour so that it would be in keeping with the Gospel; it would cause the whole assembly to stand firm against every attack, having one aim and one will; it would result in all striving together, expending energy for the faith, and would give courage that rests upon the assurance that the end is certain, vv. 27–30.

May this purpose of life characterize each one of us for the glory of God, the magnifying of Christ in our lives, and for the spiritual welfare of the assembly with which we are associated.

Aug. 21st

READING : **Philippians 2. 1-11**

THE PERFECT PATTERN

THE JOY that the apostle desired, v. 2, is that of seeing harmony in the assembly at Philippi which could only be produced by a practical demonstration of the four statements in verse 1. If we take heed to the consolation or appeal of being in Christ, we shall be likeminded; to the comfort of love, we shall have the same love; to the fellowship of the Spirit, we shall be of one accord; and to the bowels and mercies we shall be of one mind. Unity in the assembly can only be maintained when we practice the principle of not being self-centred but showing deep interest in others. Strife and vainglory are opposite to this principle and can only divide, but humility and selfless service to others produce and maintain unity.

The perfect pattern of this principle is the Lord Himself in His condescension, vv. 6–8, and moral conformity to Christ in every believer will secure perfect harmony in the assembly. The condescension of Christ from the pinnacle of glory to the ignominy and shame of the cross was voluntary and deliberate in order to secure the blessing of others. When He took the form of a bondservant it was not in place of the form of God but in addition to it, for He never laid aside His deity nor His glory, Col. 1. 15; 2. 9. He became in the likeness of men indicating that, although He became truly man, He was more than man, He was God. However, although He possessed all the attributes of Godhead as He moved among men, He never exalted Himself but humbled Himself and became obedient to the extent of death so that death—and that the shameful death of the cross—was in itself an act of obedience.

Such a description of self-renunciation for the eternal blessing of others is a perfect example for the believer to follow. Note that "this mind", v. 5, is the mind of fixing attention on the interests of others. In your thinking be as Christ, reflect in your own minds the mind of Christ. This alone will preserve harmony in the assembly.

Christ willingly emptied Himself and humbled Himself, but God exalted Him to supreme majesty, glory and dignity. In recognition of all that Jesus—the despised and rejected Man—is in His exaltation, the vast universe will be subjugated to Him and acknowledge His supreme sovereignty, vv. 9–11.

Aug. 22nd

READING : **Philippians 2. 12-30**

PRACTICE OF "THIS MIND"

THE APOSTLE in chapter 1 called upon the saints in the assembly to stand fast, exhorting them to strive together, v. 27. In the first verses of chapter 2 he mentions four facts that would produce harmony in the assembly if worked out, and he states the principle of self-denial with a deep interest in others, vv. 1–4. Having unfolded that principle in all perfection in Christ, he now exhorts the saints to obey, practising such a principle, v. 12. The assembly testimony for God, and its pleasure to God, were in danger of shipwreck by disharmony among the saints. Salvation from such shipwreck lay in each one in the assembly practising this principle. This was to be done with fear and trembling, knowing the deceitfulness of their own hearts and yet conscious of divine aid, vv. 12–13. Where there is a deep longing in the assembly for harmony, illfeeling, murmurings and disputings, which only produce dissatisfaction and suspicion, will be exterminated. This is so essential if Christlikeness of character is to be exhibited as one harmonious display in the moral darkness all around the assembly, vv. 15–16.

In vv. 17–30 the principle, seen in perfection in Christ, is seen in the lives of Paul, Timothy and Epaphroditus. In Paul we see *contentment* in esteeming others better than himself. His humility is seen in his contentment at being the lesser part of the sacrifice poured upon the major part of the Philippian assembly's testimony and service to God, vv. 17–18. The assembly is always greater than the individual servant. In Timothy we see the *character*, willing to serve all. He had a genuine anxiety for the spiritual welfare of all the saints, and to this end he willingly toiled, appreciating the value of the assembly to God, Acts 20. 28. The Philippians were acquainted with the selfless service of Timothy, Phil. 2. 19–24. In Epaphroditus we see *concern*, and thus his willingness to suffer in the service of others. Even nigh unto death he did not want to cause the assembly any distress or anxiety.

Thus the principle of humility and selfless service for the welfare and well-being of others is shown in the lives of these Christlike men who placed great value on the saints and the unity of the assembly.

Aug. 23rd

READING : **Philippians 3. 1-11**

THE PURSUIT OF LIFE

TO WRITE the "same things" shows that Paul is continuing the same subject of thinking not on one's own things. There were adversaries who were seeking their own things and thus dividing the saints, so it was needful for him to repeat the warnings. Judaistic teachers would impose an outward ritual but believers are the true circumcision, as characterized by sanctuary experience and by confidence in Christ, not in the flesh, vv. 1–3; 1 Cor. 2. 2; Gal. 6. 14; Col. 2. 11–12.

Here, Paul is a contrast to the false teachers who were placing their confidence in the flesh. The dignities that he had were now set aside for Christ. His covenantal, national, tribal, racial, ceremonial, religious and moral dignities, were counted as assets before he was saved; these he sets aside as being worthless in his pursuit along the Christian pathway. Christ had captivated his heart and thus Christ was his goal.

"That I may know him"—Christ in resurrection—in Him alone the heart is fully satisfied. He desired to be fully occupied with the Lord. Spiritual maturity is only produced by a present, personal, practical knowledge of Christ. "The power of his resurrection"—the power proceeding from Christ in resurrection, power that enables victory in the Christian conflict and produces a life of holiness and godliness. "The fellowship of his sufferings"—entering into the sufferings of reproach and rejection that the Lord experienced, Heb. 13. 13; 2 Cor. 12. 10, we suffer for righteousness' sake and through carrying out the will of God, 1 Pet. 2. 12–23; 3. 14. "Being made conformable unto his death"—although Paul was prepared to die as a martyr, we feel the thought here is of dying to sin, Rom. 6. 10, that he might be a blessing to others. As Christ in His own death dealt with sin to the eternal blessing of others, so the believer should reckon himself dead unto sin, Rom. 6. 11, in the interests of others. "If by any means I might attain unto the resurrection of the dead"—Paul was not expressing doubt as to his part in the out-resurrection but was showing his earnest desire for a present experience of living as one who had been raised with Christ. His desire was to attain to a condition that when people saw him they would see he was a heavenly man living above the world.

Aug. 24th

READING : **Philippians 3. 12-21**

THE PROSPECT OF GLORY

PAUL WOULD not have the Philippians believe that he had attained to spiritual perfection but this ideal was before him, and to this end he strove, using all his energy, whatever the cost. To apprehend is to lay hold of the purpose for which one has been saved, v. 12. As the runner concentrates on the finishing line, allowing nothing to distract, so the believer is to set aside past attainments or merits and eagerly press towards the goal. On a downward course Paul was arrested, and his course altered to an upward one at the end of which was a prize and nothing was going to distract him from obtaining it, vv. 13–14; 1 Cor. 9. 24–25; 2 Tim. 2. 5; Heb. 12. 2. The minds of those who were perfect would be like Paul's, setting aside all personal things and pressing on for the prize. All the saints should mind the same things and so produce harmony in the assembly, Phil. 3. 15–16.

Paul's character is indeed Christian character, and his desires are Christian desires; thus he is the pattern for the saints to follow, v. 17. He, along with others, had the welfare of others at heart and pursued his course out of an affection for Christ. Such characteristics were to be imitated, unlike the conduct of mere professors who only had their own fleshly desires at heart, vv. 18–19; Rom. 16. 17–18. Such was the love of Paul for the assembly that he weeps when he considers what these evil men were seeking to do. His was a true shepherd's heart and it was stirred when danger threatened. He did not cover over things, but faithfully warned, corrected, comforted or exhorted according to the need, Acts 20. 17–31; 2 Cor. 2. 4; 11. 28. If all believers valued the assembly they are in as Paul valued the assembly, then there would be perfect harmony and unity in maintaining the principles of gathering.

The believer's home is in heaven, to which he hastens and by which his life is governed. In view of this we should be looking with expectancy for the Lord to come from heaven, who, with the power whereby He is able to subject all things to Himself, will change our bodies and fashion them like unto His body of glory, Phil. 3. 20–21. Then we shall be like Him, fully conformed to His image, bearing the image of the heavenly, 1 John 3. 2; Rom. 8. 29; 1 Cor. 15. 49.

Aug. 25th

READING : **Philippians 4. 1-9**

THE PEACE OF GOD

"THEREFORE" connects this chapter with the previous one, linking the exhortation in v. 1 with the hope of the Lord's return. Saints are to stand firm in regard to this hope without being distracted at all. The believer should not be minding earthly things but heavenly things. This is the basis of the appeal to Euodias and Syntyche, v. 2. They were once yoked together, striving with Paul and others, but something had come between them. This disharmony was affecting the assembly, so Paul pleads with them to be yoked together again and this was so vital that he enlists the aid of another, v. 3. "The same mind in the Lord" would suggest harmony in subjection to the claims of the Lord. The result of this would cause them to "rejoice in the Lord", v. 4. When there is willing surrender to the Lord's will there is harmony of spirit and joy.

"Moderation", v. 5, is yieldingness, and indicates willingness to set aside personal interests in seeking the interests of others, not yielding ground as to truth for we must all "stand fast in the faith", 1 Cor. 16. 13, but yielding when it comes to our personal rights. We can well afford to yield all personal rights, for the Lord is standing by our side and He will vindicate when necessary. We must not be filled with anxiety about anything but rather be characterized by prayer, making specific requests with a spirit of thankfulness, v. 6. Such dependence upon God results in the peace of God guarding our hearts and minds in Christ Jesus, v. 7. The peace which is God's is peace that is always undisturbed by circumstances. Far better to have the peace of God than to be able to understand why we have difficulties and the problems of life, for that alone can guard our affections and our thinking.

The mind is to be taken up with those things that bring out Christian character and promote harmony in the assembly. Thinking always on things that are true, honest, just, pure, lovely and of a good report in our fellow believers, things that can be praised, would produce harmony, v. 8. "The mind controls the affections; the affections control the will; and the will controls the life" (W. Trew). Meditating upon right things will result in practising right things, and thus secure the enjoyment of the presence of the God of peace, v. 9.

Aug. 26th

READING : **Philippians 4. 10-23**

THE PROVISION FOR EVERY NEED

PAUL EXPRESSES his gratitude to the Philippian assembly for their concern for his welfare, demonstrated in the gift received, v. 10. He rejoices greatly, not because of the gift received but because of the result of this for the assembly. He was not thinking on his own things but theirs, for he had learned to be content in every circumstance, vv. 11–12. Paul had learned the secret of contentment in the enjoyment of a fellowship with Christ, the source of all his strength, v. 13. Christ is the source of power for the whole of the Christian pathway, and His grace is sufficient in every circumstance, 1 Cor. 15. 10; 2 Cor. 12. 9; 2 Tim. 2. 1. The secret of victory in life in all conditions is to draw from the infinite reservoir of strength in Christ.

In verses 14–18 Paul returns to the gift the Philippian assembly had sent him. He shows it relieved his need; it was fruit abounding to their account; it was wellpleasing to God. Their giving was not merely sympathy for Paul but a genuine offering to God. What sublime language the apostle uses regarding Christian giving! We should find a delight in giving, and do it cheerfully with purpose of heart, having first given ourselves to the Lord, 2 Cor. 8. 5; 9. 7. Such a giving will have a rich recompense, Prov. 11. 24–25; 2 Cor. 9. 6. The true value of faithfulness in giving, as in every aspect of our lives, will be revealed at the judgment seat of Christ. Faithfulness ought to characterize every department of all our lives in view of that day when "we must all appear (be made manifest) before the judgment seat of Christ", 2 Cor. 5. 10.

"My God shall supply all your need". When Paul says "my God", he is thinking of his own experience and all that God meant to him, the God whose love and care he had proved all along the pathway. With all confidence Paul could assure them that God would supply all their needs. He is the same today, supplying the needs of His people according to His infinite resources in glory in Christ Jesus. We can therefore cast all our cares upon Him for He cares for us, 1 Pet. 5. 7. Let us not doubt His love or care but let us be marked by dependence and a life of obedience. "The grace of our Lord Jesus Christ be with you all. Amen", v. 23.

Introducing Colossians

THE VALUE and importance of the letter to the Colossians is not to be gathered from its size but from the tremendous truths it reveals to us concerning the Person and the work of our Lord Jesus Christ. Written to a young first-century church, these truths are for every age, and we need them as much as they did, so to counter Satan's lies and his "fiery darts". The "Wolf" river ran through Colosse, and the "grievous wolves", Acts 20. 29, foretold by the now imprisoned Paul, were making their incursions into this little flock. All heresy seeks to degrade the Son of God and to belittle His vicarious cross-work.

It is to eliminate such insidious teachings that the apostle, with shepherd care, pens this lofty Christology, establishing finally the absolute deity of Christ together with the complete and utter sufficiency of the sacrifice of Christ to meet the just demands of God and effect reconciliation to Him. The danger was both doctrinal and practical (what you believe affects what you do), and later became known as Gnosticism. The adherents claimed to be initiated into divine secrets, claimed superior "knowledge", and entertained philosophical ideas about Christ, which relegated Him to an inferior position in an endless string of angelic mediators between God and men. The logical outcome of reducing the status of the Lord was to place less reliance on what He had accomplished, and thus supplementary practices as circumcision, angel-worship, sabbaths and abstinences were introduced. These same things in modern guise are with us today. As Elisha's meal (type of Christ) removed the "death in the pot", 2 Kings 4. 38–41, and fruitlessness was cured by salt in a new cruse, 2. 19–22, so doctrinal poisons and the moral corruption they produce are dispelled by understanding the worth and work of Christ.

The Epistle can be studied as follows:

1. 1–13	Salutation, Thanks, Prayer, Praise.
1. 14–22	Christ—His Worth and His Work.
1. 23–29	Paul—his Work.
2. 1–23	Aim, Admonition, Appropriation, Application.
3. 1–14	Resurrection, Rejection, Renewal.
3. 15 to 4. 18	Relationships and Reports.

Aug. 27th

READING : **Colossians 1. 1-20**

THE PRE-EMINENCE OF CHRIST

NEWS OF the situation at Colosse was brought to Paul by Epaphras. Paul responds with pleasure at their conversion, a prayer for their continuance, and the presentation of Christ as the answer to their difficulties. The Holy Spirit is mentioned only in verse 8, but His gracious activity is seen in their initial *faith* in Christ, their continuing *love* for all saints and their *hope* for the future as embodied in the Gospel of God's grace. From the day they heard and responded they were constituted saints, and, indwelt by the Spirit, could be guided into all truth regarding Christ, John 16. 13–14. They were the true holy ones, initiated to receive the "full knowledge" of His will with spiritual understanding, Col. 1. 9; 1 Cor. 2. 9–12.

In contrast to the harsh asceticism of the heretics, the saint is characterized by joyfulness, v. 11, and thankfulness, v. 12. Thanks are mentioned six times in this letter, and verses 12 to 14 are the New Testament counterpart of Psalm 103. Our thanks are to spring from intelligent appreciation, and we find a seven-fold revelation of the Person of Christ interwoven with a seven-fold declaration of what He has accomplished, Col. 1. 12–20. Ponder carefully these verses. The One who humbled Himself to be the lowly Jesus is the Son of God, v. 13; the Redeemer, v. 14; the visible representation of the invisible God, v. 15; John 14. 9; the mighty Creator of all things, Col. 1. 16; the Eternal God ("He is" equates with "I am", Exod. 3. 14) and Sustainer of the universe, v. 17; and, in a very intimate way, He is Head of the Church, v. 18.

All that God is resides permanently in Christ. God intends that Christ in His glorified Manhood should be pre-eminent in every sphere, not least in the hearts of His saints. Appreciating something of the Incomparable Christ, we are in the good of the peace which He has made "through the blood of his cross", v. 20, which enables us to be reconciled to God (see 2 Cor. 5. 19), and enables God to forgive us, v. 14. That same precious blood procured our redemption, v. 14, brought us out from Satan's bondage and transferred us into Christ's kingdom, v. 13. Now—glorious thought—we are made fit for heaven, v. 12. Is He not "Wonderful, Counsellor, The mighty God, The everlasting Father, The Prince of Peace"?

Aug. 28th

READING : **Colossians 1. 21-29**

CHRIST IN YOU

THE EFFECT of the cross-work of our Lord Jesus Christ is both powerful and permanent, and extends far beyond humanity to touch things in the heavens, v. 20; cf. Heb. 9. 23. The scope of Christ's *authority* is unlimited, embracing "things in heaven, and things in earth, and things under the earth", Phil. 2. 10. *Reconciliation* is confined to "things in earth" and "things in heaven", Col. 1. 20, whilst *evangelism* is limited to those "under heaven", v. 23. Whereas we do not represent the sole objects of Christ's atoning work, we certainly are included. The lovely phrase "And you", v. 21, guarantees for us a place in His scheme to bring us into a position of holiness and love.

The theme of verses 20 to 29 is "presentation". By virtue of our reconciliation we are presented to God holy and unblameable. Paul describes his special calling as evangelist, writer and teacher to present the truth to men in order that they in turn may be presented spiritually mature in Christ. He exemplifies in verse 24 what he exhorts in verse 11, "longsuffering with joyfulness". The fellowship of Christ's sufferings, Phil. 3. 10, has brought Paul to the cramped confines of a Roman prison. Yet, far from indulging in self-pity, the apostle gives himself to a written ministry, inspired by the Spirit of God, and, from the darkest of experiences, shines out the greatest and highest truths of the New Testament relative to Christ and to the Church which is His body. This particular aspect of truth was committed to Paul (see Eph. 3. 1–9) as part of his contribution to complete the Word of God. Today we have the complete canon of Scripture, which includes the revealing of those mysteries "which from the beginning of the world hath been hid in God", Eph. 3. 9. Mysteries are now open secrets to the saints, those truly initiated, because the saints have the spiritual faculty to appreciate them, 1 John 2. 20. They are the heritage of the saints, to whom God desires to make His purposes known. Verse 27 teaches the thrilling truth that the majestic Christ in all His fulness indwells the humblest believer by His Spirit, and thereby guarantees his eternal destiny. Paul endeavours to employ this glorious revelation as the means of bringing "every man" to spiritual maturity.

Aug. 29th

READING : **Colossians 2. 1-11**

COMPLETE IN HIM

THE APOSTLES' greatest joy was to hear that their children walked in truth. To them it was the assurance of spiritual health and development. In a similar way, we are exhorted to walk in Him, v. 6, a term which indicates that all our conscious activities are within the sphere of Jesus' will and approval.

The One we have received is "Christ Jesus the Lord". He is the Son of God who became Son of man, yet is also "the blessed and only Potentate, the King of kings and Lord of lords", 1 Tim. 6. 15. He is the "lofty One that inhabiteth eternity, whose name is Holy", who says "I dwell in the high and holy place, with him also that is of a contrite and humble spirit", Isa. 57. 15. The double mystery of "ye in me, and I in you", John 14. 20, is the secret of the saint's joy, his power, his "hope of glory", Col. 1. 27, and his completeness, 2. 10.

Paul's conflict (lit., agony), v. 1, is that the saints should be in the good of this assurance, enjoying the full knowledge of "the mystery of God, even Christ", the depository of all wisdom and knowledge, v. 2. In Christ we discover things which "flesh and blood" cannot reveal, Matt. 16. 17. We obtain spiritual understanding not by human speculation but by heavenly revelation, Eph. 1. 17–23, as we read God's Word and are established in the faith, Col. 2. 7.

"In Christ" is the theme of this section; no less than seven statements are made which incorporate the expressions "in him", "in whom" or "in Christ". Two of these instances, vv. 3 and 10, provide strong and clear statements regarding the absolute deity of Christ. These are plain words that cannot be gainsaid by any of the old heresies or modern cults. Christ is truly God and, as such, can say "believe also in me", John 14. 1. Our faith is therefore directed to, and reposes in, Him, Col. 2. 5. We are also directed by Him and, by reason of vital union, develop in Him, v. 6. The central consummating truth is contained in verse 10; we stand complete in Him (as the body is completed by the head) requiring nothing and no-one besides.

Aug. 30th

READING : **Colossians 2. 12-23**

WITH CHRIST

THE VITAL union that the believer enjoys with his Head is such that he is reckoned to have experienced that which Christ passed through as his substitute. Thus the theme moves from "in him" to "with him", and we have a sevenfold description of the saint's association with Christ from 2. 12 to 3. 4, commencing with death and consummating in glory. Elsewhere, Paul wrote "if one died for all, then were all dead", 2 Cor. 5. 14, and in Colossians 2. 11 he indicates that literal outward circumcision profits nothing, but that, by the death of Christ, we have undergone a spiritual circumcision in putting off the body of the flesh, described later as "the old man with his deeds", 3. 9. "Our old man is crucified with him", Rom 6. 6. By baptism we signify that we share in Christ's burial in order that we may also share in His resurrection. We are "quickened together with him", Col. 2. 13, having put on the new man to "walk in newness of life", Rom. 6. 4. In our unregenerate state we were dead; "it doth not yet appear what we shall be: but we know that . . . we shall be like him", 1 John 3. 2.

The reference to circumcision, Col. 2. 11, indicates a Judaizing influence such as was dealt with earlier by the apostles in Acts 15. Peter referred to it as a "yoke upon the neck of the disciples, which neither our fathers nor we were able to bear", and stated that it was unnecessary to salvation. The "us" in verse 14, as opposed to the "you" in verse 13, indicates the special condition of the Jews, who were under contract to keep the law but were incapable of doing so. For Jew and Gentile alike "Christ is the end of the law for righteousness to every one that believeth", Rom. 10. 4. The law was only a "shadow of things to come" but the object casting the shadow is the "body", the solid abiding reality which is Christ. Neither is the saint subject to ascetic religious ordinances which, whilst making a fair show in the flesh, achieve nothing. They would only divert the saint from his purposeful adherence to the Head, and rob him of a "full reward", 2 John 8.

The "commandments and doctrines of men", v. 22, have a terrible influence. Paul would stress "the commandments of the Lord" and "the doctrine of God", 1 Cor. 14. 37; Titus 2. 10.

Aug. 31st

READING : **Colossians 3. 1-11**

CHRIST IS ALL

WE ARE now at the heart and centre of the Epistle. Paul, the "wise masterbuilder", 1 Cor. 3. 10, has laid his foundation "which is Jesus Christ". The edifice that now arises rests solidly on the doctrine of the deity of Christ our Head and on His vital, indissoluble union with the Church which is His body. Our Head is in heaven, enthroned with God, and our soul-occupation should be with "things above". It is natural for the world to "mind earthly things" but our citizenship is in heaven, to which we now belong and "from whence also we look for the Saviour . . . who shall change our vile body . . . like unto his glorious body", Phil. 3. 20–21.

With regard to the past, Christ "is our peace", Eph. 2. 14; in the present, He "is our life", Col. 3. 4; for the future, He "is our hope", 1 Tim. 1. 1. As we have shared with Him in His death, burial and resurrection, so shall we share in His glory, His triumph and His kingdom. We once had our "portion in this life", Psa. 17. 14, alienated from God through sin. Now, being reconciled, we are subjects of the heavenly King in a land that does not own Him, but in which He has placed us as His ambassadors, 2 Cor. 5. 18–20. To speak for Christ requires a manner of life consistent with our confession; that which relates to "the old man" is to be put to death. The vices mentioned in verse 5 are very prevalent today, accepted in many cases as the norm for society, and popularized through every broadcasting medium. They have no place in the life of the child of God, Rom. 6. 1–23. Self-control is required to master the sins listed in verses 8 and 9. These sins are mainly offences of that "unruly" member, the tongue, James 3. 8. Even when lying is "one to another", it can also be against the Holy Spirit, Acts 5. 3.

The "old man" relates to our fallen Adamic nature and all that stems from it; the "new man" is a new creation in Christ after God's image and likeness. As such the new man cannot be circumscribed by ethnic, religious or social distinctions of earthly origin. In one sense Christ divides, Luke 12. 51; in another sense He unites in one body of heavenly character all those whose affections are directed to things above, and to whom "he is precious", 1 Pet. 2. 7.

Sept. 1st

READING : **Colossians 3. 12 to 4. 1**

THE NEW MAN

THE NEW life in Christ is no patch-up of the old garment, and the new man of verse 10 is very different in character from the old man of verse 9. The new wine of thankfulness and joy are features of this new man who rejoices in the knowledge that, in the divine and eternal purpose of God, he was chosen in Christ before the foundation of the world that he should be holy and without blame before Him in love, v. 12 with Eph. 1. 4. He is one of the children of God, a partaker of the divine nature, 2 Pet. 1. 4, through whom the Holy Spirit desires to manifest the seven-fold grace displayed in verses 12–14, that He might produce Christ-likeness. Just as love is the top-most rung of Peter's ladder of spiritual advancement, 2 Pet. 1. 5–7, so love is the new man's spiritual "overcoat", v. 14.

In this section the apostle addresses himself to the saints regarding their corporate life in the local church, their behaviour and attitude toward each other. Verses 12–15 are therefore addressed to all. "Humbleness of mind" is the fruitful bough that bends lowest. Paul earnestly desires that the Colossians may know the pleasantness of brethren dwelling together in unity, Psa. 133. 1, for God hates discord, Prov. 6. 19. The peace of God into which they had been brought was to rule (*lit.*, act as referee) in their hearts, Col. 3. 15.

The word "body" occurs nine times in this letter. In verse 15 it is viewed in its local church aspect; see also Rom. 12. 4–18.

The Holy Scriptures are the Word of God concerning Christ. They should have a large part in our individual and church life, v. 16, because, dwelling in us in abundant measure, they preserve us from error, make us fruitful in service and afford themes for praise and worship.

For most believers, life is a combination of church, home and work. No sphere is excluded from the Lordship of Christ, and all relationships are considered in the light of our responsibility to Him, 3. 18 to 4. 1. Most is said about servants. In one sense every saint is a servant with a heavenly Master, and all service should be rendered as unto Him.

Sept. 2nd

READING : **Colossians 4. 2-18**

FELLOWWORKERS

EVER CONSCIOUS of the power of effectual prayer, and having assured the saints of his "conflict" for them, 3. 1, Paul now requests inclusion in their intercessions. His concern is not for his personal liberation but that the truth about Christ may be more widely preached, even though this could well mean continued imprisonment for him.

The efforts of the Colossians to evangelize are to be marked by the four qualities seen in the men who brought their palsied friend to the Lord, Mark 2. 1–5. These qualities are wisdom, the redeeming of opportunities, grace and uncorruptness of speech, vv. 5, 6; essentials for the soul-winner.

This is one of the last letters that Paul wrote to a group of Christians, and in his closing greetings he mentions many individuals by name. Including Timothy, 1. 1, twelve persons are named in all, some of whom had served with Paul from the earliest days and shared his hazardous adventures. As a group, Paul's fellow-workers exemplify the teaching of 3. 11, for they comprised Jews and Gentiles, freemen and slaves. Their relationship to Christ transcended all distinctions and united them in His service. It is their loyalty and devotion to Christ that impresses Paul and, in a sense, the list might be regarded as a preview of the judgment seat of Christ.

Both Tychicus and Onesimus are called "faithful", vv. 7, 9. God is faithful and we can trust Him; we are faithful when He can trust us in His service, as in Paul's case, 1 Tim. 1. 12.

Two Gospel writers are mentioned, Mark and Luke, and it is characteristic of self-effacing Luke that Paul has to tell us he is a qualified doctor!

Instructive contrasts are afforded by Onesimus, Mark, and Demas. Onesimus had once been useless to his master but now he is profitable both to Paul and Philemon, v. 9; Philem. 11. Mark had started well but had suffered a sad relapse, Acts 12. 25; 13. 13. Nevertheless, he has been restored, v. 10; 2 Tim. 4. 11. This is surely an encouragement to any who have stumbled. Demas had made a good start and appears to be continuing well. Yet he is to finish badly, forsaking the apostle in his hour of need, 2 Tim. 4. 10. He provides a solemn warning against complacency.

Introducing 1 Thessalonians

THESSALONICA WAS an important city, both wealthy and large by Roman standards. It was situated on the Egnatian Way, a military highway joining Rome to the East. It was also a port in the north-western corner of the Aegean Sea and the capital city in the province of Macedonia. Its status and location attracted wealthy merchants and well-to-do Romans to settle there, and in these conditions evil and licentiousness flourished, much of it no doubt linked with heathendom and idol worship.

Paul's stay at Thessalonica on the second missionary journey was of short duration, but his preaching met with success and there were converts, Acts 17. 1–9. Yet immediately, these new converts felt the heat of persecution, when the unbelieving Jews stirred up such an uproar in the city that Paul was forced to depart to Berea.

Later Paul sent Timothy from Athens to Thessalonica to learn how they were progressing in the faith, 1 Thess. 3. 2. Timothy brought back a very good report of their faith and love and, together with Silas, he rejoined Paul at Corinth. It was from Corinth that both Epistles to the Thessalonians were written.

First Thessalonians was written by Paul about 53 A.D., and was one of the earliest of the New Testament writings. It does not however reflect undeveloped, immature teaching, for Paul had been a Christian for nearly twenty years at this stage and his theology was fully developed both in his mind and through his practical missionary experience.

In this first Epistle, Paul identifies himself with Silvanus (Silas) and Timotheus (Timothy), 1. 1, and tends to write in the plural. He commends the Thessalonians for their love and faith and seeks to encourage them in the midst of persecution. He reminds them of the work he did amongst them, not for personal gain or profit, but for their spiritual welfare. He answers doctrinal questions about the second coming of Christ, also difficulties in church life and personal holiness. On the whole Paul is satisfied, even thrilled with the progress made by the church at Thessalonica, and he seeks in love to strengthen them in the faith.

Sept. 3rd

READING : **1 Thessalonians 1. 1-10**

PAUL'S COMMENDATION

FOLLOWING THE salutation, 1. 1, Paul goes on to commend the Thessalonians, and gives thanks to God for three spiritual features which they displayed.

The first feature the apostle commends is their "work of faith", 1. 3, and this is primarily concerned with that time when the apostle was among them, when they "turned to God from idols", 1. 9. He goes on to give reasons for his certainty of their faith in Christ. He reminds them of the way the gospel came to them "not . . . in word only" (that is, not simply man's oratory, for that would lack power), but "in power, and in the Holy Ghost", 1. 5. It is always the Holy Spirit who, working through the preached word, produces the power that brings about conviction and conversion. Also Paul says that the gospel came "in much assurance", 1. 5. Both the apostle and the converts were given deep assurance by the Holy Spirit that the work of faith was genuine.

The second feature the apostle gives thanks for is their "labour of love", 1. 3. A great change came upon these people on becoming Christians. No longer did they "serve idols" but they now served "the living and true God", 1. 9. To labour involves cost and the word "serve", 1. 9, implies the service of a slave. This labour requires an absolute devotion to God, with no thought of personal reward. Such was the labour of love among the Thessalonians as they preached the gospel in the areas round about, 1. 8.

The third feature commended is their "patience of hope", 1. 3. This is not a sad resignation to what might happen in the future, but is a bright, eager and optimistic expectation of the Lord's future return for His people. This hope brought real joy to the Thessalonians in the midst of hardship and persecution, 1. 6.

The centre of their hope was the Lord Jesus, the One whom God raised from the dead, 1. 10. In the last verse of the chapter we have three lovely insights into the Person of our Saviour. Firstly, we wait for the One who is essentially divine, "his Son from heaven". Yet secondly, he is Jesus, the human One, and thirdly, he is the Deliverer from the wrath to come because of His work on Calvary's cross.

Sept. 4th

READING : **1 Thessalonians 2. 1-20**

SERVICE AND SUFFERING

PAUL REMINDS them of his work among them and the blessing which has been evident. He had come to them preaching with boldness, despite the persecution he had endured at Philippi, 2. 2. Yet the boldness had not been natural human courage, but an enabling of the Lord, for he was "bold in our God", 2. 2.

Three reasons gave him confidence in the gospel, 2. 3. It did not have its source in deceit, nor did it appeal to uncleanness, neither did it require guile to convince. It could stand for itself and be accepted. Also he pleased God and not men in his preaching, 2. 4. This was seen in the fact that his labour had been selfless in nature, being characterized by a lack of flattery and freedom from covetousness and self-glory, 2. 5–6. Instead he laboured with gentleness, as a nurse who cares for her own children with tender affection, 2. 7. He had also shown a willingness to devote everything, even his own soul, for their spiritual welfare, 2. 8.

Paul calls upon his readers (who can see outward actions) and God (who can see the heart and mind) to witness the truth of his statement that he behaved "holily and justly and unblameably" among those who believed, 2. 10. "Holily" describes Paul's conduct in relation to God, "justly" in relation to men, and "unblameably" in relation to self, i.e. he had no cause for reproach. Such conduct was a basis for exhortation, for he could not exhort if he were unholy.

The seal that Paul's work at Thessalonica had not been in vain, 2. 1, is his converts, 2. 12. They had accepted the Word of God, and this is proved in their patient endurance in suffering. Paul is concerned for them in persecution, and he reminds them that they are not alone in suffering. The churches in Judaea had also suffered at the hands of the Jews, 2. 14–16. Yet as the persecutors compounded their evil, the sinful nature of mankind was clearly evident, and this by contrast reveals the righteous character of God's future judgment. In allowing suffering God's purpose is working.

Finally, Paul expresses his desire to be with them and rejoices that they had stood firm even under persecution. They are his hope, joy and crown of rejoicing, and when they stand together before the Lord, they will be Paul's trophy.

Sept. 5th

READING : **1 Thessalonians 3. 1-13**

VISIT OF TIMOTHY TO THESSALONICA

PAUL CONTINUES to show concern for the suffering of the Thessalonians, 3. 3–4, but says that no one should be surprised by these afflictions because for Christians it is normal to suffer persecution, John 15. 20. Also he had previously warned them that they would suffer tribulation, so it would have come as no surprise. Such suffering, however, may have caused some to give up, and Paul's work would become vain, 3. 5.

To determine how they had borne their suffering, Paul sent to Thessalonica Timothy, who is described as "our brother, and minister of God, and our fellowlabourer in the gospel of Christ", 3. 2. These are three terms of endearment, and reveal the esteem in which Timothy was held by the apostle Paul.

Timothy's report, 3. 6–13, had been a good report, stressing the Thessalonians' faith toward God, love toward men and their particular love for the apostle Paul, which had not waned in his absence. They had a "good remembrance", 3. 6, of Paul, and they longed to see him as he longed to see them.

Such a report brought comfort to Paul who, in Athens, was experiencing "affliction and distress", 3. 7. His gloom dispersed and he was uplifted when he knew they were standing fast in the Lord. The only cloud was the difficulty he was experiencing in going back to see them. Night and day he prayed for this opportunity so that he might perfect (or complete) that which was lacking in their faith, 3. 10. Thus he wanted to build them up spiritually so that their faith would not be defective in any way.

He then exhorts them to "abound in love", 3. 12, both one toward another (as fellowbelievers), and to all men. He uses himself as an example of love. As non-Christians, he had loved them by preaching the gospel to them; as believers, he showed his love by seeking to build them up in their faith.

Their abounding love will establish their hearts "unblameable in holiness before God", 3. 13. "Heart" here indicates the whole personality, and the process of sanctification (i.e., being set apart for God) should be developed in every phase of a believer's life. The point is reinforced by mentioning the second coming, for believers living in anticipation of the Lord's soon return ought to walk in holiness.

Sept. 6th

READING : **1 Thessalonians 4. 1-12**

PURITY AND LOVE

TWO DISTINGUISHING features of Christianity should be purity, 4. 1–8, and love, 4. 9–10. These will lead to a right testimony before the world, 4. 11–12. Thus in this section Paul turns his attention to practical and doctrinal matters.

Paul exhorts them by saying they "ought to walk and to please God", 4. 1. In other words, for Christians to please God is not optional, but a matter of necessity growing out of their relationship with Christ.

Christians are called to sanctification, 4. 3–4. To sanctify means to set apart for God, or to be holy. Every believer's position is a sanctified position in Christ, but practically sanctification is a goal of life which every believer should be pursuing, Heb. 12. 14, and that involves separation from evil things. In particular Paul tells the Thessalonians to "abstain from fornication", 4. 3. It may seem strange that such a spiritual church should have such a weakness, but we must remember that the city was heathen and these Christians had been raised on paganism in which all sorts of evil was practised. So as born-again believers this was one of their short comings, and had to be rectified because Christianity has never taken its standards from the society in which it is placed, but from God Himself. So Paul exhorts that sanctification and purity need to be developed and uncleanness avoided. The power to obey this commandment to be sanctified is the Holy Spirit indwelling each believer, 4. 8.

Paul then goes on to deal with "brotherly love", which should be evident between "all the brethren", 4. 10. Brotherly love is that special love which unites children of one family. The only limit to this kind of love is in the availability of opportunities to express it. Such love characterized the believers at Thessalonica, yet Paul says "increase more and more". There is always room for growth in brotherly love.

Finally, believers are to maintain an honest testimony before the world by keeping themselves through hard work and studying to "be quiet", 4. 11. This latter statement seems to mean that Christians ought to develop a mental tranquillity and peace through total dependence upon Christ. This is a great contrast to the restlessness of the world.

Sept. 7th

READING : **1 Thessalonians 4. 13-18**

CONCERNING THE DEAD

IT SEEMS that Paul had spoken on the important subject of Christ's second coming while at Thessalonica, and the believers were eagerly awaiting this event. Yet a few had died and this raised the question of whether these dead believers would miss out on the benefits of the glorious return of Christ.

Paul now addresses himself to this subject by using the metaphor of sleep in describing the dead, 4. 13. This suggests that as sleep has its awakening so death will have its resurrection. Thus there is no need for the Christians to sorrow for a departed loved one. There will certainly be sadness at the parting, but not the awful sorrow of non-Christians who have no hope. Such assurance of the dead being raised is based on the facts of the death and resurrection of the Lord, 4. 14.

Paul then goes on to say that those left alive when the Lord returns will not precede those who are asleep, 4. 15. Indeed their dead bodies will be raised, and afterwards those still alive will go to be with the Lord. So in reality the dead in Christ, instead of missing out, will have a foremost place at the Lord's return. Paul lived in the expectation of the Lord's imminent return, and this wonderful hope has always burned brightly in the hearts of the Lord's people, no matter how long the coming has been delayed. Surely it ought to shine brightly in our hearts today.

A vivid picture is given to us of what will happen at the second coming of Christ for his people. "The Lord himself" will descend from heaven, 4. 16. There will be a commanding shout. We do not know who will utter the shout, maybe the Lord, perhaps an archangel. Anyway, the voice of an archangel will be heard, and the trumpet of God will sound. What a majestic, splendid, grand occasion it will be, with living believers' bodies being changed without the dissolution of death, 1 Cor. 15. 50–53. This is the rapture of the church.

Then will come the twofold reunion. First of all with loved ones who had died, 4. 17, then with the Lord, to begin uninterrupted union and communion with Him. Thus there was no need to sorrow any longer for the dead, but they could take comfort in the hope of that glorious reunion, 4. 18. This hope can also bring comfort to our hearts today.

Sept. 8th

READING : **1 Thessalonians 5. 1-11**

THE DAY OF THE LORD

PAUL NOW deals with a further difficulty concerning the second coming, namely its timing. Such concern must have been expressed by the Thessalonians to Timothy, who then reported back to Paul. So the coming of the day of the Lord is dealt with in this passage, not the day of the Lord itself. The rapture of the church is not a subject of Old Testament revelation for it was a mystery in those times, 1 Cor. 15. 51. However, the day of the Lord was revealed in the Old Testament, Isa. 2. 12; 13. 9–11; Joel 1. 15; Amos 5. 18; Zeph. 1. 14. The term appears to involve both judgment (tribulation) and blessing (millennium) as God intervenes directly in the affairs of the world. The great tribulation and then the millennium are to be ushered in by the rapture preceding them.

The coming of the day of the Lord will be as "a thief in the night", 5. 2. As the thief's coming is unexpected, those to whom the thief comes are unprepared. So when the world feels secure in its peace proposals, then will come certain and swift destruction, 5. 3, for that day will be a great divider between the children of light and of darkness.

Only believers are children of the light, and they are exhorted to be watchful and sober, 5. 6–8, i.e., they must be alert and in a well-balanced frame of mind. To maintain this sober-mindedness, Paul exhorts to put on the breast-plate of faith and love, and the helmet which is the "hope of salvation", 5. 8. Faith, hope and love enable Christians to be sober and to fight spiritual battles. Here the implication is to keep the armour on and always to be on the spiritual attack, for there is no armour on the back. Thus Christians must never turn back to pre-conversion sin.

"Hope of salvation" means that we will be saved. Salvation is only completed by the total removal of sin, when we stand in the presence of the Lord, 2 Cor. 1. 10. God has appointed us to obtain salvation and not wrath by the death of His Son. We must readily agree that all emphasis in our salvation is on God; he has "appointed" us. So we will escape the wrath associated with the day of the Lord, and such hope ought to comfort and edify all believers in the meantime, 5. 11.

Sept. 9th

READING : **1 Thessalonians 5. 12-28**

CONCLUDING THOUGHTS

HERE PAUL deals with believers' relationships with elders, with each other and with outsiders. Elders should be known and "very highly" esteemed in love, 5. 12–13. This is because of their difficult work and the burdens they bear as they labour in the assembly. If such men are rightly esteemed, then the assembly will submit to their guidance and admonitions. In relation to each other, believers are instructed to be at peace, 5. 13. There ought not to be schisms in a church, for that makes the testimony null and void.

Four exhortations are given to all believers. The unruly or disorderly are to be warned, the feeble-minded or faint-hearted are to be comforted, the spiritually weak are to be supported, and patience is to be exercised toward each other. These things should be evident in all assemblies of God's people. Patience should also be exercised toward all men, 5. 14, so short-temperedness should not be evident. Also they must seek to do what is beneficial to others, i.e., not evil but good.

In persecution the Thessalonians are exhorted to "rejoice evermore", 5. 16, and to "pray without ceasing", 5. 17. The latter has two aspects: firstly Christians ought always to be in an attitude of prayer, and the reflex action in any situation should be to pray, Neh. 2. 4. Also, when we have a specific prayer point, we should not cease praying for it until it is answered. This was Paul's example in chapter 1.

Paul goes on to command the Thessalonians to stop quenching the Spirit, as it seems that they frowned upon manifestations of the Spirit. They even despised prophecy, i.e., the expounding of the revelation of God, either as forthtelling (admonishing), or as foretelling (the Lord's second coming). Yet not all manifestations are to be accepted, only those that are genuine, 5. 19–21. The process of being holy is dealt with next, 5. 22–24. This is the work of God, and Paul prays that their whole being will be kept blameless. Complete sanctification will take place at the coming of the Lord.

In conclusion Paul requests prayers and solemnly binds them to read the Epistle to all, as all were to know what the apostle had to say. Finally, Paul prays for grace for his readers whom he loves so dearly in the Lord.

Introducing 2 Thessalonians

THE SECOND letter of Paul to the Thessalonians was written from Corinth about one year after he wrote the first. Although critics have sought to stress the differences in style and content of the two Epistles, there is much more evidence to indicate that the two are the work of the apostle to the Gentiles. There is a striking similarity in the opening salutation of each—both have greetings from Paul, Silvanus and Timothy, fellow-labourers in the gospel. The Epistle can be outlined as follows:—

1. Greetings and Thanksgivings, 1. 1–4.
2. The Approaching Judgment, 1. 5–10.
3. Prayer for Fulfilment, 1. 11–12.
4. The Appearance of the Lawless One, 2. 1–12.
5. Words of Comfort and Prayer, 2. 13 to 3. 5.
6. Dealing with Disorder, 3. 6–15.
7. Conclusion and Benediction, 3. 16–18.

The Epistle has three main ideas.

1. *Comfort.* The atmosphere of affliction in which the Thessalonian church was born does not seem to have diminished—rather has it intensified. Amidst their affliction Paul wants them to rest in the light of the final event of judgment, 1. 7. He commends them to the comfort of God Himself, 2. 16–17, and he desires that the Lord of peace give them "peace at all times in all ways", 3. 16 R.V. The letter was designed to bind up the wounds of those who suffered.

2. *Correction.* There were problems to be dealt with in the church at Thessalonica. Some would write, as from the apostle, to deceive, 2. 2, 15; 3. 17. Teaching was abroad which suggested that the coming of Christ had taken place and that the day of the Lord was in course. Chapter 2. 1–12 deals specifically with this. There were busybodies and disorderly brethren about, walking contrary to the traditions that had been taught. These were to be avoided, 3. 6–15.

3. *Confirmation.* The Epistle is an encouragement to the believers to continue in the things that they had learned from the apostle. They were to stand fast and hold the traditions given to them, 2. 15. Thus the Epistle is designed to establish this healthy, growing church in the things of the Lord.

Sept. 10th

READING : **2 Thessalonians 1. 1-12**

WORDS OF COMFORT

THE APOSTLE Paul was writing his second letter to the saints at Thessalonica. With his companions in service, he greeted warmly those who were dear to him in Christ. They were in "God our Father and the Lord Jesus Christ". This is not without significance. There were those who were writing with wrong intent, claiming that their letters were from Paul, 2. 2. The Thessalonians would be able confidently to accept this letter as genuine. How tactful the apostle was in dealing with the problems of his converts. He was a wise pastor—worthy of imitation.

There are three main points that Paul touched in the chapter.

1. He expressed his *pleasure* in the spiritual growth and development of the believers, vv. 3–4. This was true care for the flock. Where he could give thanks for progress he did. Growing faith, abounding love, patience and endurance in persecution, all proved that there was a deep work of God done in these once pagan people. But spiritual shepherding and care will bring lasting fruit. Paul was not just content with converts. He gave thanks for a growing church.

2. The apostle sought to comfort the afflicted believers by unfolding the *purpose* of God, vv. 5–10. Their sufferings were part of God's righteous ways. For them it gave evidence that they were counted worthy to share in God's kingdom. The manifestation of the Lord Jesus in glory was the ultimate of God's purpose. To those who did not obey the gospel this event would mean destruction. But in that day also He would come to be admired in all His saints. Notice the two stages in the coming of Christ: *for* them, 1 Thess. 4; *with* them, 2 Thess. 1. We can rejoice in God's unfailing purposes.

3. Finally Paul assured the believers of his constant *prayer*. This revealed the present concern that he had for them. He wanted to see fulfilment of the initial work of faith, through God's power. It was not enough that the future would see Jesus glorified in them; he prayed that the name of the Lord Jesus would be glorified in them then. Thus they would be seen to be worthy of God's call. How vital prayer is to the continual development of God's work in believers!

Sept. 11th

READING : **2 Thessalonians 2. 1-12**

WORDS OF CORRECTION

THERE WERE problems at Thessalonica. Paul dealt with a very serious one in this passage. Reading it carefully we see how dangerous wrong impressions can be.

In verses 1 to 3 he began with exhortation. It is quite beautiful to notice just how he began. He besought them, earnestly entreated them, by the coming (*parousia* or presence) of the Lord Jesus Christ and their gathering together unto Him. It was an interesting method of emphasis that Paul used. See Rom. 12. 1; 2 Cor. 5. 20; 2 Cor. 10. 1. The problem that the believers faced had two aspects. There were those who were purporting to write letters as from Paul. Their teaching was false. They claimed that Christ had already come and that the day of the Lord was already present. Paul exhorted the saints not to be shaken in mind or disturbed. It could be that this is why he ended the Epistle as he did, 3. 17. His genuine Epistles bore his own signatures. Notice that by his very exhortation, he emphasized that the coming of the Lord was still to be expected. They would gather together then "unto him". It was a delightful assurance that His coming was a certainty.

In verses 4 to 11 he gave an explanation. He dealt with the time factor. God was working to a timetable—this must never be forgotten. The day of the Lord could not come before there was a falling away—the apostasy. That which is still restraining today must be removed before there can be a final manifestation of lawlessness. Unrestrained evil is held back. Many feel that the "Restrainer" is the Holy Spirit in the church, which will be taken away when the Lord comes for His saints. It is evident that when evil is fully manifested it will be in a person, the man of sin, the lawless one. Unholy arrogance, satanic activities, every evil influence will emanate from him. But his destruction is sure. With the powerful light and glory of His presence the Lord Jesus will destroy him.

How important it is for believers to be established in the truth. It will be those who have refused the truth who will believe the "lie" in the time of Antichrist. It is a sober reflection that the God who sends out His truth will send to those who refuse it strong delusion to believe the "lie".

Sept. 12th

READING : **2 Thessalonians 2. 13-17**

WORDS OF CONFIDENCE

THIS PASSAGE begins with another expression of gratitude for the believers at Thessalonica. In this thanksgiving there is a lovely touch. Paul did not thank God for anything that they had done for Him, or for their response to what He had done for them. He was considering certain evidences of God's work in them and for them—that which was beyond human agency. He thanked God for His wonderful purpose in them. "We are bound", he said; it was their duty to thank God for them. They were "brethren beloved of the Lord". Can you find a more wonderful description of the relationship of believers to the Lord than this?

He considered God's *choice.* They are chosen to salvation. The mystery of that choice will always remain unexplained. It is the result of sovereign grace. But its aim and end is salvation in its widest and most complete sense. He also considered God's *claim* upon them. This was realized through sanctification of the Spirit and their belief of the truth. There is an echo here of the words of the Lord Jesus in His prayer for His own: "Sanctify them through thy truth: thy word is truth", John 17. 17. The Spirit and the word are the agencies which set believers apart, in mind and life, for God. Paul connected these great ideas with the *call* of the Thessalonians; they are called to the obtaining of the glory of our Lord Jesus Christ. It is good to note that this is the ultimate of the effectual call of God. So Paul, in a short compass of words, linked the Godhead together in the past, present and future blessing of the believers. No wonder He thanked God for them.

Against this background, Paul exhorted them to stability in their lives. They had been taught certain fundamental truths either by direct ministry of the Word or by letter from the apostle. It was essential that they stood firm. Notice that traditions of truth, soundly taught and spiritually imparted, are vital to steadfastness and spiritual well-being.

Paul committed them to the God who had loved them; everlasting consolation and good hope were theirs. This surely was the only God who could make them stable in every good word and work. The apostle's confidence in them did not waver.

Sept. 13th

READING : **2 Thessalonians 3. 1-18**

WORDS OF COMMAND

THE CHAPTER opens with a *cry* from the apostle for the prayer-fellowship of his converts. In verses 1 to 5 we are made to feel the close personal bond that existed between Paul and the saints at Thessalonica. "Pray for us", was his demand. He had two needs. First that the word should prosper. Then that the opposition of wicked and unreasonable men should be frustrated. It was not too much for the apostle, who laboured so fervently and unceasingly in prayer for his converts, to ask for prayer from them. These who opposed were men who had not the faith. It was not that they were unfaithful; they had never received the faith. They had not obeyed the gospel. How much reciprocating prayer meant in that situation!

Paul had no doubt about the loyalty of the believers. He was sure that they would obey his commands and act upon his words. It must have warmed his heart to be able to count upon their loyalty, not only to him but to the Lord as well. We can reflect here on the essential need of praying for God's faithful servants. They need our support before the throne of grace more than we can know. Dedicated prayer is vital.

As the apostle brought his letter to a close he had a serious *command* to give. There were believers who were walking disorderly. Like ships off course, they were a menace to those who were seeking to walk rightly before the Lord. Notice the force of verse 7. Now, as on many occasions, Paul drew attention to his own example of correct behaviour. How important godly example is! Sound teaching must always be backed up by practical living. Those causing the trouble were busybodies, lacking in industry. Perhaps this attitude began with a warped approach to the truth of the Lord's coming. If so, this was very sad. There are times when wrong influences among believers must be avoided. Yet in this avoidance, there must not be enmity but brotherly love.

The *conclusion* of the Epistle is beautiful indeed. Paul had spoken of the patience of Christ, v. 5 R.V. Now he commended the saints to the Lord of peace that He should give them peace at all times in all ways, v. 16 R.V. In the light of the teaching of the Epistle these are satisfying values to know and enjoy. Paul wrote the closing greeting with his own hand.

Introducing 1 Timothy

BY WAY of introduction to the first Epistle to Timothy, the following features may help to indicate the nature and content of the letter:

(1) *The Pattern of the Epistle*—It is a pastoral letter, written in the first place to Timothy as a confidential and private document, but no doubt circulated among the saints at a later date.

(2) *The Purpose*—To direct Timothy to charge false teachers to cease from propagating their subversive doctrines—and to instruct him concerning the qualifications and functions of elders and deacons, and other matters affecting the government and practice of the church.

(3) *The Protégé*—Timothy, the recipient of the letter, was Paul's genuine child in the faith, and a representative of the next generation of Christian witnesses. Though not an apostle, nor even an elder, he was the delegated apostolic envoy, charged by Paul to guard the doctrine, and ensure that spiritual protocol was observed by the elders and the saints alike, within the realm of the assembly. Prophecy indicated that Timothy had a definite niche to fill in the purposes of God, and of him much was confidently expected.

(4) *The Précis*—Each chapter of the Epistle highlights certain contrasts or comparisons.

Ch. 1: the principles of *law* and *grace* are contrasted.
Ch. 2: the functions of *male* and *female* are contrasted.
Ch. 3: the responsibilities of *elders* and *deacons*.
Ch. 4: *truth* and *error* are contrasted.
Ch. 5: the contrasts are between *older men* and *younger men*; *older women* and *younger women*; widows with *relatives* and widows who are *solitary*.
Ch. 6: the contrasts are between *masters* and *slaves* and between the *vain life* and the *valuable life*.

(5) *The Peaks*—Important truths emerge from the contents:
The Project of Salvation—Christ's *Saviourhood*, 1. 15.
The Price of Redemption—Christ's *Mediation*, 2. 5–6.
The Purpose of Incarnation—Christ's *Manhood*, 3. 16.
The Preservation of Mankind—God's *Providence*, 4. 10.
The Prospect of Sovereignty—Christ's *Kingship*, 6. 14–16.

Sept. 14th

READING : **1 Timothy 1. 1-11**

PAUL'S CHARGE TO TIMOTHY

GOD IN His *Saviourhood* gives character to the Epistle. And it is salvation in a wide sense which is implied, going far beyond the redemption of the believer from sin's dreadful doom, to his destiny of endless glory.

In verse 1 Paul draws attention to his authority for enforcing the maintenance of godly order in the church. He had been constituted an apostle of Christ Jesus by the command of God, and it was in this capacity that he committed the special charge to Timothy his genuine child in the faith. The terms of the commission were, negatively, to instruct the false teachers to cease from their subversive teaching, and, positively, to ensure that spiritual proprieties were duly observed in God's house, the assembly. The term "charge", used by Paul, is a strong one. It is not simply an appeal or a request, but a command, a commission, a mandate—a word spoken with the voice of authority. The fulfilment of the charge would cause the silencing of false teaching, and also effect the promoting of love out of a pure heart, and a good conscience, and genuine faith, v. 5. The touching reference to Timothy as being his "true child in faith", 1. 2 R.V., reveals something of the tender affection Paul bore towards the younger man, particularly now that the aged apostle sensed he was nearing the end of his life on earth for God.

The false teachers with whom Timothy was charged to deal were intent on being "law-teachers", and such teaching ran completely counter to Christianity, which is based on the principle of pure grace. There is but one legitimate use of the law today, namely, to convict and to condemn a man in respect of his sin; whereas the Christian's rule of life is the risen and ascended Christ Himself.

"*Sound doctrine*", an important truth in the Epistle, is mentioned in verse 10, and this is in harmony with the gospel of the glory of the blessed God.

In contrast to a stern law-giving God, delivering to men a code of condemnation, we now see Him acting towards us in fulness of grace as the "happy" God, declaring in the good news of salvation the prospect of endless glory. For the believer there is, therefore, *grace* and *glory* too!

Sept. 15th

READING : **1 Timothy 1. 12-20**

PAUL A PATTERN

HAVING SPOKEN of "the gospel of the glory of the blessed God" (R.V.) entrusted to him, Paul now expresses his deep thankfulness to God for such an immense privilege of being counted faithful, and being appointed unto this holy service, inwardly strengthened for the onerous task by Christ Jesus our Lord. And this was all the more astounding when he considered his own background and activities—a blasphemer, possessed of a ferocious zeal to exterminate the Christians, accounting this new religion of Christianity a growing threat to the Jewish faith of his fathers. He acted in sincerity, albeit in ignorance and unbelief. But now he magnified the mercy and grace of God abundantly displayed towards him, without affectation the self-styled "chief of sinners"; the inference was that there was none too vile or sinful for the grace of God to reach and save. Thus Paul asserts that the statement that "Christ Jesus came into the world to save sinners" can be wholly relied upon, and is worthy of acceptation on the part of everyone, v. 15.

Paul obtained mercy, not only that his own soul might be saved, but also that he might be a pattern ("outline-sketch"), displaying the longsuffering of Christ to them "which should hereafter believe on him to life everlasting". This prompts Paul's spontaneous ascription of praise to the Author of this "so great salvation": "Now to the King of the ages, incorruptible, invisible, the only God, be honour and glory unto the ages of the ages. Amen", v. 17 R.V.

The "charge" referred to in verse 18 links up with verses 3 and 5, and the carrying out of it effectively would involve Timothy in spiritual warfare, because Satanic opposition would be encountered. To conduct a victorious campaign, a steady faith *God-ward* and a good conscience *self-ward* were essential qualities. Without them, Paul warns that, as in the case of Hymenaeus and Alexander, there would be defeat and disaster.

And so it is in the case of the Christian today, a firm faith in God and a good conscience within are cardinal factors if moral shipwreck is to be avoided, and spiritual victory assured.

Sept. 16th

READING : **1 Timothy 2. 1-7**

A RANSOM FOR ALL

THE CANVAS spread before us in today's passage is a wide one—indeed, universal in its compass, for it embraces the entire human race. There is nothing narrow or exclusive in the scope of the picture. It accommodates the attitude of a Saviour-God towards sinful, rebellious mankind. He "will have (desires) *all* men to be saved, and to come unto the knowledge (acknowledgment) of the truth", v. 4. The infinite sacrifice of Christ on the cross had procured a salvation capable of meeting the needs of every man of the fallen race, and a gracious and loving Saviour-God intensely desires the salvation of all men; but of course, the personal responsibility of acceptance devolves on all. Blessed beyond words are those who have already responded by faith to the message of salvation and life!

The unlimited nature of the atonement is emphasized in verse 6, where we read the plain truth that Christ Jesus "gave himself a ransom for *all*"—the one and only mediator between God and men.

Two things stand out prominently on the extensive canvas before us: on the one hand, the *universality* of the human race, and on the other hand, the *unity* of God—it is "*all* men", but "*one* God". The teeming millions of the race of men are placed in juxtaposition to the one Almighty God, and in this context, how reassuring to learn, a *Saviour*-God. And even as God is declared to be "one", so there is but one divine Mediator, who through His Manhood, and by His sin-atoning death, is able to reconcile repentant, believing men unto God in a righteous manner, having Himself paid the ransom for all.

Now, it is against this background of the universal appeal in the gospel of God's grace towards all mankind that the exhortation for supplications, prayers, intercessions, and thanks to be made for "*all* men" (and especially for those in positions of rule and authority) is given in verses 1 and 2. Therefore, our attitude should be one of compassion and concern for our fellowmen, thus reflecting the spirit of the gospel of a gracious God. Shall we, then, widen the scope of our prayers today, to include "*all men*"?

Sept. 17th

READING : **1 Timothy 2. 8-15**

THE SEXES DISTINGUISHED

In verses 1–7 it is our relationship with those in the *world* outside which is in view; now in verses 8–15 it is our relationship with those inside the *church* which is dealt with.

Males and females are clearly distinguished as to their place and function in the church. The divine order established in creation has to be adhered to in the church.

The males have to engage in public prayer; and the females have to dress in a manner befitting those who lay claim to godliness—with modesty and discretion, their adornment being not with opulent and showy jewellery, but with commendable good works. In a word, the adorning is not to be superficial and material but spiritual and moral. Moreover, the woman has to "learn in silence" in the church, with "all subjection", v. 11. She has not to engage in teaching nor "to usurp authority over the man, but to be in silence", v. 12. This is completely in line with what Paul lays down in 1 Corinthians 14. 34, "Let your women keep silence in the churches, for it is not permitted unto them to speak". The directions are so clear, that it is difficult to see how any honest reader can fail to understand their import, especially when in 1 Timothy 2. 13-14 two reasons are given for these prohibitions which relate to the women:

(1) because of the *creation* order. The women's place in creation determines her place in the church, "Adam was first formed, then Eve", v. 13.

(2) because of the order in *transgression*, the woman's part in the fall. "Adam was not deceived, but the woman being deceived was in the transgression", v. 14. Eve was *deceived* but Adam disobeyed *deliberately*; for love of his wife he went in with his eyes wide open.

Our passage today is, therefore, a salutary reminder that the divine decree regarding the relative functions of male and female in the church cannot be set aside with impunity. There is reason and relevance for maintaining these God-given principles in our day, when some are departing directly from them. May God exercise our hearts—and if need be, our consciences—in respect of these things, and keep us faithful to His truth!

Sept. 18th

READING : **1 Timothy 3. 1-13**

CONTROL IN THE CHURCH

CHAPTER 3 introduces the subject of the house of God. Our conduct in God's house, the assembly, must have regard to the spiritual and moral proprieties befitting the sanctity of the dwelling place of God here on earth. Not only is *conduct* in the house of God dealt with, but *control* in the house is the matter particularly before us in this passage today. God's house is the figure of the church which emphasizes that this is the sphere wherein God *rules*. It is *His* house; and He expects His will to be obeyed, and His order to be observed in His own house. The question is, "Are we doing things *God's* way in His house?".

On the human level, the responsibility for the control and preservation of order in the house of God is committed into the hands of the bishops ("overseers") and the deacons ("servants"). The characteristics and qualifications of overseers are first listed, vv. 1–7, and those of the deacons ("servants") in verses 8–13. The basic function of the overseer is to "take care of the church of God", v. 5, namely, to *oversee*, to rule, to be concerned with the moral government of the local assembly in which they are in fellowship. Two terms are used in Scripture to designate these men. Here they are called "*bishops*" (*episcopos*, overseer), and this word denotes their *function*. In other places they are called "*elders*" (*presbuteros*), describing their *person*, and denoting spiritual maturity, experience and wisdom. The credentials of the overseer might be summarized as follows: *ability*, *maturity*, *integrity*, *morality*, *sobriety*, *identity* and *hospitality*.

The work of the deacons is of a different order. It is of a *material* rather than of a *spiritual* nature, relative to the temporal affairs of the assembly; and while the qualifications of the deacon are very similar to those of the overseer, they are not quite of such a high standard. In their case, being "apt to teach" is not a required condition.

It is important to observe that both overseers and deacons have a *local* charge, namely responsibility for what obtains in the assemblies to which they individually belong.

And the practical application for us all in this is surely, "Obey them that have the rule over you", Heb. 13. 17.

Sept. 19th

READING : **1 Timothy 3. 14-16**

CONDUCT IN THE CHURCH

FOLLOWING THE matter of *control* in the church, the closing section of chapter 3 is concerned with *conduct* in the church, "These things write I unto thee . . . that thou mayest know how thou oughtest to behave thyself in the house of God", vv. 14, 15. This phrase is constructed in a form which embraces all Christians, and is not limited to Timothy, nor to the overseers and deacons and their wives. A consciousness of being in the living God's house should cause us to behave with a due sense of reverence, since the living God's church stands in contrast to the house of dead idols, "the pillar and ground (groundwork) of the truth", v. 15.

It has ever been in the mind of God to have a dwelling-place on earth among men. The first man to anticipate by faith this amazing concept was the patriarch Jacob. When erecting the stone which had formed his *pillow*, to become a *pillar*, he called that place "Bethel", "The house of God".

The assembly is represented here in 1 Timothy 3 by the monumental pillar upon which the truth is inscribed and displayed to the world, for the assembly is today God's authentic witness in an unbelieving world. Moreover, the assembly in its corporate practical life is viewed as the foundation, or *groundwork*, of the truth, that which upholds the truth.

Verse 16 speaks of "the mystery of godliness", or "the secret of piety". The secret of piety is the truth concerning Christ, now fully revealed. He is the embodiment of everything that gratifies the desires of God's heart.

To present the truth of Christ is an essential purpose of the church today. How well are local assemblies fulfilling this task in their immediate areas? Are we individually contributing our quota in relation to the "pillar" and "support" activities of assemblies to which we belong?

The chapter concludes with a concise summary, expressing in three contrasting statements, the earthly life of Christ from His incarnation to His ascension, a digest of Deity manifesting Itself in humanity. These six short statements will provide us with food for thought for the rest of the day, as opportunity affords!

Sept. 20th

READING : **1 Timothy 4. 1-16**

SATANIC SEDUCTION

FURTHER CONTRASTED principles are identified in this chapter. After the reference in the closing section of chapter 3 to the "secret of piety", we are now warned of the "secret of iniquity" (lawlessness). The contrast is introduced by the first word of the chapter "But", R.V., and what a striking contrast it is! The "secret of piety" is all that is acceptable to God, as embodied and revealed in the Person of Christ incarnate; "the secret of iniquity", already at work, will reach its full manifestation in all that is evil and vile, displayed by the Man of sin.

The determined and sustained opposition of Satan against God will know no let-up, until the devil's banishment to the abyss, and eventually to the lake of fire forever. Even as he practised his sinister seduction against God's first creation in Eden, so he now employs the same tactics to disrupt and destroy the new creation—the church of God. "In the latter times", v. 1, some who had professed faith in Christ, apostatized, that is to say, deliberately jettisoned the truth, completely renounced Christianity, and thus apostasy began its development within the church. In the days when the apostle Paul was writing, the mystery of iniquity had already begun its subtle work.

These seductive teachings of the apostates (whose course, character and spurious commandments are pin-pointed) are to be refused by the believers, who have to exercise themselves instead unto godliness (or, train themselves unto godfearingness) for "godliness is profitable unto all things", for this life, and for the life to come, v. 8. You can be sure of this, says Paul in effect. It is a trust-worthy saying, it can be relied upon absolutely, and it is worthy of acceptation on the part of everyone. Therefore, "Do we really practice piety?" is the pertinent question for today!

Many pithy practical exhortations are now addressed to Timothy personally in the second half of the chapter. Some of them we may suitably apply to ourselves as we read and ponder them. For instance, "Be thou an example", v. 12, namely, Be a model of the believers, in word, in conduct, in love, in faith, in purity. What a good maxim to model!

Sept. 21st

READING : **1 Timothy 5. 1-16**

RELATIONSHIPS AND RESPONSIBILITY

DISTINCTIONS and differences again form the subject-matter of chapter 5, which remind us that Christianity is a system of truth intended to affect our relationships and conduct here below, as worked out in practical terms in our daily lives. Without doubt we are a people of an heavenly calling, whose eternal destiny is one of celestial glory. But while in this world, we must give heed to our earthly relationships. In the context of this chapter, various factors have to be taken into account in connexion with our treatment of our fellow-Christians. Age, sex and circumstances are among the matters to be considered, and our spiritual relationships in the church do not eliminate the performance of our natural duties in respect to one another.

The treatment of widows is the main teaching in the first section (although the proper attitude and approach of the younger men and women to the older men and women, and to themselves, is also laid down by Paul in the passage).

Now, a careful reading of today's portion will show that Paul alludes to *four* different classes of widows:

Class 1—Widows who are solitary, and who do not "live in pleasure", vv. 3, 5, 6 (v. 5 defines what the apostle means by "a widow indeed").

Class 2—Widows who have children or grandchildren (descendants) to maintain them, vv. 4, 7, 8, 16.

Class 3—Widows of 60 years and over who are placed on the assembly list, probably for regular support, vv. 9, 10.

Class 4—Younger widows who have the intention of re-marrying, vv. 11–15.

In these days of "the Welfare State", the case of the widows among us may not be as acute as it was in Paul's time, but surely this does not absolve those who read this Epistle from a sense of responsibility for the financial support of the dependent widow in need of help—or indeed the assembly, in the case of the solitary widow.

The Eventide Homes, provided by some assemblies, form a haven of rest for the sister in the Lord who is a "widow indeed", as well as for other Christians of advanced years who are in need of care and attention.

Sept. 22nd

READING : **1 Timothy 5. 17-25**

EXHORTATIONS REGARDING ELDERS

TODAY'S MAIN topic is the treatment of elders, that is, those responsible for leading, guiding and controlling the local church. In yesterday's portion we noted *four* classes of *widows*, and now *three* classes of *elders* are indicated:

(1) Elders who take the lead.
(2) Elders who take the lead *well*.
(3) Elders who rule well, and are *teachers* of the Word.

The saints are enjoined to "*honour*" the elders, and "doubly" so, in the case of those who, in addition to ruling well, exercise with diligence their teaching gift, labouring "in the word and doctrine". The elders are "honoured" when the saints respect their persons, and submit to their judgment in ordering the assembly affairs aright. The term "*honour*" in this context does not carry any thought of a regular salary or stipend being paid to them for acting as overseers. (The same word "honour" appears in chapter 6. 1, where its usage could not in any way imply financial recompense).

When we come to verse 20, the reference is not here limited to the "official" elders in particular, but includes all members of the assembly who sin seriously and openly in a continuous manner. Such are to be rebuked in public, so that others may be warned against a similar course. This action has to be taken with impartiality. Natural ties and personal bias must be strictly set aside, so that righteous action may be seen by all to have been taken. The unfallen angels, too, are noting what takes place in the sphere of God's assembly, v. 21.

The "laying on of hands" is mentioned in verse 22. This is an act of identification with the person in his service. Timothy is warned not to do this in a hasty manner. It required due consideration and satisfactory proof of the reliability of the individual concerned, lest he should later defect, and any spiritual damage resulting be partly attributable to the one who commended him.

Then verse 23 forms a brief aside, in which Paul counsels the sensitive Timothy to have no scruples about taking "a little wine" for "his stomach's sake", avoiding, of course, any possibility of excess.

Sept. 23rd

READING : **1 Timothy 6. 1-12**

GODLINESS IS GAIN

THE GENERAL theme in chapter 6 is, "How to enjoy life". Paul had a very full life, having passed through the whole gamut of life's experiences. He had known imprisonments, floggings, shipwrecks, privations, stoning, and experienced the range of human emotions from one extreme to the other. Yet, despite the intensity of his sufferings, his post-conversion life was suffused with holy joy and spiritual ecstasy.

No man, therefore, was better qualified from personal experience to advise on life, and how to live it to the highest advantage and the fullest enjoyment. And this is what he does in 1 Timothy 6. As we read, we find no indecision in his pronouncements. It is the sure prescription for the Good Life. Indeed, the passage is so practical and explicit, that simply to read it is to understand it—and to understand it should have, as its happy sequel, our complying with its wholesome counsel.

In today's section, Paul points out the pathway which inevitably leads to sorrow and disappointment in *this* world, and will result in loss in the world *to come*. He indicates, too, the path that leads to real joy and contentment.

Once again in the course of this letter, contrasts are in evidence. The aged apostle contrasts the quest for *material* wealth to the pursuit of *spiritual* riches. And the basic ingredient for a truly contented life is "*godliness*". This is a key-word in the passage, and it is the secret of success in Christian living, for "godliness" has to do with our vital relationship with God, and identifies with the inner life of the soul, as distinct from the externals and ceremonies of religion. It is the essence of *true* Christianity. Real enjoyment, writes Paul, comes not through *material* things, but through *spiritual* acquisitions.

"Lay hold on eternal life", v. 12, means to get a firm grip of it, to get joy from it! Take hold of it, so as to keep possession of it. What a thought to carry with us through this day! Are we in the good of this new life that Christians already possess in their souls, the very nature of which is the experimental knowledge of divine Persons? Eternal life is to know the only true God, and Jesus Christ the sent One of God.

Sept. 24th

READING : **1 Timothy 6. 13-21**

SOVEREIGN SUPREME

PAUL BRINGS this Epistle to a close by reaffirming the charge which he has committed to Timothy, and he does so in the presence of God, the Preserver of life in all its forms, the Source from which all life is derived, and before the presence of Christ Jesus, the One who in His Manhood here displayed perfect fidelity in His witness before Pontius Pilate. By the tone and setting of this section, it is clear that the apostle intended this solemn responsibility to be regarded by Timothy as a serious commitment, to be kept until the appearing of our Lord Jesus Christ. The implication of this is that, if responsibility is discharged now, glory will be revealed at the appearing of Christ, vv. 13, 14, since God, at the appointed time, will manifest in glory the Man, who during his life on earth, was God's faithful Witness.

In verses 15 and 16 we have an impressive description of God as the supreme invisible Sovereign of the whole universe, "the King of those that reign, and Lord of those that exercise lordship". He alone has immortality, and dwells in light unapproachable, and who, as to His divine essence, no man has seen, and is, moreover, incapable of seeing. What an awe-inspiring picture of the might and majesty of Him who is, albeit, designated the blessed Potentate! This remarkable description of God, in common with the similar statement in chapter 1. 16, concludes with an ascription to God, "to whom be honour and power everlasting. Amen", 6. 16. Paul's "Amen", and ours, will swell in that coming day into a resounding acclamation from the whole universe.

A further charge, to be addressed to those rich in this world's wealth, is now given to Timothy. They had not to be high-minded, but to place their trust in the living God, and not in uncertain riches. Our God is a beneficent and a bountiful Creator-God, "who giveth us richly all things to enjoy", v. 17. The materially rich are enjoined to be rich in good works, liberal in contributing of their substance to others.

Again in this chapter the expression occurs, "lay hold on eternal life", v. 19. Paul is anxious that the believers should not only possess eternal life, but realize the *quality* of this life, in a conscious experience of God.

Introducing 2 Timothy

PAUL'S SECOND letter to Timothy becomes very precious to us when we remember that here we have the last words of the apostle to be recorded in Holy Writ. During his first imprisonment, Paul could speak of "having a desire to depart, and to be with Christ; which is far better", Phil. 1. 23, but at the end of this Epistle we read, "I am now ready to be offered, and the time of my departure is at hand", 2 Tim. 4. 6.

There are marked differences in the character of the two letters which Paul wrote to this young man: in 1 Timothy 4. 1 we find the expression, "in the latter times" (or "in latter times", i.e., the times subsequent to Paul's writing of the letter), whereas the corresponding phrase in the second Epistle is "in (the) last days", 3. 1. There is no definite article in the original, for in this letter Paul outlines for us the features that have characterized all "last days"; indeed the close of each age has been marked by perilous times. The "last days" of which Paul is more directly speaking are undoubtedly the closing days of this age of grace; these days were already beginning to manifest themselves in Timothy's time. "Second" epistles (2 Cor., 2 Thess., 2 Pet., 2 John as well as 2 Tim.) have the end of things particularly in mind and emphasize the work of the enemy.

Returning to Paul's letter to Timothy, note the contrast between "*some* shall depart from the faith", 1 Tim. 4. 1, with "*men* shall be lovers of their own selves", 2 Tim. 3. 2. What was true only of certain individuals in "the latter times" is true of the mass in "the last days".

As far as Timothy was concerned, the point of the first Epistle is the ordering of the house of God, 1 Tim. 3. 15, but in the second, the emphasis is upon the ordering of himself as a servant of Christ, especially in a time of confusion and departure from the truth. There is a dark background to the whole Epistle, and there are examples of departure in each of the four chapters; in each case it is associated with the names of two men; see 1. 15; 2. 17; 3. 8; 4. 10, 14.

2 Timothy is indeed a letter written for the days in which we live, and it behoves us to pay close attention to what God has to say to us in it.

Sept. 25th

READING : **2 Timothy 1. 1-18**

TIMOTHY AND ONESIPHORUS

THE GENEALOGY of Timothy is given to us spiritually, for not only are we told that his grandmother, Lois, and his mother, Eunice, were those in whom dwelt faith without hypocrisy, v. 5, but Paul designates him "my dearly beloved son (child)", v. 2; he was saved and then served under Paul's influence. Indeed Paul had a special affection for this young man; in their separation he constantly prayed for him and had a great longing to see him.

The suggestion in verse 7 is that Timothy was of a somewhat timid nature, but nevertheless he was to stir up (rekindle) the gift of God that was in him. Are we exercising the gift that God has given to us? Timothy was not one whom God used to introduce the truth; the work entrusted to him was to stand for the truth once the truth had been delivered. The things of God are to be kept, not by mental power or by creed, but by the Holy Spirit who dwells within us. A great responsibility rests upon us to keep what has been committed to us.

The end of the chapter reveals how the majority of Christians may fall short when the real test comes. Paul was himself the true test at this time as to whether there was true affection for Christ, for he was in great reproach, v. 8. Asia had been a scene of triumph for the gospel, but now "all they which are in Asia be turned away from me", v. 15. These men did not apostatize, they simply turned away from Paul.

There is a dark background throughout the Epistle, but at the end of chapter 1 there is one bright shining light in the person of Onesiphorus. Four things are said concerning him: (i) "he oft refreshed me"—this ministry is needed today; (ii) "he was not *ashamed* of my chain", (in v. 8 Paul enjoins Timothy not to be *ashamed*, and in v. 12 he says "I am not ashamed"); (iii) "he sought me out very diligently"—some lonely saints need seeking out; (iv) "he ministered unto me in Ephesus". It took a brave man to do this; he went against the tide. Are we marked by the fear of man? Paul asks for present mercy for his house; as to the brother himself, he expresses a desire that he may find mercy of the Lord "in that day". Paul's desire has in view the coming judgment seat of Christ, for the thought of mercy goes on right through to the end.

Sept. 26th

READING : **2 Timothy 2. 1-13**

SOLDIER, ATHLETE AND HUSBANDMAN

A GREAT responsibility rested upon Timothy's young shoulders, and he would find all necessary grace in Christ Jesus; in this grace he was to be continually strengthened. This grace is available to us today. There is to be the handing down of the deposit of divine truth ("the same" emphasizes that the teaching was not to be altered in any way) from one generation to the next; indeed four generations are in view in verse 2, "me" (Paul), "thou" (Timothy), "faithful men", "others also".

Paul employs three illustrations to impress upon Timothy (and ourselves) his responsibilities: (i) a *soldier*, not on leave, but on active service ("no man that warreth"). We cannot be well-pleasing to Him if we are becoming too involved with the affairs of this life; (ii) an *athlete*—not after the race, but "striving for masteries"; the Word of God provides the guide-lines for us in the race in which we run; there is no crown unless we abide by the Scriptures; (iii) a *husbandman*, not after the harvest, but one "that laboureth"; there is no partaking of the fruits without prior arduous toil.

Suffering is the subject of the section that follows. We, as well as Timothy, are to be motivated for a life of endurance by (i) the constant remembrance of Jesus Christ, v. 8; the exhortation here is not simply to recollect facts about Him, but to remember the Person Himself; (ii) the example of Paul's own suffering, vv. 9–10; Paul's present suffering in prison was due to his relation to the gospel he preached—men may bind the Lord's servants, but they cannot bind the Word; (iii) the certainty of future reward, vv. 11–13. These latter verses set before us principles governing reward at the judgment seat of Christ. "If we died with him", v. 11 R.V.—there can be no reward unless there has first been identification with Christ in His death. "If we suffer", i.e. persevere under trials and difficulties, "we shall also reign with him"; He waits to receive His own throne, till then we are called to endure. "If we deny him" in the sense of not giving Him His rightful place in our lives, He will disown us in the matter of reward. Finally, if we are unfaithful, yet His faithfulness is unchanging. He always acts consistently with His character and this means withholding reward from those who are unfaithful.

Sept. 27th

READING : **2 Timothy 2. 14-26**

DEPARTURE FROM THE TRUTH

WE NEED to be constantly reminded of truths already known to us; there is in the Scriptures the principle of the reiteration of divine truth; see 2 Pet. 3. 1. We cannot adopt a passive attitude towards error, and here Timothy was encouraged to take an active stand against error by solemnly warning against it. A realization of the relative importance of time and eternity is an effective restraint upon trifling word battles. What is unprofitable tends to go further, and can have the effect of overthrowing what has been wrought in our hearts by the Holy Spirit.

Timothy was to give diligence to present himself before God as one tested or examined; it is not a question of winning the approval of men but of God; see Gal. 1. 10. Here we have a further illustration, that of a workman "rightly dividing the word of truth". The Word of God is to be considered with spiritual intelligence, strictly in accordance with its lines of teaching; those who teach must handle the Scriptures accurately.

Since it is inevitable that wrong doctrine leads to wrong practice, those who corrupt the truth will themselves make progress in ungodliness. Hymenaeus and Philetus were among those who affirmed that the resurrection had passed already, confusing Paul's doctrine of a future resurrection of the body with the believer's experience of having been raised with Christ; see Col. 3. 1. However, the doctrine of the bodily resurrection lies at the very foundation of the Christian faith.

The reference to "a (not "the") great house" is given by way of illustration. Paul is thinking of a great house of his day, in which would be found various vessels; whatever the vessel was made of, it had a particular use. So today, each believer has his own sphere of service and usefulness. In making the application, Paul goes beyond the figure of vessels. "These", v. 21, probably are the babblings, v. 16, of the false teachers, v. 17; there cannot be reference to the other vessels, since purging oneself from them would never make one useful. The value of the vessel lies in its being fit for use, not in its material; vessels are "unto honour" because of their being clean and set apart.

Sept. 28th

READING : **2 Timothy 3. 1-9**

FEATURES OF THE LAST DAYS

IN VERSES 2–4, 18 evils are enumerated; this list differs very little from the catalogue in Romans 1. But whilst the latter shows the gradual degeneration of the *heathen*, the former describes spurious Christianity retaining a religious form, "having a form of godliness". The list commences with "lovers of self" and ends with "not lovers of God". Self has been deified and God is dethroned. The features outlined here show clearly that the ten commandments are spurned; men infringe the first commandment by being lovers of self and not of God; the third by being blasphemers; the fifth by being disobedient to parents; the seventh by being unholy; the ninth by being false accusers; and the tenth by being covetous.

The first feature is "lovers of their own selves"; contrast the demands made by the Lord Jesus on those that would be His disciples: "let him deny himself", Matt. 16. 24. Christ Himself must be first, indeed He must be all. We need to challenge our hearts lest we become infected with the spirit of the age. The second mark is literally "lovers of money"; if men love self, then self must be gratified; it must possess and accumulate. Self has a thirst which cannot be satisfied. Out of these first two features there issues a stream of evils which are only too apparent in our day. Bearing in mind that these verses describe apostate Christendom, it is salutary for us, in these days when there is a cry from all sections of Christendom for unity at any price, to take account that our instruction is plain, "from such turn away".

If verses 2–5 depict evil men, then verses 6–9 present seducers (or imposters). Firstly their activities are described and then their victims—they specialize in the art of captivating women. Then finally their character is given; they are compared with the Egyptian court magicians, Jannes and Jambres. These men imitated what Moses did; they withstood the truth with counterfeit. The devil is a master at this. The teachings of Jehovah's Witnesses, Christadelphians and other heresies, are counterfeits of the truth; it is very difficult to counteract imitation, for imitation tends to confound people.

Sept. 29th

READING : **2 Timothy 3. 10-17**

THE DIVINELY INSPIRED SCRIPTURES

IN CONTRAST to that of the apostates, Paul reminds Timothy of what his own behaviour had been; cf. 1 Cor. 11. 1. Doctrine heads the list of the nine terms used. In these pastoral Epistles, where there is so much truth relating to the assembly, doctrine is referred to 16 times. We should be automatically suspicious of the philosophy which demands "less doctrine and more practice". "Manner of life" follows; a man's doctrine will be of little value if his conduct does not correspond with his teaching; "purpose"—Paul was not disobedient to the heavenly vision, he shrank not from declaring the whole counsel of God; "faith", namely active, living faith—"longsuffering, love, patience, afflictions". He dwells upon the subject of persecutions, vv. 11–12. The Lord Himself said, "If they have persecuted me, they will persecute you", John 15. 20. In one form or other, the godly believer will know persecution, for this is our heritage; see Phil. 1. 29. It is well to bear in mind that mocking is viewed as persecution; cf. Gal. 4. 29 with Gen. 21. 9. Evil men, 2 Tim. 3. 2–5, and seducers, vv. 6–9, begin by deceiving others but they lose the distinction between truth and error. Timothy was not to be given to change, and truth remains immutable; "and hast been assured of"—are you where you are by personal conviction?

As to their capacity, the O.T. writings are able to make one "wise unto salvation"; this declares the sufficiency of the O.T. Scriptures to lead a soul to Christ; see Acts 8. 35. They are Christ-centred, for they are designed to produce faith in Christ Jesus—this presents man's side. In origin, all Scripture (the N.T. as well as the O.T.) is warm with the breath of God. We believe in the verbal inspiration of Scripture; it is insufficient to say that the thoughts are inspired but not the words. As to their use, they are "profitable for doctrine" (this again heads the list), "for reproof" (detecting and exposing what is wrong), "for correction" (of what is wrong), "for instruction in *righteousness*" (i.e., child-training in uprightness before God). Their purpose is that the man of God (every true follower of Christ) may not be unbalanced in any area of his being; thus he will be permanently equipped "unto all good works".

Sept. 30th

READING : **2 Timothy 4. 1-8**

PAUL'S DEPARTURE

Here Paul sets before us ("thee" of v. 1 is not in the original) a solemn charge, the last of three in these letters to Timothy couched in very similar terms (see 1 Tim. 5. 21 and 6. 13). Preaching the word as a herald has the first place—not just the gospel but the whole word entrusted to us; how important it is to be able to say, as Paul, that we have kept nothing back. We must hold ourselves in readiness, not only *taking* opportunities but, where possible, *making* opportunities.

How sad that some believers have grown weary of the pure doctrines of the N.T., and sigh for something to gratify the intellect and feed the imagination. They will find plenty of so-called teachers who are willing to satisfy their demands that their ears be tickled.

Times would become worse, and Paul's own course was almost finished; four further imperatives therefore follow. Timothy must allow nothing to control him excessively; he was to be prepared to suffer hardship, for undoubtedly he would experience persecution. Although Philip, Acts 21. 8, is the only named evangelist in the N.T., Timothy is bidden to "do the work of an evangelist"; there should always be a concern for the salvation of those with whom we come into contact. Then Timothy was to fulfil the specific service entrusted to him, and this responsibility rests upon us today.

Paul then depicts his present circumstances, v. 6, views his life in retrospect, v. 7, and anticipates the future, v. 8. His whole life had been presented to God as a living sacrifice, and now the closing days of that life and his death are seen as a drink-offering poured upon that sacrifice. The time for him to strike tent, to loose his moorings and to set sail for the eternal harbour had come.

With the grand contest having been fought, the race completed and the body of Christian doctrine successfully guarded, Paul was confident that there was safely kept for him a crown of righteousness. Paul has no monopoly in this, for such a reward is open to all that love His appearing—the reference is to the manifestation of Christ when He will come to reign in righteousness; such love is demonstrated by living a life of practical righteousness now.

Oct. 1st

READING : **2 Timothy 4. 9-22**

DEMAS, MARK AND ALEXANDER

PAUL MAKES mention of certain co-workers. This letter is addressed to an individual and, in one sense, deals with individuals; no less than 23 names of people who are considered known to Timothy are mentioned. Demas, earlier commended as Paul's fellowlabourer, Philem. 24, forsook the apostle in the hour of loneliness and need. True to the principle of a moral law of gravitation, he went after that on which his heart was set. Luke, the beloved physician, who accompanied Paul in many of his journeyings and who was at Paul's side through much of his first captivity, is seen to be the apostle's only companion at this testing time. Mark, who had set out as a young man with Paul and Barnabas but had turned back, Acts 15. 38, is now given a good testimony. There is always place for recovery, and it is appropriate that the Holy Spirit should take up Mark to record the Gospel of the Perfect Servant of Jehovah. How intensely personal is this Epistle! Note the touching reference to Paul's cloke as well as the books and "especially the parchments".

There are always those who would oppose the truth, and Timothy was to be on his guard against Alexander for he had withstood Paul both in deed, v. 14, and in word, v. 15. Instead of desiring personal vengeance, the apostle leaves the matter of retribution to the Lord—and so should we in such a situation.

The apostle then refers to his recent trial at Rome; no one appeared on his behalf to testify for him. Note the Christ-like spirit of Paul, reminding us of the attitude of Stephen towards those who were stoning him, Acts 7. 60. There was, however, One who stood with him, the One who has promised always to be with each of His own, Heb. 13. 5. By the Lord empowering him and in view of his deliverance from Nero, Paul was enabled after his first trial to fulfil his ministry in proclaiming the gospel. If he had been delivered from death, in this way, v. 17, then in verse 18 Paul is considering his future deliverance by martyrdom from the activities of his enemies.

The reference to Trophimus is significant; the suggestion is that the sign gift of healing had now ceased to be in operation. Paul begins the Epistle with grace, v. 2, and ends with grace—for all saints, v. 22; he owed all to grace and so do we.

Introducing Titus

TITUS WAS a Greek, Gal. 2. 3, whose name means honourable. Paul writes to him as "mine own son", Titus 1. 4, so he was probably converted through his labours. He is not mentioned in Acts, but see 2 Cor. 2. 13; 7. 6, 13–15; 8. 6, 23; Gal. 2. 1–3; 2 Tim. 4. 10. He was sent to Corinth after Paul had written his first letter, and in difficult circumstances proved himself a partner and fellowhelper of Paul concerning the Corinthians, 2 Cor. 8. 23. Galatians 2. 1 shows that Titus accompanied Paul to Jerusalem over the false teaching concerning circumcision, Acts 15. Now he is left in Crete with an apostolic charge. Order in the churches is the substance of the charge, Titus 1. 5. The office and authority of apostles was not given to succeeding generations.

Analysis of the letter

1. 1–4	Salutation, introduction and greeting.
1. 5	The apostle's charge to Titus.
1. 5	The appointment of elders. Their character and behaviour, 1. 6–8. Their work, 1. 9–11.
1. 12–16	Cretan false teachers and their false profession.
2. 1	The things which befit sound doctrine, concerning: Aged men, 2. 2. Aged women, 2. 3. Young women, 2. 4–5. Young men, 2. 6. Titus himself, 2. 7–8. Servants, 2. 9–10.
2. 11–14	The grace of God. Its appearing, 2. 11. Its instruction, 2. 12. Its purposes, 2. 13–14.
2. 15	The ministry of Titus defined.
3. 1–2	Christian behaviour in society.
3. 3	Former foolish and sinful behaviour.
3. 4–7	The transforming effect of the kindness and love of God.
3. 8	Things to be constantly affirmed. Things good and profitable unto men.
3. 9	Things unprofitable, to be avoided.
3. 10–11	Dealing with a factious man.
3. 12–14	Closing instructions.
3. 15	Salutation, greetings and benediction.

Oct. 2nd

READING : **Titus 1. 1-16**

TRUTH AND GODLINESS

IN THE introductory verses 1–6 Paul writes as a servant, or bondman, of God. His message concerns eternal life, the believer's hope of which rests upon the faithfulness of "God that cannot lie". This reminds us of "the God of truth", Isa. 65. 16; "the God of hope", Rom. 15. 13; "the God of love and peace", 2 Cor. 13. 11. The message entrusted to Paul originated in God's promise "before the world began". Cf. 2 Tim. 1. 9 where the same words are used of God's purpose and grace.

We are not apostles as was Paul, but we are bondservants of righteousness, Rom. 6. 18; and of God, 6. 22. So let us be faithful with the gospel, and have confidence in the word of the God who cannot lie, even "God our Saviour". Titus was reminded that the saints lived among Cretans who, by contrast, were "always liars". Truth and godliness are joined together in verse 1. Genuine knowledge of the truth is seen in godly character and conduct. In this way the saints were to be distinct from the Cretans. So must we, by our lives, show the transforming power of the truth we have received.

Certain things needed attention, and the first matter on which the apostle offers his guidance is the appointment of local elders. They must be morally irreproachable, and qualified as verses 6–9 indicate. The great need for true elders is felt on every hand, but only the Lord can raise up the men with the required moral and spiritual character. We may propose elders, or they may assume responsibility of necessity, but it is the Holy Spirit who makes them, Acts 20. 28. A man's service, particularly when standing before the saints, is effectual only if he is a godly man. No reference is made to his material possessions, or prominence in a secular sphere. The reason why such a high standard is required lies in the words, "as the steward of God". He must be one who holds to "the faithful word", in order to be able to convict and rebuke false teachers by it. His sound, or healthful, teaching produces godliness. This is still the objective in ministering the Word, and only those who are godly men can serve God in this way.

Oct. 3rd

READING : **Titus 2. 1-10**

THINGS BEFITTING SOUND DOCTRINE

THIS SECTION details things which become sound doctrine. False teachers, referred to in 1. 10–16, were corrupt in motive and character. Their works were a denial of their profession. Sound teaching is like spiritual hygiene, resulting in healthy character and conduct.

Aged men, v. 2; aged women, v. 3; young women, v. 4; young men, v. 6; and overseers, 1. 5–8; are to be sober. Discretion and self-restraint over fleshly desires are in view. Present days are marked by lack of restraint, and this leads to lawlessness. The value of one's Christian service and influence can be lost or greatly reduced through one serious indiscretion. Aged men are to be grave, v. 2. It does not suggest being miserable, but points to seriousness of purpose that earns respect. An elderly man who is never serious will not gain the confidence of believers who need help. We do not apologise for gravity as if it misrepresented Christian life. The gospel is serious when we are said to be a savour of life, or a savour of death, unto those who hear, 2 Cor. 2. 16.

Aged women are to reveal holy deportment, are not to speak indiscreetly, and in their influence on younger sisters are to teach good things, vv. 3–4. Young women who are married have a work for God in the home and family, of such value that it cannot be measured. Failure in us causes the Word that we believe to be rejected by those who see our inconsistencies, particularly at home. It is here where the words apply, "that the word of God be not blasphemed", v. 5.

Young men are to avoid the extremes of thought and word, and guard against the lusts associated with youth, v. 6.

As to Titus, and it applies to all who teach the saints, he was to be a pattern of good works, v. 7, while his teaching was to be untainted, serious and sincere. No one should lightly regard the work of teaching the saints, nor should one forget that a teacher is also to be a pattern. The section closes with an exhortation to live in a way that adorns the teaching of God our Saviour. The good doctrine is to be beautified as it is clothed by our lives.

Oct. 4th

READING : **Titus 2. 11-15**

THE SHINING FORTH OF GOD'S GRACE

THESE MAY be thought to be the key verses of this Epistle. How beautiful their subject! It is the shining out (the *epiphany*) of the grace of God. It has shone out in the One who was full of grace and truth, John 1. 14. The purpose of this is stated as "bringing salvation", Titus 2. 11 R.V. The first mention in Scripture of the grace of God is Genesis 6. 8, and it brought salvation to Noah and his family. May we never forget what we owe to the grace of God. The desire of God is the salvation of all men, but many are indifferent. Titus 2. 12 brings in the instructions of grace for those who are saved. Ungodliness and worldly lusts are to be denied. Life is to be sober or discreet, 1. 8; 2. 2–4, 6, righteous and godly, or pious in this present age. This passage sums up the letter.

God's grace has brought us salvation, and it now instructs us how we are to live while awaiting the age to come. This will be ushered in by another shining forth of the great God and Saviour Jesus Christ. The falling away and ungodliness that will mark the close of the present age will be followed by righteous administration, and submission to Christ, Zech. 14. 16, 20–21; Jer. 3. 17; Isa. 60. 18–22; Psa. 72. In Titus 2. 13 the rapture of the saints is linked with the later manifestation with Christ; see 1 Thess. 4. 13–18; Col. 3. 4. Are we still looking for the blessed hope and glorious appearing? Let us show by the way we live that our hearts' affections are centred on pleasing the Lord now. Our present portion is grace, while glory awaits us.

Our great God and Saviour Jesus Christ gave Himself for us. What a gift of grace and love! Read these words again in Gal. 1. 4; 2. 20; Eph. 5. 25; 1 Tim. 2. 6. He was the ransom price to release us from all iniquity. The Son hates iniquity, Heb. 1. 9. How great the purpose of Christ when He gave Himself, first to redeem us from all iniquity, then to have us for His own possession, purified and living to do only good. These were the things that Titus was to teach and encourage. Similar remarks about commanding, teaching and not being despised were made to Timothy at the same time, 1 Tim. 4. 11-12. Society then was opposed, as it still is, but the believers then, as now, are to be submissive, for the teaching is God's.

Oct. 5th

READING : **Titus 3. 1-15**

THE KINDNESS AND LOVE OF GOD

THE FIRST two verses relate to conduct in society, where active good, inoffensiveness and law-abiding are to be shown. Racial or class hatred would be quite wrong in us. Principalities and powers, v. 1, are of earth's order, while those of Eph. 1. 21; 3. 10; 6. 12; Col. 2. 10, 15 are of heaven's. It becomes us to show meekness to all men, Titus 3. 2. The truth is to be received meekly, James 1. 21, and practised in the same way. Have we not once been hateful, and slaves of various lusts and pleasures?, v. 3; yet God has saved us according to His mercy, v. 5. He said to sinful Israel, "I am merciful", Jer. 3. 12. Like the apostle we can say, "I obtained mercy", 1 Tim. 1. 16.

We have in this Epistle the outshining of God's grace, 2. 11; then of the glory of our Lord Jesus Christ, 2. 13, (cf. 1 Tim. 6. 14 and Matt. 24. 27); while here in verse 4 we have that of the kindness and love of God our Saviour toward man. It is from the Greek word meaning "*love . . . toward man*", that we get our word *philanthropy*. This is the only reference to God's philanthropy. The same word occurs in Acts 28. 2, but there it applies to men. The One who has acted in kindness and highest philanthropy toward us is God our Saviour, and He has saved us, Titus 3. 5, justified us by His grace, v. 7, and made us heirs of eternal life, v. 7.

Verse 5 describes what God has done for us when, according to His mercy, He saved us. The passage says nothing about deliverance from sin and wrath, but speaks of the washing of regeneration and renewing of the Holy Spirit. The first is an entirely changed state. Regarding this, J. N. Darby has written, "A change of position, a new state of things". Matthew 19. 28 is the only other occurrence of the word, and refers to a new state on earth when the Son of man shall sit on the throne of His glory. Our old state was described in verse 3; the new one brought about by the Holy Spirit is continued by His work of renewal in our lives.

Artemas is not mentioned elsewhere, but Tychicus is in Acts 20. 4–5, etc. He is a beloved brother, a faithful minister and fellow-servant in the Lord—proof of the washing of regeneration and renewing of the Holy Spirit in his life.

Survey of Paul's Four Personal Letters

When we come to read 1 and 2 Timothy, Titus and Philemon, we have left behind Paul's letters to the saints in general, and to the churches in particular, and have reached those which he addresses, for a variety of reasons, to some of his most intimate friends and fellow-workers. The apostle had many notable friends, from Barnabas and Silas, Priscilla and Aquila, Luke and Epaphroditus, to the households of Chloe, Stephanas and Philemon where his welcome was always assured. It is likely that he wrote letters to many of them from time to time, but, be that so, God has only permitted these four to be preserved. These alone are given to us to convey God's mind on the various matters with which they deal.

Timothy was in Ephesus; Titus in Crete; Philemon at home in Colossae; and Paul, the aged warrior of the Lord, in prison probably at Rome. Look at a map and note how much sea and land separated him from them. Think of the differences in their ages and circumstances at the time of his writing, but remember how closely they were knit together in the life in Christ, and in the Spirit's work of perfecting that life in all believers everywhere.

Life in Christ, being in God, is always in love; hence he writes to Timothy, his dearly beloved son, that the end of the charge he had given him was, "love out of a pure heart", 1 Tim. 1. 5. To Titus, his own son after the common faith he writes, "Greet them that love us in the faith", Titus 4. 15. While Philemon, his dearly beloved and fellow-labourer, must have been deeply moved to read "for we have great joy and consolation in thy love", Philem. 7.

These letters range over matters affecting the churches and homes of the saints, and the relationships in both. They warn of perils, and counsel in things vital to godliness. But withal, they are from the heart to the heart; from one who was, as it were, an old, battle-scarred general to younger officers and men enlisted in the cause of Christ. Here, where all are on active service, clear, confident notes are sounded in the way things are turning out. These are born of a settled conviction that the foe has been routed, and all the spoils of the victory are soon to be shared.

Oct. 6th

READING : **Philemon 1-9**

PEN PICTURES OF PHILEMON

THE EPISTLE to Philemon is a delightful gem of inspired writing which is all too often passed over without due consideration. It contains in embryo much precious truth, suggestive and practical, which teaches us as Christians how to comport ourselves among the members of the new society into which faith in Christ has brought us.

Paul appears in this private letter in the role of a mediator. Indeed, the purpose in his writing was to present his plea on behalf of a runaway slave, Onesimus, who had been converted through Paul's preaching, and must now return to his original owner—a Christian master called Philemon, a fellow-labourer with Paul and a beloved brother in the Lord.

The Epistle is an intensely human document, written with extreme delicacy and gracious finesse, yet revealing on Paul's part mature wisdom and understanding of the human reactions to life's circumstances.

Three main characters come before us in the touching little drama—Paul himself, the writer; Onesimus, the defecting slave; and Philemon, the wealthy owner. And woven into the fabric of the opening section we find a pen picture of Philemon, the addressee. He was a fine character, an ardent Christian, a dearly beloved brother in the Lord. He was a man characterized by faith and love. Not a dreamer, nor a romantic, but a saint whose love and faith found practical expression and were in constant exercise. The recollection of Philemon's positive godly living filled Paul with praise and thanksgiving. Do many Christians find such occasion for thanking God on account of our lives and deeds? Can it be said that we, too, refresh the hearts of the saints?

An arresting expression in respect of Philemon's faith occurs in verse 6, "the communication of thy faith". Faith is not fanciful but fruitful; not mystical merely, but missionary. It is a virile principle that vents itself visibly and palpably in practical deeds, to meet the needs and ease the burdens of fellowsaints in material things. This communication of faith has its fruit in the consolation of love.

Oh, that we like Philemon, might have a real living faith which expresses itself in terms of Christian practice!

Oct. 7th

READING : **Philemon 10-25**

PAUL'S PLEA TO PHILEMON

THE MAJOR part of this private letter is taken up with the presentation of Paul's plea on behalf of the absconded slave Onesimus. With all the skill and mastery of an able advocate, Paul builds up a strong argument in his appeal to Philemon for the reinstatement of the former worthless slave.

Embodied in this short Epistle, we may discern some sixteen points most deftly introduced by Paul to press home his appeal. We can note here but a few of them:

(1) *That* for Philemon not to receive Onesimus would constitute a glaring inconsistency with his previous conduct as a Christian—"hearing of thy love and faith, which thou hast toward the Lord Jesus, and toward all saints", v. 5.

(2) *That* Paul's plea is made in the logic of love rather than in the apostolic authority—"though I might be much bold in Christ to enjoin thee that which is convenient, yet for love's sake I rather beseech thee", vv. 8–9.

(3) *That* Paul was now an old man and his word should therefore be treated with added respect—"being such an one as Paul the aged", v. 9.

(4) *That* Paul the pleader was also Paul the prisoner—"being . . . now also a prisoner of Jesus Christ", v. 9.

(5) *That* Paul was intimately related to the one for whom he pleaded—"I beseech thee for my *son*". Onesimus was Paul's spiritual son, v. 10.

(6) *That* Onesimus was now a converted man. His whole life had been transformed. He now lived up to the meaning of his name ("profitable"), v. 11.

(7) *That* to part with Onesimus would be a sacrifice for Paul—"whom I would have retained with me . . .", v. 13.

(8) *That* to complete the pattern of divine purpose Philemon must receive Onesimus back forever, "For perhaps he therefore departed for a season, that thou shouldest receive him for ever", v. 15.

As we ponder the significant phrases, do they not remind us of the interposition of another Mediator who acted on our behalf—the divine "Daysman", our blessed Lord Himself—who "suffered for sins, the just for the unjust, that he might bring us to God"? He paid our debt and set us free.

Introducing Hebrews

THOUGH WE are not informed as to who wrote this Epistle, its message places beyond doubt the identity of the recipients. The reference to the fathers, the tabernacle and the day of atonement confirms the title in the A.V. There must be a reason for there being no mention of the writer, but this should not be a matter of contention.

The two themes of the Epistle are the Priesthood of Christ, and His sacrifice. The Epistle is one of interesting comparisons; chapters 1–6, what is partial and complete; chapters 7–10, what is temporal and eternal; chapters 11–13, what is earthly and heavenly. As a "word of exhortation", 13. 22, its message is threefold: "Let us go on", 6. 1, advancement; "Let us draw near", 10. 22, approach; "Let us go forth unto him", 13. 13, association.

There are recurring parentheses in the Epistle, in which the writer desires the reader to test whether or not he has faith, whether or not he is a Christian. The main parentheses are 3. 1 to 4. 13; 5. 11 to 6. 20; 10. 23–39. In those early days there were Jews attracted to Christ and Christianity, but this was no more than an extension of their Jewish beliefs and practices. They were not established in the once-and-for-all character of the sacrifice of Christ, nor in the fulfilment of the types, and indeed in many other matters. It is not, therefore, in this Epistle the possibility of a Christian's faith becoming weak, nor a Christian going back into the world; it is rather that of a Jew attracted to Christ and Christianity going back to the types, and thereby denying their fulfilment in Christ. There was involved in such an act a renunciation of Christ and His sacrifice. Many readers of this Epistle would have been saved from heartache had this been understood. Child of God, you may fail Christ but you will never renounce Him; your faith at times may be weak, but you will never lose it.

When asked if the word *better* was the key word of this Epistle, a believer replied, "What about *perfect* and *eternal*? We will be better only when we are perfect, and we will not be perfect until eternity".

Note: "New Trans." is often used throughout this Epistle; see *Abbreviations* on page 4.

Oct. 8th

READING: **Hebrews 1. 1–3**

THE SON OF GOD

In times past God spoke "in the prophets" in many parts and in many manners; each revelation was partial and imperfect. They spoke to the fathers, not to the patriarchs, Rom. 9. 5, but to the whole nation, 1 Cor. 10. 1. "At the end of these days" (R.V.), God has spoken, not simply by His Son, nor in the Son as He did in the prophets, but "in Son". The absence of the article, or possessive pronoun before "Son", means that God has spoken in One in this character, in One His equal. Divine revelation is now complete and perfect. The Son is not merely the Messenger, He is the Message and the Message is final. We are the recipients; God has spoken unto us. In time past the sun was seen to be rising slowly until, in these last days, it has reached its meridian in a cloudless sky and we bask in its splendour.

But who is this Son who is God's final revelation? The future shall witness His incalculable wealth as the "appointed heir"; the past witnessed His creative power, "he made the worlds"; the present witnesses His transcendent Majesty, He has sat Himself down "on the right hand of the Majesty on high". The order is significant; first His appointment to heirship then His creatorship. It is right that mention of His heirship should follow the reference to His Sonship in verse 2, but there is a deeper and richer thought here. He was the appointed Heir before He made the worlds, hence "all things were created by him, and for him", Col. 1. 16.

Yet there is more! In verse 3 we learn three things: *What He is,* as the brightness of God's glory (no cloud of glory now). He is the collective expression of every divine attribute, as the express image of God's substance. He is the perfect representation of God's essential being. *What He does,* "upholding all things by the word of his power". He is the Steersman of all things that He made; "having made purification of sins" (R.V.) He has made purification available to all. *Where He is,* "set himself down on the right hand of the greatness on high", New Trans. The grammar of the last two statements of verse 3 tells us that by Himself He made purification of sins, and by Himself He has sat down.

Oct. 9th

READING: **Hebrews 1. 4–14**

THUS IT IS WRITTEN

THE WRITER finds seven O.T. Scriptures to confirm what he has been saying about God's Son. Psalm 2 and 2 Samuel 7 confirm that God has spoken "in Son". Psalms 97, 104 and 45 refer to the Son as heir of all things. Psalm 102 refers to the Son who made the worlds. Psalm 110 refers to the Son who has sat down on the right hand of the Majesty on high.

In verse 5, as in every instance where Psalm 2. 7 is quoted, reference is to our Saviour's birth. It was then in Manhood that He inherited the more excellent name that was His eternally. With what pleasure God must have looked on that Holy Babe and said, "Thou art my Son". 2 Samuel 7. 14, quoted in verse 5, refers to the perfect reciprocity that existed between Father and Son when the Son was here.

Psalm 97. 7 (Greek) projects the mind to His future appearing. When he came to Bethlehem, He was given as the Only-begotten; when God brings Him back again it will be as the First-begotten. When He was given as the Only-begotten, the angels directed their praise to God, Luke 2. 13–14; when God brings Him back again He will direct the worship of all the angels of God to His Son. What a day! Angels beyond numbering, Heb. 12. 22, worshipping the Son! Psalms 104. 4 and 45. 6–7, quoted in verses 7–9, anticipate His coming kingdom, when as God immutable He will sit on His throne, while angels are transformed in accordance with their mission. But He is still Man, and His God has anointed Him above His fellows.

Psalm 102. 25–27, quoted in verses 10–12, refer to the end, when the One, who made the worlds and now upholds them, will fold them up. Then will be the day of God, the day of eternity. But when all will have been changed, He remains the same.

Psalm 110. 1, quoted in verse 13, brings this thrilling chapter to a close—the Son is sitting on God's right hand. In verse 3 He sits in His own right on the right hand of the Majesty on high. In verse 13, by divine assent, He sits on God's right hand until His enemies are made His footstool. While the Son sits, angels are "sent out for service" (New Trans.), and they serve those who shall be heirs of salvation—you and me!

Oct. 10th

READING: **Hebrews 2. 1–9**

LAW AND GRACE

Verses 1–4 belong to chapter 1. Now we learn why the writer has emphasized the superiority of the Son of God to angels. It is that he might compare law with grace. In verses 5–9 we learn of the superiority of the Son of man to angels, yet to be seen in the world to come.

Considering verses 1–4: "Lest haply we drift away from them", v. 1 R.V., envisages the possibility of drifting away (as a ship from its moorings), from the anchor of the soul because there is no vital link by faith. "If we have been negligent of so great salvation", v. 3 New Trans., involves a wilful act following a profession. Here we have the first steps in apostasy. The question is asked in verse 3, "How shall we escape?". This is dealt with by comparing the solemnity of the law and the certainty of judgment for disobedience, with the surpassing greatness of the Gospel; and, by implication, the certainty of judgment for neglect. The word spoken by angels is the law; see also Acts 7. 53; Gal. 3. 19. This word was stedfast; every violation must be punished. If this was so of the word spoken by angels, how much more in the case of this "so great salvation", since there is involved not merely angels but the three Persons in the Godhead. The Lord had spoken, God had attested, and the Holy Ghost had distributed.

In verses 5–9 we learn that "the world to come" will not be subject to angels but to man, the Son of man, Jesus. The quotation from Psalm 8 is intended to show that the dominion forfeited by Adam because of disobedience will be more than restored in the Son of man in the world to come. Jesus, now crowned with glory and honour, is the pledge of this. Nothing shall be left that is not put under Him. Even angels, which are greater in power and might than men, 2 Pet. 2. 11, shall be made subject to Him, though for a little while He was made lower than them. Now we can appreciate the future of Jesus, "nothing that is not put under him", v. 8; His past, "made for a little while lower than the angels", 9 R.V. marg; His present, "crowned with glory and honour", v. 9.

Angels shall worship the Son, 1. 6; all things will be made subject to the Son of man, 2. 8.

Oct. 11th

READING: **Hebrews 2. 10–18**

THE INCARNATION

NOW WE learn of our own future, our past, and our present. Our Captain is leading us as sons to future glory, v. 10. Our Lord claimed us as His brethren when He rose from the dead, vv. 11, 12. Our Lord treasures us as God's children, His love-gift to Him now, v. 13.

If we include verse 9 in this section we may observe three steps in our Saviour's incarnation, and its threefold purpose.

First Step, v. 9, "made a little lower than the angels". No angel could have taken our place, since angels do not die, Luke 20. 36. We therefore thank our God for One who, with a view to the suffering of death, was prepared to be made lower than angels.

Second Step, v. 14, He took part in flesh and blood. Our Saviour was no mere emanation of deity. He was a real Man, though with a difference. Whereas the children are "partakers" in flesh and blood without lot or choice, He voluntarily "took part" in the same.

Third Step, v. 17, "in all things . . . made like unto his brethren". Not only did He partake in "flesh and blood", but He became a tripartite Being: He had a human spirit, soul and body.

The First Purpose in His incarnation recorded here was to deal with the devil who had the power of death, v. 14. The devil had neither absolute power nor unrestricted delegated authority in the matter of death. He only had strength given to exercise that power by permission. We bless God that the devil has been rendered inactive in this matter, as far as we are concerned.

The Second Purpose, v. 17, was "to make propitiation for the sins of the people" R.V. "Reconciliation", v. 17 A.V., is always for "people" and never for "sins". Reconciliation is persons brought near; propitation is sins expunged. Praise God all our sins are put away for ever!

The Third Purpose, v. 18, "he is able to help those that are being tempted" (New Trans.). Thank God for the One who helps us when we are under temptation, when the pressure is on.

Satan, sins and the present need of saints are thus all taken account of.

Oct. 12th

READING: **Hebrews 3. 1–19**

THE SIN OF UNBELIEF

THE SANCTIFIED brethren, 2. 11, and sons being brought to glory, 2. 10, are now addressed as "holy brethren, partakers of the heavenly calling", and called upon to consider the Son of chapter 1 sent to them by God as their Apostle, and as the High Priest of chapter 2 representing them before God.

In verses 1–6 the subject is God's house in this present day. Moses was in God's house as a servant; Christ is over God's house as a Son. "He that built all things is God", v. 4, is an indirect reference to the deity of Christ. If Moses was "in God's house", vv. 2, 5, we are God's house, v. 6. Holding fast, v. 6, is not a means of salvation, it is simply an evidence of it.

In verses 7–19 the subject is God's rest in the future. The recurrence three times of "to day" indicates urgency. It is an urgent matter to examine the heart, not for coldness, but for the possibility of having erred, or having a hardened or an evil heart. The trouble could be deep seated. It is not a matter of a temporary lapse, but rather of an irreversible state. The example of the nation of Israel makes this clear. Of whom did He sware in His wrath that they should not enter into His rest?, v. 11. It was a nation who, though they saw His works forty years, had hardened hearts which remained unchanged, vv. 8, 9. It was a generation who always erred in their heart and did not know His ways, v. 10. Theirs was an evil heart of unbelief that turned away from the Living God, v. 12. The appeal to brethren in verses 12, 13 need not alarm. God always addresses men on the ground of their profession until it may be proved false. It was thus our Lord dealt with Judas Iscariot.

Both the R.V. and the New Translation help us into an understanding of verses 16–19. There is a series of questions and answers. Who provoked? All that came out of Egypt, v. 16. With whom was He displeased? Those who sinned, whose carcasses fell in the wilderness, v. 17. To whom did He sware that they should not enter His rest? Them that believed not, v. 18. What was their sin? Not weakness of faith, but the unbelief of an apostate nation, v. 19.

Oct. 13th

READING: **Hebrews 4. 1–16**

FEAR AND BOLDNESS

VERSES 1–13 conclude the first parenthesis and continue the subject of the rest. Rest for man which was in the mind of God in creation, and repeated by Him in the law, and a long time after in the Psalms, has not yet been realized. God will not, however, be diverted. Despite failure on man's part, the promise of rest is still left, v. 1; it remains, v. 9. This rest is future; that we have not ceased from our own works is an evidence of this, v. 10. Man's experience in Eden, v. 4, and in Canaan, v. 8, foreshadowed this rest, but very inadequately. This is God's rest, vv. 1, 3, 5, 10,—God resting in His love when everything is in accord with His holy nature, and man resting there too.

The exhortations "Let us . . . fear", v. 1, and "Let us . . . give diligence", v. 11 R.V., are given against the background of Israel's failure. "We have had good tidings preached unto us, even as also they", v. 2 R.V.; though the messages were different, each offered rest. Wherein did they fail? They did not hear with faith, v. 2; because of unbelief, vv. 6, 11. The only condition for entering this rest is stated "For we enter into the rest who have believed", v. 3 New Trans. We therefore have the appeal. "Let us therefore give diligence to enter into that rest", lest any man fall after the same example of unbelief, v. 11. It is not, therefore, a question of weak or strong faith, but of faith or no faith. Verses 12, 13 present important means to test faith: the Word of God and the eye of God. The child of God may fear exposure by God's Word, and the searching of God's eye, but recognizing their necessity, will not avoid them. Resting now by faith in the Lord Jesus, the believer is assured of enjoying God's rest eternally—resting in God's love.

In verse 14 the Priesthood of Christ is resumed from 2. 18. The believer is furnished with all that is required to hold fast. *What we have*, v. 14,—a Great High Priest in heaven in whom are combined deity and Manhood. *What we have not*, v. 15,—an unsympathetic high priest. Because of the unfailing ministry of our Great High Priest we have the unlimited resource of a throne of grace, with mercy and grace always available to help, v. 16.

Oct. 14th

READING: **Hebrews 5. 1–14**

SELECTED AND SUMMONED

OUR LORD is now presented as fulfilling the two pre-requisites for priesthood—*Selected from among men*, v. 1, *Summoned by God*, v. 4. The O.T. priest selected from among men was established for men. His work was in sacrifice, v. 1, and compassion, v. 2. Sacrificing involved the people's worship (gifts), and failure (sacrifice for sins). Compassion was extended, not as a legal duty, but as a moral obligation because of his own weakness. His own infirmity made it necessary to offer for his own sins. He was summoned by God, because his office was an honour that could not be assumed, v. 4. If his priesthood was an honour bestowed, v. 4, Christ's is a glory added, v. 5. Psalm 2, referring to the Son of God's incarnation, quoted in verse 5, and amplified in verses 7, 8, confirms our High Priest was selected from among men. Psalm 110, referring to His resurrection, quoted in verse 6, and amplified in verse 9, confirms He was summoned by God. What a High Priest is ours! Selected from among men, He suffered every trial that could assail Holy Manhood and endured them all. In the days of His flesh, praying and weeping, He cried to Him who was able to save Him out of death by resurrection when His trials were over. Summoned, too, by God in resurrection, God saluted Him a Priest forever who would know no interruption and have no successor. He has become also the Author of eternal salvation. All who are of the obedience of faith are assured they have a Priest forever and blessings eternal.

The following parenthesis, 5. 11 to 6. 20, is necessary before the subject of Melchisedec is taken up again.

Verses 11–14 are in the nature of a rebuke. Having progressed somewhat, they had "become dull of hearing", v. 11 R.V.; they had "become such as have need of milk", v. 12 R.V. They had degenerated to deafness and infancy. Instead of being teachers they required teaching; instead of solid food they needed milk. They had associated what had been introduced by Christ with what belonged to the law, instead of recognizing that the law was but the first principles (rudiments) of the beginning of the present oracles of God. They were not babes spiritually in the sense of 1 Corinthians 3. 1, 2, but rather dispensationally as in Galatians 4. 3.

Oct. 15th

READING: **Hebrews 6. 1–8**

US; THEM; YOU

BY OBSERVING a change of pronoun in this chapter we may notice its threefold division. Verses 1–3, profession: "let us"; verses 4–8, apostasy: "to renew them"; verses 9–20, reality: "better things of you".

In verses 1–3 the writer associates himself with those who had been attracted to Christ, amongst whom were certain in danger of drifting away, 2. 1, and turning away, 3. 12. The exhortation in verse 1 is "to leave" and "to go on". To leave the word of the beginning of the Christ (New Trans. and R.V. marg.) was to recognize that Christ's earthly ministry was a beginning that led up to what He secured in His death and resurrection. To go on to perfection ("full age", 5. 14) was to have faith in a Risen Saviour, the Author of eternal salvation, and a Priest for ever. To fail was (i) to lay again their O.T. foundation of repentance from dead works and faith toward God, instead of repentance toward God and faith towards the Lord Jesus Christ; (ii) to retain the doctrine of baptisms and not accept one baptism; (iii) to revert to the laying on of hands on both people and sacrifices, something quite different from the act of fellowship and identification among the early Christians; (iv) to hold to a general resurrection not an eclectic resurrection; (v) to fear eternal judgment and not rest on eternal salvation.

In verses 4–8 there is the possibility of apostasy. None of the statements in verses 4, 5 imply conversion. (i) "Once enlightened" is mental illumination, as 10. 26 "the knowledge of the truth", and not the divine illumination of 2 Cor. 4. 6. (ii) "Have tasted of the heavenly gift", as with those who wondered at His gracious words, Luke 4. 22. (iii) "Were made partakers of the Holy Ghost", not possessors. (We are told in Luke 5. 10 that James and John were partners with Simon, and in 5. 7 that they beckoned their partners in the other ships. The second word in Greek translated "partner" is used here. They shared in the same profession, but not the same business). (iv) "Tasted of the good word of God" may be likened to the seed that fell upon stony places, Matt. 13. 20, 21. (v) "Tasted . . . the powers of the world to come" may have involved a miracle of healing, but without conversion.

Oct. 16th

READING: **Hebrews 6. 9–20**

THE ANCHOR OF THE SOUL

To FALL away is a wilful act of desertion by a nominal Christian. The case here is of a Jew renouncing Christ after some kind of profession. Such an one could not be renewed again unto repentance nor conversion, seeing he had never had that experience. Having in the first instance changed his mind about Christ, then reverting to his former position, he declared that Christ was justly crucified and exposed to scorn; "crucifying for themselves (as they do) the Son of God, and making a show of (him)", v. 6 New Trans. A child of faith will never do this. The effect of the Gospel is likened to the earth that drinks in the rain: diverse results are produced, the herb-yielding ground receives blessing, the brier-yielding ground is condemned to burning; cf. 2 Cor. 2. 16.

In verses 9–20 those are addressed who by their work and labour of love have shown evidence of salvation. For such there is exhortation and encouragement. Because of future hope they are exhorted to be diligent, v. 11, and because of present trials not to be slothful but patient, v. 12. Abraham is cited as an example of patience. A promise was made to him before Isaac was born, Gen. 12. 2; when Isaac was offered up it was confirmed by an oath, 22. 16. Not until Isaac was sixty years of age and twins were born to Rebekah, was the promise of verse 14 received. God's word, and God's oath in which He vouched His own integrity, v. 13, enabled Abraham patiently to endure. What was their encouragement (strong consolation)?, v. 18. By two unchangeable things, His word and oath, God has shown His counsel (purpose) to be unchangeable. Having fled to Christ for refuge to lay hold upon the hope of blessing in Him, we have a hope which, though unseen and heavenly (within the veil), is an anchor of the soul both sure and steadfast. Jesus, too, has entered within the veil for us as our Forerunner, the pledge of our admission one glorious day. In the meantime He is there in our interests having become an High Priest after the order of Melchisedec.

Safe to land no shadows enter, on that radiant shore;
Past the pangs, the pains, the partings,
Hushed the storms for evermore.

Oct. 17th

READING: **Hebrews 7. 1–28**

THE ORDER OF MELCHISEDEC

"AFTER THE order of Melchisedec, and not . . . after the order of Aaron", v. 11, is the subject of this chapter. The Aaronic order was: "not suffered to continue by reason of death", v. 23; that of Melchisedec: "a priest for ever", vv. 17, 21.

The greatness of Melchisedec, priest of the Most High God, and as having no recorded genealogy and neither birth nor death, is brought before us as a type of God's Son. He was superior to Abraham, he received tithes from him and blessed him. He was superior to the Levitical priesthood; he received tithes on a voluntary basis, but they because of command. They received them and died, but Melchisedec liveth (figuratively). Levi, yet in Abraham's loins, paid tithes to Melchisedec when Abraham did.

The need for a different Priest arose because both the priesthood and the law were imperfect and provisional, vv. 11, 19. For two reasons our Lord's Priesthood required a change in the law concerning priests. He sprang out of Juda and not Levi, v. 14. Our Lord's Priesthood is after the power of an endless life, the Levitical priesthood was after the law of a carnal commandment (physical deformities debarred, and death terminated), v. 16. The Levitical priests, having a temporary calling, were made without a binding oath, v. 21; a change could be made. Since our Lord is a Priest by oath, vv. 20, 21, there can be no change. We are now blessed with a better hope; we can draw nigh unto God, v. 19; and Jesus, a Priest for ever by divine oath, is our surety of all the blessings of a better covenant.

How blessed then we are! We have a High Priest who, after the pattern of Aaron, intercedes and saves, and after the order of Melchisedec continues ever in an unchangeable Priesthood.

Our Lord's Priesthood is not based on sacrifice as was the Levitical priesthood; His is by word of oath. During the seven days of consecration of the Levitical priesthood, a daily sin offering was offered for the high priest and his sons. Our Priest required no daily sacrifice; His offering was once and it was Himself that He offered. What a Priest, then, is this! He is a King-Priest, v. 2; He continues ever, v. 24; He is a divine Priest, v. 28.

Oct. 18th

READING: **Hebrews 8. 1–13**

SOMEWHERE; SOMEWHAT

WE THINK now of our Lord as Minister of the true tabernacle, vv. 1–5, and Mediator of a better covenant, vv. 6–13.

Having been *selected* from among men and *summoned* by God, ch. 5, He must now have *somewhere* to officiate, 8. 1–2, and *somewhat* to offer, 8. 3–5. Earthly priests offer gifts according to the law, and serve in what is a copy and shadow of heavenly things. Our High Priest is a Minister of the true tabernacle, the pattern of which was shown to Moses, vv. 2–5. Having offered Himself once, He is now in God's presence in the eternal value of that sacrifice. This, again, makes His priesthood unique, seated, v. 1, serving, v. 2. A sitting priest was unheard of, but now a Man as Priest sits where no angel ever sat, 1. 13. Here, then, is the chief point, v. 1 R.V.; the High Priest we have is the Man of the shame of the tree now sitting on the throne of the Majesty in the heavens, in all the eternal efficacy of His once-for-all sacrifice. Aaron is eclipsed.

He is also the Mediator of a better covenant established upon better promises, v. 6. The first covenant was a contract between God and the fathers; its promises depended upon the terms being kept, but the fathers continued not in those terms, even though God took them by the hand, v. 9. The new covenant is not made with man as in verse 9; it is consummated as regards the house of Israel and the house of Judah, v. 8 New Trans. God assumes every obligation, and its terms are not therefore "*thou shalt*" as in first covenant, but "*I will*", vv. 10–12. It is a better covenant! What of the better promises? God's laws will be put into their renewed mind to know and do them, written in their purified hearts to love them; the promises will rest on what God Himself shall be to His people, v. 10. All shall know the Lord in themselves, v. 11 New Trans., by reason of the Spirit's anointing. God will be propitious to their unrighteousnesses, and will never in any wise remember their sins and iniquities, v. 12. Our Lord as Mediator of this better covenant lives to make good to man the better promises. The first covenant is now antiquated; Moses is eclipsed. While this chapter makes Israel the beneficiaries, we shall see in chapter 10 that we now enjoy the better promises.

Oct. 19th

READING: **Hebrews 9. 1–10**

A WORLDLY SANCTUARY

WE ARE now shown the temporary and limited character of the ceremony under the first covenant. Verse 1 speaks of its divine service and its worldly sanctuary. Verses 2–5 describe the worldly sanctuary, and verses 6–7 the divine service and in 8–10 we have the conclusion.

Verses 2–5. The tabernacle was "a sanctuary of this world", v. 1 R.V., as to its location. As "set up", v. 2 New Trans., there were two compartments divided by a veil; each had their articles of furniture. The first was the sanctuary, "Holy place", v. 2 R.V. Then there was the Holiest of all, or "Holy of holies", v. 3 R.V. The reference to the golden censer, but not to the golden altar, suggests the day of atonement when the censer linked the golden altar in the Holy place with the Holy of holies. The expression "which had", v. 4, and not "wherein", v. 2, indicates the golden censer did not have a permanent place in the Holy of holies.

Verses 6–7. In the divine service we are told the priests went always into the Holy Place, each morning to trim the lamps, morning and evening to burn incense, and every Sabbath to replace the loaves. Into the Holy of holies the high priest entered one day each year and not without blood, offered both for himself and the errors of the people.

Verses 8–10. The conclusion was this: while the worldly sanctuary had a standing, the way into the holiest (heaven) was not made manifest, v. 8. The "*first* tabernacle", v. 8, is obviously the whole structure, and not as in verse 6. The word for "holiest of all", v. 8, is different from that in verse 3, but the same as in 10. 19; it therefore refers to heaven. As for the divine service, the gifts and sacrifices could never give peace of conscience, v. 9.

Verse 9 speaks of "the time now present", R.V.; verse 10 of the "time of setting things right", New Trans. What a privileged people we are! The tabernacle in terms of practicality, though not enlightenment, has served its purpose—the way into the holiest is now manifest. The sacrifices and ordinances of the flesh, imposed as a burden, have served their temporary purpose; things have been set right, and we have peace of conscience. But more of this later!

Oct. 20th

READING: **Hebrews 9. 11–28**

"BUT CHRIST"—"FOR CHRIST"

VERSES 11–23 are particularly Jewish. Note the reference to "dead works", v. 14, "transgressions" under the first covenant, v. 15. In verses 11, 12 we see the anti-typical High Priest of the anti-typical tabernacle and holy place; His own blood is of such value that He has entered the holy place once for all because the redemption He has obtained is eternal. He therefore needs not to enter every year, v. 7. In verses 13–15, we have the Mediator of the new covenant; by His blood the conscience can be purged, by His death the promise of eternal inheritance may be received. In contrast with the ignorant, involuntary, physically perfect animal sacrifices, Christ's sacrifice was intelligent (eternal Spirit), voluntary (offered Himself) and of moral perfection (without spot), v. 14. Animal blood procured external sanctification, v. 13, but Christ's blood, inward purging, v. 14. The retrospective character of the death of Christ vindicated God in dealing with transgressions under the first covenant, so that Jews called before and since Calvary receive the promise of eternal inheritance, v. 15.

In verses 18–23 we return to the first covenant and blood-sprinkling. It would appear there is a grouping together of different occasions of blood-sprinkling to emphasize that this was an essential element in God's dealing with Israel. (i) Verse 19: God dwells with them, Exod. 24, and journeys with them, Num. 19. (ii) Verse 21: so that they might serve Him, Exod. 29; Lev. 8.

In verses 24–28 we have three appearings. In verse 24 Christ now appears before the face of God *for us* in all the eternal efficacy of His shed blood, (this is the high priest in the Holy of holies making atonement for his family, Lev. 16. 11, 14). In verse 26, once in the consummation of the ages He has "appeared to put away sin", (this is the sacrifice slain, Lev. 16. 11, 15) referring to Calvary. In verse 28 "unto *them* that look for him shall he appear the second time without sin unto salvation", (this is the high priest emerging from the Holy of holies to deal with the scapegoat to procure the nation's forgiveness, Lev. 16. 20, 22) and refers to our Lord's future appearing for Israel's salvation.

Oct. 21st

READING: **Hebrews 10. 1–39**

ISRAELITE, BELIEVER, APOSTATE

In verses 1–14 the old order of sacrifices as a means of sanctification is taken away, and the sacrifice of Christ established, v. 9. Those sacrifices in themselves neither expressed God's will nor gave Him pleasure, vv. 5, 6. The yearly and daily repetition proved their inefficacy, vv. 1, 11. Peace of conscience was unknown, past guilt remained, v. 2; assurance for the future was never enjoyed, the offerer never made perfect, v. 1. God's Son by the offering of His body has accomplished God's will and procured our sanctification, vv. 6–10. The Saviour having offered Himself once, v. 10, has sat down for ever, v. 12, and the sanctified ones are now perfected for ever, v. 14.

In verses 15–25 believers of this day are beneficiaries of the new covenant. Israel and Judah are not mentioned as in chapter 8. Whereas 8. 8 reads "*to them*" New Trans., yet now the Holy Ghost is a witness "*to us*", 10. 15. Since for us now there is "no more offering for sin", v. 18, and no more remembrance of sins, v. 17, we move inwards to worship, vv. 19–22, look forward with assurance, holding fast the confession of our hope", v. 23 R.V., and think outwards in terms of others, vv. 24, 25.

In verses 26–39 we learn the true character of the apostate. He has received the knowledge of the truth, v. 26, has been enlightened, v. 32 R.V., but sins wilfully, v. 26, and is an adversary, v. 27. There being no thought of weakness nor a temporary lapse, the writer emphasizes his habit and boldness, having wilfully turned his back on the one Sacrifice; God has nothing else to offer, v. 26, but inescapable judgment, v. 27. To have despised Moses' law meant death without mercy under two or three witnesses; to sin wilfully means much sorer punishment, because the witnesses involved are the three Persons in the Godhead, vv. 28, 29. Could it be that some, having been enlightened and having accepted that they had a better and enduring substance, had suffered loss in vain? It was all a matter of living by faith or drawing back. The "little while" till He should come is the test of faith. If the Israelite "comes", v. 1, the believer "enters", v. 19, the apostate "draws back", v. 38.

Oct. 22nd

READING: **Hebrews 10. 1–39**

ENTER AND DRAW NEAR

AS FOR the Israelite, vv. 1–14, "no more conscience of sins" was never attained, v. 2; the Christian, vv. 15–25, "no more offering for sin" is required, v. 18; for the apostate, vv. 26–38, "no more sacrifice for sins" can be offered, v. 26.

The Work of Christ, vv. 11–14. Having offered one voluntary vicarious sacrifice, our Saviour, in virtue of a finished work, has sat down to perpetuity in a place that declares unmistakably His acceptance, v. 12. His foes shall yet be subdued, v. 13, and in the meantime His friends, as far as their sins are concerned, are perfected to perpetuity, v. 14.

The Witness of the Holy Spirit, vv. 15–18. The Holy Spirit bears witness to a new covenant vastly different from the old, where there was a continual remembrance of sins, v. 3. The believer now enjoys a plenary and perpetual remission of sins which "I will never remember any more", v. 17 New Trans.

The Worship of the Saints, vv. 19–22. In virtue of the work of Christ, and the witness of the Spirit to the remission of sins, God now invites us to enter the holiest with boldness, v. 19, and to draw near in full assurance, v. 22. This boldness is a result of complete remission, this assurance because of full acceptance. We enter by a newly slain and living way; not only is the efficacy of the Sacrifice ever present, but there is no threat of death to those who enter. We enter because of a finished work: "the blood of Jesus", v. 19; we draw near because of an unfinished work: "a great priest", v. 21 R.V. If the apostate draws back, vv. 38, 39, the believer draws near, v. 22; if the apostate has "an evil heart", 3. 12, the believer has "a true heart"; if the apostate has a "heart of unbelief", 3. 12, the believer has "full assurance of faith". The blood for our guilt, and the water for our new birth, v. 22, entitle us to do what no priest before would have dared to do.

I hear the accuser roar of ills that I have done,
I know them all and thousands more.
  Jehovah findeth none.
Why stand we then without with fear?
The blood of Christ invites us near.

Oct. 23rd

READING: **Hebrews 11. 1–40**

THE JUST SHALL LIVE BY FAITH

Ante-deluvian Age, vv. 1–7. Faith substantiating hope, so necessary for converted Jews, was not something new, (see vv. 9, 10); nor was evidencing the unseen, (see vv. 7, 13, 27). Obtaining "a good report" had been experienced too; see vv. 4, 5, 39. Following the introduction, vv. 1, 2, we have faith acknowledging a Creator-God, v. 3, recognizing the need of a Saviour-God, v. 4. Thereafter faith expressed itself in pleasing God, vv. 5, 6, becoming separate from the world, v. 7.

Patriarchal Age, vv. 8–22. If Noah became heir of a position, v. 7, Abraham was heir of a place, vv. 9, 10. In Abraham, v. 8, we see the obedience of faith; in Sarah, vv. 11, 12, the reckoning of faith. In verses 13–16 there is the faith that refuses to go back. If Sarah reckoned God faithful and received a son, v. 11, Abraham reckoned God able and renounced a son, vv. 17–19. We have the nature of faith's blessing, "things to come" v. 20, and the extent of it, "both the sons of Joseph", v. 21. In verses 21, 22 faith in God's promise is undiminished in death; Jacob worshipped when promised burial in Canaan, and Joseph gave commandment to be buried there.

Egyptian Bondage, vv. 23–29. Now we see that faith is stronger than fear. Moses' parents feared not the king's commandment, v. 23, and Moses himself feared not the king's wrath, v. 27. In verse 28, in connection with the passover, there was safety, and in verse 29, in their passing through, there was separation.

The Land of Canaan, vv. 30–40. Two incidents associated with faith describe Israel's entry into Canaan: "walls . . . fell down" and "the harlot . . . perished not", vv. 30, 31. After the identification of persons marked by faith during the days of the judges and the monarchy, v. 32, there follows a specification of remarkable acts of faith. In verses 33, 34 we see the successes of faith, in verse 35 the sufferings of faith, and in verses 36–38 faith in apparent defeat.

The closing verses 39, 40 afford us a humbling conclusion. Those Old Testament worthies whose faith shames us will not be perfected without us. God, in fact, has provided "some better thing" for us, and not the least the glorious possibility of being caught up without dying in bodies of glory.

Oct. 24th

READING: **Hebrews 12. 1–11**

JESUS OUR EXAMPLE AND ENCOURAGEMENT

The Race, vv. 1–2. As our Example, we are to fix our eye upon Jesus where He is now. Whereas the joy was set before Him, the race is set before us. There is need of endurance; Jesus endured the cross; we are to run the race with patience (endurance). We are compassed about with witnesses, and beset with sin; our need is twofold. Firstly, to look away from those heroes of chapter 11 who obtained witness because of their faith, and fix our eye on Jesus who began and completed the path of faith without wavering; to fix our eye on Jesus who, for the joy that was set before Him, endured crucifixion, despised shame, and is set down at the right hand of God, not in virtue of His finished work as 10. 12, but a completed course. Secondly, every cumbrance and the besetting sin of falling out of the race must be laid aside. For the Hebrews, the danger was their life-long association with a worldly sanctuary and its attendants that belonged to sight and not faith.

Chastening, vv. 3–11. For our encouragement, we are to consider Him as He was here. Significantly we are told that whereas the opposition to Him was from sinners, to us it is from sin. The need again is endurance, and it must be noted that whereas Jesus endured contradiction, we have to endure chastening. Chastening is the parental education and correction of a child. God's business, however, is different from that of our earthly fathers. They, for the short time we are under their jurisdiction, chasten as seems good to them, and they are by no means infallible, yet we reverence them. The chastening of God, the Father of our spirits, is always for profit, He makes no mistakes; should we not then be in subjection to Him? The source of chastening is the Lord, v. 5; the subjects are sons, v. 7; the scope, "all are partakers", v. 8. Four responses to chastening are mentioned: (*a*) "despise", v. 5, is to be careless as to the purpose; (*b*) "faint", v. 5, is to give up because of failure; (*c*) "endure", v. 7, is to endure the trial so as to learn the lesson; (see R.V.); (*d*) "exercised", v. 11, is to mean business as the gymnast, with every muscle tense. If the Lord is source, v. 5, then love is the motive, v. 6, and our profit is the object, v. 10.

Oct. 25th

READING: **Hebrews 12. 12–29**

SINAI AND SION

VERSES 12–17 conclude the foregoing section and introduce the next. To help the weak, drooping hands require to be lifted up, feeble knees strengthened and straight paths made for the feet. To see the Lord, peace and sanctification must be pursued. Watchfulness was needed, lest there be among them an apostate failing of the grace of God, having the poisonous effect of a root of bitterness. Esau, who forfeited blessing for a morsel of meat, is cited as an example of an apostate who chose the temporal instead of the eternal. By his deliberate choice, Esau discovered, despite his tears, his father could not repent; the blessing was irrevocably Jacob's.

To expose the folly and seriousness of apostasy, we are told what Christianity is not, vv. 18–21, and what it is, vv. 22–24. To apostatize was to go back to what could be touched, the law with its fearful accompaniments of death and judgment foreshadowed at Sinai. To this the Christian has not come, but to Mount Sion symbolizing the establishment of a kingdom in Christ. The great and future kingdom age is brought before us in verses 22–24, and to this, by faith, the Christian is already come. There is the heavenly city for which Abraham looked; a universal gathering of the serried ranks of angels; the assembly of those enrolled in heaven sharing in the birthright; God with everything under His scrutiny; the Old Testament saints made perfect; Jesus the Mediator of the new covenant for Israel and Judah on the earth, and the blood of sprinkling that secures earthly blessings. The apostate, a profane person, chooses what is palpable, and forfeits what is of faith. If there was no escape for those who refused the oracles from Sinai, how much more those who refused the oracles from heaven offering eternal redemption. The shaking of the earth accompanying the oracles of Sinai cannot be compared with a future shaking, when all that is not of God is removed and an everlasting kingdom remains. To the believer this is not something to fear, but a promise to cherish; it is the establishment of the new creation. Remembering, however, God's character, we seek with grace to serve Him now with reverence and fear.

Oct. 26th

READING: **Hebrews 13. 1–25**

ESTABLISHED WITH GRACE

Verses 1–6, *Practical.* Brotherly love is hospitable, "Be not forgetful of hospitality", v. 2 New Trans.; sympathetic, "Remember them that are in bonds" v. 3; pure, "Let marriage be had in honour" v. 4 R.V.; content, "Be ye free from the love of money; content with such things as ye have", v. 5 R.V.

Verses 7–17, *Doctrinal.* Jesus Christ remains when faithful leaders pass on. Grace establishes when there is danger of wavering. We have an altar, neither tangible nor visible; it is Calvary in remembrance, and this precludes those who serve the type. Christ suffering outside the gate was a fulfilment of that sin offering that was burned and not eaten. The place of His suffering not only fulfilled a type, it signified the setting aside of all that the camp of Israel represented. All who are now set apart to God are set apart from Judaism and its present day counterpart. For the converted Jew, reproach was certain, but it was His reproach: he now had nothing abiding here; even Jerusalem was soon to be destroyed, but a heavenly city was assured him. A new twofold sacrifice was his: a heart continually expressing its joy to God through Christ, and its kindness to men. He also had leaders to watch over his soul. What was his by grace is ours too.

Verses 18–25, *Hortatory.* The writer requests prayer, recognizing the saints needed him, and trusting that his conscience and conduct were worthy of this request. Now he prays for them, that they may be perfected in every good work of grace to do God's will as declared in this Epistle, and at the same time that God through Jesus Christ may do in them what is pleasing to Him. If God had brought their fathers up out of the Red Sea with Moses and Aaron as their shepherds, Isa. 63. 11, the God of peace had brought again from the dead the Lord Jesus as their Great Shepherd. If, after their fathers had been brought up out of the Red Sea, they were given a covenant of condemnation, then their Great Shepherd had brought out of death an everlasting covenant ratified in His own blood that assured them of everlasting blessing. Compared with what might have been written, the Epistle was but few words.

Introducing James

THIS EPISTLE was written by James, one of three well-known persons of this name in the New Testament; the son of Zebedee, Matt. 10. 2; the son of Alphaeus, Matt. 10. 3; and James, the Lord's brother, Gal. 1. 19. It is unlikely that it was written by the son of Zebedee, or the son of Alphaeus. James, the Lord's brother, one of the reputed pillars of the church, Acts 15. 13; Gal. 2. 9, the leader of the circumcision party, 2. 12, was possibly the author of an epistle intended to make a great appeal to Jewish believers. He abode in Jerusalem, whence the letter was sent to the twelve tribes of the dispersion, James 1. 1. These may have been Jews scattered among the Gentiles before the first advent of Christ, John 7. 35, and who later believed on Him. Or possibly they were believers scattered after the persecution of Stephen, Acts 11. 19. They were Jewish Christians, James 2. 1. But from the Epistle it would seem they lacked a virile, active faith. They had turned from the Judaism of works to a merely passive faith in Christ. Where these scattered believers lived we are not told. The Epistle seems to have been a circular one. The time of writing is uncertain, but it was early in the history of the church, before a clear-cut distinction had been made between the synagogue and church gatherings, before Acts 15, to which chapter no reference is made in the Epistle. It was in all probability written about A.D. 45, and is reckoned the earliest book of the New Testament.

The subject matter of the letter is the practical outworking of Christianity, and consists of exhortations and reproof. It exhorts poor believers to patience and prayer, and rebukes the worthless faith and boastful talk of the rich. James has a style of writing peculiar to himself; he sets out positive and negative aspects of his themes; he quotes freely from the Old Testament —passages familiar to those brought up in the synagogues, and which have a relevance to present-day believers. He gives principles applying to Christians of all ages, which should be taken to heart by all to whom its exhortations apply. His teaching is like that of the Sermon on the Mount, to which there are about thirty references, but no quotations, for the Sermon had not yet been committed to writing.

Oct. 27th

READING : **James 1. 1-18**

TEMPTATIONS

JAMES AT once deals with a practical problem, temptation, v. 2, a word that may be understood in a good or bad sense, to do good, or entice to sin; the context decides which meaning. Trials are the experiences of all believers, 1 Cor. 10. 13, and are diverse in origin. They are not so much examples of our failure, as a question of how we react to them. James says that we ought to find joy in such experiences, 1. 1–4, to prove if we do really trust God. Can we patiently wait for Him to remove them, to produce perfection in us, Christlikeness, Eph. 4. 13, with no grace lacking in our lives, the ability to conduct ourselves in trials? We are told how to get this wisdom—by asking God, who gives it liberally—freely. How to ask is important—positively, in faith; negatively, without wavering, unlike the waves—uncertain, doubleminded—one who looks to God, or to himself, being unstable—fickle. The believer should glory in these trials, whether poor or rich: if poor, to rejoice in God's deliverance; if rich, to rejoice in being brought low, learning how not to depend on riches, since they ultimately pass forever. The result of these trials is seen in verses 13–18. He who endures is blessed by God, receiving the crown of life, the reward for winning, 1 Cor. 9. 25. The second man, James 1. 13, is also tempted. But "tempt" here is used in a bad sense—enticed to sin. This test is not of God. He cannot do evil, nor does He tempt man to do so. How could such a God tempt to evil those whom He has begotten through the Word of truth, the Gospel?

An example of God's good giving and perfect boon is seen in His gift of life, v. 18. This was His set purpose for our good. His giving is seen in that He brought us forth by the word of the truth of the gospel—the good news. His resultant boon is the perfect outcome, in "that we should be a kind of first-fruits of his creatures". "Firstfruits" suggests the best, very close to God, just as Israel was the best among the nations, Jer. 2. 3. The outcome that God looks for in us through our trials is a patient endurance that merits the crown of life.

There is no "variableness" associated with the Father and His gifts, v. 18, contrasting with the wavering and double mindedness, vv. 6, 8, when faith is lacking.

Oct. 28th

READING : **James 1. 19-27**

THE WORD OF TRUTH

James impresses on his brethren how they should treat the Word of truth, by which they were begotten, 1. 18. They ought to *listen* to the Word, and *talk* less about it. Ceaseless talking often develops into controversialism and wrath. Such wrath hinders the spread of the gospel, for it does not demonstrate the righteousness of God.

In this passage James uses three metaphors to describe the Word of truth, and the lessons that may be learned from them. (1) A plant, v. 21—one meekly planted in the clean soil of a heart uncontaminated from overflowing malice. This will bring salvation. (2) A mirror, vv. 22–24; this reveals man's activity, not his hearing. If a man is a hearer rather than a doer, he may look into one of these eastern mirrors, made of burnished metal, usually a mixture of copper and tin, not giving a very exact picture. In this mirror he will see his natural face, but on going away he will forget what he saw, an unprofitable use of the mirror. (3) The perfect law of liberty, v. 25, described in Romans 8. 2 as the law of the Spirit of life in Christ Jesus, making us free from the law of sin and death. The man who looks into such a law will continue to do so; he will not easily forget what he sees. He will be blessed in such an act, by its permanence.

James finishes this teaching by warning against self-deception—a man thinking he is religious, when he is not. This is evident in a believer who cannot bridle his tongue, thus declaring the vanity, the emptiness of his profession of religion. Genuine religion, in the sight of God, is indicated not by what a man thinks about himself, but rather by the outward manifestation of religion—visiting the fatherless and widows. This is the negative side of religion—he does not forget the orphans and widows. The positive side of religion is evident in the believer keeping himself unspotted from the world that defiles, the world that is at enmity with God, James 4. 4. Spotlessness is a condition of unworldliness. Active charity and moral purity constitute pure religion.

Note. In verse 22, we read of a doer of the *word*, while in verse 25, we find a doer of the *work*, contrasting with "hearers only" and a "forgetful hearer".

Oct. 29th

READING : **James 2. 1-13**

RESPECT OF PERSONS

THE PRACTICE of Christianity does not always express itself in right conduct, 1. 22. This is seen in the partiality that characterizes some believers, 2. 1. "Brethren" here must be Christian brethren, as the words "our Lord Jesus Christ" imply. "My brethren" suggest those who have a common faith in Christ. James would query the faith of those who show partiality, and he gives an example of respect of persons in the reception into fellowship of those of different social standing—rich and poor. This social standing was obvious by the clothes they wore, yet those who received them gave to the rich the place of favour, and to the poor the inferior place. This is partiality, and shows them to be judges with evil thoughts, unfair thinking. God did not thus receive them at the first. This state of affairs may be all too common in our gospel meetings to-day. We make a fuss of important people, and pay little attention to poorly-clad folk. This ought not so to be, else we "became judges of evil thoughts".

This is different from the way God treated the poor; them He reckoned rich in faith, and established them as heirs of the coming kingdom. Your treatment of the poor is strange, for it is the rich who are your opponents, and mark it by drawing you before the courts, in contrast to God who called you by His name, Acts 15. 17. If you treated the poor as God does, you would fulfil His will, and the royal law of love, James 2. 8. But if you prefer some persons over others, the royal law condemns you as transgressors. Loving one's neighbour as oneself means fulfilling the royal law, and includes loving all the poor. Keeping the law means keeping it as a unified whole, v. 10, and demands that we love all, not just merely the rich. Breaking one part of the law means breaking it all, for it is disobedience to the law. So with respect of persons. In violating this statute, Lev. 19. 15, so trivial, so easily forgotten, the authority of the whole law is violated. Thus the respecter of persons is a transgressor, both of the Mosaic and of the royal law. God's present judgment under the law of liberty is without mercy to those who show no mercy, but to those who show mercy to others God's mercy glories in withholding judgment.

Oct. 30th

READING : **James 2. 14-26**

FAITH AND WORKS

PAUL, IN dealing with faith, mainly has before him the faith that leads to conversion, while James here considers the faith of a man after supposed conversion. He contrasts two kinds of faith—the faith that is not accompanied by works, 2. 14–20, and faith associated with activity for God, 2. 21–24. Two questions are asked concerning such faith: (i) What profit is there in his faith, if it is not combined with good deeds?; (ii) Can such faith save him from eternal punishment? The answers to both questions are negative. The first question is seen when a brother is ill-clad and hungry, obviously in need, but all he gets is good advice, and no practical help. There is no profit in such dealings for the destitute. A word of faith by itself without works is dead—it is non-functioning. James says that good works are the outward proof of an inward faith, not merely the words of the orthodox Israelite, 2. 19.

Abraham's offering of Isaac proved the reality of his faith; it was a faith that produced works. His response to God's command showed that he trusted God to raise Isaac again, to fulfil the promises in which he had so firmly believed, Gen. 15. 5–6; Heb. 11. 17–19. In his treatment of the subject of justification by faith Paul condemns the substitution of works for faith. Paul deals with legalism, James with antinomianism. But Paul also has a place for the manifestation of works after faith, as something that God has ordained for the believer, Eph. 2. 10. Abraham was justified by his later works when he offered Isaac on the altar, showing how works made faith perfect. This was the fulfilment of Genesis 15. 6. God knew Abraham's faith in Genesis 15, but it was fulfilled before men in Genesis 22.

Another example of the co-operation of faith with works is found in Rahab. She is a great contrast to Abraham, teaching us that all classes are included in this doctrine. He was a mighty man of wealth, she a simple woman; he was a Hebrew, Gen. 14. 13, she was a Gentile; he was the associate of kings, she was a harlot. Yet in common with Abraham she had a living, active faith in God, a faith that was accompanied by works, a faith that brought justification. Her faith was shown to be sincere, for all generations of men to discern.

Oct. 31st

READING : **James 3. 1-6**

THE POWER OF THE TONGUE

JAMES, IN this chapter, enlarges upon his exhortation of 1. 19, "be . . . slow to speak". He deals with restraint in the use of the tongue. Whilst the tongue is a great asset, it is also a great liability, for we must give an account in the future judgment of how we used it. It is a great privilege to have such a member, but it also represents a great responsibility.

The subject is introduced by a warning against the rash desire to be masters, whose work is largely done through the use of the tongue. James writes, "be not", *lit.*, "become not", indicating a keen desire for this honour, on account of the sense of importance associated with the position, even though frowned upon by the Lord, Matt. 23. 7–12.

Three reasons are given for not seeking this place of supremacy. (i) The word "many", v. 1, is emphatic, as though to suggest that already there were too many. (ii) We teachers, as a class, says James including himself, are exposed to a more searching scrutiny at the judgment seat of Christ, Matt. 12. 36. (iii) We all, including masters, are prone to stumble others. The tongue is the most difficult member of the body to control. Three metaphors indicate for us the power of the tongue. The first two, the bit and the helm, depict its power for good, because of the control it can effect. The bit is inserted into the horse's mouth; the animal must obey—a great task for a small item. So the tongue controls man's body, walk, works and thoughts. The second metaphor, the helm, though small, controls a large ship, even when influenced by outside forces, e.g., gales. The harmful effect of the tongue is seen in the ravages of a fire. In verse 6 James likens the tongue to a spark that can produce a world, a large amount, of iniquity among our other members. The wrong use of the tongue, a wrong word, unintentionally spoken, can cause a brawl, with flying fists.

The tongue inflames the course of nature—the whole round of life that started at birth. How great a disaster is produced by one little slip of the tongue! The tongue is set on fire by hell—it is the devil and his angels who urge on all this destruction. What a harmful little member is the tongue! Let us take great care of how we use our tongues.

Nov. 1st

READING : **James 3. 7-18**

THE USE OF THE TONGUE

TO EMPHASIZE the impossibility of controlling the tongue, man's ability as a tamer is first noted. Man can tame all kinds of animals, birds, serpents, but no one can tame the tongue. How inconsistent! With it we bless the Lord. Man uses it also to curse men, made like God. How absurd to use the tongue for such a combination! Even nature condemns such inconsistency. A fountain does not send forth from the same orifice sweet water and bitter; fig trees do not bear olives. The tongue is unnatural if it send forth two kinds of speech from the same mouth.

The two kinds of use of the tongue are seen in verses 13–18: spurious wisdom in verses 14–15, confusion, disorder in the church, every evil work in verse 16. True wisdom is from above—Spirit-inspired, pure, like God. Its outcome is seen in verse 18; its fruit is righteousness, the result of peace being sown amongst believers, whose souls are bent on peace. Good works, in 2. 18 the evidence of faith, are here the evidence of wisdom—spiritual gifts used for works done to others, not words spoken to others, 2. 16. Meekness is the effect of wisdom on the master himself, and indicates one who has followed the Lord's example, Matt. 11. 29. It is the opposite of self-assertion and boasting.

In verse 14 spurious wisdom is characterized as lacking meekness. Such a master is marked by bitter envying and strife in his heart. Let not a master boast in such wisdom; it belies the truth by which he has been begotten, 1. 18. The origin of such wisdom is seen negatively, as not being from above, not of God, whence good wisdom comes, 1. 5, 17. Positively, it is described as being earthly (earth-centred), sensual, (*lit.*, soulish, holding to natural rather than to spiritual things), self-seeking, devilish, demon-inspired, v. 6,—like the word of demons, cunning, deceitful. The outcome of spurious wisdom is confusion, disorder in the church, every evil work.

The origin of true wisdom is from above. It is like God—Spirit-inspired, peaceable, gentle, easily entreated, full of mercy, full of good fruits, Spirit-produced, Gal. 5. 22, impartial, without hypocrisy, sincere, real, with no deceit. Its fruit is righteousness.

Nov. 2nd

READING : **James 4. 1-17**

STRIFE IN THE LOCAL CHURCH

HAVING SET forth peace as the effect of the teaching of true wisdom, 3. 18, James now deals with the opposite, strife in the assembly—all too common to-day. He shows the origin of strife—it is due to wordly desires, which men cannot obtain, because they ask amiss, merely to consume it on their lusts. This friendship with the world is enmity with God, and the Scripture does not speak in vain, that is, it can be depended upon. Nor does the Holy Spirit who dwells in us cause us to envy. God gives grace to the humble, and resists the proud. The remedy for this strife is given in ten exhortations in verses 7–10. Strife between brethren becomes evident by a believer having a wrong attitude towards his brother, vv. 11–12, speaking evil of his brother and the law, which implies judging the law, and not doing it. God alone is the law-giver, and He alone is fit to judge a man, and to execute the sentence. He is able to save and to destroy. He has absolute supremacy and absolute power.

Strife also reveals man's wrong attitude towards God, his wrong actions, vv. 13–16. The man given to strife boasts as to an occasion being under his control to do what he pleases, to go wherever he wants, and is confident of success. But verse 14 denounces the man who forms his own plans. All such schemes are envisaged in verse 13 as foolish. James asks, "what is your life?". He answers his own question by saying that the life is a vapour, to indicate the transience of life. Note the opening words of verse 15, "For that ye ought to say". Connect this verse with "ye that say", v. 13. Ye say the things of verse 13 instead of saying, "If the Lord will". Instead they boasted in their own plans. Herein lay their fault; they did not recognize God's sovereignty, His right to rule their lives. Rather should they acquiesce with His will.

James sums up the subject in verse 17. Note the three proper relations to God in the chapter—submission, v. 7, humility, v. 10, dependence, v. 15. If we fail to do these things we sin against God. Rather let us go in for them with the whole heart. They will keep us from strife, and enable us to glorify God. We must not reckon in our business plans without God.

Nov. 3rd

READING : **James 5. 1-11**

RETRIBUTION TO THE UNJUST RICH

JAMES HAS a severe reproof for some rich men. These may be unbelievers, or possibly rich men who unjustly oppressed believers. In Scripture men are not condemned for merely possessing wealth, but for the abuse of it, Gen. 13. 2. Men may turn to sin because of riches, either in gathering or in abusing it. James tells them to weep because of afflictions in store for them, either in this life—the loss of securities, James 5. 2–3; ill-health, v. 3; or in the life to come. Riches hoarded for self, and not used for helping others, cause distress, for their owners find them perishing, or corroded. Their health may become ruined. Accusing voices reach the ears of God. Workers must be paid their wages promptly, which otherwise are "kept back by fraud".

The rich men whom James warns had been living in pleasure, v. 5; they were given to licentious living, satisfying their hearts' desires. They were like animals being fattened for slaughter, Jer. 12. 3. Believers today are sometimes given too much to luxurious living. Rich men, too, used their wealth to control the courts, and oppress the poor. James would remind them that the judgment is near, when all wrongs will be righted. The poor should be patient. Three examples of patience are set before them: (i) the husbandman, (ii) the prophets, (iii) Job. The husbandman waits with patience for the early rain, in October, to germinate the seed, and for the latter rain, in April and May, to ripen the fruit. Suffering Christians are called on to follow the example of the husbandman, "ye also". The suffering saint is encouraged to note the example of the prophets; the example of Job is quoted. They must copy two things, (*a*) suffering evil, and (*b*) being patient. In James 1. 12 we are taught the happiness of those who endured (same word as here) temptation. Now he tells of the blessedness of Job, because of his endurance. Job endured to the end of his trial; he continually bore up under his sufferings; he complained to men, but he did not renounce God. James reminds us that in the book of Job we see the end of the Lord—what God finally did for Job, that the Lord was very pitiful, *lit.*, great-hearted. Job had a happy ending.

Nov. 4th

READING : **James 5. 12-20**

SUFFERING AND THE TONGUE

ANOTHER THING that James impresses on the suffering saint is the right use of the tongue as he passes through a trial. He must not swear, that is, be extravagant in his speech. There is no need to add an oath to reinforce what is said. A simple affirmation is sufficient. Nor does it imply taking an oath in court. How to use the tongue in various circumstances is given in verses 13–20. James deals particularly with the use of speech in the case of one afflicted with an illness. If any is afflicted let him pray, that is, the sick man by himself, asking God for patience and wisdom, 1. 5. Then the sick man's duty is to call the elders of the church to him, possibly because of the association of his illness with sin, which he would confess to the elders—not necessarily men with the spiritual gift of healing. Next we get the elders' duty. They must first anoint the sick man. The use of oil, v. 14, may have been (i) medicinal, but the only medicinal use of it in the New Testament seems to have been for dressing wounds, (ii) symbolic of the Holy Spirit, working a cure. The latter is the more likely here. Anointing with oil does not mean its employment by the elders, medically to heal the man. The prayer of faith saved him. The second duty of the elders was to pray. This was their function, distinct from the apostles who could heal. The prayer of a righteous man is stressed. See the example of Elijah—a man like ourselves. He prayed for rain to be withheld, and no rain fell for three years and six months. After that time Elijah prayed again, and rain fell, and the earth brought forth fruit. These two references to Elijah's prayer life show the miraculous effect of prayer. It was energetic, and accomplished much. So God will do for the believer today. Let us learn to pray as if we really mean it.

James would encourage the brother who seeks to reclaim a backslider. It would seem from verse 20 that the error was nipped in the bud, before it proceeded to gross sin (a multitude of sins), to bring discredit on the testimony; it demanded a just punishment—death, possibly physical death. "Confess" means that the sick man acknowledged that the sickness was due to his sin. This is not a public confession, but in private—to the elders, or to the person wronged.

Introducing 1 Peter

PETER WRITES as an elder with a true shepherd's heart, leading the flock for their good. But he speaks as a chosen and an authoritative apostle who was a witness of, and for, the sufferings and the glory of the Christ, 5. 1; 2 Pet. 3. 2; Matt. 17. 1, 2; Luke 1. 2; Acts 1. 2; 3. 15; 4. 20; 5. 32. The Lord had chosen him to open the door of faith to the Jews, Acts 2 (and later to the Gentiles, Acts 10; 15. 7).

It was to suffering saints that he wrote. They suffered for righteousness' sake, and for Christ's cause. There are four allusions to sufferings: 1. 6, 7; 3. 13–17; 4. 12–19; 5. 9. The Lord's suffering and victory are brought before them for encouragement and assurance of ultimate triumph. As we read this Epistle may we, in our day, "Remember them that are in bonds, as bound with them; and them which suffer adversity", Heb. 13. 3.

The Epistle is full of Christ. Peter speaks of the Son of the Father, who is our Lord, 1. 3. His deity is asserted in 3. 15 R.V. He was foreordained to the work of the cross, 1. 20. His perfect walk is left as an Example, 2. 21. His substitutionary death as the Lamb of God and His exaltation are stated, 1. 18, 19; 2. 24; 3. 18; 4. 1; 1. 3, 21; 3. 22; 4. 13.

Oh tell us often of thy love,
Of all thy grief and pain;
And let our hearts with joy confess
That thence comes all our gain.

"The true grace of God wherein ye stand", 5. 12, is the overall theme of the Epistle. It states their standing. What God has done for us in Christ by His abundant mercy, 1. 3, and His grace, forms the basis of comfort and strengthening in adversity, 1. 3, 10, 13; 3. 7; 5. 10.

Our calling should produce character. It follows that we "should show", 2. 9; "wherefore gird up the loins of your mind", 1. 13; "wherefore . . . as newborn babes, desire the sincere milk of the word", 2. 1–2. Objective truths of grace should find echoes in subjective experiences. Knowing our standing should move us to enquire of our state, Phil. 2. 19.

Nov. 5th

READING : **1 Peter 1. 1-12**

FOUR BLESSINGS

TODAY'S PORTION shows four blessings into which the believer has been brought:

(1) Made to be the object of eternal counsels, thus being elect according to the foreknowledge of God, v. 2. Love was in that choice, Eph. 1. 4, 5 R.V. marg.; Deut. 7. 6–8.

(2) Made to be sanctified (set apart) by the Spirit's power to *obedience* to the Gospel, vv. 2, 22; 2. 7, 8; 3. 20; 4. 17; 2 Thess. 2. 13. Thus we personally come under the sprinkling (application) of the once-shed blood of Jesus Christ, Heb. 10. 22; 12. 24.

(3) Begotten again to an inheritance which is *incorruptible*, for no dust of death can settle upon it. It was purchased not by corruptible silver and gold, vv. 18, 19. Being born again not of corruptible seed, he has escaped the corruption that is in the world, 2 Pet. 1. 4, so should put on the incorruptible adornment of a meek and quiet spirit whilst awaiting the day when the corruptible shall put on incorruption, 1 Pet. 3. 4; 1 Cor. 15. 53. Again, the inheritance is *undefiled* by enemy encroachment and spoliation, Psa. 79. 1. Furthermore, it is *unfading*, for it is eternal in its beauty. Meantime it is kept in heaven for those who are kept for it, 1 Pet. 1. 4, 5.

(4) The certain hope of seeing the absent Lord, who will bring salvation to perfection, vv. 5–9. The prophets of old searched as to when and in what circumstances the sufferings and the glory of Christ would secure this salvation, v. .10. Angels, too, show intense interest therein, v. 12.

Whilst rejoicing with unutterable joy, there may be seasons of manifold (varied) testings of faith, if need be. Faith is more precious than gold. Its proving in the fire of affliction will prove it to be what it surely is, v. 7. In such trials "heaviness" is real and not wrong, but the outcome will be unto His praise and glory. The trial is but for a "moment", but the weight of glory will be eternal, 2 Cor. 4. 17.

Note that New Testament believers are personally brought into the relevance of Old Testament revelation: "unto us" this truth was also ministered, v. 12. Other similar passages are: "unto us", Acts 7. 38; "for us also", Rom. 4. 24; "to us" as a witness by the Holy Spirit, Heb. 10. 15.

Nov. 6th

READING : **1 Peter 1. 13-25**

OBEDIENT CHILDREN

APPROPRIATELY it was in a wilderness that the voice cried "repent", for it declared all flesh is as grass and all the goodliness thereof is as the flower of the grass. The Spirit blows upon it and it withers, v. 24; James 1. 11. Faith accepts the fact of man's ruined condition.

Obedience commences the believer's life making him to be a child of obedience, characterized by obedience in all things, v. 14; Matt. 28. 20. But this demands girding up the loins of the mind, in purposeful preparation for action, as the pilgrim girded his loins for the journey, and the priest for sanctuary service, 1 Pet. 1. 13; 2. 5.

Being free from the stupor and excitement of influences that cause unbalanced living, he hopes for the grace and glory which his Lord will reveal at His return, v. 13.

Yet there is the danger of allowing the former wilful living to fashion to a pattern utterly different from that to which the believer was committed in the gospel, v. 14; Rom. 6. 17 R.V.; 12. 2. It was the Holy One who called and made them to be the called-ones, 1 Pet. 1. 15; Rom. 1. 6; 8. 30; 1 Cor. 1. 9. Moreover, it was the Holy One who caused it to be a "statute for ever" that we put a difference between holy and unholy, maintaining *soberness* in serving the Lord, (see Lev. 10. 1, 3, 9, 10; 11. 4).

Although it is upon a Father that we call, reverential fear is demanded, which will keep from unholy ways, v. 17, will give guidance, Psa. 25. 12, will bring sweet fellowship among saints, Psa. 89. 7, and result in not withholding the best from Him, Gen. 22. 12.

The imperatives of holiness are obeyed, as the persuasion of the great ransom is allowed to move the redeemed, and as the deliverance from aimless living is acknowledged as being through redemption in the blood, vv. 18, 19.

This redemption was no afterthought, but was of the eternal counsels of God, for Christ was foreordained to this end. So our faith and hope are in God, who has so purposed and provided.

Nov. 7th

READING : **1 Peter 2. 1-10**

HE IS PRECIOUS

SEEING THAT the Word has effected the new birth, and is a Word that endures for ever, 1. 23–25, it naturally follows that we should feed upon it, 2. 2; James 1. 18, 21. We tasted the Lord's grace at conversion; now we are to cultivate the proper spiritual appetite for the truth. Just as newborn babes desire milk, so are we earnestly to desire the spiritual, unadulterated milk of the Word. (We are not to be babes, but to desire nourishment and life.)

But to have this appetite for the Word which is "without guile" (R.V.), there must be the decisive putting away of all guile, and hypocrisies, and all evil speaking, v. 1.

We have come (that is drawn near, approached) to Christ, v. 4; Lev. 21. 17, 18, 21, 23, and found him to be the Chief Corner Stone as foundation. But to those who rejected Him, He became a stumbling stone, 1 Pet. 2. 7, 8; Matt. 21. 42; Acts 4. 11. To the believer He is precious, 1 Pet. 2. 4, 6, 7, and He shall never let us be confounded.

Besides being the living stones built on Him, we are the priesthood to offer up spiritual sacrifices such as our bodies, Rom. 12. 1, 2; 2 Cor. 8. 5; Psa. 110. 3 R.V. marg.; our praise and thanksgiving, Heb. 13. 15; our giving, Heb. 13. 16; Phil. 4. 18; and our prayer, Psa. 141. 2. Let us firmly bind such sacrifices to the altar of devotion, and so proclaim the excellencies of our Lord, 1 Pet. 2. 9; Psa. 118. 27.

Priesthood is the *common* and blessed portion of all believers, so they are a kingdom of priests, Rev. 1. 6. By contrast, gifts in the churches are *variously* distributed, Rom. 12. 6.

Again, we are now a people, who formerly were only scattered sinners, v. 10. We are "a people for God's own possession", v. 9 R.V.; Exod. 19. 5, 6; "mine saith the Lord . . . a peculiar treasure", Mal. 3. 17 R.V. marg.; "mine" says the Lord Jesus, John 17. 10. To make us His, He gave Himself for us, Titus 2. 14, so we are bought with a price, 1 Cor. 6. 19, 20. Further, to make us His, He called us by name, Isa. 43. 1, and put His comeliness upon us, Ezek. 16. 8, 14.

Nov. 8th

READING : **1 Peter 2. 11-25**

STRANGERS AND PILGRIMS

BEING ASSOCIATED with his Lord, the believer finds that he is a stranger in the world, for the world knows him not, as it knew not his Lord, 2. 11; 1 John 3. 1.

Abraham the "Hebrew" (which means the one "passing through", or "the one from the other side") readily confessed to others that he was looking for a heavenly city, and that he was a sojourner. So God was not ashamed to be called his God, Gen. 14. 13; 23. 14; Heb. 11. 16.

Jacob began his pilgrimage with his staff, and ended by leaning on it, Gen. 32. 10; Heb. 11. 21. Of old God spoke to Israel, stating that they were strangers and sojourners with him, Lev. 25. 23. This the psalmist gladly confessed: "I am a stranger with thee, and a sojourner, as all my fathers were", Psa. 39. 12. Taken out of the world by the drawing power of his Lord, the believer is sent into it for pilgrim testimony by life and lip, John 17. 6, 14, 18.

But the servant will find persecution and misrepresentation as did the Lord, v. 12, 15; John 15. 18–20. In this Christ is the Example, whose steps are to be followed. Though reviled and threatened, He was without guile and threatened not, but committed His cause to the righteous Judge, awaiting His vindication, 1 Pet. 2. 21–23.

The nullifying of such evil accusations is by honest (noble, seemly) behaviour, which will glorify God in the day of His visitation either in judgment or in giving repentance, v. 2; Luke 19. 44; Isa. 10. 3; Rev. 11. 13.

Believers are to submit to the established government, not out of fear but "for the Lord's sake", for He has ordained such for the punishment of evil doers, v. 13; Rom. 13. 1; John 19. 11. However, God's claims are paramount, Acts 4. 18, 19.

The fear of God can regulate all relationships, vv. 13, 14, 17, even bringing a slave and master together in Christ, Philem. 16.

Whilst Christ's sufferings are exemplary, v. 21, primarily they are substitutionary: "his own self bore our sins" bringing us to God. But we died with Him unto sin, to live unto righteousness, v. 24; Gal. 1. 14; 2 Cor. 5. 15.

Nov. 9th

READING : **1 Peter 3. 1-12**

DIVINE ARRANGEMENTS

LAWLESSNESS AND insubjection increase in these end times, and will yet produce the lawless one who will epitomise man's constant attitude of exalting himself against God's order, 2 Thess. 2. But submission to divine arrangements is most becoming to believers who profess to acknowledge One who is sovereign in His disposals. Submission to every ordinance of man for the Lord's sake, 1 Pet. 2. 13, and submission of servants to masters are good for society.

In the sphere of the home there are the God-ordained relationships, practical recognition of which will bring blessings that even many unbelievers would fain enjoy, Eph. 5. 22; 6. 1, 4, 5, 9. The pagan world of that time would be shocked by the revolutionary thought of "giving honour to the wife", 1 Pet. 3. 7. In their thinking and writings, she was but a "thing". Even among the Jews this was so, too.

When the gospel is received, it not only imparts eternal blessings, but it also gives proper value to human relationships. Whilst "in Christ" there is neither male nor female, yet each has a responsibility. Inferiority is not implied in being submissive to this, for as Servant and Man Christ owns headship in God, a truth that does not impair His co-equality, 1 Cor. 11. 3; Rom. 9. 5; Gal. 3. 28.

The believing wife, whose husband was antagonistic to the word of the gospel, was in a vexing situation, v. 1. Yet, without a further word of oral testimony, he may be won as a spiritual gain to her, and as a mutual heir that comes with life in Christ, v. 7. What shall be the testimony that wins him? It is her chaste behaviour that comes of her reverential fear of God, and the ornament of a meek and quiet spirit.

In this meekness the holy women of old beautified themselves. The fashions have changed through the centuries, but this adornment is always up-to-date among those that are Sarah's daughters, vv. 5, 6.

The believing husband, like all believers, has been brought into the knowledge of God, and should live accordingly, so that both enjoy their spiritual heirship together. What a testimony to their Lord!

Nov. 12th

READING : **1 Peter 4. 10-19**

GOD GLORIFIED IN ALL THINGS

EVERY BELIEVER has received at least one gift (*charisma*). The gifts are "manifold", being many and varied, v. 10; Rom. 12. 3; 1 Cor. 12. 11; Eph. 4. 7.

In the lists given in 1 Corinthians 12, Romans 12, Ephesians 4, and here in verses 10–11, there are twenty or more gifts, and these lists do not purport to be exhaustive.

As the human body has many members, each having its peculiar function, so the varied gifts of Christ. If the whole body were an eye only, or an ear only, it would be grotesque. Variety produces functional unity, 1 Cor. 12. 17, 29, 30. (Note that priesthood is not among the "gifts", for it is common to all believers).

It is the victorious and absent Lord who is the Giver. These gifts are to be used faithfully in stewardship during His absence, v. 10; Eph. 4. 8; Luke 19. 13; Matt. 25. 14. Faithfulness is the pre-eminent requisite demanded of stewards, 1 Cor. 4. 2; Matt. 25. 21, 23.

The Lord gives according to His sovereign will, Eph. 4. 7, 8, as the Spirit wills, 1 Cor. 12. 11, and as God wills, 1 Cor. 12. 18, 28. One can earnestly desire the best gifts for the good of others and for God's glory, 1 Cor. 12. 31; 14. 1; 1 Tim. 3. 1; Exod. 36. 2, but the Lord's sovereign disposal is final. Christian character is for all, Christian *charismata* (gifts) are varied.

Having received the gift, v. 10, it is to be ministered for the profit of others, not for self-display or pleasure, that God in all the service may be glorified, v. 11.

Two kinds of ministry are mentioned in verse 11: oral ministry and ministry in deeds. The spoken word is to be God's message from the holy oracles, Rom. 3. 2; Acts 7. 38, uttered in reverence and authority. The service in deeds is to be "with the strength that God supplieth", R.V., evidencing divine enablement to do so, and not man's fleshly vigour.

Suffering for Christ is again referred to in verses 12–16. "Rejoice" with exultation, v. 13, and know that you are privileged thus to be associated with the sufferings of Christ and with the glory to be revealed, v. 13!

Nov. 13th

READING : **1 Peter 5. 1-14**

THE FLOCK FED

THE LORD'S gracious ministry to Peter in both restoring and re-instating him is very precious and encouraging. The Lord had prayed for him, not that he should not fail through his self-assertiveness, but that his faith should not fail. The root of the matter, his faith, was preserved, Luke 22. 31–34. But Peter was to be "converted" and re-commissioned in a most telling fashion, John 21. 15–22. Peter's thrice-repeated "Lord; thou knowest that I love thee" is thrice answered by the Lord "feed my lambs . . . sheep". When Peter wrote this Epistle, he had been doing this for thirty years, so rightly he could describe himself as an elder tending the sheep, v. 1.

Elders are firstly to take heed to their own behaviour, and then to pastor (tend) the flock, v. 2; Acts 20. 28. Like good shepherds they go before, leading by example, (Rom. 12. 8 "ruleth", *lit.* "stand before, take the lead", 1 Thess. 5. 12). But they also are *among* the sheep, 1 Pet. 5. 2. Was Peter recalling the Lord's words in the upper room: "I am *among* you as he that serveth"?, Luke 22. 27. Again, "all of you be clothed (*lit.* girded with an apron)", v. 5, is an echo of the Lord girding Himself with a towel and serving in gracious lowliness, John 13. 4. "Gird yourselves with humility to serve one another", 1 Pet. 5. 5 R.V.

Faithful shepherds keep eternity in view when the Chief Shepherd shall appear to crown with unfading glory. As the Good Shepherd He had the cross; as the Great Shepherd He has the crook; as the Chief Shepherd He will have the crown and give crowns, John 10. 11; Heb. 13. 20; 1 Pet. 5. 4.

Whilst the readers are suffering, the God of all grace will give grace as they humble themselves under His dealing, assured that He who called them to eternal glory will do it, in spite of the roaring lion, vv. 6, 10. Their anxiety (for themselves, their loved ones, etc.) was decisively to be cast upon Him, and not just cast aside, knowing that "he careth for you", v. 7; Luke 10. 40; Mark 4. 38.

Peter's restoration was truly of abounding grace, but Mark's also is encouraging to all, v. 13; Acts 15. 38. Had he written his Gospel by now, or was he yet to write it? Peter's influence is generally recognized in it.

Introducing 2 Peter and Jude

PETER HAS two main messages in his second Epistle, both concerning what the Lord could do; first the deliverance of "the godly out of temptation", and secondly keeping "the unrighteous under punishment unto . . . judgement", 2. 9 R.V. He was also moved to speak in a prophetic mode of things that were going to happen in the future; namely the appearance of false teachers, 2. 1; the initial success of their allurings, 2. 2; but their eventual swift judgment, 2. 1; 3. 7.

While warning of these evil men and their attacks, Peter gives his readers ample means of defence against them. Like so many of his Old Testament counterparts, although the things they prophesied certainly would come to pass, any one generation that was willing to heed the warnings could escape them in their day. There are three principal ways of escape given by Peter:

Adding what God has provided, 1. 10;
Reading what God had written, 1. 19;
Looking for what God is going to do, 3. 11–14.

There are no spiritual situations of which the believer has been left unaware, then or now. The Scriptures are our complete answer to today's difficulties, 2 Tim. 3. 16. It is sad that the events that Peter warned about (as Paul had done before him, 2 Tim. 3), Jude reports some time later to have started to happen; cf. 2 Pet. 2. 1 with Jude 4. Many details of Peter's prophecy are recorded by Jude as having become awful fact. The terrible indictment against Jude's readers is that they knew this already, for Jude only seeks to remind, Jude 5, 17. Realizing the threat that existed, Jude now calls upon every believer to be a defender of "the faith which was once delivered unto the saints", v. 3.

Neither Epistle is intended for comfortable reading, since they are meant to stir and waken, although had things been otherwise, Jude intended to write comfortable words about the salvation he shared with his audience. However, certain men had slipped in secretly among the saints, and were already showing their true colours by denying any form of spiritual authority, although ready to show respect to any who could further their cause.

Nov. 14th

READING : **2 Peter 1. 1-11**

ADDING WHAT GOD HAS PROVIDED

PETER'S MINISTRY in chapter 1 is that of reminding, particularly of what God had given to the saints:

Each one had obtained an equally precious faith, v. 1.
His divine power had granted all things that pertain to (relate to, are necessary for) life and godliness, v. 3.
He had granted His precious and exceeding great promises to those who had escaped from corruption, v. 4.

God had thus dealt with their past, provided for their present needs, and had promised a great prospect. Peter then reminds them of their responsibility: *give* in the light of what God had given to them, v. 5. They were to give "diligence", that is, to hasten to do, to exert themselves; this diligence was to be directed into specific tasks, all involving adding.

They did not have to add faith, for this God had given, but they were to add to (or in) their faith; neither were they dependent on their own energies or resources for the material to add, for His divine power had already granted them all the things that were necessary for life and godliness. However, like a builder, having had all the necessary materials delivered to the site, the believer must get to work and build the house! He must build with God's materials, 1 Cor. 3. 11–16, and in God's power, Phil. 2. 13; Psa. 127. 1.

Virtue, knowledge, self-control, patience, godliness, love-of-the-brethren and love; these are the sevenfold graces that should characterize our profession of faith. Their possession and abundance lead to the certain promise that we will not be idle or unfruitful. Their lack spells spiritual disaster—blindness, short-sightedness and spiritual amnesia, 1. 9.

"Wherefore . . . brethren, give diligence to make your calling and election sure", that is, sure to you and others, not to God, who when He elects is certainly sure. "For if ye do these things (i.e., diligently add), ye shall never fall". Peter was a man who had stumbled, Matt. 26. 31–35, and had learned his lesson the hard way. He wants us to learn in a less painful way. For those who are faithful in this matter, there is a special welcome home!, 2 Pet. 1. 11.

Nov. 15th

READING : **2 Peter 1. 12-21**

A LIGHT IN A DARK PLACE

IF ADDING assures the readers of their spiritual fitness to prepare for the coming battle, then reading sharpens their spiritual intelligence. The Scriptures, and especially the prophecies, should be heeded, v. 19, because first they shine as a lamp in a dark place (cf. Psa. 119. 105) making them indispensable in dark days, and second, because they originate from the moving of the Holy Spirit in their writers and are not private interpretations of God's messages to men. They are thus effective weapons in the fight against false doctrine, Eph. 6. 17. The inspired writings of Paul were going to be misused by the false teachers; they were going to take the difficult passages and twist or torture them and, like some poor victim on the rack, they were going to make them say what they wanted to hear. This is the mark of the false teacher—he cannot refute the plain teaching of Scripture, so he has to twist the difficult passages to try to make them support his arguments. The Scriptures forewarn, and should therefore forearm us against such, 2 Pet. 3. 17.

For Peter it was not enough that they had heard what he had to say before; indeed, he intended going on reminding them about these things, and would write them down so that his reminders would live on after his approaching departure. Peter felt very happy about teaching these things, because they were not "cunningly devised fables", for Peter had been an eyewitness of His majesty, a majesty that was shown in the Lord Jesus receiving the divine commendation "This is my beloved Son, in whom I am well pleased", Matt. 17. 5. Peter knew all the circumstances of this wonderful moment, and wanted no one to forget its truth.

The readers were going to be attacked by clever men, and they could not refer to their own experiences as could Peter, but they had (written) prophecies which to-date had never been disproved. Indeed, inasfar as they had thus far been fulfilled, they were absolutely correct, making it even more sure to the readers. They were to be their guide, weapon and comfort until the battle is won, and the day dawns, when darkness will be gone forever. As Jude was later to show, the Old Testament still has vital truth for the believer, even today.

Nov. 16th

READING : **2 Peter 2. 1-10**

THERE WILL BE FALSE TEACHERS AMONG YOU

WHEN GOD speaks in truth, Satan subsequently lies, e.g., Gen. 3. 4. Satan is the great initiator of the false—he has his false prophets, Matt. 24. 11; false Christs, Matt. 24. 24; false apostles, 2 Cor. 11. 13; false brethren, 2 Cor. 11. 26; Gal. 2. 4, and also false teachers as Peter now warns. But note how subtle Satan is, for it is now the age of the teacher, when the foundation work of the apostles and prophets is over, Eph. 2. 20; so it is with false teachers and not false apostles or prophets that Satan now tries to deceive.

These false teachers would first of all infiltrate themselves, Jude 4; Gal. 2. 4, and then just as secretly introduce their destructive heresies. The word heresy had the meaning of choice, and came to mean the choice of an opinion contrary to that usually held. How different from those holy men of God who spoke as they were moved by the Holy Spirit, and did not introduce their own opinion; see 2 Pet. 1. 20, 21.

The principal doctrine that the false teachers held was the denial of the Lordship of Christ. The word used here for Lord is not the usual one, but here has the meaning of "absolute master" a word used only of divinity by the Greeks. The fact that He is the Lord who bought them does not mean that these men were believers, for all the world is bought, but only believers are redeemed. This is their cardinal point, and it is this denial that will bring upon them swift destruction.

They were experts at inventing teaching, moulding it to suit what their followers wanted to hear, and indeed they would be successful in their allurings, for many would be their close adherents. The true teaching of God has no attraction to the flesh, but always brings joy to the new man.

In all these difficulties, there was one truth to cling to, namely, "the Lord knoweth how to deliver the godly . . . and to reserve the ungodly unto . . . judgment to be punished". This truth is evident from sacred history, vv. 4–9, Noah and Lot being able to witness to the former, and hell-bound angels and inhabitants of Sodom and Gomorrha being able to witness to the latter. These false teachers follow in a long line of those who only follow the flesh, who are selfwilled and daring, taking no notice of spiritual authority.

Nov. 17th

READING : **2 Peter 2. 11-22**

THEY HAVE FORSAKEN THE RIGHT WAY

THESE FALSE teachers rush in where angels fear to tread; they ignore the example of these mighty creatures, and in doing so become subhuman, behaving like the animals whose whole life is summed up as "born . . . taken and destroyed," v. 12 R.V. They act as creatures without reason, blaspheming in matters of which they have no knowledge or understanding; cf. 1 Pet. 2. 15. Although they are set on destroying the things of God, God will destroy them; their hire for wrongdoing will not be the popularity and material gain they expected, but will be themselves being wronged.

Whereas for the believer the present is a time for godly activity, for these men it is a time for mere pleasure seeking. While they feast with the saints, they cannot cease from sin; cf. 1 Pet. 4. 1. Not only were these men a danger to themselves, but they were enticing unstable souls. It is the work of the "God of all grace" to make us spiritually stable, 1 Pet. 5. 10; this stability (or establishing) is done by means of the truth, 2 Pet. 1. 12. The plain truth of Scripture is the source of our stability; the spiritually unstable can only twist the hard-to-be-understood passages, 3. 16, but the warning is ever there that the beloved can lose this stability (but not salvation) if they are carried away with the error of the wicked, 3. 17.

The motives of the false teachers soon became clear: they loved reward. For a time they had their reward, cf. Matt. 6. 2; some followed hoping for satisfaction, but "these" were springs without water. Their enticing was couched in great swelling words, giving hope of great freedom to live as you like; those who were only just converted, and who were only just getting to know the truth properly, were the special target. We remember the words of the Lord Jesus to Peter, "Feed my Lambs", John 21. 15.

The false teachers knew the right way, but were actively forsaking it, v. 15; their initial contact with the saints had brought some change in their life, even if only to conform temporarily to be accepted, but now they had completely rejected the good influence of the saints, and now were in a worse state than ever. They had turned back from the holy commandment delivered to them, v. 21.

Nov. 18th

READING : **2 Peter 3. 1-18**

THE DAY OF THE LORD WILL COME

THE UNPLEASANT things Peter had to say are almost finished, and now he is able to think of the saints, whom he calls "beloved" four times in this chapter. The remembrance of the Word of God always stirs the sincere mind. Among the great swelling words of vanity of the false teachers was the question "Where is the promise of his coming? for since the fathers fell asleep, all things continue as they were". They, like everyone else, had the Old Testament to read, but they made themselves wilfully ignorant of its truth. They particularly ignored the accounts of the creation and the flood, because it is these events that prove that God can step in and openly display His power.

The believer, on the other hand, is not to be ignorant of the fact that time in itself is no limitation to the Lord. God's time always comes, and with it a display of His power and holy character; but in the meantime He is longsuffering, not willing that any should perish, and that all should come to repentance, v. 9.

The day of the Lord is that period of time in which He will once again openly intervene in the affairs of this world. It is true that He is at work in His world today, but in such a way that men can ignore it; however the time is coming when men will be forced to acknowledge that there is a God, and this God is holy in character and is powerful. That day will come as a shock to unbelievers.

The believer, on the other hand, is at least to be looking for such things, 3. 14; and better he should be earnestly desiring them, 3. 12. Looking for these things in the future should have its effect in the present. As Peter exclaims, "what manner of persons ought ye to be in all holy conversation (living) and godliness". "What manner", W. E. Vine tells us, originally meant "From what country", and later, "of what sort". The implication is clear; if we are looking for a day in which "dwelleth righteousness", then we should live now as if we were living then. Paul had spoken to them about the same things, so from the mouths of two witnesses they had heard the truth; this should have been enough to set them on their guard against false teachers. See Jude 17.

Introducing the Epistles of John

When the Lord spoke to Ananias concerning Saul of Tarsus, He said, "he is a chosen vessel unto me, to bear my name before . . . kings". This Paul did, and published *the gospel of salvation* according to the revelation he received from heaven. John was a different character. He was a companion of the four other better-known apostles—Peter, James, Andrew and Philip. He never showed himself as their leader, but nevertheless had a real influence on them. His was a contemplative, retiring spirit. Like the apostle to the Gentiles, John was chosen to bear the name of the Son of God before his fellow-believers. Like Mary who sat at the Master's feet and heard His word, John became a close associate of the Lord Jesus as he contemplated His Person. To John we owe much of our knowledge of *our Saviour, the Son of God.*

The ministry of John is twofold. Firstly, it is written, secondly, oral. In the case of his written ministry, John makes it very clear that he is not writing to replace the Word of truth. He writes to them "because ye know it", 2. 21. He does not lay down edicts for the church, but he brings into clear relief those things which they already knew, saying, "ye need not that any man teach you", 2. 27. This leads us to the importance of giving "attendance to reading" the Word of God, and to meditation upon it, as our daily food, 1 Tim. 4. 13. The gift God has given to His church through written ministry should never replace that daily exercise, any more than it should be despised or neglected. Its function should rather be to confirm the ministry of the Holy Spirit to our hearts as He says, "Study to show thyself approved unto God, a workman that needeth not to be ashamed, rightly dividing the word of truth", 2 Tim. 2. 15.

But what of John's oral ministry? In his second and third Epistles he says he will not write. Where he can come "face to face" with his loved ones he will do so, whether this is in the home, as of the elect lady for her mutual benefit; or with Gaius concerning difficulties in the church. It will be seen what wisdom and tact there is in this. It seems that he reserves his pen, ink and paper for those too distant for him to visit.

Nov. 19th

READING : **1 John 1. 1-10**

THE TRUE FELLOWSHIP

TODAY WE live in a world of such rush and care that men turn from it to the quietudes of the hills, valleys and rivers—those places of natural peace which can restore to them that mental rest which has been eroded by the stresses and cares of daily life. To the believer John gives a recipe which is more sublime, and yet fundamental to his spiritual wellbeing. In the simplest of words he says, We *heard*, we *saw*, we *contemplated*, and we *handled*, of the Word of Life. Paul declares, "faith cometh by hearing, and hearing by the word of God", Rom. 10. 17, and the Psalmist says of the blessed man, "in his law doth he meditate day and night", Psa. 1. 2. Further, Bonar writes "Here, O my Lord, I see Thee face to face; Here faith can touch and handle things unseen".

That which John learned of the Word of life is still for us today. We may hear the Word of God by the Holy Spirit communicating to us that Light which in essence God is. We, by faith, may see "the glory of God in the face of Jesus Christ", 2 Cor. 4. 6. We may contemplate that glory until, again with the Psalmist, we say, "One thing have I desired of the Lord, that will I seek after; that I may dwell in the house of the Lord all the days of my life, to behold the beauty of the Lord, and to inquire in his temple", Psa. 27. 4. Ours is the most blessed position, for "the only begotten Son, which is in the bosom of the Father, he hath declared him", John 1. 18.

John, declaring what has been made good to him in his own experience, now wishes all believers to share it. "Our fellowship", says he, "is with the Father, and with his Son Jesus Christ". True fellowship this! But how can it be attained? Thomas Binney, in his hymn "Eternal Light, Eternal Light" surely shares, and answers the question.

Light and truth are inseparable; sin and darkness go hand in hand: therefore we are brought to see His unsullied holiness to which the slightest spot of sin is conspicuous, and must be cleansed if that fellowship is to be maintained. We see also the provision for that cleansing, and the need for confession of sin if it is to be obtained. Finally, we are shown the conditions in which it thrives, and reasons why it is forfeited. May we learn to enjoy this true fellowship.

Nov. 20th

READING : **1 John 2. 1-11**

THE LIGHT AND THE DARKNESS

In the presence of God sits One by virtue of a completed work. He perfectly satisfies the Father, and has undertaken to see through all matters pertaining to His children. The purity of the light in which God dwells demands sinlessness; the nature of man is sinful. Whilst, in view of fellowship with God sin should not mark us, there will be occasions when it does by reason of our nature: therefore it is necessary that One should be before Him continually to plead our cause. This One is Jesus Christ the Righteous. We dare not trade upon this provision of God which is made to provide against our inadvertent failure: a provision which appeals against the wrath of God for all sins (ours and the world's) during His longsuffering in the day of grace. Jesus Christ then is the propitiation (the place of favour) through whom we may know God.

But what confidence can we have of knowing God? The keeping of, or watching over, His commandments, His precepts, to guard them from loss or injury is the evidence of our knowledge of Him, for he that does not know Him will have no desire to cherish them. In the believer the love of God is formed and perfected, and his desire will be to walk as His Saviour has done—in constant communion with the Father.

If the believer does so walk in love, he will find himself living in the light of the divine presence, and so the truth of the light will be revealed which is both in Christ and the believer. The true Light shines always, and, as each soul finds that true Light, so the darkness for that one passes, since light and darkness cannot dwell together.

What do we mean by the darkness? It is not that we are in a place where light is not, and we grope; nor is it alone that God is light and we have no understanding of Him (although these things are true): but rather is it that—as the word used here does not mean darkness, but *THE* darkness—we have the domination of Satan: the authority of the darkness. So that he that hates his brother is of that kingdom, says John. To John there are no "half-ways"—it is the light or the darkness. May we be found loving our brethren, and have no cause of stumbling in us.

Nov. 21st

READING : **1 John 2. 12-29**

THE CHRIST AND THE ANTICHRIST

IN THIS PORTION the apostle speaks of his written ministry. He says, "I write", "I have written", "I have not written". In these statements he clearly shows the purpose of his writings—they were to encourage those who knew the truth, and therefore to substantiate the Word of God to them. It was not to advance something new, but to cement what had already been made known to them, whether young, full-grown, or mature in the faith; so that the teachings of those opposed to Christ—who makes the Father known—may not turn them away from Him.

There is a system (which includes what we would accept as good, right, and honourable) formulated from the will of man without God, and energized by Satan, which is called in Scripture, the world. Too often it is clouded by our thoughts as that which is bad in man, and we can thereby be deceived. It is found in Genesis 3, where Eve "saw that the tree was good for food" (the lust of the flesh); "and that it was pleasant to the eyes" (the lust of the eyes); "and a tree to be desired to make one wise" (the pride of life). Herein is the will of man shown, and the principles of the world system; and, says John, love of the world, and love of the Father are so opposed that a man *cannot* have both. To accept the one is to deny the other. The tempo of this denial seems to gather momentum as time passes, so that the apostle says, "it is the last time (hour)" and there are many antichrists—not the man of sin—but those opposed to the doctrine of Christ in its purity. They separate themselves from the company of believers that it might be known whence they are.

The believer has the anointing of the Holy One—the Spirit of truth indwells him, and therefore he is endowed with knowledge as to what truth is, and what is the doctrine of this world system. He is aware of the One who is righteous, and also that those who practise righteousness must be of Him. Because of this the believer is exhorted to abide in the Spirit who has taught him that in so doing he may have confidence and not shame in the day of the Lord's coming.

In accepting the Son, the believer also accepts the Father, and is thus placed in a new sphere. May we appreciate more effectively the implications of this new relationship.

Nov. 22nd

READING : **1 John 3. 1-10**

CHILDREN OF GOD AND OF THE DEVIL

OUR LAST meditation brought us to the point where those who practised righteousness are begotten of God. Now we are to see something of the characteristics of the family of God and, conversely, the family of the wicked one.

The motivating thought permeating the family of God is the kind of love extended to us. Could there be any greater gulf than that which divided man with his natural lusts and the unmerited love which God "shed abroad in our hearts by the Holy Ghost"? What manner of love! But this is not all. He goes further: "it doth not yet appear what we shall be: but . . . when he shall appear, we shall be like him", v. 2. That is, we shall be righteous, pure in every aspect, and "conformed to the image of his Son". Fellow-believer, can you begin to imagine what this will mean? But then John says, "every man that hath this hope in him (set on Christ) purifieth himself, even as he (Christ) is pure", v. 3. Such should be the ambition of every child of God. He may sin, but he will not live or continue in it, for he comes to the One in whom sin is not, to have his sins taken away. Let us keep short accounts with God.

The nature of the devil is that of "a murderer from the beginning" and he "abode not in the truth", John 8. 44. This nature is imparted to his children, as the love of God is to His. Murder springs from hatred, pride, jealousy, and every evil work. We cannot but expect then that the world will hate us, "because it knew him not"—the God in whom dwells righteousness and love bringing forth peace.

Now the apostle elaborates on our knowledge that he "that doeth righteousness is born of him", 2. 29. Those practising righteousness are righteous, as He is. The difference is clear-cut: "all unrighteousness is sin", 5. 17, and "he that committeth sin is of the devil", and also "he that loveth not his brother". Christ "was manifested, that he might destroy (undo) the works of the devil", so making it possible for believing men to practise righteousness, and to love their brethren. Let us follow Him who said, "I must work the works of him that sent me, while it is day", John 9. 4. In doing this it will be abundantly clear as to which family we belong.

Nov. 23rd

READING : **1 John 3. 11-24**

LOVE AND HATE

IN THE WORLD-SYSTEM dominated by the will of unregenerate man, emotions which are the outcome of that will are evident. Pride may be disturbed by another's actions. We may brood over these until envy, anger, temper, and hatred result. Actions, or words, commensurate with these emotions take place, in some instances fatally. Whoever does not love the brother dwells in death—that must mean apart from God; and hatred of the brother is one and the same as murder—the thought being father of the deed—therefore eternal life does not dwell in him. Cain sought to do the right thing by the wrong method (that of his own will), despite the teaching about approach to God that his parents must have made known to him. His pride was disturbed because of the acceptance of his brother's offering. He carried a grudge and slew his brother.

This principle obtains in the world. Therefore hatred of those who do not practise it may become evident.

Another principle obtains in these born of God which is opposite to hate. It is demonstrable (not demonstrative) love. It shows itself by caring for those in adverse circumstances, not just with "cold charity", but with succouring deeds and, if necessary, with life itself. We may feel we could give our lives for *Him*, but to do so for our brethren—any of the household of faith—may cause more consideration. Yet He laid down His life for those who had given Him nothing! The love God commands is both active and in truth. It has no ulterior motive, but is crystal clear in its purity.

Our hearts, or consciences, respond to our self-consciousness, and, like those of Romans 2, accuse or excuse us. The heart, like our nature, is sin-stained and, whilst used by God at times to constrain or restrain, is not infallible. God is; and knows all things. What comfort this! But we must remember that His righteous judgment of our motives can only uphold our *righteous* actions. We then have boldness towards God when our hearts are not pointing the accusing finger, and we are keeping His commandments, loving our brethren practically! Under these conditions, and no other, we may receive the things we ask of Him. This means He will enjoy our obedience, and we His indwelling. This is by the gift of the abiding Spirit.

Nov. 24th

READING : **1 John 4. 1-6**

TRUTH AND ERROR

JOHN, THE apostle of love, very gently and yet very positively spells out the truth of the two realms in which man may live. He moves forward through his Epistle, but in a way which leaves room for repetition of a statement in order to bring home its import. From one standpoint or another John clearly shows that the two spheres for man's choice are entirely opposite. They cannot be mixed and hold together. John also makes clear that man has a responsibility towards both, and must choose one or the other: the one to his eternal good, or the other to his everlasting sorrow.

It has been said that the Father wills; the Son works; and the Spirit witnesses. This statement can be applied in this Epistle, and the reading today bears upon it. If there is one thing above another to which the Holy Spirit witnesses it is to the Person and deity of the Lord Jesus Christ. We may accede to the fact that Jesus Christ is divine—is God, and yet not accede to His incarnation. To hold such a view militates entirely against the divine purpose for that incarnation, and therefore is "antichrist". To deny His incarnation is to deny His deity and His pre-existence, for without it these would be impossible. If then false prophets are gone out into the world, 2. 19; 2 John 7, it can only be that, "moved by the spirit" of error, they seek to falsify the doctrine of the Christ. How necessary to have a good understanding of the Word, and to know the indwelling of the Holy Spirit that we may discern between the Spirit of truth and the spirit of error—not in the head, but in the heart; not theoretically, but practically.

The witness of each is clear. One is of the world; the other of God. Because God has given His indwelling Spirit, 3. 24, we cannot but overcome; for His Spirit (the Spirit of truth) is greater than the spirit in the world (the spirit of error). Therefore, while we listen to Him and allow *His witness to Christ* to flow from us by life and lip, we will be more than conquerors through Him that loved us.

In the last chapter and this, knowledge of His indwelling and witness are assured us. Let us imbibe these teachings of John that fruit may abound to His glory.

Nov. 25th

READING : **1 John 4. 7-21**

LOVE AND FEAR

OUR READING today is one of emphasis by repetition. Much of what the apostle says here has been said in earlier chapters, but John feels the need for a re-statement. This he does in a progressive way. He writes of the manifestation of the love of God with a number of "Herein(s)": He sent His Son that we might have life; He has given us of His Spirit that we might dwell in Him; and He has given us boldness because He reckons us as He reckons His Son in the world. "Herein" starts each of the three subjects under review, and we now turn to note some of the comments.

As the nature of God is light, so it is love. We have seen that light is absolute; we see now that love also is absolute. God is love—nothing can change, diminish or mix with that. Love is complete in itself. It is manifested to us in God's *purchase* of the gift of life for us through His Son. The quality and magnitude of that love is seen in His gift and its effect—a place of favour for us. Because of this we too should love, not with mere natural fellow-feeling or sentimentality, but as God Himself—when we were enemies! This shows we have life—are born of God. Absence of it shows the converse.

Next we have the *preservation* of that life. We dwell in Him. He has given us of His Spirit to assure us that we do. By confession of the Lord as Saviour and Son of God we dwell in that absolute love, and so love dwells in us. Surely this enables us to love our brethren.

Further, the *perfecting* of our love is related to God's dealings with us. His Son is not of the world. All that is true of that sphere *cannot* apply to Him—He is not under its judgment: and God reckons us as He does Him! Blessed position! We do not fear Him, because love is perfected in us both, and this fearlessness before Him should give us more courage before men.

His is the love; ours the response. But it can only be practical and real as we love our brethren. Otherwise it is no more than a lie to claim that we live in, or love, God. Lord, teach us the *meaning of love,* that we may live as Thou hast done in this world!

Nov. 26th

READING : **1 John 5. 1-15**

TESTIMONY AND CONFIDENCE

TO THE BELIEVER who is tempted to doubt his acceptance in the sight of God, belief in this opening verse must give assurance. Does he *believe* that Jesus is the sent One of God? If so, he *is* born of God and therefore must be accepted as His child. Also, to each person so born there must be the evidence of love to all others in "precious blood" relationship with him in the family of God. We may not hold with what others do, but we must be careful about despising them, Luke 18. 9–14. In this statement the keeping of God's commandments shows our love for our brethren and not the reverse. We have already noted what is meant by "the world", and perhaps thought of ourselves outside it. We may be wiser to search deeper and find it in us also! The faith we are given must first be seen to be victorious over the world *in* us before it can be over the world *outside* us! Who is the overcomer? The one who holds Jesus to be the Son of God.

In verses 6–8 we have a statement difficult to understand, and one on which there is divergence of opinion. Let us consider it in its setting. At least four times in today's reading the Lord Jesus Christ is referred to as the Son of God. He is also spoken of as the Christ. These titles brought together clearly show us His pre-existence and His incarnation—His Manhood. At the beginning of His public ministry one "saw, and bare record", and again at the end of this ministry, John 1. 34; 19. 35; and, if we include the testimony of the centurion, Mark 15. 39, we find those testimonies to be "This is the Son of God". So the apostle continues: "I have written unto you that believe on the name of the Son of God; that ye may know that ye have eternal life", and this assurance will inspire continued faith in Him.

We have noticed a number of things which are simple in themselves but are designed to give us knowledge of the fundamental facts of our faith. "Hereby we know" the apostle repeats. Now we are to have confidence as knowing His will and make our petitions, not with the suffix "if it be Thy will", but according to it. If we do this His ear is always open to us, and, being in line with His desires, petitions will be answered. How we should study the Word to ascertain the Lord's will.

Nov. 27th

READING : **1 John 5. 16-21**

DISCERNMENT AND DEVOTION

THIS FINAL portion of John's Epistle brings us to a very practical effect of knowing the will of God. We know He has "no pleasure in the death of the wicked", Ezek. 33. 11; therefore very careful discernment must be exercised in the prayer of those who know that "the petitions that we have asked (marg.) of him" are answered. It would be just as serious a matter to make request for one who had sinned a sin unto death as it would be to assume that sin in one who had not done so. Both would be contrary to the will of God. Nor can we take "the easy way out"; for we should know the will of God—then the matter would not cause difficulty. We think of Nadab and Abihu, Num. 3. 4; the ten spies, 14. 11; Korah, Dathan and Abiram, 16. 27, 32–33; Uzzah, 2 Sam. 6. 7; the "man of Judah", 1 Kings 13; and Ananias and Sapphira, Acts 5, who each died an unnatural death in connection with their behaviour before the Lord. In each case it seems that presumption in one form or another marked those who died. Let us heed the warning given in Numbers 15. 30 and 31, noting the marginal reading in Newberry; also the Lord's word in Matthew 12. 31–32 concerning blasphemy against the Holy Spirit. If these incidents recorded in Scripture are for our learning, how careful we should be, as the Psalmist was, when he prayed "Keep back thy servant also from presumptuous sins", Psa. 19. 13.

John now clearly states again where each man is—either devoted to the Father, keeping himself there, so that the wicked one cannot attach himself to him; or lying helpless and unconscious in the grip of that wicked one.

In closing his Epistle John sums up all that he had been warning them against in the previous chapters with another simple exhortation, lovingly given, "Little children, keep (guard as with a sentinel) yourselves from idols". An idol is something which can be seen, but the things of which he has been writing are not all visible to the physical eye, though they should be evident to spiritual discernment. The true God is invisible and will never be seen except through Jesus Christ, who is also that eternal life of which John speaks. May we each enter into the fulness of the apostle's ministry.

Nov. 28th

READING : **2 John 1-13**

THE HOME CIRCLE

IN DAYS WHEN the sanctity of the home is being threatened, it is well to think on this Epistle given by the Holy Spirit for the home circle. It exemplifies Paul's word in Titus 2. 5, "keepers (*guardians*) at home", in a delightful way. This sister kept open house and sought to bring up children in the way of *truth*. How important! Particularly when linked with love, as here. Truth is basic, pure and unalterable. It is mentioned first. Love is emotional, often base and vacillating, but shines brightly when anchored to truth.

The testimony of this good lady is reflected by that guardian work in the home which brought some of her children to walk in truth, and no doubt her prayers were still for the rest, even as her sorrows would be over them. This the elder with "all they that have known the truth" recognized, as he enjoyed the hospitality of this home in his pastoral care over it in person and by letter. Now he further encourages her in the commandment of the Lord to walk in love. No doubt she had been doing this, but he reminds her that a home established in truth should be energized by love.

The elder brings into stronger relief fundamental truth for their further meditation and strength. This is the doctrine of Christ, which is central to the Christian home. It embraces the deity of Christ; the unity between the Father and the Son; the sending and coming of the Son and His incarnation; His perfect, sinless Manhood leading to His atoning death, resurrection, and ascension; His glorification; and His high-priestly office. What nobler themes to meditate upon in the home circle! What better to guard the home from the onslaughts of that which savours of the anti-Christian influences at work outside it!

Surrounded by forces of truth, love, and the teachings of Christ, we are equipped to withstand the messengers of evil who deny these doctrines to us. They will not even be given entrance to the home circle. As Christ *took part* of blood and flesh to sanctify His children, Heb. 2. 14, so, by our not greeting these evil persons, we do not *take part* in their wicked works, but remain separated to Him who has called us from darkness to light. May Christ fill our home circle!

Nov. 29th

READING : **3 John 1-14**

THE SPHERE OF THE LOCAL CHURCH

THE THIRD EPISTLE complements the second as two pages of an open book, giving practice after precept. The elder continues his pastoral work by commending spiritual vitality and caring for physical weakness. In the second epistle evil was outside seeking admission through those who brought not the doctrine of Christ: in this one, evil is inside the assembly casting out those who would go forth for His name's sake.

We learn about hospitality in home and assembly from the praise of Gaius. Not only had he brought these brethren, and strangers, home and cared for them, but had also helped them on their way in a manner worthy of God himself. The present must be provided for, yet the future must not be forgotten. As they moved to other assemblies, those going forth in complete dependence on the Lord reported the kindness of Gaius. This should give us the desire to imitate him.

To each man the Creator has given an individual personality, which now expresses itself in flesh which is tainted by sin. Some personalities are very strong, as Diotrephes shows. He desires the place of Christ in the assembly—the pre-eminence. This caused the elder much sorrow. Perhaps John thought of the day when he forbad one casting out demons in the Lord's name and heard His rebuke, "Forbid *him* not: for he that is not against us is for us", Luke 9. 50. This shows the seriousness of hindering, by not receiving, those who, in sincerity, seek to serve the same Lord.

Further, Diotrephes refused the position of John as an elder and would not receive him—apostle though he was—and those who walked in the truth with him. He spoke evil of them in the assembly. Not only so: he excommunicated those who would have received them. What a salutary warning to all God's leaders in assemblies, as well as to each believer! Let us cultivate meditation in the doctrine of Christ, in order to avoid the efforts of the flesh which are after the mind of man, however good those efforts *may* appear.

The apostle Paul enjoins the Philippian believers, "Look not every man on his own things, but every man also on the things of others. Let this mind be in you, which *was* also in Christ Jesus", 2. 4–5. May He form His selfless mind in us.

Nov. 30th

READING : **Jude 1-11**

DEFENDERS OF THE FAITH

JUDE CLAIMS no special relationship with the Lord Jesus, even though he was His kinsman according to flesh. He does, however, remind the believers, to whom he was writing, about their special relationship: "preserved, called, beloved". They did, however, have a great need for "mercy, peace and love" to be multiplied. They needed these divine gifts in abundance to be able to cope with the spiritual crisis facing them. Although Jude was eager to write about the salvation he shared with these "beloved", events had changed his subject matter; it was not now what the Lord had done for them, but what they had to do for the Lord. They were strenuously to defend the faith (the sum of what Christians believe) that had been once for all delivered to the saints (for safekeeping) by the Lord.

False teachers had crept in unnoticed, but had now drawn attention to themselves. Although people were shocked by them, it should be no surprise because, if they remembered the words of Old Testament Scripture and New Testament apostles, they would have been prepared for them.

From the readers' knowledge, Jude draws out examples from Old Testament times based on the characteristics of those who had crept in: unbelief, (cf. Num. 14); disobedience, (perhaps Gen. 6); loose-living, (fornication and homosexuality, Gen. 18, 19); insolence to spiritual dignities, (ct. Michael the archangel with Korah, Num. 16); seeking material gain from religious deception, (Balaam, Num. 22–24). These were characteristics that brought certain judgment, indeed, eternal fire, (cf. Matt. 18. 8; 25. 41, etc.).

Jude uses the expression "these" to describe the false teachers; see vv. 8, 10, 12, 16, 19. This impersonal expression stands in contrast to the words "beloved" in verses 3, 17, 20. Only in this situation where there are those who are devoid of the Spirit, v. 19, and therefore are "none of his", Rom. 8. 9, can we rightly speak of "us and them". These men sought to pull down that which was good, and elevate that which was bad; they spoke of liberty and tolerance, but were really motivated by jealousy, greed and pride, (as Cain, Balaam and Korah). Let us remember that grace is ours for service and witness; cf. Rom. 12. 3–8 with Jude 4.

Dec. 1st

READING : **Jude 12-25**

REMEMBER, BUILD YOURSELVES UP, AND PRAY

ALTHOUGH THE false teachers had come in among the saints with no spiritual credentials, it seems, from the figures Jude uses to describe them, that soon much was expected of them. However, those expectations were unfulfilled, for they were shepherding themselves, v. 12 R.V., clouds without water, trees without fruit, v. 12, and wandering stars; cf. v. 13 with Matt. 2. 1–12. They were now uncontrolled and shameless in their behaviour, but although they seem to have gone unchecked so far, they were soon, as Enoch had prophesied thousands of years before, to be the objects of divine judgment.

"These" were men of "big, boastful words" (Weymouth), who cultivated certain individuals so that they seemed for a time to have been tolerated, but soon they denied "the only Lord God, and our Lord Jesus Christ"; they deny dominion and "speak evil of dignities . . . (and) of those things which they know not"; they were murmurers, complainers and mockers. The arrival of Jude's letter must have brought things to a head; once the letter had been publicly read and generally acknowledged to be true, the behaviour of the false teachers (if they had not left already) is predictable; railing at the elders, apostles and Jude, they would separate themselves, and possibly take some unstable souls with them who would be attracted by promises of greater (so-called) liberty.

We can imagine the state of the assembly after this crisis; exhausted and in a state of spiritual shock. They now had to rebuild their (no doubt shaken) assembly life. Instruction is now given on this subject. Those who had left were destructive and did not have the Spirit, whereas the true believers were to build themselves up on their most holy faith, praying in the Holy Spirit (note the stress on "holy"), and to be merciful to the doubters, v. 22 R.V.

Opportunity had to be given to reassert the pre-eminence of the Lord God, to whom alone be glory, majesty, dominion and power, before all time (before angels fell, because of their denial of these divine qualities); now (when these false teachers are heading for swift judgment for their denial); and unto all ages (when all deniers of the Lord Jesus will be judged).

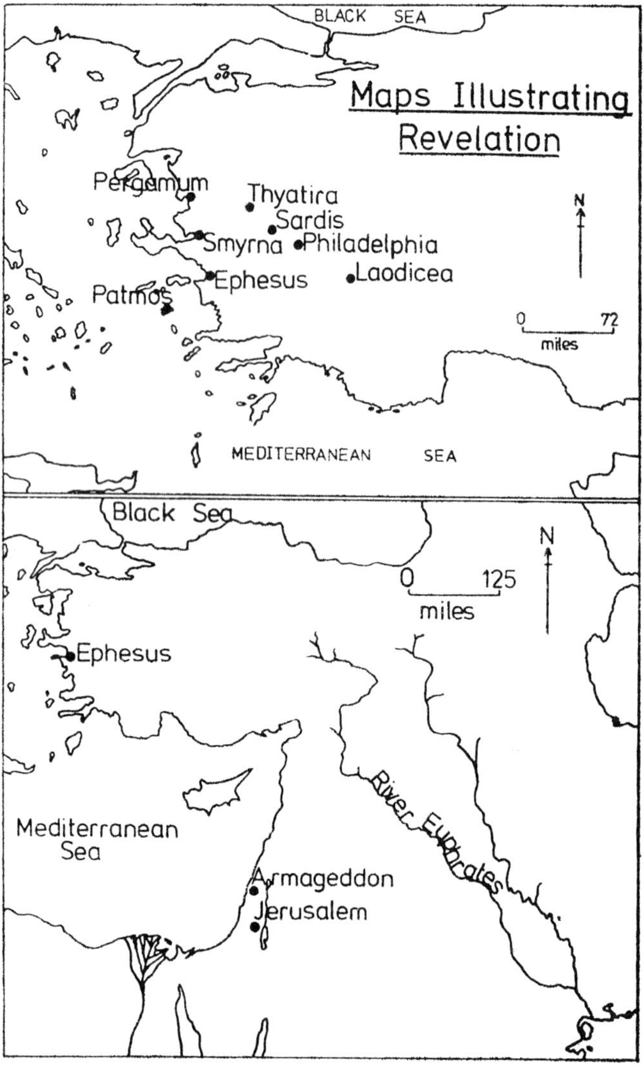
BLACK SEA
Maps Illustrating Revelation
Pergamum
Thyatira
Sardis
Smyrna
Philadelphia
Ephesus
Laodicea
Patmos
N
0 72
miles
MEDITERRANEAN SEA
Black Sea
N
0 125
miles
Ephesus
Mediterranean Sea
Armageddon
Jerusalem
River Euphrates

Introducing Revelation

THE BOOK is one of judgment where all are judged in the light of holiness. As symbols are used, interpretations by equally good men vary, and we must remember that, having strong convictions, we know only in part.

All, however, must be fully assured that the book is dominated by the One to whom the Father has committed all judgment; so that, not only are present and future things unveiled, but the majestic Person of our Lord is seen, at the end using His own sweet name of Jesus.

An analysis of the contents reveals an orderly pattern of sevens, and the purposes of God prospering in the hands of His Servant who purges the earth by judgments, leading to the eternal state where all is in harmony with God.

After an introduction and the first great vision of our Lord, chapters 2 and 3 consist of messages to seven churches in Asia. Then one is transferred from earth to the throne of God, at which point many believe that the Church will be raptured to be with the Lord Jesus.

From chapters 6 to 16, seven seals are opened by the Lamb, seven trumpets sounded, and seven bowls of wrath poured on the earth. The three series may be consecutive or concurrent, but not co-extensive. If concurrent, all terminate just before the appearing of our Lord. Chapter 7 is an interlude between the sixth and seventh seals. The trumpets follow the same pattern; a little is said about the first four, more about the fifth and sixth; there is another interlude in chapters 10 and 11, and then the seventh trumpet sounds. The next four chapters fill in details, particularly of the activities of the devil, the beast and the false prophet. There is no interlude between the pouring out of the bowls; they end in the overthrow of the cities of the world. In chapters 17–18 the whore and her end are described, and details of Babylon's fall. All is now ready for the return of the King who executes judgment on a godless and unrepentant world. The millennial kingdom is seen, followed by the last judgment. Chapters 21 and 22 bring us into the glories of eternity, and the conclusion of the book warns, invites and promises—best of all His own words, "I come quickly".

Dec. 2nd

READING : **Revelation 1. 1-8**

THE CURTAIN DRAWN ASIDE

THE SECRETS of the Lord are with those who fear Him. To John the final secrets are made known. They were revealed by the Lord Jesus for the instruction and blessing of His people, and had been given Him by the Father. In His days on earth He had said, "I have given unto them the words which thou gavest me", John 17. 8. He hides nothing from His own that is for their good, and His words, come to us through the Spirit, are life indeed.

The salutation of grace and peace comes to the Lord's people from the Triune God, the eternal God, the "seven spirits" before the throne, and Jesus Christ. Grace comes first, for peace is only possible through the working of God's love. Matchless grace and peace are both God's gifts ministered through the Spirit and resulting from the work of the Son. He, the faithful witness on earth, bore witness in word and work to the Father, and was "faithful unto death", the death deserved by us. But He is the first begotten of the dead, for God raised Him from the dead and in His exaltation is "the prince of the kings of the earth". To Him who is supreme we have given our allegiance.

Well, therefore, may we with all who love Him join in the song of praise. It is a song of love unknown!, for He loveth us. He loved us unto death, He loves us in His life, and He will go on loving us through eternity. It is the song of the free, for He has "washed (or loosed) us from our sins in his own blood". It is the song of those who have been lifted from the dust to be kings and priests to the God who is His Father. "To him be glory and dominion for ever and ever, Amen."

The section closes with a solemn reminder that the manifestation of Christ in glory, the joyous consummation to the believer, Col. 3. 4, will at the same time bring wailing to all the world that rejected Him. Such a reminder should have a sobering effect upon all as we live our lives in a world that is fast hastening to ultimate ruin. For a repentant Israel the manifested Lord will be the One who comforts, but for an unrepentant world it will be the wailing of final doom.

Dec. 3rd

READING : **Revelation 1. 9-20**

THE JUDGE OF HIS PEOPLE

JOHN WAS an old man, lonely and an exile on the Isle of Patmos. It was on a Lord's Day that the first great vision was given to him by the Spirit of God. The vision was one of his glorified Lord. Although John had laid his head on the breast of the Lord Jesus in the days of His flesh, he was now over-awed by the majesty of the vision that, as with Daniel, he became as one who is dead. What, therefore, must have been the joy and encouragement of John when he felt the touch of the Lord's right hand, and heard His gracious words, "Fear not". Still he touches our spirits and speaks to our hearts, causing us to rejoice.

The revelation of our Lord is as the judge of His people, for judgment always begins at the house of God. Here, as in Ezekiel's day, the Lord says "begin at my sanctuary", Ezek. 9. 6.

The words of our Lord to John are a wonderful revelation of His character: I am the First and the Last and the Living One. Without beginning, without ending, the Lord of eternity and the source of all life, He is the Eternal God to be adored as such. The mystery of His Being defies analysis and the exploration of our finite minds. "No man knoweth the Son, but the Father", Matt. 11. 27.

His first statement reveals His Godhead, the second His amazing grace. He, the Lord of life and eternity, became dead. Well might Charles Wesley write, "'Tis mystery all, the Immortal dies". It was by the grace of God that He tasted death for every man, and as we remember that He died for us, we bow before Him, and thank Him from our hearts.

But He is "alive for evermore". Amen! Because He died and has emerged triumphantly, He is now the Lord of life and death with absolute authority, and has the keys of death and the grave.

This then is the glorious and triumphant One who commissioned His servant to write letters to the seven churches in Asia. In the power of the Spirit, these have application to all churches throughout the age of grace, letters to which we do well to take heed.

Dec. 4th

READING : **Revelation 2. 1-7**

LOVELESS ORTHODOXY

THE LORD speaks by His Spirit to the churches. They are subject to His control, for He holds the stars in the right hand of His power. He walks in their midst, discerning all, justly commending what is good and condemning what is evil, and at the same time, seeking their fellowship, even as at the beginning, "the Lord God walking in the garden in the cool of the day", Gen. 3. 8.

The church at Ephesus had persisted in obedience to her Lord, and for the sake of His name had not grown faint-hearted. Clearly they had also profited from the warning given some years before by Paul who had spoken of false teachers arising from among themselves, Acts 20. 30. Workers and teachers of evil had both been utterly rejected.

Alas! there was something vitally wrong with these believers. They had left their first love. Our Lord desires first of all the affections of the heart. A cold correctness, a loveless orthodoxy can lead only to the complete destruction of effective witness to Him who is the Lord of love. A passion for truth without love quickly leads to carping criticism and heresy hunting, while service will become mere "stern duty", instead of the response of loving obedient hearts.

How necessary, therefore, to heed the solemn yet gracious injunction, to remember, to repent, and to return to "the first works"! If thus convicted in our heart of coldness, we are to look up to the height from whence we have fallen. Bathed in the sunshine of the love of Christ,

> "What peaceful hours I once enjoyed
> When first I knew the Lord!" (Cowper)

Our Lord remembers; "I remember . . . the love of thine espousals", Jer. 2. 2.

With the call to remember comes too the call to repent. All to whom our Lord thus speaks should return to the place where first the altar of devotion was created, and weeping out tears of real repentance seek the renewal of the fellowship of love with the Risen Lord.

The tree of life, growing in luxuriant abundance in glory, is promised to the overcomer.

Dec. 5th

READING : **Revelation 2. 8-11**

SUFFERING FOR HIS SAKE

OUR LORD told His disciples, "in the world ye shall have tribulation", John 16. 33. The church at Smyrna was proving the truth of this prediction and to them, and to all who suffer like them, He sends this message of sympathy and encouragement. He is the "first and last", the Eternal, and this in marked contrast with "ten days" of tribulation, "Our light affliction which is but for a moment", 2 Cor. 4. 17. Some of His people would be done to death, but He had Himself become dead, robbing death of its sting, and had triumphed over death, for it was the Living One who spoke.

He understands His people's tribulation, the harrowing experience through which they were passing and would yet pass. He knows all about their poverty, the forcible spoiling of their goods. But in heaven they have an enduring substance, an inheritance that is unfading; therefore, they are rich indeed. One of the hardest things of all to bear was the slander of the synagogue, no longer of the Jews but of Satan, for they had, alas, become the determined adversaries of the gospel.

He who knows the end from the beginning, knew that there were still deeper waters through which His own must pass, and that soon (the things thou art about to suffer). For some it would mean imprisonment, severe testings, and death, but the Lord says, "Fear none of those things". Two things He says for their encouragement: (i) The tribulation will last ten days, possibly a proverbial expression for a brief period (Gen. 24. 55; Dan. 1. 12), but long or short when the tenth day had ended, our Lord would say, thus far, "but no further", Job. 38. 11. (ii) He also bids them look beyond the suffering of the present to the crown of life which He promises to those who are faithful unto death.

Our Lord had said, "Be not afraid of them that kill the body, and after that have no more that they can do", Luke 12. 4. Now He assures His own that the overcomer shall not be hurt of the second death.

The words of a twentieth century Chad martyr are worth recording, "I have served my Lord for thirty years, and I am going to see Him today" (Echoes of Service).

Dec. 6th

READING : **Revelation 2. 12-17**

COMPROMISE

PERGAMOS WAS a great religious centre of the pagan world. Among the many pagan deities worshipped the most prominent was the Pergamene god, Aesculapius. He was given the title of "saviour". This, and his symbol of a serpent, were regarded with special abhorrence by the Christians living there, and their environment would have been one of extreme difficulty.

How gracious is our Lord! Before He exposes evil, He commends what is good. He recognized the peculiar difficulties of their situation where Satan thus held sway. He still says to those in like conditions, "I know . . . where thou dwellest". In such circumstances they had remained loyal, and had even had one of their number martyred.

It is true to say that human society would be impossible without a measure of compromise. That this is also true of the local assembly is clear from such a statement as, "Let your moderation (yieldingness) be known unto all men", Phil. 4. 5. When, however, it is a question of tempted compromise with what is manifestly evil, those things which our Lord hates, then there must be no compromise. We say with Martin Luther, "Here I stand; I can do no other. God help me!".

The church at Pergamos had compromised. There was recognized evil in the church, and our Lord whose word is as a sharp two-edged sword which divides asunder rebukes His people for this. There is, and must be, no walking together of good and evil, for light can have no fellowship with darkness. The God whom we worship is Light and "in him is no darkness at all". Balaam with his greed and the attempted seduction of God's own, or the Nicolaitanes with their practices of evil—with such there must be no compromise.

Our Lord Himself will deal with the evil if there is no repentance, but for the overcomer there will ever be within the inner, hidden man the sweetness of feeding upon Him who is the "bread of life". As the heart knows its own bitterness, so also it alone can know the secret, inner joy of the Lord's gracious approval, for there will be given a white stone with a name written, that none other knows or can know, saving the one who receives it.

Dec. 7th

READING : **Revelation 2. 18-29**

TOLERATION

THERE COULD be no more solemn introduction to a letter than that to the church at Thyatira. The Son of God speaks to His people in all the dignity that such a title implies, and His character is such that He cannot for one moment tolerate evil. His eyes, scorching in their intensity, search out the inner thoughts and motives of the heart, and His feet are as of burning brass.

His church had grown in love, her acts of service were more, her faith had increased and she still endured. Indeed, the last works were more than the first, in favourable contrast with the Ephesian church which had left her first love. How good it is when the Son of God can commend real progress in the path of faith. But, with all this progress, evil was tolerated within the assembly, as old leaven which would taint and spoil the whole.

We live in a day when toleration is looked upon as a positive virtue. Should one venture to speak out against evil, then that one is dubbed as being intolerant, bigoted, and grossly lacking in "Christian charity"! Jezebel was a Tyrian princess and wife of Ahab. Introducing the Tyrian Baal into Israel, she had the prophets of the Lord slain and was utterly unscrupulous and domineering. She came to a terrible end. Such an evil woman is the picture of what was tolerated in Thyatira; whether she represented a single domineering woman, or a party within the church, we cannot say. Her teaching led to the seduction of the Lord's servants to commit fornication and to eat things sacrificed to idols. This may be taken absolutely literally in the context for these things were the usual accompaniment of paganism. If the sinners continued unrepentant, anguish, great tribulation, and death would be their portion, and all the churches would learn to fear Him who searches the hearts and would see that "if any man defile the temple of God, him shall God destroy", 1 Cor. 3. 17.

The Lord is coming! For the faithful there is the call to hold fast. The overcomer, obedient to the end, will share with Christ in the power and glory that belong to Him who is the Bright and Morning Star. Therefore, hold fast!

Dec. 8th

READING : **Revelation 3. 1-6**

FORM BUT NOT POWER

ALL FULNESS dwells in our Lord Jesus. He has the seven Spirits of God, and holds the seven stars in His right hand, thus revealing Himself to the church in Sardis as the One with fulness of wisdom and of power. The church had acquired a reputation for being alive, but the Lord pronounces it to be dead. Someone has recently written, "A church is in danger of death when it begins to worship its own past—when it is more concerned with forms than life—when it loves systems more than Jesus Christ". John Bunyan said, "Christian men should be living men. Take heed of being painted fire, wherein there is no warmth, and painted flowers, which retain no fragrance, and painted trees wherein is no fruit". Such was the church at Sardis, having all the form but not the power; having the reputation to live, but dead.

The quickening voice of the Lord calls upon His people to wake up and revitalize those things which remain to them and are about to die. A similar call was made by Paul in Ephesians when he quoted, "Awake thou that sleepest, and arise from the dead, and Christ shall give thee light", Eph. 5. 14. This is no time to be spiritually alseep. Our Lord still says what He said in the days of His flesh, "And what I say unto you I say unto all, Watch", Mark 13. 37.

It is not too late for repentance, but if His people remain asleep, then He will come upon them unexpectedly as a thief in the night. This can have no reference to our Lord's second coming, but it implies an act of sudden judgment.

There were a few, even as in Malachi's day, who feared the Lord and thought upon His Name. He knows His own; they had not defiled their garments. To these overcomers there was given a threefold promise. As they had maintained their purity, so would they be clothed in white robes. When a citizen died, his name would be erased from an earthly city roll. This could not happen in the city of God for names are recorded there in the book of living ones. On earth they had confessed their Lord, so He would confess their names before His Father and in the presence of angels.

Dec. 9th

READING : **Revelation 3. 7-13**

A LOVE LETTER

IN SPIRITUAL terms Philadelphia is a splendid place in which to live, for it is the place of brotherly love. Those who dwell there are obedient to the new commandment which our Lord gave to His disciples, "That ye also love one another", John 13. 34.

The letter has no condemnation, no complaint, only love and encouragement from Him who is true. He who has the keys of the prison also has the key of the palace. When He opens no one shuts, and when He shuts no one opens. For the church in Philadelphia the door was open, for in spite of their having but little strength, they had kept His word and had not denied His name. The reference to the key certainly reminds us of what is said of Eliakim in Isaiah 22. 22. Our Lord opens to His people the rich storehouse of His grace. Are they poor? Here is unimaginable wealth. Are they weak? Here is the all-sufficiency of His strength. There would appear also to be a reference to the door of opportunity, in the light of what immediately follows. Such would be their witness, that those who were their determined enemies would come bending before them, recognizing that they were beloved of the Lord. The letter is rich in Old Testament allusion. and verses such as Isaiah 61. 9 should be compared with what is written here.

Believers in Philadelphia were already being tried but, having patiently endured, the Lord promises them immunity from the hour of temptation which would come upon the world. He knows how to keep His own!

For the first time in these letters, the Lord Jesus holds out to His people the promise of His near return, both for encouragement and also as an incentive to hold fast. We must not allow the crown of the Lord's approval to be lost, or taken from us. Here the figure is not of someone taking something for himself, but simply depriving the possessor of what he treasures.

The strength of a pillar in the temple would be given to the overcomer, engraved with the name of God, His city, and the new name of our Lord. Then we shall learn new aspects of the glory of the Christ who loves us.

Dec. 10th

READING : **Revelation 3. 14-22**

LAODICEA

THERE CAN be few sadder paragraphs than that of today's reading, for here a message is sent to a church in which the Lord could find no pleasure. Indeed, such was their condition that they were likened to tepid water, so distasteful that the Lord says, "I will spue thee out of my mouth"! Yet it should be noted that this severe displeasure is spoken from a heart that still loves in spite of all, for "as many as I love, I rebuke and chasten", and the call to repentance is made even to such.

The Laodiceans had a high opinion of themselves! They were congratulating themselves on being rich, having increased goods to themselves, and asserting their self-sufficiency. If we truly know our Lord, and truly recognize what we are, then we must humble ourselves to the dust and confess, "Nothing that's good have we; nothing apart from Thee—Jesus our Lord".

By His words our Lord, as it were, puts the mirror of truth for them to see themselves as they really are, objects of the utmost poverty and degradation, to be pitied for their blindness. Will they listen to advice? Then they may come, and from Him who speaks may buy the true riches, purity of garments, and ointment for their eyes that they may truly see. What will all this cost them? Nothing, and yet everything! Our Lord is the giver of all that is good, and we are bankrupt sinners having nothing wherewith to pay. But to receive what He offers will cost us every bit of our pride, our arrogance, our self-sufficiency.

Having called upon His people to be zealous and repent, the Lord then utters to the individual that glorious call which is so often used in gospel preaching and singing, but was first of all made to those in a church that had become lukewarm. "Behold", He cries, "I stand at the door, and knock". These people were so self-satisfied that they did not miss the presence of the Lord among them. May this at times be true of us? He calls to the individual to hear His voice, and open the door, for He never forces an entry. If we truly desire Him, then His promise is sure. He sups with us and we with Him, for the invited guest becomes the Lord.

Dec. 11th

READING : **Revelation 4. 1-11**

GOD'S THRONE

AFTER THESE things, "the things that are", (where so much failure had been exposed, but we may joyfully add, where much had brought pleasure to the heart of the glorified Lord), John in the Spirit is taken up to a scene where all is perfect to see "visions of God", Ezek. 1. 1. Man is bounded by time and sense, so that if he is to learn something of the Eternal One, he must learn by symbols which will convey the truth to him. The symbolism should be compared with visions given to Old Testament prophets, to the tabernacle or temple, where "every whit of it uttereth his glory", Psa. 29. 9 marg.

The throne of God is seen for ever established in the heavens, for God is ever supreme. Happy are those who ever recognize that "God is still on the throne". One is seen upon that throne, at least not directly, but God shows Himself as a vision of dazzling purity and radiance, all surrounded by a rainbow. "The brightness of His glory and fire of His judgment are ever girded by the refreshment and surety of His mercy and goodness" (Alford).

Round the throne there are twenty-four thrones upon which sit elders clothed in white and crowned. Some speak of these as angels, but they are more probably representatives of the church in glory and redeemed Israel, Rev. 21. 12, 14. Seven lamps of fire are burning before the throne, these being the seven Spirits of God, the Holy Spirit in all His fulness. Round the throne also were four living creatures (a better expression than "beasts"). Their description should be compared with that of the seraphim in Isaiah 6, and the cherubim in Ezekiel 1. Whom or what do they represent? Interpretations vary, but in the context of each of these passages, they appear to be a high order of angelic being, principalities and powers in heavenly places, Eph. 1. 20, 21. Ceaselessly they declare the thrice-holy character of the eternal God, while the elders abase themselves in worship, ascribing glory and honour to the Lord by whom all things were created. They exist for His pleasure, and were for that purpose brought into being. Thus at the start of the vision of glory, the holiness and power of the Eternal are extolled.

Dec. 12th

READING : **Revelation 5. 1-7**

THE LAMB OF GLORY

THE VISION of chapter 4 continues, and the right hand of the Eternal One is seen stretched out. On it rests a book, a roll filled with writing on both sides, but it cannot be read before seven seals which seal it have been broken. What is this book and what does it contain? Possibly it is the complete record of all the final purposes of God. When the call is made for one who is worthy to draw near to take the book, John weeps bitterly for none was found worthy. He thinks that now the contents of the book will never be known. His weeping is ended by the words of an elder. One has been found who is worthy!

Here we are introduced to the second great vision of the many glories of our Lord, not now as the awesome spectacle of the Son of man, but as that of a Lamb! John is bidden to look at One who is the Lion of the tribe of Juda, the Root of David, and who had overcome to open the book; "The lion hath roared, who will not fear?", Amos 3. 8. This is the Lion of the kingly tribe of which Jacob had said, "The sceptre shall not depart from Judah", Gen. 49. 10. He is the One from whom David sprang, and of whom David had said, ". . . my lord", Psa. 110. 1. And yet, as John looks, he sees one who overcame neither by fierceness, nor kingly might, but by the meekness of self-sacrifice; he sees a lamb with all the marks of sacrifice and death upon him, for He was as it had been slain. But the Lamb was standing in the power and energy of life. The mind reverts to what John told us in his Gospel, "he showed unto them his hands and his side. Then were the disciples glad when they saw the Lord", John 20. 20.

Two more things are said of the wonderful Lamb of God. The Lamb has seven horns. Even a superficial reading of the Revelation will show that the number "seven" is used again and again. It is the perfect number indicating completion or fulness. Though the Lamb is seen in meekness, yet to Him belongs fulness of power, and He has seven eyes which we are told are the seven Spirits of God sent forth into all the earth. There is nowhere out of the range of the perception of Him in whom dwells the fulness of the Spirit.

Dec. 13th

READING : **Revelation 5. 8-14**

HEAVEN'S MUSIC

AND NOW the scene of glory witnessed by John bursts into a song to the accompaniment of the harps of the elders and the sweet incense of the prayers of the saints. The Lamb has taken the roll from the outstretched hand. The song is new in that the occasion and the circumstances are new. "On earth the song begins; in heaven more sweet and loud". It is a song of praise acclaiming the worthiness of the Lamb, for He was slain.

His death has accomplished three great things. It has brought redemption by the blood of His sacrifice. The full scope of the redemptive purpose of God for the church is now realized, freedom from all that sin has meant in the way of bondage, defilement and corruption. It has been made available for all mankind even as our Lord commissioned His disciples when He said, "Go ye into all the world, and preach the gospel to every creature", Mark 16. 15. The judgment of Babel has been completely reversed, for the redeemed are out of "every kindred, and tongue, and people, and nation".

More than this, however, flows out from the sacrifice of Calvary, for those same redeemed ones, glorified with Christ, have been made a kingdom of priests. Here is the full realization of what Peter wrote, "Ye . . . are built up . . . an holy priesthood, to offer up spiritual sacrifices, acceptable to God by Jesus Christ, . . . a royal priesthood . . .", 1 Pet. 2. 5, 9. On earth we show forth His praises, in heaven we do so perfectly! The idea of a "kingdom of priests" first arose in Exodus 19. 6 before the restricted Levitical priesthood was established. There is no restriction now for believers, nor in the future.

The last great statement of the song is "and we shall reign on the earth", A.V. On earth the church is poor, and made of small account by the world. Often suffering and persecution have been the lot of the Lord's own. But, "If we suffer, we shall also reign with him", 2 Tim. 2. 12.

His death had appeared a negation of all those things now ascribed to Him by innumerable angels; power, riches, wisdom, strength, honour, glory, and blessing. Then John hears the whole creation owning the One upon the throne and the Lamb. As we hear the praise, we say with the living ones, "Amen", and with the elders bow in silent adoration.

Dec. 14th

READING : **Revelation 6. 1-17**

THE BEGINNING OF THE END

THREE SERIES of solemn visions are now given to John. The first concerns the opening of the seals of the book. God, who has dealt in longsuffering with men, is now about to do His strange work, and His judgments will be abroad. Until towards the end of the book the church is not mentioned as being on earth, so it seems that there is truth in writing, "the opening of the seals ushers in the terrible judgments to fall upon this earth after the church has been caught up to glory" (Van Ryn).

On the opening of each of the first four seals, John is called upon to "come and see". How different from the gracious invitations couched in the same words in his Gospel ! Four horses and riders appear. The first is a crowned victor on a white horse. Here surely is a figure of the anti-Christ energized and accepting authority from Satan. The red horse symbolizes war. The black horse implies the need to husband resources. Last, Death personified, and the grave appear. Power is given to these riders to kill a quarter of all mankind. These things have been known throughout history, but in the great and terrible day of the Lord they will be much intensified. Alas for man that the Prince of Peace is rejected, and that true peace is never more than an illusive dream for those who know not God.

The opening of the fifth seal reveals the souls of martyred ones, their blood calling, as did Abel's, for vengeance. If, as it would appear, the opening of the seals is co-extensive with the three and a half years of great trouble, then these are the many of the saints slain during that great persecution not yet over at this stage.

One cannot possibly conceive a more terrible scene than that depicted at the end of the reading when the sixth seal is opened. The great and terrible day of God's wrath has come. In a day of "darkness, and not light", Amos 5. 18, the powers of heaven are shaken and the whole earth reels like a drunken man. Terror strikes every heart; small and great cry out for a hiding place from the face of God. Who can stand when God ariseth? It is God who has saved us from so great a death, and from our hearts we thank Him.

Dec. 15th

READING : **Revelation 7. 1-17**

SEALED AND COMFORTED

THE JUDGMENTS of God are ever exercised with discrimination. To the four angels who were given power to hurt the earth and the sea the command was given to wait for the sealing of the servants of God. This sealing should be compared with the words, "come not near any man upon whom is the mark", Ezek. 9. 6. In our own dispensation, when we believed in the Lord Jesus, we "were sealed with that holy Spirit of promise", Eph. 1. 13. In all ages "the Lord knoweth how to deliver the godly", 2 Pet. 2. 9.

In today's reading those who are sealed as the servants of God are described as belonging to the tribes of Israel, 12,000 from each tribe. There is no reason to suppose that they are any other than the godly remnant of Israel in the darkest hour of that nation's history before the dawn of the day of which Paul spoke, Rom. 11. 26. One must ask the question, "Are we to understand the numbers as literal or symbolical of the very large number of Jews who in their distress turn to the Lord?". Their cry in that dark hour will be, "Oh that thou wouldest rend the heavens, that thou wouldest come down", Isa. 64. 1.

From the sealed ones on earth John looks again to the throne of God and the Lamb, where he sees an innumerable company, clothed in robes of white, with palms of festal joy, the symbol also of victory. With a loud voice ("when the praise of heaven I hear, loud as thunder on my ear . . .") they ascribe their salvation to God and the Lamb. This evokes further worship and praise from the angels, elders, and living creatures.

John is told that they have come out of the great tribulation. Two main views are held; that these are those who have suffered for Christ in that last time of trouble; or that it is called the great tribulation as being the sum of all the trouble through which Christ's own have passed, as He Himself said, "in the world ye shall have tribulation", John 16. 33. The scene is a brief and glorious view of what it will be to be there. The Lamb still shepherds His flock and leads them to living fountains of boundless joy, and God wipes away all tears.

The heavenly blessings described in verses 15-17 take place before the "first resurrection". It is interesting to compare these with 21. 3-4 referring to the eternal state.

Dec. 16th

READING : **Revelation 8. 1-13**

THE TRUMPETS SOUND

THE READING begins with the opening of the seventh seal which is followed by half an hour's silence. Dependent on the believed timing of the new series of visions (see the Introduction) the silence of heaven may be thought of as the almost oppressive hush which precedes a terrible storm. If, however, the seventh seal marks the end, then as one has said, "The half-hour is the beginning (one would say personally, "the symbol") of the rest of eternity", the sabbatical rest that awaits the people of God.

What follows immediately is a new series, the blowing of seven trumpets, the sounding out by angels of the solemn judgments of God upon an unrepentant world. How different is the sounding of these trumpets from that which shall be heard at the rapture when the Lord Himself shall come for His church! As in the case of the opening of the first four seals, so the first four trumpets are sounded in quick succession. Judgment which has waited long is now no longer delayed. The first brings disaster to the earth; the second, utter pollution by blood of a third part of the seas, destroying a third of all living creatures in the seas, and a third of all ships upon the waters. When the third is sounded, a star called Wormwood falls upon rivers and fountains, poisoning water on which man's life depends, and causing many a person's death. For these there was no tree to cut down to make sweet the waters of Marah, neither was there an Elisha to take a new cruse of salt to pour upon the poisonous water and declare, "Thus saith the Lord, I have healed these waters", 2 Kings 2. 21. The fourth angel sounds and the created heavens, sun, moon and stars, created to give light and to be for times and seasons, have a third of their shining taken away. The gloom of the day of wrath is already descending, but there is still more, and worse to follow.

Before the remaining trumpets sound, an angel is heard loudly proclaiming three woes. Man could no longer be ignorant that God was at work, but there is no repentance—such is man's folly. We should urgently make known the gospel of grace, mercy and peace through our Lord Jesus.

Dec. 17th

READING : **Revelation 9. 1-21**

HORROR LET LOOSE

THIS CHAPTER is one of the most sombre in the book. Here is given an insight into the dark mysteries of evil and what happens when restraint is taken away from demonic forces. It should act as a very solemn warning to our own generation where there is an increasing tendency to dabble in the occult. This characterized the nations around Israel, as they entered into the promised land, Deut. 11. 9-14; "the Lord thy God hath not suffered thee so to do".

A star fallen from heaven may well refer to Satan himself, this short statement being a preview of what is described later. Did not our Lord say, "I beheld Satan as lightning fall from heaven"?, Luke 10. 18. The star must be an intelligent being, for a key is given with which he opens the abyss, the dark prison of fallen angels, and later, during the millennium, of Satan himself. The opening of the prison is immediately succeeded by horrific events. One can hardly accept that literal locusts are meant, for we are told that their prince is the destroying angel, Apollyon. Our Lord said, "The thief cometh not, but . . . to destroy", John 10. 10. Here the devil's minions are free to wreak their destructive forces on godless mankind. None who is sealed as God's own must be touched. For five months (possibly literal) men are subjected to agonizing experiences, torture wrought by these evil spiritual forces. So terrible are they, that men long for death as the only escape they can imagine, but even that is denied them.

The blowing of the sixth trumpet signals the loosing of four evil angels. Their work is to incite and energize a great army, and because Euphrates must be the river of that name, we may gather that the vision is of a great invasion from the East. With the present expanding world population, the enormous numbers present no problem. The army causes a toll of human life greater than any known in past ages.

The final verses indicate the stupendous folly of man. He refuses to repent of his demonism, idolatry, violence, and corruption. In Noah's day the whole race had been corrupted and here we see the solemn fulfilment of the Lord's words, "as the days of Noe were, so shall also the coming of the Son of man be", Matt. 24. 37.

Dec. 18th

READING : **Revelation 10. 1-11**

SWEET AND BITTER

TODAY'S READING is a parenthesis between the sixth and seventh trumpets. All true messengers of God are clothed with the dignity that is suited to His ambassadors. Nathan Cole in New England said of the young Whitefield, "It seemed as if he was clothed with the authority of his God". Such here is the magnificence of the messenger, "another mighty angel", that many most respected commentators have said was the Lord Himself, but it may humbly be stated that in all places where the Lord is seen, the reader is left in no doubt as to who it is. The angel is clothed with a cloud, but there is also a rainbow, for judgment is still mingled with mercy; see Ezek. 1. 28. He claims for God the sovereignty of this world, and seven thunders are heard. Many have tried to say what their message was (even papal anathema!) but when God seals, for us it is an end of enquiry.

There would now no longer be delay, for the end was at hand, and the mystery of God would be finished when the seventh trumpet sounded.

In contrast to the sealed messages, the little book in the hand of the angel is open. Here there are no secrets. A scripture student will readily compare a similar incident in Ezekiel 3, and as we thus note the wonderful harmony of God's Word, we thank Him for giving us His Book.

What John ate and digested would be what was about to be revealed. One must first assimilate for oneself the Word of God, before passing it on to others. It is always sweet to His servants, "sweeter also than honey and the honeycomb", Psa. 19. 10. The taste is sweet, but the digesting is bitter! Who can but rejoice when the Lord of glory is revealed; who can but weep over the lost! Oh, that we might enter more into the spirit of our Lord who wept over a doomed nation, even as Jeremiah cried, "Oh that . . . mine eyes (were) a fountain of tears" as he thought of the coming disaster, Jer. 9. 1. Yet he also had found God's words to be sweet, "I did eat them . . .", 15. 16.

The final verse will cause us no difficulty if we read, "*concerning* many peoples" (Alford).

Dec. 19th

READING : **Revelation 11. 1-19**

THE LORD IS KING

THE PARENTHESIS continues. Later an angel measures the city of God, but here it is a temple, and the three and a half years of the Gentile profanation indicates the period of "Jacob's trouble". That the literal Jerusalem is meant is clear from the words, "where also our Lord was crucified", v. 8. A Jewish temple is thus envisaged, having been rebuilt either for sacrifice or as a religious centre.

In this city two great witnesses are raised up to prophesy for the Living God. He is never without His witnesses even in the darkest hours. The symbol of the olive trees and candlesticks should be compared with the vision of Zechariah 4. Those circumstances have long passed, and the vision here is yet to come, but at all times, even in ours, the message is true, "Not by might, nor by power, but by my spirit, saith the Lord", Zech. 4. 6. We do not know who the two witnesses are, but they exercise powers possessed by both Moses and Elijah. Their witness is completed in spite of the malice of the evil one, for those who truly do the will of God are kept until their work is done. But when it is ended, the beast (first mentioned here) makes war against them, and they are killed. Their bodies lie unburied in the street that all may gaze, gloat, and be glad, so greatly does darkness hate the light. But great fear comes to that evil generation for the Spirit of life enters into the two and they ascend into heaven, as did Elijah, he in the sight of his friend, but these in the sight of their enemies. A great earthquake causes death and destruction, and the terrified people give glory to the God of heaven.

The seventh trumpet sounds. At last a great cry goes up declaring that the kingdoms of the world have become the kingdoms of our Lord and of His Christ. When our Saviour stood before Pilate, He was asked, "Art thou a king then?". Yes, indeed, our hearts exclaim and He shall reign for ever and ever. Once again heaven is seen as the centre of worship. There is seen the true ark of the covenant, the throne of God founded on justice and judgment, but also the symbol of the covenant mercyof our God, through the precious blood that was shed for us sinners.

Dec. 20th

READING : **Revelation 12. 1-17**

SATAN CAST OUT

IN ALL records it becomes necessary to go back in time to fill in details. This would appear to be what happened in the visions now granted to John. The earliest promise of man's redemption was made in Eden. The enmity between the woman's seed and the serpent reached its climax in the crushing of the serpent's head. Today's reading gives a panorama of the story of that enmity, the evil one trying to destroy the seed who was to come through the covenant people, "of whom as concerning the flesh Christ came, who is over all, God blessed for ever", Rom. 9. 5. The hostility of the devil reached its climax when our Lord came, and at the cross it seemed as if evil had triumphed. But the very moment of that seeming defeat was one of greatest victory. "He death by dying slew." The purpose of God ever was that man should have dominion, and that purpose is to find fulfilment through the promised seed, the One now exalted to God's throne.

The enmity of the evil one is turned especially on the woman (the faithful remnant of Israel), but there is found a refuge for her for 3½ years, Isa. 26. 20, 21. The accuser of the brethren was cast down to the earth, as our Lord had said, "now shall the prince of this world be cast out", John 12. 31. In this overthrow he will no longer have access to the heavenlies. This casting out goes on until he ends eternally in the lake of fire. The words of Isaiah may be applied, "How art thou fallen from heaven, O Lucifer, son of the morning!", Isa. 14. 12, and heaven rejoices. No accusation was upheld, for the blood of the Lamb has fully dealt with our guilt, and by this and by faithful witness the saints overcome. Though heaven rejoices, the world has every cause to be fearful, for he, who is the embodiment of all that is evil, has come among men to give vent to his anger, for he knows that soon he will be where he would not. His malice is directed against the remnant of those from whom had come the One who had brought about his defeat. A flood is poured from his mouth, but all in vain, for "when the enemy shall come in like a flood, the Spirit of the Lord shall put him to flight", Isa. 59. 19 marg.

Satan therefore attempts further damage through the two beasts introduced in the next chapter.

Dec. 21st

READING : **Revelation 13. 1-18**

A TRINITY OF EVIL

JOHN IS now upon the shore of the sea which cast up its filth. Daniel had in his day seen four beasts arise; John sees only one, having features belonging to each of the four. They had been representative of great Gentile powers. The one now seen had a head looking mortally wounded but wonderfully healed, a first horrible caricature of the Lamb who was slain, but lives again. The language of the reading forbids us to think in general terms of a state, but rather of an individual, energized by the dragon, Satan. This individual, the embodiment of all that is anti-Christian and, therefore, anti-Christ, is given power for the 3½ years. He blasphemes the Holy God; he hurls defiance against the throne of God, and not only exercises for a time universal power, but also makes war with those who are true to God. In these terrible conditions the true character of the saints will be seen, not in armed resistance, but in patient endurance for His sake. Has not this been true at all times?

This terrible ruler also claims for himself divine honours as had been done by Roman and other emperors. For the saints to say that Caesar is Lord and to offer incense to him would be a denial of Christ, an offering to Caesar what belongs to God alone.

Another beast arises, this one from the earth, in appearance different, but in character the same as the first, so that the "trinity" of evil is complete. Looking gentle, but in speech ferocious, this one acts as prophet to the first, causing men to worship him, and deceiving men by the satanic power in him. Cowper said, "He that hates truth shall be the dupe of lies". Paul had said long before, "God shall send them strong delusion, that they should believe a lie", 2 Thess. 2. 11.

As God seals His own, so will there be a mark to show that men belong to this evil trio. Failure to worship the beast or to receive the mark will mean death. Is the number of the beast a symbol of the highest that man can reach in his struggle to be like God? In that nightmare world will be seen what Swinburne blasphemously wrote, "Glory to man in the highest".

Dec. 22nd

READING : **Revelation 14. 1-20**

HARVEST AND VINTAGE

ONE HUNDRED and forty-four thousand faithful followers of the Lamb are now seen on the mount Sion. It is not possible in few words to point out problems that arise. Clearly those seen must be identified with the same number in chapter 7, but debate arises as to whether this is the earthly mount Sion, or the heavenly. Certain statements made, however, are such as should stimulate us in our work and witness. There is the joy expressed in a new song which only they can learn; there is such devotion that they follow the Lamb wherever He goes. They are virgins, for they have not allowed themselves to be seduced from single-hearted love for the Lamb; cf. 2 Cor. 11. 2–3. Guileless in speech and without fault before God's throne—this is the witness of the Spirit.

The everlasting gospel is always for all men, that they should fear God, a fear which will produce repentance and faith. The only ground of the forgiving love of God is the cross of Christ.

An angel is seen with the prophetic announcement of the fall of Babylon, the fact of which is given in detail later. Again an angel appears warning of the doom of the worshippers of the beast, but the endurance of the saints is such that they continue in their loyalty to God and the faith of Jesus. This will inevitably lead to their martyrdom, but how blessed are those who die in the Lord! The Spirit adds His "Amen". It will be specially true in that day, and also today, for they rest from their labours.

Two visions are now given which briefly give, as would seem, the whole scope of the days at the end. First, the Son of man is seen reaping the harvest, gathering the wheat into His garner, the much fruit of His suffering unto death. This is followed by the vintage. Our Lord described Himself as the true vine; the Old Testament speaks of the vine of Israel; but here it is the vine of the earth with its ripe fruits of utter corruption, fit only for the winepress of God's wrath. The work of execution is performed by two angels. The visions should be compared with the relevant parables of our Lord.

Dec. 23rd

READING : **Revelation 15. 1-8**

BOWLS OF WRATH

THE READING is of the most solemn significance, and this is emphasized by the use of the words "Great and marvellous". In this new series, John is to see the completion of the wrath of God poured out upon an unrepentant world. First of all, however, as preparation for what is to follow, he sees those who have triumphed in the tribulation of those days, and he hears their singing. They stand on what looks like a sea of glass, which, as we know from chapter 4, is in front of the throne. It is there as a wonderful pavement before God's throne, as glass, for there is neither storm nor restlessness in the presence of God; it is like crystal, for one is in the presence of dazzling purity and sparkling joy. Here it is seen as mingled with fire, for it is the day of judgment.

The victors sing the true expression of heaven's joy. They sing the song of Moses. Is it the song of Exodus 15, or Deuteronomy 32? We do not know, but either tells of the faithfulness and power of God towards Israel. In the context of the reading, the end of the latter song is peculiarly appropriate, "for he will avenge the blood of his servants . . . and will be merciful unto his land, and to his people", Deut. 32. 43. They also sing the song of the Lamb for, even as with all redeemed ones, they are there because of the shedding of His precious blood. These final judgments will cause all nations to come and worship the One who alone is holy.

And now the last solemn acts of judgment are about to begin. Seven angels are seen issuing from the temple, and to each is given by one of the four living creatures a golden bowl filled with the wrath of the Eternal God. As in Exodus when mount Sinai was enshrouded with a thick cloud and no Israelite dared to approach, so now, the brilliance of the heavenly scene is shut out by a pall of smoke, and none can draw near until the angels have ended their mission. As we ponder these things, we rejoice that "ye are not come unto . . . blackness, and darkness", but we should also with true godly fear serve our God, remembering that He "is a consuming fire", Heb. 12. 18, 29.

Contrast the ark, temple and glory, 11. 19; 15. 8, with the tabernacle and temple, Exod. 40. 21, 34-35; 2 Chron. 5. 7, 14.

Dec. 24th

READING : **Revelation 16. 1-21**

THE LAST PLAGUES

IN RAPID succession the seven angels pour out the bowls of wrath on men and creation.

The first falls in the form of a grievous sore on men who have worshipped the image of the beast. For their hurt there is "no balm in Gilead". Their physical condition now reveals their inner rottenness. The sea becomes corrupted as the blood of those who have died; no more can it sustain life. Rivers and fountains are also polluted. They become blood, and John hears an angel ascribe righteousness to God, for have not these who are now suffering shed the blood of God's saints? The cry of the souls under the altar is answered, for God has said, "Vengeance is mine; I will repay", Rom. 12. 19. Another angel is heard, recognizing the justice of God's ways. We also say, "Shall not the Judge of all the earth do right?", Gen. 18. 25.

Then the sun itself is affected and men are scorched by its great heat. Once again it is said that instead of crying for mercy, men blaspheme God and refuse to repent and give Him glory; such is the delusion of the devil and the hardness of the human heart.

The throne of the beast suffers next and his kingdom is smitten with a plague of darkness. Men gnaw their tongues in their agonies, but, for the second time in the reading, we learn that there is no repentance.

Events move very rapidly towards the end. Euphrates dries up so that there is no great barrier from the east to the valley of Megiddo, and evil spirits from the "trinity" of iniquity stir up the leaders of the world to gather their forces for the final conflict when the Lord appears. The call of the Lord to His servants is to keep awake, and to us also it is said, "Awake thou that sleepest, . . . and Christ shall give thee light", Eph. 5. 14.

The outpouring of wrath is completed with the pouring out of the seventh bowl, for a great voice from the throne cries, "It is done"; the whole earth shakes, the cities of the nations are shattered, islands and even mountains disappear, and upon mankind falls the hail which God had "reserved against the time of trouble", Job. 38. 23.

Dec. 25th

READING : **Revelation 17. 1-18**

THE GREAT HARLOT

THE BEAUTIFUL figure of the relationship between husband and wife is used by Paul to describe the union between Christ and His Church. She is the bride of Christ. In awful contrast to the purity and devotion of the bride, today in the reading we have a description of what may be reasonably regarded as a world religion utterly opposed to Christ. Babylon the Great, therefore, must here be regarded as the world's religious centre. An unbiased historian once wrote to the effect that the most important study of a culture is its religion. The use of the figure of a harlot need cause no surprise if we remember the many times that Old Testament prophets speak in such terms of apostate Israel; e.g. Hosea. Here, then, is man's religion in its final outcome, in stark contrast to the true faith, and a fearful caricature of it. We are arrayed in God's sight in the purity of Christ; the harlot is clothed with gorgeous robes and every sign of magnificence and wealth. Into our hands has been placed the cup of salvation, but she has a golden cup full of all that is ugly and vile—the cup of demons. The Church is glorious without spot or blemish; the character of the harlot is displayed in the name on her forehead. Her words are blasphemous and she kills the martyrs of Jesus. The true Church takes upon her lips the name of her Lord with hushed and holy awe.

But the harlot comes to a violent and fearful end at the hands of those with whom she was so closely allied, and with whom she committed her abominations. In the vision at the start, she is seen riding on the beast who has received authority from a strong federation of powers. Their aim is deliberately to take up arms to resist the Lamb, the returning Lord of lords and King of kings. They are about to rush to their destruction against God, against the "thick bosses of his bucklers", Job 15. 26. Before doing so, however, they turn in their fury upon the harlot and tear her to pieces. So ends man's religion.

Is Babylon of that day to be the same city, pagan Rome, almost certainly the primary subject of the vision? We do not know. Will it be a new Babylon?

Dec. 26th

READING : **Revelation 18. 1-24**

THE FALL OF BABYLON

THE EMPHASIS today is on the commercial prosperity of Babylon. Her magnificence is great, but a swift and sudden end comes. As destruction is about to fall, a call is made to the people of God to come out, lest they suffer with the ungodly. The practical import of this for us is that we should have no part in the greed and love of gain of our modern world. A very solemn warning against this was given to Timothy by Paul, 1 Tim. 6. 10, 17, and our Lord Himself declared that we cannot serve God and mammon.

When the men of Babel built a tower, the top was to reach heaven, but of Babylon it is declared that her sins had reached as a foul heap to the heavens; therefore her judgment was just. In one day she who said in her pride, "I . . . shall see no sorrow", experiences utter catastrophe and is burned to the ground.

The great of the earth who had lived luxuriously from her wealth stand off in great fear, bewailing her. So also do the merchants whose trade has now come to nought. Among the merchandise are the bodies and souls of men. The picture was before Bunyan's mind when in his masterpiece he described "Vanity Fair". While we must needs use the things of the world, we must not abuse them; see 1 Cor. 7. 31. We must beware of entering into the spirit of commercial Babylon which denies that a man's life does not consist in the abundance of the things he possesses. The things that endure are laid up in the heavens for those who love God.

While kings and merchants loudly lament, heaven rejoices in the bringing low of this heap of iniquity. As the end of the chapter is read, there is a terrible finality in the repetition of the words, "no more at all". This is the end of man's world, his religion, his politics, his commerce and his arts. From now on the Lord rules as King, and His will alone is supreme.

The true character of Babylon, as seen by the Lord, is exposed at the end, for He had said, "there is nothing covered, that shall not be revealed", Luke 12. 2. In Babylon was found the blood of all that were slain upon the earth. This was the enormity of her sins.

Dec. 27th

READING : **Revelation 19. 1-21**

THE RETURNING KING

HERE IS the climax of the whole book. The King Himself appears! The appearance is heralded by a chorus of praise, ending with the great finale, "Alleluia: for the Lord God omnipotent reigneth".

In the whole book reference is made to three suppers. The first is in the Laodicean letter where the Lord will sup with those who in love respond to His call. The second is the marriage supper of the Lamb, where is fulness of joy, the joy of the Lord who gave Himself for His Church, that this spiritual union might be accomplished. The bride is fully prepared, adorned in garments of purity and holiness, even as Paul had written, "a glorious church, not having spot, or wrinkle, or any such thing", Eph. 5. 27. In that unparalleled scene of festal joy, how blessed are all who are called to share! The revelation is affirmed as the true sayings of God, and it is all so wonderful that John fell down to worship the angel, but was forbidden to do so, for worship belongs to God alone.

The final supper is a grim one, the end of those who die in the great overthrow. Of old when great armies marched any distance to battle, it was said that the soldiers would look up and curse the carrion birds flying overhead, for they knew their significance.

Between these two last suppers the King appears through the opened heavens. The description is one of awesome majesty. In His names we learn the devotion of His humanity, for He is Faithful and True; we hear the declaration of His deity, for He is the Word of God; and in the third name we see the demonstration of His sovereignty, for He is King of kings, and Lord of lords. Surrounded by the hosts of heaven He comes to execute justice upon the earth, and with the sword of His mouth to slay the wicked. The folly of man is such that the King is met by the world's forces, led by the beast and false prophet. The issue of such a confrontation could not be for one moment in doubt. The leaders are taken alive and cast into the lake of fire.

The King has returned to take up the place which was His in virtue of the victory of His cross.

Dec. 28th

READING : **Revelation 20. 1-15**

THE MILLENNIUM AND AFTER

THE REVELATION ends what began in Genesis. There in Eden the serpent beguiled Eve, and sin with its untold ruin came into the world—a ruin that would have been irreversible, had it not been for God's redemptive purpose. Here, except for a very short time, the serpent will deceive no more for he is imprisoned in the abyss.

The golden age of righteousness and peace, spoken of by Israel's prophets, arrives at last. There will be unbroken harmony between heaven and earth, for the angels of God will ascend and descend on the Son of man; see John 1. 51. The saints shall reign with the King, as a priesthood to God, for, "If we suffer, we shall also reign with him", 2 Tim. 2. 12. Even then, too, we shall know our present "light affliction" has worked an "eternal weight of glory", 2 Cor. 4. 17. Here is the first resurrection, and the rest of the dead remain in their graves until the millennium is passed. Comparison should be made with the great chapter on resurrection, 1 Cor. 15, especially verses 20-26.

For mankind this period may be regarded as a last probation, and it is shown that, in spite of all the wonders of the reign of the King of glory, the heart can know no real change apart from regeneration. When for a short while the devil is released, there is a world-wide rising against the King and His people, and the beloved city is besieged. Fire destroys the insurgent, and the devil is cast into the lake of fire. The millennium merges into eternity.

Before the eternal state is described, the last solemn judgment of the dead is seen. These words should be read with great awe and, perhaps, with a minimum of comment. Let us ever beware of adding to the Word of God what is not there, especially of painting lurid pictures of the lot of the damned which are usually the figments of imagination from the Catholic Church of the Middle Ages, used to scare ignorant people into submission. When our Lord spoke of Gehenna, people knew He used as a figure the rubbish heap outside the city with its ever-burning fires, but, as Campbell Morgan pointed out, "the fact is always of greater force than the figure".

Dec. 29th

READING : **Revelation 21. 1-8**

ALL THINGS NEW

Now we are given by the Spirit of God a wonderful glimpse into eternity, and we hear the words from the throne, "Behold I make all things new". The old things have passed away for ever.

There is a new creation both of heaven and earth. Of the old it was said that even the heavens were not clean in God's sight and, as for the earth, so fair in the beginning, it had been corrupted; but now all is new and unspoilt. There is no more sea, for in the Word of God the sea is spoken of as being restless, casting up mire and dirt, stormy, and, in a practical sense, separating loved ones. Even as John was shown these visions, he was separated from his fellow-believers on the mainland. None of these things will be found in the new creation.

John sees a new city, holy; the new Jerusalem; the city of God coming down out of heaven. A city should not be thought of primarily as a geographical place, but rather as the community that comprise it. The glory of this new city, adorned as a bride for her husband, is described in some detail in the next reading.

There is a new condition, a wonderful and abiding relationship between God and men, when will come to pass the absolute fulfilment of the name Immanuel, God with us.

For all there are entirely new conditions of life. How little we can understand the positive meaning of these things, but God graciously tells us what will be known no more: no more death, no more sorrow, nor crying, and no more pain. Every shadow will have passed away, every pang gone, and God will wipe away all tears. Now the creation groans in pain, but "He'll bid the whole creation smile".

Once again the truth and faithfulness of the words of God are confirmed. Not one thing is left undone; all is fulfilled, for He is the Beginning and the End.

For a moment the seer is brought back to the reality of the world in which he lives. The invitation of the gospel is still for men to drink freely of the water of life. Encouragement is given to the believers, and a very solemn warning to the unregenerate sinner.

Dec. 30th

READING : **Revelation 21. 9-27**

THE HEAVENLY CITY

THIS PASSAGE has truly been described as a spiritual revelation of eternal verities. Once again John is in the Spirit, and sees the city of God from the top of a high mountain. It is from the heights that the best views can be had, and to be on such a spiritual height and to see such things, one can well rejoice and exclaim, "What hath God wrought!", Num. 23. 23.

Looking upon the city, John sees seven wonderful things. He sees her beauty, for she has the glory of God, who is the perfection of beauty, upon her. When man makes his idols, they are ever hideous. Our God has revealed His glory in the incomparable Lord Jesus who is altogether lovely. She has a wall great and high, telling of her security, and the city's universality is seen in that the gates are towards each point of the compass. Note that both Israel and the apostles of the Lamb are associated with this city. In the measuring of it, one is reminded of Paul's great prayer in which we read, "what is the breadth, and length, and depth, and height", Eph. 3. 18.

The earthly city had a sanctuary set apart from other parts; but in the city of God there is no separation, yet its sanctity is such that there is no temple! The whole is one sanctuary, for all is pervaded by the immediate presence of the Lord God Almighty and the Lamb. Its clarity, also, is such that there is no need of any created light. God, who is Light, is abiding there, and also the Lamb whose life is the light of men.

When the Lord was here, His purity contrasted sharply with the impurity of Herod's temple, John 2. 16; instead He spoke of "the temple of his body", v. 21, manifested when the Lamb is the temple of the heavenly city, Rev. 21. 22.

On earth it is a great honour to receive the freedom of a city, but in the spiritual realm all enjoy the privileges of absolute liberty. The gates are never shut. It was at night that the gates of a city were closed, but here night can never come.

John is finally reminded of the spotless purity of the holy city. There is no spot or stain, nothing to mar and nothing that is ugly; all is utterly true. The inhabitants are those whose names are in the Lamb's book of life, even as our Lord had said to His disciples, "rejoice, because your names are written in heaven", Luke 10. 20.

Dec. 31st

READING : **Revelation 22. 1-21**

I COME QUICKLY

MORE IS now told of the city of God, and the book ends with sundry exhortations, a promise and a prayer.

The water of life flows as a mighty river, with its source at the throne. This is for ever associated with the work of the cross, for it is the throne of God and the Lamb. Such a river, ever pure and bright, and radiant with boundless joy, is the fitting symbol of the fulness of life of the Spirit of God. Where the river flows, there grows the tree of life in abundance with a continuous variety of pleasant fruits of which all who live for ever may freely eat. Its foliage is luxuriant, for the health of the peoples (not "healing", for there is no disease there!).

Where there are such conditions, there can never be another curse such as blighted the first creation; there, in unclouded light, the light of the glory of God and the Lamb, the Lord's servants will find joy in unfettered service, and best of all, they will see His face, no longer through a glass darkly, but face to face! Bunyan wrote, "which when I had seen, I wished myself among them".

Three times our Lord says, "I come quickly". He comes; blessed are they who keep His words! He comes that He may reward His own according to their work. He comes, the Bridegroom of our hearts, and with John we respond, "Amen. Even so, come, Lord Jesus".

In conclusion, there still comes the message to give to men, that all may drink freely of the water of life. There is yet the solemn reminder that "the time is at hand", and an implied exhortation not to delay, else change will be impossible, for "where the tree falleth, there it shall be", Eccl. 11. 3.

It is "I Jesus" who speaks to His servant, for He ever bears that precious Name. For Him we wait and serve, and while here, His grace is unfailing. In conclusion, the words of Augustine are worth recalling, "He therefore loves the coming of the Lord, not who asserts it is near at hand, or who asserts it is not at hand, but, rather, who, whether it be near or far off, awaits it with sincerity of faith, constancy of hope and fervour of love".

Index